Illustrated WPF

Written and Illustrated by
Daniel Solis

Apress®

Illustrated WPF

ISBN-13 (pbk): 978-1-4302-1910-1

ISBN-13 (electronic): 978-1-4302-1911-8

Printed and bound in the United States of America 9 8 7 6 5 4 3 2 1

President and Publisher: Paul Manning
Lead Editor: Ewan Buckingham
Editorial Board: Clay Andres, Steve Anglin, Mark Beckner, Ewan Buckingham, Tony Campbell, Gary Cornell, Jonathan Gennick, Michelle Lowman, Matthew Moodie, Jeffrey Pepper, Frank Pohlmann, Ben Renow-Clarke, Dominic Shakeshaft, Matt Wade, Tom Welsh
Coordinating Editor: Anne Collett
Copy Editor: Kim Wimpsett
Compositor: v-prompt
Indexer: BIM Indexers and e-Services
Artist: Daniel Solis
Cover Designer: Anna Ishchenko

Distributed to the book trade worldwide by Springer-Verlag New York, Inc., 233 Spring Street, 6th Floor, New York, NY 10013. Phone 1-800-SPRINGER, fax 201-348-4505, e-mail orders-ny@springer-sbm.com, or visit http://www.springeronline.com.

For information on translations, please e-mail info@apress.com, or visit http://www.apress.com.

Apress and friends of ED books may be purchased in bulk for academic, corporate, or promotional use. eBook versions and licenses are also available for most titles. For more information, reference our Special Bulk Sales–eBook Licensing web page at http://www.apress.com/info/bulksales.

The source code for this book is available to readers at http://www.apress.com. You will need to answer questions pertaining to this book in order to successfully download the code.

*I would like to dedicate this book to
Sian, and to my parents—Sal and Amy,
and to Sue.*

Content at a Glance

Contents

About the Author

Dan Solis holds a Bachelor of Arts degree with majors in biology and English. He initially worked in research on the structure of bi- and tri-metal crystals, until he found that he enjoyed programming much more than working in a lab. He also holds a Master of Science degree in computer science from the University of California at Santa Barbara, where he concentrated on programming languages and compiler design.

Dan has been programming professionally for more than 20 years, with more than half that time working as a consultant and contract programmer, including several projects for Microsoft Consulting Services. His consulting projects have ranged from programs for mutual fund analysis and supply chain management to systems for missile tracking. He has also taught courses on various programming languages, Windows programming, UNIX internals, and a number of other topics, in both the United States and Europe.

Dan's first programming language was C, but he soon became intrigued by the journal articles about a new language being developed called "C with Classes." Eventually that language was renamed C++ and released to the world. He began using C++ as soon as he could get access to a compiler, and he eventually started teaching training seminars on the language as well as continuing to code.

With the advent of C#, .NET, and WPF, he has moved on to enjoying the myriad advantages of the new platform and has been working with them enthusiastically ever since.

Acknowledgments

I want to thank Sian for supporting and encouraging me on a daily basis, and I want to thank my parents and brothers and sisters for their continued love and support.

I also want to express my gratitude to the people at Apress who have worked with me to bring this book to fruition. I really appreciate that they understood and appreciated what I was trying to do and worked with me to achieve it. Thanks to all of you.

Introduction

With WPF, Microsoft started from scratch and built a UI framework that is more logical, powerful, and integrated than previous frameworks. But it's *different* from previous frameworks, and you need to understand its structure and paradigms to use it effectively.

One of the reasons WPF has a reputation of having a steep and extensive learning curve is that we, as programmers, think that all UI frameworks are pretty much the same, just with different API classes, methods, and parameters. In the case of WPF, however, this definitely is not case. The result is that when programmers just jump from another framework to WPF without learning the basics, they're frustrated that everything seems so different.

The purpose of this book is to teach you the fundamentals and mechanics of WPF programming as quickly and simply as possible, while giving you a firm grasp of what's actually going on under the covers. To do this, I've used a combination of text, figures, bulleted lists, and tables.

Many of us think visually. To us, figures, bulleted lists, and tables help clarify and crystallize our understanding of a concept by cutting through the clutter of pages of dense paragraphs of explanation. My experience was repeatedly confirmed, when, in several years of teaching programming, I found that the pictures I drew on the whiteboard were the things that most quickly helped students understand the concepts I was trying to convey.

Illustrations alone, however, aren't sufficient to explain the vast and powerful framework that is WPF. The goal of this book is to find the best combination of words and illustrations to give you a thorough understanding of the framework, eliminating the steep learning curve, and to serve as a reference when you're done.

Audience, Source Code, and Contact Information

This book was written for intermediate to advanced programmers who want to write Windows programs using the WPF UI framework. It assumes that you're familiar with C# and that you have some experience with Visual Studio.

You can download the source code for all the example programs from the Apress web site. And although I can't answer specific questions about your code, you can contact me with suggestions for the book at dansolis@sbcglobal.net.

I hope this book makes learning WPF an enjoyable experience for you! Take care.

Dan Solis

CHAPTER 1

Introduction to Windows Presentation Foundation

What Is Windows Presentation Foundation?

The Path to the Screen

Documents and Fonts

Graphics and Animation

Styles and Control Templates

Separating Visual Design from Coding

WPF Prefers Vector Graphics

System DPI Independence and WPF Units

XAML Browser Applications (XBAPs)

The Other Parts of .NET

Silverlight

What Is Windows Presentation Foundation?

Windows Presentation Foundation (WPF) is a platform for developing and running visually rich .NET programs. It consists of two elements:

- A set of DLLs designed for creating Windows programs with the following characteristics:

  - Richly visual user interfaces

  - Strong and extensive data binding

- A public application programming interface (API), allowing our programs to access those DLLs and use their powerful capabilities

The purpose of this book is to explain this programming framework and how it is designed to be used. Once you learn this, you'll have the tools you need to write programs that delight your users as never before.

Some might argue that a richly visual interface is just so much fluff and not essential to the functionality of a program—particularly a business program. I disagree. I think that programs that are well designed and visually pleasing are less taxing on the users and improve morale and efficiency.

WPF is designed to run on PCs running Windows Vista and Windows 2008 Server, and it can be run on Windows XP and Windows Server 2003 if they have .NET 3.0 or later installed. WPF gives us the tools to create programs our users will be excited to use—and that we will be excited to develop.

In this chapter, I will give a high-level description of what WPF encompasses and how it improves over previous platforms such as the Microsoft Foundation Classes (MFC) and Windows Forms (WinForms).

The Path to the Screen

Since output to the screen is an essential part of a Windows program, let's start by looking at the path from the program to the screen.

Most computers today have graphics cards that are capable of producing amazing graphics. Except for games, though, most applications make little use of those capabilities. Part of the reason for this is that in order to really access the graphics cards' capabilities, programmers have had to delve into the complex realm of DirectX programming.

Ideally we'd like to be able to have our programs be able to do some of the fancier things that take advantage of the graphics cards' capabilities—but without the steep and extensive learning curve of graphics programming. This is exactly what WPF promises. This does *not* mean, however, that you'll want to use WPF for game programming. It's not designed for that and would not give you the flexibility or performance of programming directly using DirectX.

Games and DirectX

At the high end of the video performance spectrum are the game programs, which present animated, interactive 3D worlds on the screen. These programs push the huge processing power of today's graphics cards to their limits. To do this, many of them use a special set of APIs called *DirectX.*

DirectX is a set of APIs for producing high-performance graphics and multimedia under Windows (and the Xbox). As shown in Figure 1-1, it includes APIs for graphics, audio, and input. The one for producing 2D and 3D graphics—called *Direct3D*—is the one were interested in.

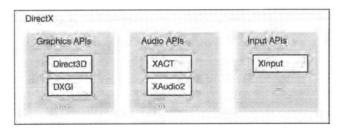

Figure 1-1. *DirectX is the name for a set of multimedia APIs.*

Direct3D maps its API onto the low-level hardware instructions of the graphics card. This allows programs to take advantage of hardware acceleration, making them much faster. Although this gives the programmer an immense amount of control and additional execution speed, it is much more complex than general-purpose programming frameworks such as Windows Forms or the Microsoft Foundation Classes, and it's quite a bit of work.

Since the significant effort required to use Direct3D generally outweighs its benefits in most consumer and business programming situations, the graphics power of video cards has remained largely untapped.

Windows Forms

At the heart of the Windows operating system is the User32 DLL. This component performs windows management and many of the other functions we associate with the appearance and behavior of the standard UI components, including implementing and rendering buttons, list boxes, text boxes, and so on. The Win32 API is a large collection of C language functions that give access to the functionality built in to the Windows operating system.

Another important component of the operating system is the GDI DLL. GDI stands for *Graphics Device Interface*. GDI is an abstraction layer and API for displaying graphical objects, and it allows scaling and rendering on different output devices. Because GDI and its newer C++ based version, GDI+, are software libraries, their performance on complex shapes can be poor in comparison with the rendering that video cards are capable of producing.

Previous frameworks such as Microsoft Foundation Classes and Windows Forms are implemented as wrappers around the functionality supplied by User32 and GDI. Figure 1-2 shows the architecture of a Windows Forms program.

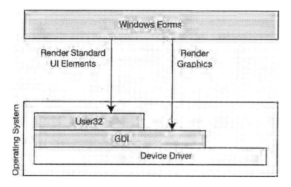

Figure 1-2. *Windows Forms programs render their objects using User32 and the GDI.*

The disadvantages of this architecture are the following:

- *Inefficient*: Since the rendering process is done in the operating system software, it doesn't take advantage of the graphics processing power built into today's graphics cards.

- *Locked-in implementation*: Since the functionality and presentation of the UI elements is built into the operating system, there is little you can do to customize them, other than to build custom controls with the look and behavior you want. This severely limits the amount of original style you can include without investing in a fair amount of work.

Rendering Under WPF

Under WPF, the path from the processor to the screen is entirely different from in Windows Forms. The new engine sends *all rendering* to Direct3D. Even simple text gets the full power of the graphics card's capability. And it's all done without any extra work required by the programmer.

Figure 1-3 shows the architecture of a WPF program.

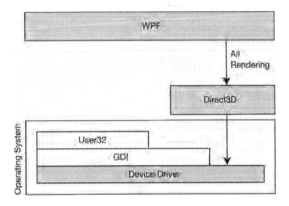

Figure 1-3. *All the visual rendering in WPF programs goes directly to Direct3D. This allows greater flexibility and enables hardware acceleration for much of the work that would have been done in software.*

Documents and Fonts

In previous programming frameworks, the support for text consisted mainly of labels, text boxes, and Rich Text Format controls. WPF, however, goes far beyond that. Besides improving these controls, it introduces two new ways of producing text-based programs:

- *Flow documents* allow their text to flow according to the size and shape of the window.

  - Like HTML, when the user changes the dimensions of the window, the text is readjusted and laid out to fit the new size and shape.

  - Unlike HTML, flow documents support multiple columns and built-in pagination.

- *Fixed documents* are similar to Adobe PDF documents. The text and all formatting are fixed and unchangeable by the end user.

  WPF also adds extensive support for scalable font standards such as OpenType and ClearType.

Graphics and Animation

WPF has built-in support for vector-graphic 2D and 3D shapes. Unlike previous programming frameworks, though, shapes are more than mere visual objects on the screen. For example, shapes are capable of the following:

- Shapes can be filled with solid colors, gradients, images, or even video.

- Shapes can behave like controls, including such things as hit testing and keyboard and mouse input.

WPF has built-in support for animation. *Animation* refers to changing the display in small ways very quickly over time so that an object appears to move or change.

For example, you might place a small graphic at the top center of the window and then, at a certain point, move it down several pixels every 1/60th of a second until it reaches the bottom. To the end user, this would appear as a smoothly moving object. WPF's built-in animation support makes animating objects simple.

Styles and Control Templates

A *style* is a named set of property settings, much like Cascading Style Sheets styles in HTML or like paragraph styles in Microsoft Word. When you apply a style to an element, it sets that element's properties to the values set in the style. This makes it easy to get a consistent look and feel among the elements of a program.

A *template* is similar to a style. A *control template* determines how a control is displayed. The look of standard Windows controls is built into the operating system, and previous frameworks used thin wrappers over the operating system's API to display the controls. If, however, you wanted a control to have a different look, you had to write a custom control, which involved a lot of work.

In WPF, however, the "look" of a control is not built into the operating system but is just a template that you can change. So if you don't like the look of a control with the default template, you can easily change it.

Separating Visual Design from Coding

Good programmers aren't necessarily artistic as well. This results in a lot of mediocre-looking programs. To remedy this, some companies use designers and graphic artists to help produce more attractive user interfaces.

The way this has usually worked is that graphic designers produce the artwork and give it to the programmers, who then code the UI to look like the artwork. This is certainly better than having programmers produce the artwork from scratch, but it would be even better if the graphic designers could produce the visual aspects of the UI directly and let the programmers stick to coding the behavior.

WPF allows this separation of labor. If you so choose, you can separate the graphic design from the coding implementation by using a new markup language called XAML (which rhymes with "camel" and stands for *eXtensible Application Markup Language*) to produce the visual aspects of the UI, while coding the behavior of the program using C# or Visual Basic.

WPF Prefers Vector Graphics

Digital images are stored in one of two ways, either as bitmap images or as vector graphics. In the past, most images in programs have been bitmap images. WPF uses and encourages the use of vector graphics in many places that have used bitmaps before.

Bitmap Images

Bitmap images, which are also called *raster graphics* or *raster images*, have the following characteristics:

- Conceptually, a bitmap image is a two-dimensional rectangle of pixel settings that make up the image. The information that's stored is the following:

  - The width and height of the rectangular image—specified in pixels.

  - The number of bits that represent a single pixel. This is specified as *bits per pixel* and is called the *color depth* of the image.

  - The color and position of each pixel.

- Some bitmap formats use compression to make the file size smaller. These include formats with the extensions .jpg, .tiff, .gif, and .png.

  - These aren't usually called *bitmaps* even though they technically are.

  - These formats use either *lossy* or *lossless* compression. Formats with lossy compression don't contain all the data about the image and can result in loss of detail. Formats with lossless compression contain all the image's information.

- Other bitmap formats don't use compression. These include formats with extensions .bmp and .dib.

  Table 1-1 lists some of the common file extensions associated with bitmap images.

Table 1-1. *File Extensions for Common Bitmap Image Formats*

Bitmap Image File Extensions			
.jpg	.tiff	.gif	.png
.pcx	.bmp	.dib	

▓ **Note** The GIF format was originally pronounced, by its creators, as "jif." Now, however, it's also widely pronounced as "gif" as in "gift" (although that still sounds wrong to me).

Bitmap Images and Screen Size

Since a bitmap image is a rectangular matrix with a fixed number of pixels, the size of the image on the screen depends on the screen's resolution.

- With a high-resolution screen, the pixels are packed closer together, resulting in a smaller image on the screen.

- With a low-resolution screen, the pixels are spread further apart, making the image on the screen larger.

For a given resolution on a given monitor, the size of a bitmap image is completely determined; it is a fixed rectangle of a set number of pixels high and a set number of pixels wide.

If you want your program to make a bitmap image larger on the screen, the larger image will take up more pixels. Your program will therefore have to figure out what to put in all those new pixels that are spread throughout the larger image. There are various extrapolation methods for coming up with the values for these pixels. Some of these methods are better than others, but the results are usually not as good as the original image.

Vector Graphics

Vector graphics are stored completely differently. Whereas bitmap images are stored encoding a specific number of pixels laid out in a rectangle, vector graphics don't deal in pixels. Vector images have the following characteristics:

- They're stored as a set of mathematical formulas representing geometric shapes, points, and curves comprising the image.

- Because the formulas specify relationships, the actual size of the image on the screen doesn't matter. It can be scaled infinitely.

Figure 1-4 shows the difference between a bitmap image and a vector image that have each been expanded to 200 percent of their original sizes. The bitmap image shows jagged edges where the pixel values have been interpolated. The vector image is much smoother.

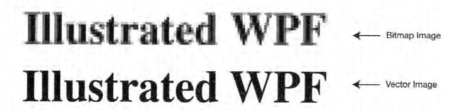

Figure 1-4. *A bitmap image and a vector image that have been expanded to 200 percent of their original sizes*

Table 1-2 lists some of the common extensions associated with vector graphic files.

Table 1-2. *File Extensions for Common Vector Graphic Formats*

Vector Graphics File Extensions		
.svg	.cgm	.pdf
.eps	.hpgl	.swf

System DPI Independence and WPF Units

To lay out a window on the screen, Windows must make an assumption of how many dots (or *pixels*) per inch (dpi) a screen has. In the past, most monitors had 96 pixels per inch. Some, however, could have up to 120. Windows has a setting called Font Size, which allows the user to set the value to 96 dpi, to 120 dpi, or to a custom value. On Windows Vista, the option is called *DPI scaling*.

Previous programming frameworks used pixels as the unit of length. Programmers generally assumed that systems would have 96 pixels per inch and coded accordingly. But if the user changed their Font Size setting from 96 dpi to 120 dpi, there were interesting consequences:

- Things that were 1 inch long at 96 dpi (that is, 96 pixels long) became only 0.8 inches long at 120 dpi because the 96 pixels were closer together.

- Although fonts were scaled uniformly, other components of the window were not, resulting in odd-looking and sometimes unusable screens.

Figure 1-5 illustrates the size of a window on a screen as it might be sized on a system set at 96 dpi and then at 120 dpi.

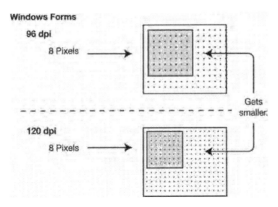

Figure 1-5. *Windows Forms and previous frameworks are pixel-based, so when you change the system resolution through the Font Size setting, the sizes of the windows and UI elements change.*

One of WPF's significant features is that it changes that situation:

- Instead of using the density of actual pixels to laying out the UI, WPF uses "device-independent pixels," or *dip*.

- Each dip represents 1/96 of an inch—regardless of how many actual pixels that length corresponds to.

- If the user changes the dpi from 96 to 120—instead of the size changing, WPF can use the greater density of pixels to render greater detail, as illustrated in Figure 1-6.

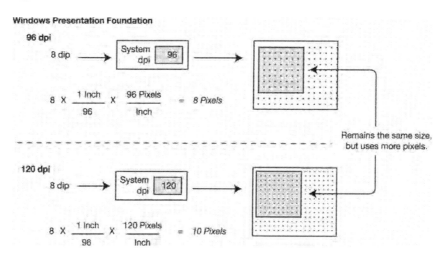

Figure 1-6. *WPF takes into account the value that's set as the system dpi. When the dpi changes, WPF adjusts so that the rendered screens remain the same size.*

▓ **Note** The Font Size setting (system dpi) is different from the *monitor resolution*. If you set the *monitor* to a higher resolution setting, then everything will shrink proportionately. This is independent from the Font Size dpi.

XAML Browser Applications (XBAPs)

Before WPF, we had basically two styles of programs—rich-client applications and browser applications.

- *Rich-client applications* run on the local machine and are characterized by the following:
    - The UI consists of one or more windows.
    - Navigation is provided by the program, using buttons, tabs, and so on.
    - Rich functionality with a range of powerful controls that are executed on the local machine and use the power of that processor.

- *Browser applications* run on the web server and are characterized by the following:
    - The UI consists of a single window hosted by a browser.
    - They use hyperlinks and the browser's Back and Forward buttons for navigation.
    - They use less powerful controls, which are often executed on the server rather than on the local machine—leaving much of the PC's power unused.

WPF introduces a new style of program, called an XBAP, that combines some of the features of these two styles. XBAP stands for *XAML Browser Application*. XBAPs have the following characteristics:

- Like a rich-client application, an XBAP has the following characteristics:
    - It runs on the user's local machine rather than on a web server and can therefore use the processing power of the local machine.
    - It has rich, powerful controls that can take advantage of the user's local processing power.

- Like a browser application, an XBAP application has the following characteristics:
    - It uses only a single window, hosted by a browser.
    - It uses hyperlinks and the browser's Back and Forward buttons for navigation.

The Other Parts of .NET

WPF is one of four major components that were released for the first time in .NET 3.0. These components, which as a group were called WinFX during their development, supplied Microsoft's latest paradigms for important areas of computing. Although this book covers only Windows Presentation Foundation, I'll introduce all four components here:

- *Windows Presentation Foundation (WPF)*: The purpose of WPF, as described throughout this chapter, was to produce a framework for building programs with rich visual content.

- *Windows Communication Foundation (WCF)*: WCF is a new communication infrastructure based on web services. It's designed to allow developers to produce service-oriented systems that can securely and reliably communicate with each other.

- *Windows Workflow Foundation (WF)*: WF is a programming framework allowing programmers to develop systems that implement *workflows*. A workflow is a process, or sequence of actions and inputs, that defines a task from the beginning to the end. Workflows can be sequential, or they can be state machines, where different input values move the process to different states.

- *Windows CardSpace (WCS)*: WCS is a programming framework allowing programmers to connect user identity systems from different trusted sources—producing an "identity metasystem."

Figure 1-7 illustrates that .NET 3.*x* is a superset of .NET 2.0.

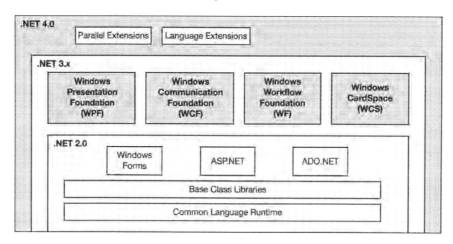

Figure 1-7. *The .NET 3.x Framework contains all of .NET 2.0, plus four additional major components.*

Silverlight

WPF is a Windows-based, rich-client technology. This means that it's not designed to run on other platforms such as the Apple operating systems or on Linux. Also, it's not designed for web-based applications.

To address this, Microsoft introduced a much smaller, lightweight product called Silverlight. Silverlight is designed for web applications regardless of the operating system on which the browser is running. Its goal is to do for web-based applications what WPF does for rich-client applications.

The important things to know about Silverlight are the following:

- Silverlight is a plug-in designed to enable rich content similar to Adobe's Flash browser plug-in and similar to WPF rich-client applications.

  - It's cross-browser, meaning that it's designed to work not only with Internet Explorer but also with all the major browsers such as FireFox, Opera, and Safari.

  - It's cross-platform, in that the browser using Silverlight can be running on a non-Windows platform such as the Macintosh or Linux.

- Because it is a browser plug-in, its runtime size is extremely small, unlike that of WPF.

- Because Silverlight's size must be kept small, its API (and hence its functionality) is a subset of WPF's.

- You can use Visual Studio and C# to create web sites that use Silverlight.

Summary

This chapter gave you a high-level overview of some of the important features of WPF, including the following:

- Unlike previous platforms, WPF allows your programs to make use of much more of the processing power of today's graphics cards to produce visually exciting programs. You saw that it goes directly to Direct3D rather than using the slow software rendering of User32 or GDI.

- WPF gives native support for documents, providing automatic pagination and allowing for dynamic flow of text from one page to the next—all using modern font technologies.

- WPF allows you to control the look of visual components in a way similar to Cascading Style Sheets—using styles and control templates.

- WPF allows you to separate the visual design from the coding so that graphic designers can supply the visual design while programmers code the behavior.

- WPF introduces a new type of rich-client application called an XBAP, which runs inside a browser—taking advantage of the simplicity of the interface and people's familiarity with it.

- Finally, you saw where WPF fits into .NET 4.0, .NET 3.x and.NET 2.0.

CHAPTER 2

■ ■ ■

Overview of WPF Programming

What Is an API?

WPF programming is a large topic with lots of areas to cover. Most of the chapters in this book address one or two topics and cover them in detail. This chapter and the next, however, are different. In these chapters, I'll cover a number of topics that will lay the groundwork for the rest of the text.

In Chapter 1, I told you that WPF programming is often split between a markup language called XAML and code written in C#. In this chapter, I'll concentrate on showing how to build a program using only C# with no XAML. I think it's important for you to understand this process so that you can see how XAML maps to C# (which of course maps to .NET). In Chapter 3, I'll introduce Visual Studio's WPF Project template, which combines XAML and C#.

In this chapter I'll start by showing you a simple WPF program and pointing out some of its parts. I'll then introduce the WPF Class Library and the compilation process. I'll end the chapter with an introduction to the Window class.

In the rest of the book, I'll be covering the WPF API, which allows you to write WPF programs. The API is a set of types—mostly classes—that the programmer uses to build programs. To use the API effectively, you must learn the following:

- What classes and other types make up the API

- The purposes and characteristics of these types

- The unifying ideas about how these types are to be used together to form a whole program

Although the API is a set of types, when referring to the members of the API, I'll generally refer just to *classes*, since the vast majority of the types making up the API are classes. If something refers only to classes, I'll point that out.

A Simple WPF Program

In Chapter 1, I described, at a high level, the features of WPF. In this chapter, I'll start to explain how to use the WPF programming framework, beginning with one of its most fundamental classes—the Window class.

Before I talk about the Window class, though, look through the code in Figure 2-1. This code is a full WPF program. Notice the following about the code:

- Line 11 creates an object of type Window.

- Line 12 sets the Title property of the window to the string "My Simple Window". This string is displayed at the left end of the title bar on the running program.

- Line 13 sets the Content property of the window object to the string "Hi there!". This is displayed in the client area of the window.

- Line 15 creates an object of type Application.

- Line 17 passes the window object to the application object and sets the application running.

```
1    using System;
2    using System.Windows;
3
4    namespace IllustratedWPF.HiThere
5    {
6        class Program
7        {
8            [STAThread]
9            static void Main( )
10           {
11               Window myWin   = new Window();          ←──── Create the Window object, and set two
12               myWin.Title    = "My Simple Window";            of its properties.
13               myWin.Content  = "Hi there!";
14
15               Application myApp = new Application();   ←──── Create the Application object.
16
17               myApp.Run( myWin );                     ←
18           }                                                  Associate the Window object with the
19       }                                                     Application object, and start the
20   }                                                         application running.
```

Figure 2-1. *A complete WPF program that displays a window with a title and content*

When you run this program, it simply displays the window shown in Figure 2-2, which shows the title and the content.

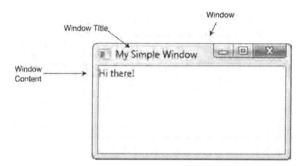

Figure 2-2. *The window includes the Title and Content as set on the window's properties.*

Most of the code in the listing should be pretty clear to you, although you might be unsure about the STAThread attribute. This attribute specifies the *single-threaded apartment* model of threading, which comes into play if the program needs to use COM. When that's the case, this threading model helps ensure reliable communication between the components of the program.

Most programs, however, don't need to use COM at all, in which case it's never initialized. But if it *does* need to be initialized, the system needs to know to use the single-threaded apartment model.

Even if you know your program won't use COM, you must include the STAThread attribute on the Main method, as shown in the following code. Without it, you'll get a compile error.

```
[STAThread]
static void Main()
{
    ...
```

Creating the Simple Program

I'll start by showing you how to build a simple WPF program. For this first program, you won't use Visual Studio's WPF Application template but will instead use the Console Application template. This will allow you to build a bare-bones WPF program without the distractions of XAML and multiple source files.

In Chapter 3, you'll build the same program using the WPF Application template, which is designed for both C# and XAML. For this chapter, however, I want you to see WPF programming at its simplest. All the references to Visual Studio in this book refer to Visual Studio 2008 or Visual Studio 2010, so after this I'll refer to it only as Visual Studio.

The program you'll build, like all WPF programs, uses the three DLLs that comprise the WPF Class Library. These contain the API for writing (and running) WPF programs. Figure 2-3 illustrates the connection between your program and the WPF Class Library.

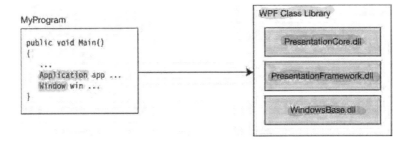

Figure 2-3. *The namespaces containing the definitions of the classes in the WPF framework are contained in three assemblies. WPF programs use the types defined in the WPF Class Library.*

In general, throughout this book I'll assume that you're familiar with Visual Studio and don't need hand-holding to create the programs listed. But in order to make sure we're all on the same page at the beginning, I'll walk through the steps of creating the WPF program shown in the previous section.

The following sections describe the process in two ways. In the section "Just the Facts," I've listed what you need to do to re-create the program. You can use this section if you're thoroughly familiar with .NET programming.

The section following that, called "Step-by-Step," goes into more detail and includes screenshots at each stage. Use whichever approach suits you best, according to your experience and inclination.

Just the Facts

If you're an experienced C# programmer, follow these steps to create the program:

1. Using Visual Studio, create a new project of type Console Application (*not* WPF Application), and call it MySimpleProgramConsole.

2. In the Solution Explorer, open the Properties window, and change Output Type to Windows Application.

3. In the Solution Explorer, under References, look at the .NET tab, and add references to the following assemblies:

   – PresentationCore

   – PresentationFramework

   – WindowsBase

4. In the Program.cs file, do the following:

   a. Add the [STAThread] attribute before the Main method declaration.

   b. Add a using statement for System.Windows.

   c. Copy the code for method Main from Figure 2-1.

   That's it. Run the program to view the (less than exciting) window.

Step-by-Step
The following steps are a more detailed description of creating the initial program:

1. Start Visual Studio, and select File ➤ New ➤ Project from the menu.

2. In the New Project dialog box, do the following:

    a. Select Windows from the "Project types" pane.

    b. Select Console Application from the Templates pane.

    c. Above and to the right of the Templates pane is a drop-down box where you can select the version of the .NET Framework. Make sure the version is greater than .NET 2.0.

    d. Select a name (MySimpleProgramConsole) and a location for the project. Figure 2-4 shows the New Project dialog box.

    e. Click the OK button.

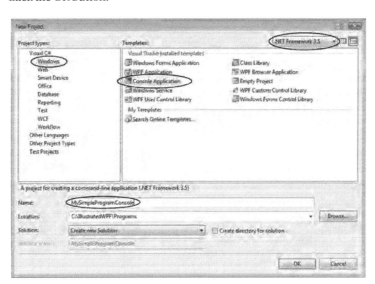

Figure 2-4. *The New Project dialog box*

When you click the OK button, Visual Studio prepares a bare-bones console application workspace for you. When it's done, you'll see a window, named `Program.cs`, in the workspace, as shown in Figure 2-5. Your screen might look just a bit different if you have your Window Layout option set to Tabbed Documents instead of Multiple Documents. You can set your preferred window layout by selecting Tools ➤ Options.

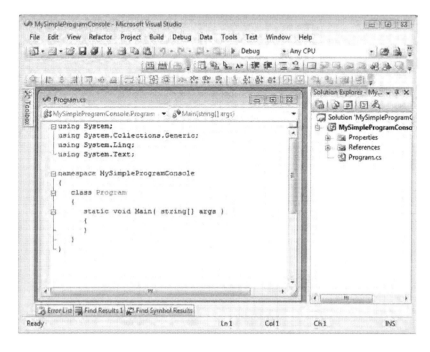

Figure 2-5. *The skeleton program produced from the Console Application template by Visual Studio*

In the Solution Explorer on the right, right-click References, and the Add Reference dialog box will pop up. Select the .NET tab. While holding down the Control key, select `PresentationCore`, `PresentationFramework`, and then `WindowsBase` from the list. Holding down the Control key allows you to select all three references at once. Click OK. Figure 2-6 shows the Add Reference dialog box with the first two of the three references selected.

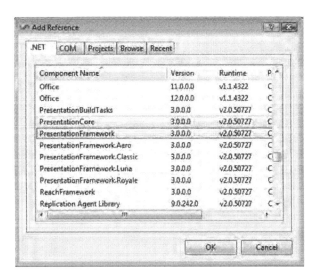

Figure 2-6. *Add references to PresentationCore, PresentationFramework, and WindowsBase.*

When you've added these references, you should be able to find them in the References folder of the Solution Explorer, as shown in Figure 2-7.

Figure 2-7. *When the References folder in the Solution Explorer is expanded, you should be able to see the three DLLs that contain the WPF API.*

By adding these DLLs to the list of references, you're telling Visual Studio where to find the classes and types used in the program.

In the Solution Explorer, right-click the project name—MySimpleProgramConsole—and select Properties. This pops up the project's Properties window. In the Application tab on the left, change "Output type" from Console Application to Windows Application, as shown in Figure 2-8, and save the file.

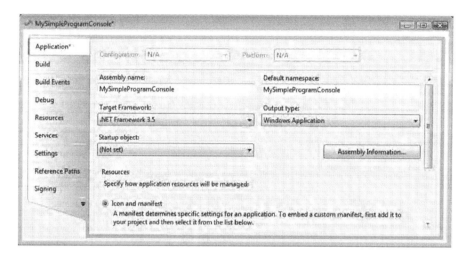

Figure 2-8. *Change the output type from Console Application to Windows Application.*

Now that you've added the references, you can modify the code in the Program.cs window in the following ways:

- Replace the three using statements referencing System.Collections.Generic, System.Linq, and System.Text with a using statement for System.Windows. (It wouldn't actually hurt to leave them in the code, but I want to pare the program down to its essentials.)

- Add the [STAThread] attribute before the Main method.

- Add the following code to the body of method Main:

```
Window myWin  = new Window();          // Create the Window object.
myWin.Title   = "My Simple Window";    // Set the title.
myWin.Content = "Hi there!";           // Set the window content.

Application myApp = new Application();  // Create an Application object.
myApp.Run( myWin );                    // Start application running.
```

Now, when you run the program, it will produce the window shown in Figure 2-9.

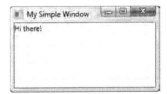

Figure 2-9. *The simple WPF window contains a title in the title bar and content in the client area.*

The Compilation Process

For this simple program, the compiler takes the source file and produces the executable, as shown in Figure 2-10. The directory structure is also shown in the figure. When the project is in the Release configuration, the folders labeled Debug would be labeled Release instead.

This simple process is in stark contrast to the set of files that will be used and produced by the examples in the next chapter that use both C# and XAML.

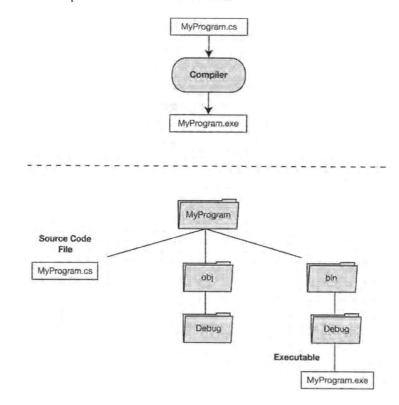

Figure 2-10. *The compiler takes the source code files and produces the executable file in the bin directory.*

The Application and Window Classes

Now that you've seen the very basics of a WPF program, it's time to start learning about the classes used in WPF programs. I'll start with the Window class here and introduce the Application class in the next chapter.

As in the case with the program you just created and ran, most minimally functional WPF programs contain an instance of the Application class and one or more instances of the Window class. You can think of a WPF program as a single Application object and one or more Window objects as represented in Figure 2-11.

- The Application object supports and hosts the Window objects.

- The Window objects comprise the user interface and present the data.

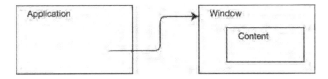

Figure 2-11. *A minimal, useful WPF program usually consists of an* Application *object with one or more associated* Window *objects.*

The Window Class

A program is displayed to the user using windows on the screen. Traditionally, these have been opaque rectangles that contained elements for displaying data and graphics to the user, and controls that allow the user to control the program and supply data. WPF allows a lot more flexibility and style in the presentation of data, but the *basic* model is essentially the same.

Every window on the screen is the visual representation of an instance of the Window class. In this section, I'll describe some of the basic characteristics of windows and the Window class. In later chapters, I'll cover the components and controls used to populate a window.

The Window class is part of the System.Windows namespace.

The Components of a Visual Window

Figure 2-12 shows a standard window and its parts. The two main components are the following:

- The *client area* is the area in the center of the window. This is where you put the content that comprises your user interface and that makes up your program. For the most part, this area is yours to do with as you want.

- The *nonclient area* is the border around the client area, containing the icon, the window title, and various buttons. You don't have to worry much about dealing with this area, because the operating system takes care of it.

  - This area is also called the *window chrome*.

  - You can set the look and behavior of the window chrome by using the WindowStyle property, which I'll describe a bit later.

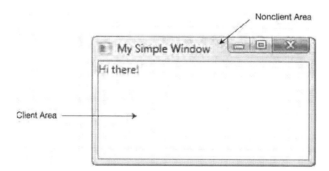

Figure 2-12. *The parts of a standard window*

Creating a Window

The following code shows how to create a main window on the screen. It includes the following actions:

- Declare a class that derives from the Window class, and use the constructor to configure it the way you want by setting the appropriate properties.

- In Main, create an instance of the derived class and have the window display itself on the screen using the Show method.

```
using System;
using System.Windows;

namespace CreateSimpleWindowCode
{           Class derived from Window
                            ↓
   class MyWindow : Window
   {
      public MyWindow()                         // Constructor
      {
         Width     = 300;
         Height    = 200;
         Title     = "My Simple Window";
         Content   = "Hi There!";
      }
   }

   class Program
   {
      [STAThread]
      static void Main( )    Create Window Object.
      {                            ↓
         MyWindow win = new MyWindow();
         win.Show();

         Application app = new Application();
         app.Run();                    ↑
      }         ↑            Create Application object.
   }      Set application running.
}
```

- This code produces the window shown in Figure 2-13.

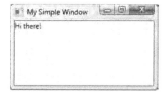

Figure 2-13. *The resulting window*

Important Properties of a Window

When you look at a window on the screen, you'll see several things. These include the client area, which consists of its content and background, and the nonclient area, which consists of the window border and the window bar at the top. The appearance of these items is controlled by five properties: Title, Content, Foreground, Background, and WindowStyle.

The Window object is illustrated in Figure 2-14.

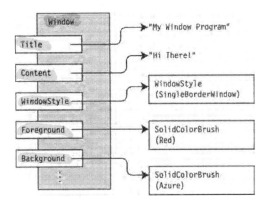

Figure 2-14. *A few of the many important properties of the Window class*

WindowStyle

The WindowStyle property gets or sets the characteristics of the nonclient area, including the border style and the buttons shown in the window bar.

The values that the WindowStyle property can accept are the following:

- SingleBorderWindow: This is the default style. It has the following:

    - A plain single border around the client area

    - A minimize, maximize, and close button in the window bar

    - An application icon in the window bar

- ThreeDBorderWindow: This is similar to the SingleBorderWindow value, but the inside of the border is beveled.

- ToolWindow: This is like the SingleBorderWindow value but doesn't have the icon or the minimize or maximize buttons in the window bar. Also, the border is thinner.

- None: This style has a thin border and no window bar.

The following code produces the top-left window shown in Figure 2-15. You can produce the other three windows by changing the WindowStyle property.

```
[STAThread]
static void Main()
{
   Window win = new Window();
   win.Height = 75; win.Width = 300;
   win.Title = "WindowStyles";
                              WindowStyle
                                   ↓
   win.WindowStyle = WindowStyle.SingleBorderWindow;   // Set property
   win.Content     = win.WindowStyle.ToString();

   Application app = new Application();
   app.Run( win );
}
```

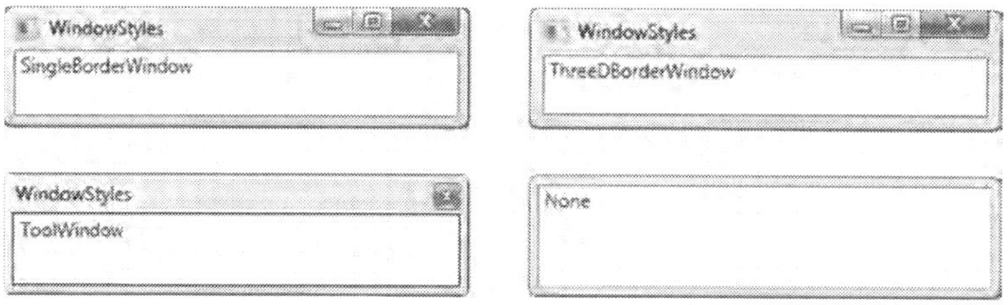

Figure 2-15. *Examples of the four different values of the WindowStyle property*

Content

Unlike previous frameworks for building Windows programs, the content of a Window object *always consists of a single object*. That object might, in turn, contain other objects—but it's still a single object. I'll explain much more about this in Chapter 5 and Chapter 6.

For example, the following code creates a button and assigns the button as the content of the window:

```
public MyWindow()
{
    Title = "My Program Window";
    Width = 300; Height = 200;

    Button btn  = new Button();    // Create a button.
    btn.Content = "Click Me";      // Set the button's text.
        Set the button to be the window content.
                      ↓
    Content = btn;
}
```

Figure 2-16 shows the resulting window. When first looking at this window, some people have trouble seeing the button immediately. That's because it *takes up the whole window*.

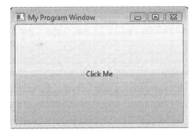

Figure 2-16. *A button as the content of a window*

35

If you add the two following lines to the previous constructor, the button looks much different, as shown in Figure 2-17. I'll explain much more about the size and placement of controls in Chapter 4.

```
btn.HorizontalAlignment = HorizontalAlignment.Center;    ← Additional line
btn.VerticalAlignment   = VerticalAlignment.Center;      ← Additional line
btn.Content = "Click Me";       // Set the button's text.
```

Figure 2-17. *A button centered in the window*

Summary

This chapter was the first of two chapters that gives you a shotgun view of a broad range of topics you need to know in order to start understanding WPF. It covered the following:

- You started by looking at what a programming framework is and how you use it.

- You saw a very simple WPF program that used only C# to create a simple window on the screen.

- You then saw the compilation process and the files and directory structure produced by Visual Studio.

- Finally, you got a short introduction to the `Window` class, which is central to WPF.

CHAPTER 3

■■■

WPF Architecture and Applications

The previous chapter was a gentle introduction to the WPF programming framework and the mechanics of building a program using just C#. In this chapter, I'll cover more of the architecture of WPF and introduce the XAML markup language.

Using Visual Studio to Create a WPF Program

In the previous chapter, I showed you how to build a WPF program from the ground up, using only C# code and the Console Application template. Most WPF projects, however, are not developed that way. Instead, they use a combination of both XAML and C#. Visual Studio 2008 and Visual Studio 2010 have a project template called WPF Application that produces a bare-bones WPF application using XAML and C#. This section shows you how to create a simple program using this template.

Step-by-Step

The following steps will show you how to create a small WPF program called MySimpleProgram:

1. Begin by opening Visual Studio. From the File menu item, select New ➤ Project, as shown in Figure 3-1.

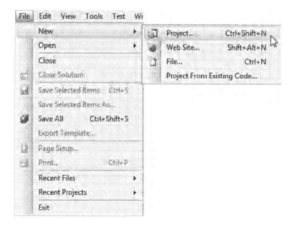

Figure 3-1. *Create a new project using the Project menu item.*

2. Figure 3-2 shows the New Project dialog box. In that dialog box, do the following:

    – In the Project types pane on the left, select Windows.

    – In the Templates pane on the right, select WPF Application.

    – In the Name text box, enter MySimpleProgram.

    – Fill the Location text box by using the Browse button on the right to browse to the directory where you want Visual Studio to place the solution.

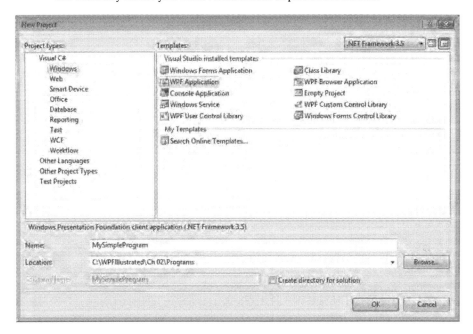

Figure 3-2. *Select the WPF Application template from the New Project dialog box.*

3. When you've selected the template, name, and location, click the OK button, and Visual Studio will prepare a bare-bones WPF solution workspace for you. When it finishes preparing the solution, there will be either two windows in the workspace or two tabs—named Window1.xaml.cs and Window1.xml. Figure 3-3 shows the configuration with windows. If only the XAML window opens, you can click the + sign in front of Window1.xaml in the Solution Explorer on the right, and double-click the .cs file to open it.

    As an aside—you can choose to have documents in separate windows, as shown in Figure 3-3, or have documents in separate tabs by choosing options via the Tools ➤ Options menu.

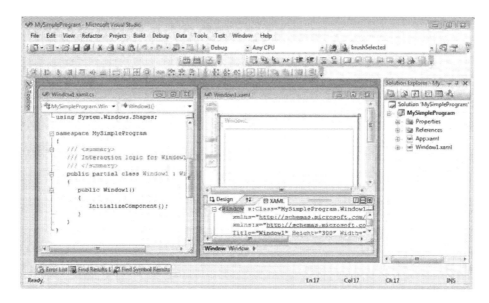

Figure 3-3. *The WPF Application template produces a minimal WPF program with two classes, each with a XAML file and a C# code-behind file.*

4. Close Window1.xaml, and widen Window1.xaml.cs, as shown in Figure 3-4. Below the line with the call to method InitializeComponent, add the following two lines, as shown in Figure 3-4.

```
Title    = "My Simple Window";
Content  = "Hi there.";
```

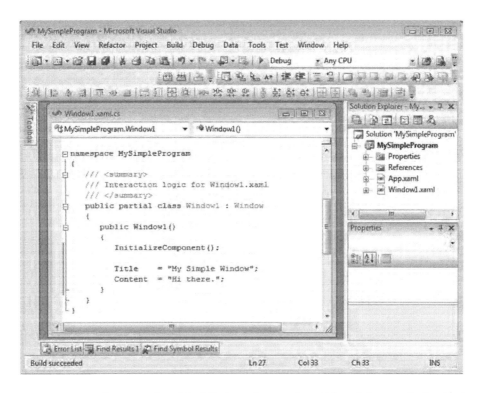

Figure 3-4. *You can set the properties of the Window1 class, such as Title and Content, in the class's constructor.*

When you compile and run this program, it will produce the same output window as the simple console application program presented in Chapter 2 and shown in Figure 3-5.

Figure 3-5. *When the program is compiled and run, it produces the simple window with a title and content in the client area.*

Source Code Generated by the Template

Now that you've used the WPF Application template, let's look more closely at what Visual Studio produced for you. This template produces a program called MySimpleProgram, consisting of two classes, as shown in Figure 3-6. One class is called App and is derived from the Application class, and the other is called Window1 and is derived from Window.

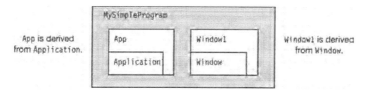

Figure 3-6. *The WPF Application template produces a program with two class—one derived from Application and the other derived from Window.*

Each of the two classes is implemented as two source code files, placed in the solution folder, as shown in Figure 3-7.

- Two of the files implement class App—one XAML file and one C# file.

- The other two files implement class Window1—one XAML file and one C# file.

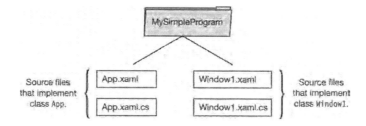

Figure 3-7. *Using the WPF Application template, Visual Studio produces four source code files. Each of the two classes is implemented as a XAML file and a C# file.*

What Is XAML?

XAML is an XML-based markup language for specifying and setting the characteristics of classes. Most WPF programs use both C# and XAML.

- XAML is used mainly for specifying static and visual aspects of the UI by setting properties of class objects.

  - Most XAML is produced by UI layout tools such as Expression Blend, rather than being coded by hand.

  - UI layout tools such as Expression Blend are often used by graphic designers rather than programmers.

- C# is used mainly for specifying most of the active parts of a program such as the flow of control and message handlers.

For example, you might use XAML to place a button on a window and to set all its visual characteristics. But you would use C# to write the message handler that's called when the button is clicked.

The two default XAML files Visual Studio generates for you are shown in Figure 3-8. Don't worry about the details of the code, since I'll be covering the syntax of XAML in Chapter 4.

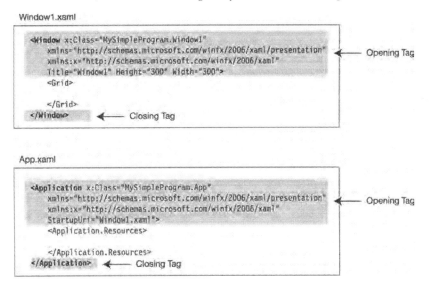

Figure 3-8. *These two XAML files are generated by default by Visual Studio.*

Logical Trees and Visual Trees

Like all XML, XAML specifies a node that contains other nodes. This containment structure forms a tree where each node can contain other nodes.

The top of Figure 3-9 shows the XAML for a simple window that contains a panel with a TextBlock and a button. Again, don't worry about the details of the XAML. Notice, though, that the structure is such that elements, like Window and StackPanel, contain other elements, to form a tree of elements. WPF works with two trees—the logical tree and the visual tree, as shown in the figure.

- The *logical tree* comprises the elements as they are listed in the XAML. These include panels and controls you will generally use.

- The *visual tree* includes the parts that make up the controls and panels. You don't generally have to deal with these. But you need to be aware of the visual tree because it's referred to in the literature, and you also might need to deal with it if you need to do some more advanced tinkering.

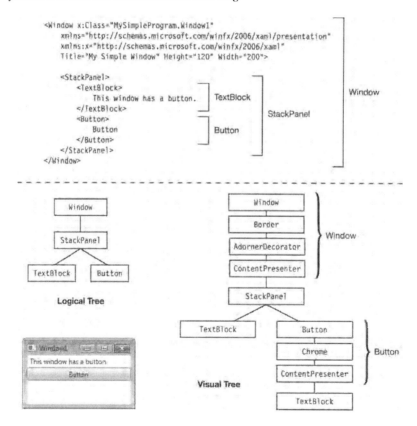

Figure 3-9. *The XAML creates a logical tree and a visual tree.*

The Compilation Process

For a program using both XAML and C#, the compilation is a two-step process. In the first step, the compiler takes each XAML file and translates it into two files, as shown in Figure 3-10.

- One file is a C# file that contains code to load the XAML and connect various components and handlers at run time. You can look at this file, but don't bother modifying it, because it's generated by the compiler and will overwrite any changes you make.

- The other file is a condensed version of the XAML file, called a *BAML* file.

    - BAML stands for Binary Application Markup Language.

    - This version of the XAML code is tokenized to make it more efficient for loading and parsing at run time. It isn't designed to be human-readable.

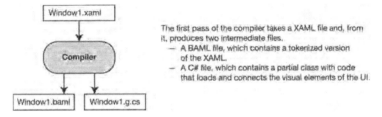

Figure 3-10. *The compiler's first pass translates the XAML into two intermediate files.*

In the second step, the compiler takes the C# files and the BAML files and produces the executable, as shown in Figure 3-11.

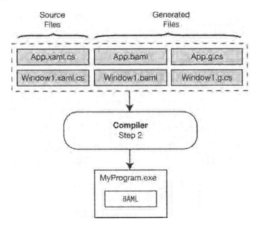

Figure 3-11. *The compiler takes the source code files and produces a set of intermediate files and then produces the executable file from the intermediate files.*

47

Figure 3-12 shows the directory structure produced by Visual Studio when it generates a project from the WPF Application template. This structure shows the output after compilation, when the project is in the Debug configuration. The four source code files are in the project folder, along with two other folders, as shown.

- The bin folder, shown on the right, contains a subfolder containing the executable. The subfolder is called either Debug or Release, depending on whether you're in Debug mode or Release mode.

- The obj folder contains a subfolder containing intermediate files generated by the compiler.

  - You shouldn't ever have to do anything with these files. As a matter of fact, if you change anything in these files, your changes will be lost when the compiler overwrites them at the next compilation.

  - The App.baml file will appear only if you add elements to the App.xaml source file. Otherwise, it would add no content, so the compiler doesn't bother generating it.

  - The subfolder under obj is called either Debug or Release.

- When it's in the Release configuration, the folders labeled Debug would be labeled Release, instead.

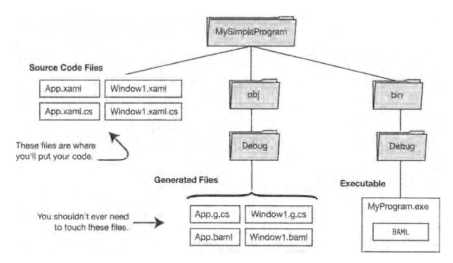

Figure 3-12. *Visual Studio and the compiler produce a directory structure with the source files in one directory, the intermediate generated files in another directory, and the executable in another.*

How the Files Are Used

You already know that the `Application` and `Window1` classes each have a C# source file, a generated C# file, and a XAML file, which is translated into a BAML file. You know the roles of the source files, but the roles of the generated files are the following:

- The generated BAML files are a condensed and more efficient translation of the XAML files. They are optimized for faster loading and interpreting at run time, since, at run time, the program loads these files into memory.

- The generated C# file has an extension of `.g.cs`. This file contains the code to load the BAML from the executable and connect it up to create the UI. The *g* in the extension stands for *generated*.

The compiler takes the C# source file and the generated C# file, and uses the partial classes in each to create the complete class, as illustrated by Figure 3-13. (Unless you look carefully, you might miss the `Connect` method in `Window1.g.cs`. It's an explicit interface implementation, and its fully qualified name is `System.Windows.Markup.IComponentConnector.Connect`.)

```
public class Window1 : Window
{
    public Window1()                                                    From
    {                                                              Window1.xaml.cs
        InitializeComponent();
        ...
    }

    public void InitializeComponent()                                   From
    {                                                              Window1.g.cs
        // Load the BAML
    }


    void System.Windows.Markup.IComponentConnector.Connect(int connectionId, object target)
    {
        // Connect the controls, fields and event handlers.
    }
}
```

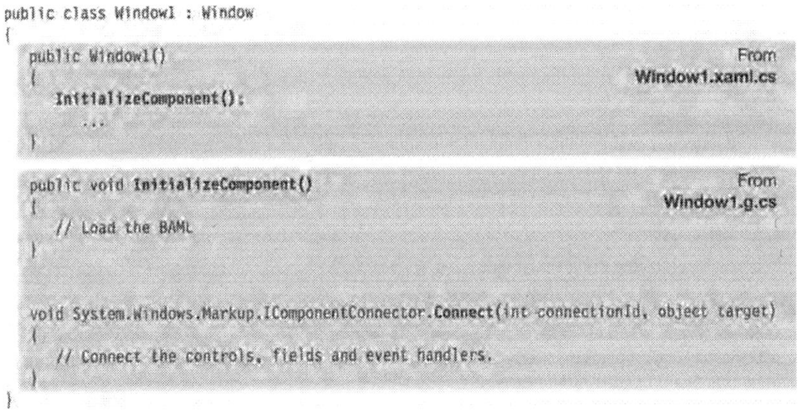

Figure 3-13. *The partial class declarations in a class's source C# file and generated C# file are combined into a single class by the compiler.*

When the program is creating an object of class Window1, the following tasks are performed:

1. The Window1 constructor is called.

2. The Window1 constructor calls the class's InitializeComponent method, which loads the UI tree and connects all the pieces and event handlers.

Figure 3-14 shows the Window1 class object, the BAML embedded in the assembly, and the UI tree produced by calling the InitializeComponent method.

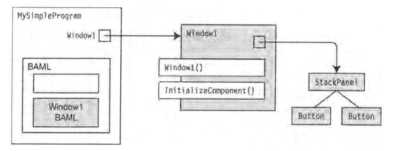

Figure 3-14. *The constructor for class Window1 calls the InitializeComponent method, which loads the Window1 BAML from the assembly, and constructs the tree of UI elements.*

The WPF Architecture

Now that you're familiar with the process of creating a WPF program, it's time to start looking at WPF's architecture and some of the classes that make up the WPF API. As mentioned previously, WPF is a set of assemblies. These assemblies are split between two layers, as illustrated by the shaded boxes in Figure 3-15.

- The *Managed WPF layer* is a set of classes and types built using the .NET Framework—which means that it is managed by the Common Language Runtime (CLR). This layer contains the three assemblies that comprise the WPF API:

  - The `WindowsBase` assembly contains many of the fundamental types you'll use in building WPF programs, including the `Application` and `Window` classes.

  - The `PresentationFramework` contains the classes and types that make up the API for programming in WPF. This is the layer most of your code will interact with.

  - The `PresentationCore` contains the low-level classes and types that are the building blocks used by the `PresentationFramework` above it.

- The *Media Integration layer* is unmanaged code and maps the WPF constructs to DirectX. DirectX, in turn, maps them to the graphics card. This module is unmanaged code so that it can be as efficient as possible.

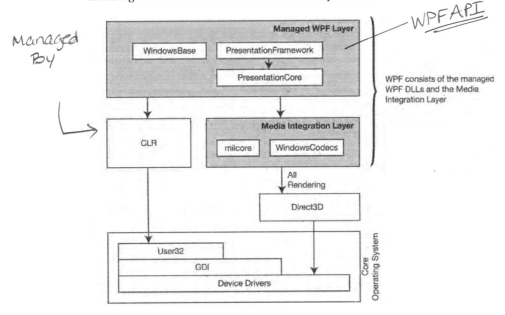

Figure 3-15. *The high-level architecture of WPF contains a managed layer and an unmanaged layer.*

More About the Window Class

In the previous chapter, you got a very short introduction to the `Window` class. In this chapter, I'll cover the `Window` class a bit more and then discuss the `Application` class.

In the previous chapter you saw that, in a simple case, the content of a window can contain text. The text is considered the *foreground* of the window, and the space around it is called the *background*. Unless you specify otherwise, the foreground is black, and the background of the window is painted white. But you can make both of these far more interesting.

The foreground and background of a window are each painted by a `Brush`. Which brush to use in each case is stored in the window's `Foreground` and `Background` properties.

A *brush* is a graphic that can be used to paint an area. There are six types of brushes, which fall into the three categories shown here:

- A `SolidColorBrush` paints the surface using a single color.

- A `GradientBrush` starts its stroke painting one color and transitions to another color by the end of the stroke. There are two types of gradient brush—`LinearGradientBrush` and `RadialGradientBrush`.

- A `TileBrush` paints an area with an image. There are three kinds of `TileBrushes`, which differ in the types of image used. They are `ImageBrush`, `DrawingBrush`, and `VisualBrush`.

Figure 3-16 shows the six types of brushes. The three classes Brush, GradientBrush, and TileBrush are abstract classes. In this chapter, I'll introduce the `SolidColorBrush`, `LinearGradientBrush`, and `RadialGradientBrush` classes and cover the others in Chapter 18.

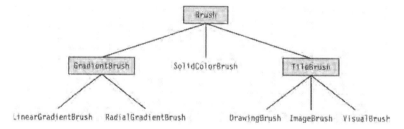

Figure 3-16. *Six types of brushes are available for painting a background. Each brush type paints with a different type of graphic.*

SolidColorBrushes

A SolidColorBrush paints an area with a single color. The SolidColorBrush class is derived from Brush and references a Color object, as shown in Figure 3-17.

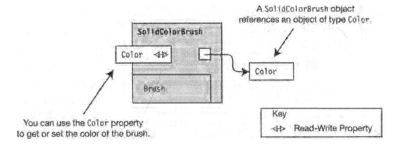

Figure 3-17. *The Color property of the SolidColorBrush class gets or sets the color of the brush.*

WPF provides a class called Brushes that can supply SolidColorBrush objects of 141 predefined colors. Figure 3-18 illustrates the Brushes class.

- Each color brush is represented by a static, read-only property with the color's name.

- The brushes returned by the Brushes class can't be modified.

The following code shows how to use the Brushes class to assign a brush to the background of window win:

```
win.Background = Brushes.Blue;
               ↑          ↑
          Class Name   Property
```

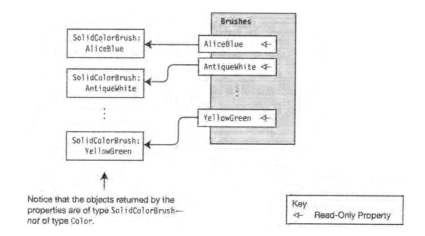

Figure 3-18. *The static properties of the Brushes class return SolidColorBrushes of 141 predefined colors.*

Creating Colors

The Brushes class returns preconstructed SolidColorBrush objects that can't be changed. Much of the time that's fine. Sometimes, however, you want greater control of the brush. You might, for example, want a color that isn't included in the standard 141 colors, or you might want to be able to change the color of the brush. In these cases, you can create your own SolidColorBrush objects.

If you want to create a SolidColorBrush that's not one of the 141 colors available, you'll have to create your own Color object and supply it to the brush. To do this, you'll need to understand how WPF represents colors.

The System.Windows.Media namespace contains the Color struct, which is used to represent colors.

- The Color struct has four main properties that represent the characteristics of a color:

    - The A property represents the opacity of the color.

    - The R, G, and B properties represent the three primary additive colors—red, green and blue. When you combine them in various proportions, they produce different resulting colors.

- The A, R, G, and B properties are of type byte, so each property can have a value ranging from 0 to 255. If the value of the A property is 0, the color is completely transparent. If its value is 255, the color is completely opaque.

- The string representation of a Color object is an eight-digit hexadecimal value, where the A, R, G, and B values are each represented by two hex digits.

Figure 3-19 summarizes the important information about the Color struct.

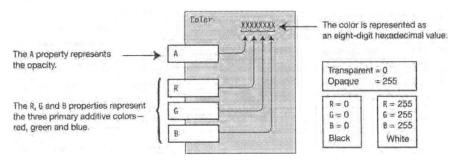

Figure 3-19. *The Color struct uses four main properties to set the color represented by the object.*

To create a Color object with a particular color, do the following:

- Use the constructor of the Color struct to create a new object.

- Set the four properties to values between 0 and 255, inclusive.

Once you have your new color, you can use it in the constructor for the SolidColorBrush to create a brush with that color. For example, the following code creates an object of type Color and sets the values to create a medium blue. The string representing this Color object is #FF6496C8.

```
[STAThread]
static void Main()
{
    Window win = new Window();
    win.Width = 250; win.Height = 150;
    win.Title = "Creating Colors";
                    Use the constructor to create a new object.
                                    ↓
    Color MyColor = new Color();

    // Set the properties to values between 0 and 255.
    MyColor.A = 255;          // 0xFF
    MyColor.R = 100;          // 0x64
    MyColor.G = 150;          // 0x96
    MyColor.B = 200;          // 0xC8
                    Use the constructor to create a new SolidColorBrush object.
                                    ↓
    SolidColorBrush scb = new SolidColorBrush( MyColor );
                                                  ↑
    win.Background = scb;                  Your Newly Defined Color
    win.Content = MyColor.ToString();   // Produces the string #FF6496C8

    Application app = new Application();
    app.Run( win );
}
```

Creating your own Color objects, however, can be tedious, so the WPF framework supplies a class called Colors, which defines 141 common colors. This class is similar to the Brushes class you saw previously. But instead of returning SolidColorBrush objects, it returns Color objects.

- The class has 141 properties, each of which returns a Color object of a predefined color, as illustrated in Figure 3-20.

- The properties are static, so you must use the class name along with the property name.

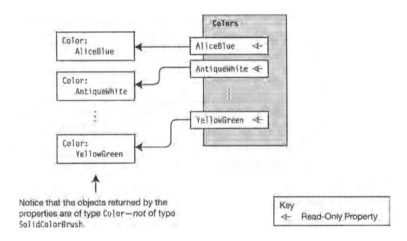

Figure 3-20. *The Colors class provides 141 properties that return Color objects of predefined colors.*

You can use objects from the Colors class in the constructor of a SolidColorBrush. The following code shows an example. It creates two new SolidColorBrushes and uses them to set the colors of the background and the foreground of a window.

```
                            Predefined Color from Class Colors
                                         ↓
win.Background = new SolidColorBrush( Colors.CornflowerBlue );
win.Foreground = new SolidColorBrush( Colors.Crimson        );
                                       ↑        ↑
                                     Class   Property
```

I've found that people are often confused about the relationships between the three classes Brush, Brushes, and SolidColorBrush. The following are the important things to understand with regard to their relationships:

- Brushes and SolidColorBrush are both concrete classes. Brush, however, is the abstract class from which SolidColorBrush derives.

- The properties of class Brushes return objects of type SolidColorBrush—not objects of type Brush—since there can be no objects of type Brush. A more accurate name for class Brushes would have been SolidColorBrushes—but that's not the way it is.

Figure 3-21 shows the relationships between these classes.

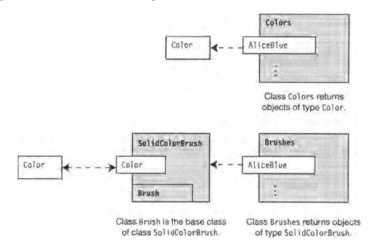

Figure 3-21. *The relationships between classes Brush, Brushes, and SolidColorBrush*

Gradient Brushes

A SolidColorBrush paints with a single color. A *gradient brush* has a stroke that starts with one color and gradually changes to another. WPF supplies two types of gradient brushes—*linear gradient brushes* and *radial gradient brushes*.

Figure 3-22 shows examples of two gradient brushes. In these examples:

- The gradients go from white to black.

- The linear gradient brush starts on the left edge and goes to the right edge.

- The radial gradient brush starts at the center and goes outward.

Linear gradient brush going from
white on the left to black on the right.

Radial gradient brush going from
white in the center to black on the edges.

Figure 3-22. Gradient brushes going from white to black

Linear Gradient Brushes

The LinearGradientBrush class has a number of constructors, each of which allows you to specify the characteristics of the gradient in different ways. The most straightforward constructor requires two colors and two points. The syntax is the following:

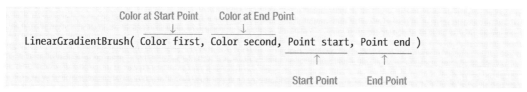

In determining the start point and the end point, the coordinate system for linear gradients uses a sliding scale that goes from 0 to 1.

- Regardless of the actual size of the item being painted:
  - The height is always considered to be a distance of 1.
  - The width is always considered to be a distance of 1.
- Even if the user changes the size of the window or the object, the edges are still considered 1 unit long.

Figure 3-23 illustrates the sliding coordinate system. Even with rectangles of different sizes, the edges are always considered to be of length 1.

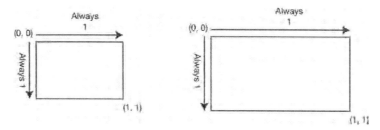

Figure 3-23. *Regardless of the actual size or proportions of the window, as far as the gradient is concerned, the window is always 1 unit wide and 1 unit high.*

For example, the following code creates a rectangular window with a linear gradient. It uses white and black as its start and end colors, and it uses the top-left corner (0, 0) and the bottom-right corner (1, 1) as the start and end points, respectively.

```
[STAThread]
static void Main()
{
   Window win = new Window();
   win.Height = 200; win.Width = 275; win.Title = "Linear Gradient Brush";

   // Create the end points.
   Point first  = new Point( 0, 0 );  // Start point
   Point second = new Point( 1, 1 );  // End point

                                Start Color      End Color     Start      End
                                    ↓                ↓           ↓          ↓
   LinearGradientBrush lgb =
      new LinearGradientBrush( Colors.White, Colors.Black, first, second );
                                                 ↑
                                            Constructor
   win.Background = lgb;       // Apply the brush to the background

   Application app = new Application();
   app.Run( win );
}
```

This code produces the window shown in Figure 3-24.

Figure 3-24. *A linear gradient from the four-parameter constructor.*

RadialGradientBrushes

Using a RadialGradientBrush is similar to using a LinearGradientBrush. Actually, it's even simpler because, by default, a RadialGradientBrush always starts at the center of the canvas and progresses to the outer edges. Therefore, you don't have to specify the start and end points.

The following is the syntax for the constructor of a simple RadialGradientBrush.

```
                              Color at Start Point
                                      ↓
RadialGradientBrush ( Color first, Color second )
                                         ↑

                              Color at End Point
```

The following code creates a rectangular window whose background is painted with a radial gradient brush:

```
[STAThread]
static void Main()
{
   Window win = new Window(); win.Height = 200; win.Width = 275;
   win.Title = "Radial Gradient Brush";
                              Color at Center    Color at Edges
                                      ↓                ↓
   RadialGradientBrush lgb =
      new RadialGradientBrush ( Colors.White, Colors.Black );
                               ↑

                          Constructor
   win.Background = lgb;

   Application app = new Application();
   app.Run( win );
}
```

This code produces the window shown in Figure 3-25.

Figure 3-25. *A linear gradient from the two-parameter constructor*

The Application Class

The Application class is the harness that hosts your program and the infrastructure that allows it to run. Every WPF application has a single instance of an object of the Application class. Some of the important things to know about the class are the following:

- The Application class starts your program running and manages the messages that drive it.

- The Application class is a member of the System.Windows namespace. This is different from the Application class for Windows Forms programs, which is in the System.Windows.Forms namespace.

    Figure 3-26 illustrates the Application class and some of its important members.

- The Run method starts the program running and calls the OnStartup method, which will be described later in this chapter.

- The Current property is a static property that returns a reference to the program's Application object.

- The ShutdownMode property can hold one of three values of the ShutdownMode enumeration. The value specifies the condition on which the application should be shut down. The enumeration values are the following.

    - OnLastWindowClose: The application closes when its last window closes.

    - OnMainWindowClose: The application closes when its main window closes.

    - OnExplicitShutdown: The application closes only when its Shutdown method is called.

- The StartupUri property holds the location of the UI to start when the application starts.

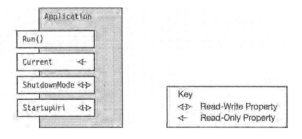

Figure 3-26. *The members of the Application class manage the life cycle of the application.*

Handling Application Events

During an application's lifetime, it goes through various stages, such as startup, activation, deactivation, and shutdown. Some of these stages are signaled by events. If you want your program to execute its own code when these events occur, you can write handlers and attach handlers to the events.

Application Lifetime Events

The Application class has seven events that can be raised at various points in an application's lifetime. The following five are the most common:

- Startup is raised by the Run method when the application is first starting up.

- Exit is raised when the application is closing down.

- Activated is raised when the application becomes the foreground application.

- Deactivated is raised when a different application becomes the foreground application.

- SessionEnding is raised when the Windows session is ending. This usually means the computer is shutting down.

You can associate methods (event handlers) with an application's events, using either markup or code. Then, when those events are raised, your event handlers will be called. The naming convention for the event handlers is to preface the name of the event with the string App_.

The process for attaching a handler to an event is the following:

1. Create an event handler for the event. The *event handler* is a method with the following characteristics:

    - It contains the code you want executed when the event is raised.

    - It has a return type of void and has the signature shown in Table 3-1. By convention, the name of the handler starts with App_ followed by the name of the event. Notice that the second parameter is specific to the event.

2. Add the event handler to the Application object's event, as shown in the following code. Now, whenever event Startup is raised, it will invoke method App_Startup. (Variable app in this line of code is an object of type Application.)

Each event has a corresponding method that raises the event. The name of the method consists of the name of the event, prefaced by the word On. Table 3-1 has the names of these methods. Figure 3-27 shows the pattern, using event Startup. The process is the following:

1. When the OnStartup method is called, it raises the Startup event.

2. The Startup event invokes any methods attached to it. In the figure, method App_Startup is attached to the event—so it is invoked.

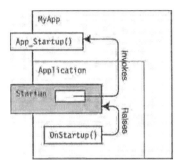

Figure 3-27. *When the OnStartup method is called, it raises the Startup event, which invokes your event handler method App_Startup.*

Table 3-1. *Common Events Associated with the Application Class*

Event Name	Raises Event	Signature and Return Type of Handler
Startup	OnStartup	void App_Startup(object sender, StartupEventArgs args)
Exit	OnExit	void App_Exit(object sender, ExitEventArgs args)
Activated	OnActivated	void App_Activated(object sender, ActivatedEventArgs args)
Deactivated	OnDeactivated	void App_Deactivated(object sender, DeactivatedEventArgs args)
SessionEnding	OnSessionEnding	void App_SessionEnding(object sender, SessionEndingEventArgs args)

The following code is an example of adding a handler to the Startup event.

- It declares a method name App_Startup with the appropriate signature and contains the code to be executed when the application starts. In this case it just shows a message box.

- In Main, it adds the handler to the event.

```
class MyWindow : Window
{
    public MyWindow()
    {
        Width = 300;  Height = 200; Title = "My Program Window";
        Content = "This application handles the Startup event.";
    }
}

class Program        The Startup Event Handler
{                              ↓
    static void App_Startup( object sender, StartupEventArgs args )
    {
        MessageBox.Show( "The application is starting.", "Starting Message" );
    }

    [STAThread]
    static void Main()
    {
        MyWindow win = new MyWindow();

        Application app = new Application();
        app.Startup += App_Startup;        // Add the handler to the event
                ↑              ↑
            ( Event )      (( Handler )
        app.Run( win );
    }
}
```

UI Elements Contain Content

WPF is designed to present content. Most UI elements are designed to contain either one item of content or a collection of items. Oftentimes, the content or items can contain their own nested content, and so forth.

Three classes from which a large portion of controls are derived are shown as the first three classes in Figure 3-28, which also lists classes derived from those classes. Their content properties are the following:

- The Content property can contain a single item of content.

  – Controls derived from the ContentControl class inherit this property.

  – Notice from the figure that both the Window class and the Button class are derived from ContentControl. A button can contain the same types of content as a window.

- The Items property is a collection that can contain multiple items of content.

  – Controls derived from the ItemsControl class inherit this property.

  – An example is the Listbox control, which uses the Items property to hold the items displayed in the list box.

- The Children property is also a collection of UI elements. The Children property is inherited by classes derived from the Panel class.

- The HeaderedItemControl class is unusual in that it contains a reference to a single item of content, as well as a collection of items.

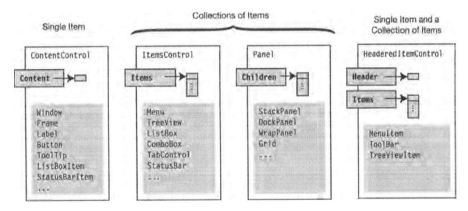

Figure 3-28. *Most UI elements are designed to hold either a single item of content or a collection of content items, as shown in the first three class boxes. But this is not ironclad, as shown in the fourth base class, which has both.*

67

The Class Inheritance Hierarchy

This section will introduce you to the class structure underneath the user interface elements. The user interface elements are contained in the Managed WPF layer, shown in Figure 3-29.

For most purposes, you will use the classes in the PresentationFramework assembly, which are derived from classes in PresentationCore. You won't, however, generally need to go down into the PresentationCore classes.

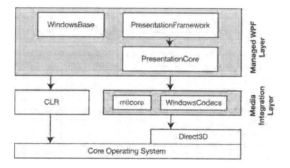

Figure 3-29. *Most of the user interface elements you'll use in your programs are contained in the PresentationFramework assembly of the Managed WPF layer.*

Figure 3-30 gives a closer view of these two layers. Throughout the rest of this book I'll be explaining the details of how to use the classes and types derived from class FrameworkElement shown in the PresentationFramework part of the figure. But in this section I'll give you a brief description of three of the classes from which they are derived—FrameworkElement, UIElement, and Visual.

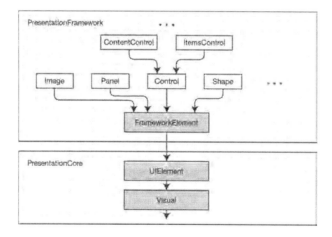

Figure 3-30. *Part of the WPF class hierarchy. The FrameworkElement class is the base class from which most of the visual elements in the PresentationFramework layer derive.*

Although these classes are base classes that you won't generally need to use or think about, it is useful to at least have an understanding of their parts in the inheritance hierarchy of the classes you *will* be using.

- The FrameworkElement class is the building block class from which most of the important elements in the presentation framework derive. It implements support for the following:

  - The logical tree model, which allows XAML to use logical items rather than the full visual tree items.

  - Styles—which are like cascading style sheets for UI elements. You can set characteristics associated with a style and then assign the style to various UI elements.

  - Refinements of animation support defined in some of its base classes.

- The UIElement class is the base class for the FrameworkElement class and implements support for the following:

  - Layout of the object—including sizing and positioning

  - Focus and input issues for the object, including keyboard and mouse input

  - Lower-level animation support

- The Visual class is the base class of UIElement. It implements support for the following:

  - The bulk of the rendering tasks. This is its most important function.

  - Hit testing, as well as determining the boundaries of the bounding box of an element.

For now, these are the main things you should know about these classes. They do much of the low-level work of the controls and UI elements that are built on top of them.

Summary

This chapter was the second of two chapters that gave an introduction to a number of topics that will serve as a foundation for your learning about WPF. In this chapter, I covered the following:

- You learned how to create a WPF program using Visual Studio's WPF Application template. As part of this you learned the following:

    - The default set of files supplied by Visual Studio

    - The directory structure of WPF projects

- You learned about the steps performed by the compiler and the files used and produced at each step.

- You got a short introduction to the XAML markup language.

- You learned about the architecture of WPF and the different layers involved.

- You got more information about the `Window` class and a description of the `Application` class.

- You learned about the new WPF concepts of logical and visual trees and got an introduction to the concept of content and containment in WPF.

- Finally, you got an introduction to the class inheritance hierarchy.

The chapters following this one will be much more focused and methodical, since they generally concentrate on only one or two topics.

CHAPTER 4

■ ■ ■

XAML

A Tree of Objects

One of the most important concepts of WPF is that the user interface is a tree of WPF class objects. That tree has a single node at the top, and each node in the tree can have zero or more child nodes.

In Chapter 2, you saw that you can use C# to instantiate WPF class objects and connect them explicitly, creating the tree.

But the tree structure is exactly the type of structure produced by an XML document. The WPF designers used that fact to create a variant of XML, called XAML, for creating trees of WPF objects. (XAML stands for *eXtensible Application Markup Language.*) A XAML parser interprets the XAML markup and produces the tree of WPF objects, as illustrated in Figure 4-1.

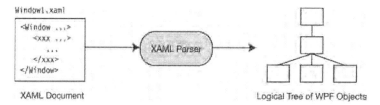

Figure 4-1. *The XAML parser interprets the XAML document and produces the tree of WPF objects, which constitutes the user interface.*

The purpose of this chapter is to explain the syntax and semantics of XAML documents and how the XAML parser interprets them.

Some of the first things you should know about XAML are the following:

- XAML is case sensitive, and follows most of the other XML syntax rules also.

- In a WPF program, although XAML is mostly used to specify the user interface, it can also be used to specify other .NET objects such as the Application object.

- As you saw in Chapter 2, WPF programs don't need to use XAML at all. You can write WPF programs completely in C#, or other .NET languages.

- XAML isn't limited to WPF.

  - Windows Workflow Foundation (WF) also uses XAML—but uses it to specify the structure of workflows, rather than to produce UIs.

  - Silverlight uses a subset of WPF XAML to build user interfaces for web applications.

- XAML source is called either *markup* or *XAML code.*

Although you can write WPF programs without using XAML, using XAML along with C# has some benefits over C# alone:

- Using them together allows you to separate the UI visual design from the coding of the behavior. This allows a graphic designer to produce the visual design and a programmer to code the behavior.

- XAML can be more compact and simpler than C# code.

This second point might be surprising, since C# has a lean and sparse syntax, and XML and its derivatives have a verbose syntax. Given that, it might be surprising that the XAML specification of a particular UI construction is generally shorter and less complex than the C# construction.

XAML is simpler and more compact because it's specialized for a particular purpose and streamlined syntactically for it. C#, on the other hand, is a general-purpose programming language. It allows you a vast amount of control of your code, but the disadvantage is that you must do everything explicitly.

Using XamlPad

Throughout this chapter and the rest of the book, I'll be providing lots of XAML markup to illustrate various points. Microsoft has created a utility called XamlPad, which parses XAML and displays the output. It's an excellent tool for playing with XAML, without having to create new solutions or projects in Visual Studio. You'll probably want to use it to try the various bits of sample code in this chapter.

XamlPad is installed in the Tools folder when you install the latest Windows SDK. To get the latest SDK, go to msdn.microsoft.com/downloads, and find the "Windows SDK" link. Click that, and it will take you to the SDK download page. From there, download and install the SDK.

Creating the UI Structure

When using C# to create a WPF user interface, you must create the UI structure explicitly, which consists of the following tasks:

- Create the UI WPF objects using the new operator.

- Explicitly specify which objects contain which other objects.

Figure 4-2 shows these steps, and Figure 4-3 shows the logical tree produced by the code and the resulting window.

```
class Program
{
    class MyWindow : Window
    {
        public MyWindow()
        {
            StackPanel sp = new StackPanel();     ⎫
            Button btn    = new Button();          ⎬  Create the objects explicity.
            TextBlock txt = new TextBlock();       ⎭

            btn.Content = "Click Me";              ⎫
            txt.Text    = "Illustrated WPF";       ⎬  Hook up the containment
            sp.Children.Add( txt );                ⎬  structure explicitly.
            sp.Children.Add( btn );                ⎭
            Content = sp;
        }
    }

    [STAThread]
    static void Main( )
    {
        Application app = new Application();
        MyWindow win = new MyWindow();
        app.Run( win );
    }
}
```

Figure 4-2. *Using C#, you must explicitly create the WPF objects and connect them to create the logical tree.*

Figure 4-3. *The logical tree created by the code and the resulting window*

When you create a user interface structure using XAML, the process is simpler than with C#. XAML allows you to create the WPF objects and the logical tree at the same time by specifying a nested tree of elements.

Figure 4-4 illustrates the XAML version of the same user interface structure created with the C# code. The logical tree and the resulting window are the same as shown in Figure 4-3. Don't worry about the syntactic details of the XAML, because I'll start describing that in the next section, but notice that the containment structure is specified using simple nesting, as in XML.

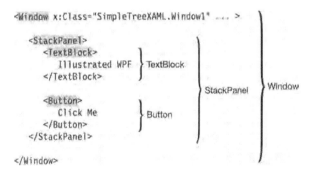

Figure 4-4. *XAML uses nesting to declare a logical tree of .NET objects.*

XAML Trees

Every XAML file contains a *XAML document*, which specifies the UI's logical tree. The important things you need to know about XAML trees are the following:

- A XAML tree is made up of *elements*.

- Elements must be properly nested. The nesting structure of the elements determines the structure of the XAML tree and hence the structure of the UI.

- The top, or outer, element is the *root element* and contains all the other elements.

Object Element Syntax

Objects in the UI are represented by XAML elements. For example, Figure 4-5 shows the logical tree for a simple UI with four objects. The XAML markup producing that logical tree comprises four elements—one corresponding to each of the objects in the logical tree.

Using XAML elements to represent WPF class objects is called *object element syntax*, because each XAML element represents a WPF object.

Figure 4-5. *The nesting of the elements in the XAML document forms a tree of WPF objects*

The Syntax of Elements

The default syntax for an element comprises three parts—the *start tag*, the *content section*, and the *end tag*, as shown in Figure 4-6. The following code shows an example of an element representing a WPF Button object. Notice the following about the code:

- The start tag opens with an open angle bracket (<) and closes with a close angle bracket (>). Immediately to the right of the open angle bracket is the type name of the element. Using object element syntax, the type name must match the name of the WPF class.

- The end tag starts with the two-character string, an open angle bracket followed by a slash, which is followed by the type name of the element. The end tag signals the end of the element.

- The content section is the area between the start tag and the end tag; it can contain text, other elements, or white space. Any nested elements might, in turn, contain other nested elements.

- Whatever is in the content section of the element is assigned to the default content property of the class. I'll discuss that a bit more shortly.

Figure 4-6 summarizes the syntax of a simple element.

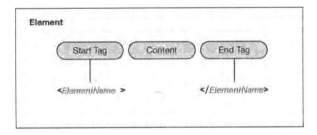

Figure 4-6. *The syntax of a simple element*

Attribute Syntax

If the only property you need to set on a class object is the default content property, you don't need to do more. If, however, you want to set other properties of the object, you can do that by assigning to XAML *attributes*, using a form called *attribute syntax*.

For example, the Button class has many properties that control the way the button looks and acts. You can set these properties using attributes, as shown in the following markup. In this case, it sets the values of two of the button's properties—Width and Height.

```
  Element
   Name        Attribute      Attribute
    ↓              ↓              ↓
<Button Width="100" Height="50">
    Click Me
</Button>
```

The important things to know about attributes are the following:

- Attributes must be placed inside the start tag, following the element name. They cannot be in the content area or the end tag.

- The syntax of an attribute consists of an identifier that is a property name, followed by an equals sign, followed by a string demarcated by a set of double quotation marks or single quotation marks.

- An element can have any number of attributes, which must be separated by white space—*not commas*.

Figure 4-7 summarizes the syntax of attributes, as well as elements with attributes.

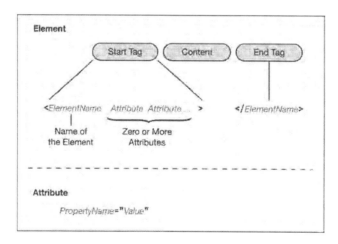

Figure 4-7. Syntax of an element, showing the position and syntax of attributes

Empty Elements

Sometimes an element doesn't need content. For example, you might want a button with no text, or anything else, on it. You can specify such an element in two ways:

- You can place the end tag immediately after the start tag or with only white space between the tags.

- You can use the *empty element tag* syntax.

    - This form consists of a single tag, instead of a start and end tag.

    - The tag has the syntactic form of a start tag—including allowing attributes—but uses the /> string as its end delimiter instead of >.

The following markup illustrates these two techniques. Both elements create identical buttons.

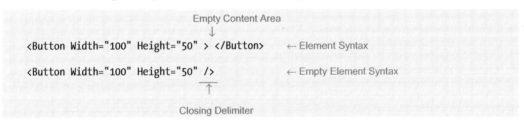

Figure 4-8 summarizes the Empty Element syntax.

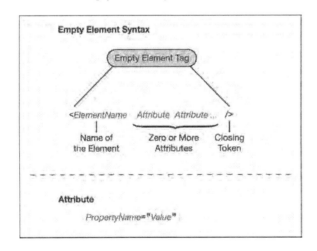

Figure 4-8. *The syntax of the empty element tag, which is used for elements that don't specify content*

More About Object Element Syntax

The elements you've looked at so far are called *object elements*, because they produce .NET objects. These elements are the foundation of a XAML document. Some additional things you should know about them are the following:

- The element name can be either a .NET class or a .NET struct. Throughout the text, however, to avoid awkwardness, I'll just refer to the element name as a *class name*.

- The element name must exactly match the name of the corresponding .NET class. Remember that XAML is case sensitive.

- When creating an object from the XAML element, the XAML parser always uses the class's parameterless constructor. You cannot specify a different constructor.

- The element is translated into a class object in the following steps:

    a. Create the object, using the parameterless constructor.

    b. Set the default content property of the class object with the content part of the XAML element. (I'll describe more about the default content property in the next section.)

    c. Set the other class object properties to the values assigned to in XAML attributes.

The Default Content Property

Many WPF visual elements display content to the user, such as the label on a button. I'll describe *content* in more detail in Chapter 6, but for our current discussion of XAML, you need to know the following:

- Every WPF class that can have content has a property that is specified as its default content holder. I mentioned this a bit earlier when describing the content section of the element syntax.

- This default content property is specified using the ContentPropertyAttribute attribute in the class declaration. (This is a .NET attribute, not a XAML attribute.)

The declaration of the default content holder might not be on the class itself, however. You might have to burrow down the inheritance tree a bit to find it.

For example, if you go to the documentation for the WPF Button class, you won't find mention of this attribute. But if you go down past the ButtonBase class to the ContentControl class and look at the C# section, you'll find the following declaration. The parameter of the attribute contains the string "Content", which specifies that for all classes derived from this one, it is the Content property that is the default content holder.

```
                  Attribute          Content Property
                     ↓                    ↓
[ContentPropertyAttribute("Content")]
public class ContentControl : Control, IAddChild
{ ...                          ↑
                   Class Name
```

Different classes have different default content holder properties. For example, if you were to drill down from the ListBox control to its base class ItemsControl, you'd find that the ContentProperty in this case is the Items property.

For simple content, rather than placing content between the start tag and the end tag, you *could* use attribute syntax. For example, the following markup shows four button instantiations that are semantically equivalent. They all produce identical buttons.

The first button instantiation uses simple object element syntax, with the content between the start and end tags. The second puts the content in the start tag by using attribute syntax. The third does the same as the second but uses the empty element syntax for the start tag. The fourth is the same as the third except that it includes the class name as part of the attribute name.

```
<StackPanel>
    <Button>Click Me</Button>                 Object Element Syntax
    <Button Content="Click Me"></Button>      Attribute Syntax
    <Button Content="Click Me"/>              Attribute Syntax, Empty Element
    <Button Button.Content="Click Me"/>
</StackPanel>          ↑ Attribute Syntax, Empty Element, Qualified Name
```

Type Converters for Attributes

If you look at the attribute in the following line of markup, you might notice something puzzling. From Chapter 3 you know that the Background property of a Button must be set with an object derived from the Brush class, but the attribute sets it with the simple string "Blue". As a matter of fact, attribute syntax requires that attributes be set with strings.

```
<Button Background="Blue"> ...
```

So, how can you assign a string to a property that requires some other type? The short answer is that the XAML parser converts it for you. The parser uses the class and property name to check the type of the property, and uses a TypeConverter for that type to convert the string to an object of the type required by the property. Figure 4-9 illustrates the process.

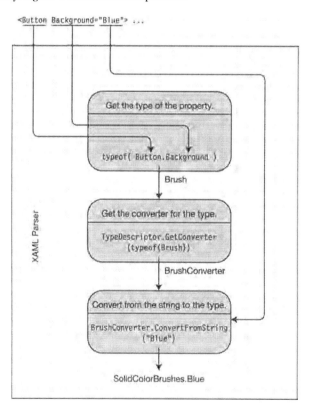

Figure 4-9. *The XAML parser converts the string value assigned to the attribute to the object type required by the property.*

Property Element Syntax

So far, you've seen classes as elements and properties as attributes. That's a very clean classification, but it's not always possible to use something as simple as an attribute for a property. To address this, XAML also provides another syntax for setting the values of more complex properties. This is called *property element syntax*, and has the following characteristics:

- The property is listed, not as an attribute inside the start tag, but using element syntax nested in the content part of the object element.

- The element name uses a two-part name in dot-syntax notation. The name consists of the class name and the property name, separated by a period (dot), as shown in the following syntax code:

```
        Class Name      Property Name
            ↓               ↓
<ElementTypeName.PropertyName>
    Value
</ElementTypeName.PropertyName>
```

- The property element tag cannot contain any attributes.

- Notice that although it has the syntax of an element, *it does not produce an object*. It *sets a property* on an object.

Figure 4-10 shows the use of both attribute syntax and property element syntax to set the Background property of a Button object. Both forms produce the same object structure, as shown at the bottom of the figure. Notice how much simpler and easier it is to read the attribute syntax version.

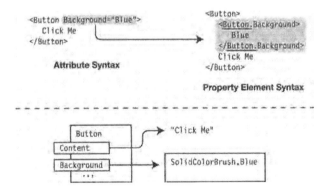

Figure 4-10. *The Button object using either the attribute syntax or the property element syntax specifies the same object structure.*

Regular attribute syntax works well when a property value is simple and can be expressed by a simple string—like the Background property of Button, as shown in the previous example. In that case, the simple string on the right side of the assignment operator is much easier to read than the property element syntax.

Some properties, however, are too complex to be set with a simple string. They might, for example, contain multiple items or complex parts. The following markup shows an example of this. It sets the Background of the Button, not to a simple brush but to a LinearGradientBrush. In this case, specifying the LinearGradientBrush requires too much information to use a simple string, and therefore requires the property element syntax. Other properties can be even more complex.

```
<Button>
    <Button.Background>
        <LinearGradientBrush StartPoint="0,0" EndPoint="1,1">
            <GradientStop Color="Red"  Offset="0.0" />
            <GradientStop Color="Blue" Offset="1.0" />
        </LinearGradientBrush>
    </Button.Background>
    Click Me
</Button>
```

■ **Note** In general, you should use attribute syntax if possible, since it's simpler and easier to understand. Use property element syntax only for complex attributes that can't be handled by attribute syntax.

Attached Property Syntax

Attached properties are a special type of property that is defined in one class but used in another. I'll explain attached properties in detail in Chapter 7. Here I just want to describe their syntax, since it looks similar to property element syntax.

The following markup shows an example of using an attached property. If you look at the Button declaration, you'll see an attribute assignment to a property called Grid.Row. Notice that the class name is Grid—not Button. That's because the Row property is not declared in the Button class but in the Grid class. This is an attached property.

```
<Button Grid.Row="2">Click</Button>
                ↑
        Attached Property
```

You can distinguish an attached property from property element syntax by the fact that in an attached property the class name is different from the class being instantiated, while in property element syntax, the class name is the same as the object being instantiated.

Reviewing the XAML Syntax Forms

Although the XAML syntax forms are quite simple, they can sometimes be confusing when they're first encountered. Figure 4-11 summarizes the concepts.

Name	Function	Example
Object Element Syntax	Create WPF class objects	`<Button>Click</Button>`
Attribute Syntax	Set the properties of a WPF class object	`<Button Width="40">Click</Button>`

Property Element Syntax	Set the properties of a WPF class object	`<Button>`
		`<Button.Width>`
		`40`
		`</Button.Width>`
		`Click`
		`</Button>`

Attached Property Syntax	Set an attached property on a WPF class object	`<Button Grid.Row="2">Click</Button>`

Figure 4-11. *A summary of the XAML syntax forms*

Top-Level Elements

As mentioned earlier in the chapter, every XAML document must have a single, top-level element. Three classes are used by WPF programs as top-level elements—Window, Application, and Page.

You've seen that Window and Application are used in Visual Studio's WPF Application template to build standard WPF applications. The Page class is used to build applications that use page-based navigation, which I'll cover in Chapter 14. XamlPad also uses the Page class.

Code-Behind and Object Names

Although this chapter concentrates on XAML syntax, you need to remember that the XAML produces the instantiation of class objects and performs an initial setting of some properties. Most of the actions performed by these objects are done in the C# part of the partial class—called the *code-behind*.

There's a difference you might not have noticed between creating class objects with C# and creating them with XAML:

- Objects created in C# have names. For example, the button created in the following line of C# code has the name btn:

  ```
  Button btn = new Button();
  ```

- Objects created in XAML, by default, don't have names. For example, the following button created in XAML doesn't have a name:

  ```
  <Button>Hi There</Button>
  ```

If an object created in XAML doesn't have a name and it's not manipulated by the code in the code-behind, then there's no problem. If, however, you need to manipulate the object from the code-behind, then the object needs a name.

Many classes have a Name property, which you can set using an attribute, if you need to manipulate the object, as shown in the following line of code. Using this form, you can now refer to the button in the code-behind with the name myButton.

```
<Button Name="myButton">Click Me</Button>
```

Some classes, however, don't have a Name property. In this case, you can use a XAML construct for assigning a name, as shown in the following line of code. Using this format you can also refer to the object as myButton in the code-behind.

```
<Button x:Name="myButton">Click Me</Button>
```

Namespaces

As you doubtless know by now, every object element in the XAML tree refers to some .NET class or struct. To create objects of these types, the XAML parser must know where to find their definitions. This information is passed to the parser using XAML namespaces.

Some of the important things to know about namespaces are the following:

- A XAML namespace is a case-sensitive string that represents a collection of .NET types.

- Namespaces are assigned using the `xmlns` attribute in the start tag of the root element of the XAML document.

- If you want to use a class as an element in your XAML markup, you must give the XAML parser the namespace that contains the class.

- Two standard namespaces represent the WPF classes and the XAML classes. Their names look like web addresses. These are shown in the following lines of markup:

```
xmlns="http://schemas.microsoft.com/winfx/2006/xaml/presentation"
xmlns:x="http://schemas.microsoft.com/winfx/2006/xaml"
```

Figure 4-12 illustrates XAML markup specifying the two standard namespaces, which are shown in gray boxes.

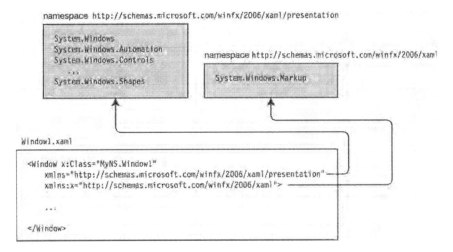

Figure 4-12. *WPF XAML documents contain the two standard namespace declarations that represent the WPF classes and the XAML classes.*

The Syntax of Namespaces

The syntax of using XAML namespaces is not the same as that of C#. In C#, when you place `using` statements with namespace names at the top of the source file, you can then use the types in those namespaces without further qualification (assuming, of course, that you also have a reference in your solution to the assembly containing the namespace).

In XAML (and XML), it works differently. One, and only one, namespace can be the *default namespace*.

- You declare the default namespace using the keyword `xmlns`, followed by an equals sign, followed by a string that is the name of the default namespace.

- When you use types from the default namespace, you can use the type names directly, without further qualification. For example, the examples you've seen so far have used classes like `Button` and `TextBlock`, which have been in the default namespace.

- You can set the default namespace to be any namespace, but it makes the most sense to set it to the namespace that contains the WPF types, which is the namespace `http://schemas.microsoft.com/winfx/2006/xaml/presentation`.

Other namespaces must each be assigned a *prefix*.

- You declare a nondefault namespace using the keyword `xmlns`, followed by a colon, followed by a string, followed by an equals sign and the name of the namespace. The string following the colon is called the *prefix*. Generally, you want the prefix to be a *short* string so it's easier to use.

- When you use a type from a nondefault namespace, you must use the prefix, followed by a colon, followed by the type name.

For example, the following markup shows a simple XAML document that contains two elements—Page and Button. In the opening tag of the Page element, you see two attribute assignments that specify the namespaces. Although these strings look like web addresses, they are arbitrary, unique strings that Microsoft has assigned to represent the set of types.

- The first attribute assignment sets the default namespace to the string http://schemas.microsoft.com/winfx/2006/xaml/presentation. This namespace contains the WPF types.

- The second attribute sets the namespace that contains types used by XAML. Its prefix string is the letter x.

Production: The arrow associated with the "No Prefix String" annotation in the code below should point to the blank space between "xmlns" and the equals sign.

```
   No Prefix String                    Namespace Name
           ↓                                ↓
<Page
    xmlns ="http://schemas.microsoft.com/winfx/2006/xaml/presentation"
    xmlns:x="http://schemas.microsoft.com/winfx/2006/xaml">
       ↑                              ↑

   Prefix String        Namespace Name
    <Button>Click Me</Button>
</Page>
```

Using Classes from Other Namespaces

You'll need to use the two standard namespaces in pretty much every WPF XAML document you create. Occasionally, however, you might need to use a type from a different namespace. The most common sources are the .NET system library—mscorlib—or your project's namespace.

As you saw in the previous sections, XAML namespace names are just unique strings that aren't parsed. If you want to use a .NET namespace that is not a XAML namespace, you must use a special syntax to tell the XAML parser you want to use a .NET namespace. .NET namespaces are called *CLR namespaces*.

To specify a CLR namespace called, say, OtherPart, which is declared in your project, you would use the following syntax. Most of the string is boilerplate text, but you have to substitute in the prefix you want and the name of the namespace. For a namespace in your project, the prefix local is often used.

Notice that the string being assigned to the prefix starts with the string clr-namespace:. This keyword string tells the XAML parser that the string needs to be parsed rather than being used as the name of a XAML namespace.

If the namespace is in another assembly, the process is similar, but you must also include the assembly name—without the .dll extension.

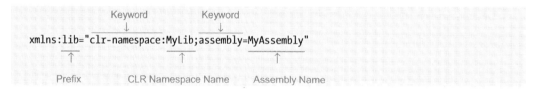

For example, suppose you've developed some visual elements in your project that you'd like to use in the XAML. If the name of your project's namespace is FunWithNamespaces, you can declare a prefix for it in the XAML, as shown in the following tag:

```
<Window x:Class="FunWithNamespaces.Window1"
    xmlns="http://schemas.microsoft.com/winfx/2006/xaml/presentation"
    xmlns:x="http://schemas.microsoft.com/winfx/2006/xaml"
    xmlns:local="clr-namespace:FunWithNamespaces">
```

Define New Prefix   CLR Namespace Name

To use a button named MyButton that you've defined in your project, you can use it in the XAML, as shown here:

```
<local:MyButton>Hi There</local:MyButton>
```

Qualified Element Name   Qualified Element Name

Example Using Namespaces

We can flesh out the previous snippets and make them into a full program:

1. Start by creating a new solution named FunWithNamespaces.

2. Add a new class called MyButton in a file called MyButton.cs. Replace the boilerplate code in the class with the following code:

```
using System;
using System.Windows;
using System.Windows.Controls;
using System.Windows.Media;

namespace FunWithNamespaces
{
    public class MyButton : Button
    {
        public MyButton()
        {
            Background = new LinearGradientBrush( Colors.White, Colors.Gray,
                            new Point( 0, 0 ), new Point( 1, 1 ) );
        }
    }
}
```

3. Replace the contents of the Window1.xaml file with the following markup. Notice that the fourth line declares the prefix for the namespace of the current project. The sixth line instantiates an object of the defined button.

```
<Window x:Class="FunWithNamespaces.Window1"
    xmlns="http://schemas.microsoft.com/winfx/2006/xaml/presentation"
    xmlns:x="http://schemas.microsoft.com/winfx/2006/xaml"
    xmlns:local="clr-namespace:FunWithNamespaces"          Declare the prefix.
    Title="Namespaces" Height="125" Width="180">
    <local:MyButton>Hi There</local:MyButton>             Instantiate the button.
</Window>
```

When you run the program, you should get the window shown in Figure 4-13.

Figure 4-13. *Window produced by XAML using a locally defined button*

Markup Extensions

As useful as XAML is, there are certain things it can't do on its own. For example, one of the biggest things it can't do is evaluate values and perform conditional logic at runtime.

For example, suppose you wanted to create a button with the label "Before Noon" if the button was instantiated before noon and with the label "After Noon" if instantiated after. In XAML there's no way to do conditional logic at runtime to set the text to one string or the other.

Notice also that in all the examples you've seen so far, when we've assigned a value to a property, we've either used a value type value or created a new object and assigned it to the property. What we haven't done is assign an already existing, nonstatic object to a property. As a matter of fact, XAML doesn't have a syntactic construct for this either.

These are just two examples of things that pure XAML can't do. To handle these types of situations—and others that require runtime evaluation—XAML has to have a "hook" to outside code that it can call at runtime. That code must be able to perform whatever runtime actions need to be performed and be able to return the value or object reference that the XAML needs to complete its assignment to the property. The construct that provides this service is called the *markup extension*.

- A markup extension is a hook to a class outside the XAML.

- A class designed to be used by a markup extension is called an *extension class*.

- A markup extension replaces the string on the right side of the equals sign in an attribute assignment. It starts with an open curly brace and ends with a close curly brace.

- Since markup extensions are used as the right side of an attribute assignment, they're placed in the start tag of an object element. (There's also a form where they can be used in property element syntax, but I won't be covering that.)

Markup extensions have the following form:

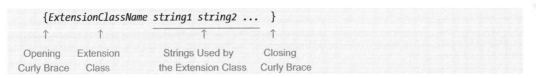

For example, the following markup shows a button where the Style property is set with a resource, using a markup extension. (Don't worry about the details of Style properties and resources right now.) The StaticResource markup extension takes a parameter—in this case the name SomeStyle—and searches the program's resources to find one with that name. If it finds it, it returns its reference, which is then assigned to the Style property. It does this search at runtime.

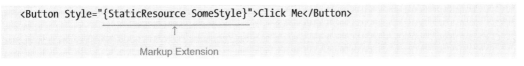

93

Markup extensions have the syntactic forms shown in Figure 4-14.

- The name of the extension class is always the first string inside the open curly brace. There's never a comma following the class name.

- Following the class name there can be zero or more strings. These strings must be separated by commas.

The strings following the class name can take one of two forms. Either they can be simple strings with no equals signs or they can be property/value pairs, with the property and the value being separated by an equals sign.

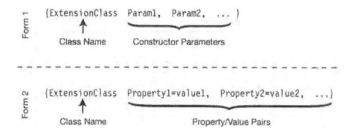

Figure 4-14. *The two syntax forms for markup extensions*

Figure 4-15 illustrates what happens at runtime, when the markup extension is encountered. If the markup extension is of the first form and has *n* number of constructor parameters, then the XAML parser finds the extension class constructor with *n* parameters and uses that constructor to create the extension class object.

Otherwise, if the markup extension has property/value pairs, the parameterless constructor is called. Once the object is constructed, its properties are set according to the values in the property/value pairs.

Either way, once the object is constructed and its properties set, the XAML parser calls on the extension class object to return the result object it needs.

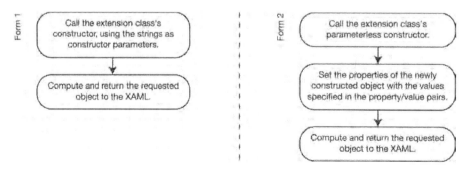

Figure 4-15. *The processing flow of the two forms of markup extensions*

Example Creating a Markup Extension

In this section, we'll create a markup extension in our current project's namespace. This markup extension will be able to label a button with the time the button was created. Generally you won't be creating your own markup extensions, but it will be useful for you to see how it's done. Creating one will also remove the mystery that so often surrounds them.

Besides showing the time it was created, the button's label also includes a string that we send into the markup extension. Once we create the markup extension, we'll be able to use it in the XAML, as shown in the following markup. Some things to notice about the markup are the following:

- The name of the extension class is ShowTime, and it's declared in our current project's namespace, which is called MarkupExtensions.

- Before we can use the extension class in the XAML, we must declare the project's namespace prefix. The fourth line assigns it the prefix local.

- The first use of the markup extension uses the constructor parameter form. The second uses the property/value form.

```
<Window x:Class="MarkupExtensions.Window1"
    xmlns="http://schemas.microsoft.com/winfx/2006/xaml/presentation"
    xmlns:x="http://schemas.microsoft.com/winfx/2006/xaml"
    xmlns:local="clr-namespace:MarkupExtensions"        Include the namespace.
    Title="Markup Extensions" Height="120" Width="175">
                              Extension Class    Constructor Parameter
                                     ↓                  ↓
    <StackPanel>
        <Button Content="{local:ShowTime First}"></Button>
        <Button Content="{local:ShowTime Header=Second}"></Button>

    </StackPanel>                    ↑                  ↑
                              Extension Class    Property/Value Pair
</Window>
```

This markup produces the window shown in Figure 4-16. The label of the top button starts with the string "First", which was sent into the markup extension as a constructor parameter. It's followed by a string representing the time the button was created.

The second button starts with the string "Second", which was sent to the markup extension as a property/value pair, where the string "Second" was assigned to the markup class's property named Header.

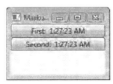

Figure 4-16. *Buttons labeled at runtime, using markup extensions*

To create the project, do the following:

1. Create a new solution called MarkupExtensions.

2. Create a new class called ShowTime, in a new file called ShowTime.cs. This will be the extension class. Set the contents of this file to be the following code.

3. Set the markup in Window1.xaml to match that shown in the markup on the previous page.

Some important things to notice about the following extension class code are the following:

- The extension class *must* derive from class MarkupExtension, which is located in the System.Windows.Markup namespace.

- The class *must* implement a method called ProvideValue with the signature and return type as shown in the following code. This is the method the XAML parser will call to get the object it needs.

- The following class provides two constructors to match the two forms we want to use from the XAML.

- The class declares a string variable called header to store the string sent in from the markup extension, and it declares a property called Header to access it.

```
using System;
using System.Windows.Markup;

namespace MarkupExtensions
{
    class ShowTime: MarkupExtension
    {
        private string header = string.Empty;
        public string Header
        {
            get { return header; }
            set { header = value; }
        }

        public ShowTime(){ }                    // Constructor

        public ShowTime( string input)          // Constructor
        { header = input; }

        public override object ProvideValue(IServiceProvider serviceProvider)
        {
            return string.Format("{0}:  {1}",
                        header, DateTime.Now.ToLongTimeString());
        }
    }
}
```

White Space

By default, when the XAML processor processes a document, sequences of white space between a start tag and an end tag are replaced with a single space. This is called *white space consolidation*. The characters considered white space are the space character, the tab character, and the new line character.

For example, the following three button declarations have varying amounts and types of white space between the words *Click* and *Me*. But they will produce identical-looking buttons, with a single space between the words *Click* and *Me*.

```
<StackPanel>
   <Button>Click Me</Button>

   <Button>Click       Me</Button>

   <Button>
       Click
       Me
   </Button>
</StackPanel>
```

Figure 4-17 describes the process of white space consolidation.

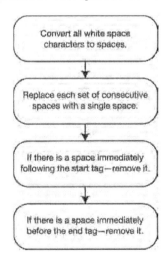

Figure 4-17. *White space in the content area of an element is consolidated.*

If for some reason, however, you need to have the XAML parser leave the white space exactly as you place it, you can set the xml:space attribute to the value preserve, as shown in the following line of code. In this example, the text of the button will have five spaces between the words "Click" and "Me."

```
<Button xml:space="preserve">Click     Me</Button>
                  ↑
          Preserve white space
            as entered.
```

Special Characters

Some characters—such as the left-angle bracket (<) and the right-angle bracket (>)—have special meaning to XAML. If you were to try to use them in the content section of an element, it would confuse the XAML parser. For these, and several other characters, you must use special strings that tell the parser to insert the corresponding character.

These special strings are called *character entities*. All the character entities start with the ampersand character (&) and end with a semicolon. Since the ampersand marks the start of a character entity, the ampersand character itself needs a character entity, in case you need to insert an *actual* ampersand character. Table 4-1 gives a list of special characters and their corresponding character entities.

Table 4-1. *Special Characters*

Character	Character Entity
Ampersand (&)	&amp;
Less than (<)	&lt;
Greater than (>)	&gt;
Nonbreaking space	
Apostrophe	&apos;
Quotation mark (")	&quot;

Summary

In this chapter, you learned that a WPF user interface is represented internally by a tree data structure. You can create this UI tree explicitly, in the code-behind, or you can use the XAML markup language. Some important things to remember about the XAML tree are the following :

- A XAML tree consists of a set of properly nested elements, with a single root element.

- Each element in the tree represents a .NET object. The element name is always the name of a .NET class.

- Each element can include assignments to attributes.

    - An attribute corresponds to a property of the .NET object represented by the element.

    - Regardless of the type of the property, the value assigned to an attribute is always a string. The XAML parser converts the string to a value of the appropriate type.

The XAML syntax includes four types of constructs:

- Object element syntax: This construct consists of the tags that specify the elements of the tree. This includes the attributes in the opening tag of the element.

- Property element syntax: The types of some properties are too complex to be specified by a simple string. In these cases, you can use property element syntax, which nests a set of property element tags in the content section of an element.

- Attached property syntax: This construct allows you to attach the property of a different .NET object to the element.

- Markup extensions: These constructs allow the .NET object to perform runtime actions to assign a value to a property.

CHAPTER 5

■ ■ ■

Layout

Layout in WPF

Before WPF, user interfaces generally consisted of windows with statically placed controls. The programmer set the height and width of a control and placed it at a certain coordinate position on the window or panel, where it stayed. (To be fair, you could also dock controls to edges.)

In WPF, the layout of visual elements is much more dynamic. One of the goals of the WPF layout system is that visual elements should resize and rearrange intelligently when the size of the available window real estate changes. When a window grows or shrinks, the visual elements it contains should automatically change size and position appropriately.

For example, Figure 5-1 shows a window where the buttons in the panel on the left rearrange depending on the amount of space available, and where the image in the right pane also changes size depending on the amount of space available.

Generally, your UI will consist of one or more panels that contain visual elements. In this chapter, I'll describe the options WPF provides for setting the size and layout of your UI.

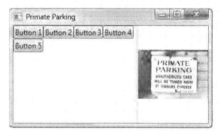

Figure 5-1. *Four views of a window showing how when windows and panes change size, the visual elements in a WPF UI can automatically change size and position.*

Chapter Conventions

This chapter contains many samples of XAML to illustrate specific points. The XAML for the window containing the visual elements is pretty much the same each time, except for the name of the window and its size.

Rather than clutter the samples with the boilerplate part of the code, in each section I'll just list the XAML for the specific visual element. Figure 5-2 shows an example of a whole XAML tree. The nongrayed markup is the boilerplate code, and the grayed markup shows where the XAML for the specific visual element should be placed.

```
<Window x:Class="MarginsPadding.Window1"
    xmlns="http://schemas.microsoft.com/winfx/2006/xaml/presentation"
    xmlns:x="http://schemas.microsoft.com/winfx/2006/xaml"
    Title="" Height="150" Width="135">
    <StackPanel>
        <Button>Button 1</Button>
        <Button>Button 2</Button>            Specific Visual Element
        <Button>Button 3</Button>
    </StackPanel>
</Window>
```

Figure 5-2. *XAML samples throughout the chapter illustrate specific visual elements. To compile and execute properly, they should be placed in the boilerplate template.*

Also, most of the examples use the Button class as the visual element. This is only because the Button class is easy to use, is simple visually, and displays nicely on the screen, showing the size of the element. Almost all the examples could use other elements in place of the Button class. In Chapter 6, you'll start seeing other elements and how easy it is to use them.

The Layout Process

As I mentioned, in previous frameworks, you set the size of an element and placed it on the panel, and that was it. It didn't move, and it didn't change size. Although that simplicity was nice, it also meant that the elements couldn't adapt as windows and panels changed sizes.

With WPF, you can make the layout of your elements adapt intelligently to changing window sizes, but it adds some complexity to the process of designing layouts. In WPF, whenever a window or container changes size, it recalculates its layout and those of its child elements.

The layout process is done in two steps, called *measure* and *arrange*:

- *Measure*: During the measure phase, the window, panel, or container asks its child elements what size they would like to be. Each child calculates that value by first asking its child elements the same question. This is done recursively down the element tree. When an element receives its answers from its children, it calculates its ideal size and returns that value to its parent.

- *Arrange*: When the parent receives all the requested sizes from the children, it calculates how much it will actually give each one and lays them out on its surface. The child elements, in turn, lay out their children.

Figure 5-3 illustrates the measure process for the elements in the window shown on the right side of the figure. The numbers in the diagram on the left represent the order of the calls and calculations.

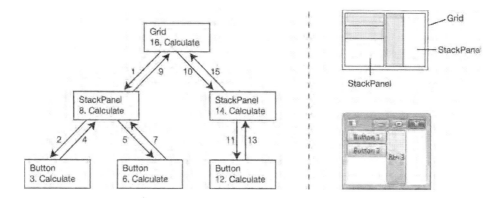

Figure 5-3. *During the measure phase of layout, an element determines the amount of space it needs by first asking its children to calculate how much space they need. The process progresses recursively down the element tree.*

The best practices for using WPF discourage setting actual sizes for visual objects. Instead, it's the programmer's job to select the right configuration of containers for the objects and to set the properties of the objects and containers so that they behave intelligently and elegantly when areas change size or when content changes size.

In many cases, the default behavior is that the size of an object is automatically set by the WPF layout system to be just large enough to hold the content. This is particularly handy when internationalizing a system and words and sentences are different lengths than they were when developed in the primary language.

Setting the Requested Size of Elements

As you saw in the previous section, the sizing and layout of a panel and its elements is a process that involves both the parent and its child elements. The size and alignment properties you set on the child element are used in the measure and arrange negotiations to determine the layout.

Some of the important properties you can set are the following:

- `Width` and `Height`: Even though the philosophy of WPF is to not set actual sizes for things, there are times when you need to do just that. You can assign values to these properties to set an actual width or height.

- `MinWidth`, `MaxWidth`, `MinHeight`, and `MaxHeight`: Instead of setting a fixed width or height, you can set a range within which the actual width or height must remain.

Figure 5-4 shows a panel with two buttons and an image. Notice how the elements react when the width of the window is first increased and then decreased.

- The first button has `MinWidth` and `MaxWidth` set and is constrained to stay between 125 units and 200 units. In the second screenshot, it has reached its maximum limit, leaving white space on either side. In the last screenshot, it has reached its lower limit and is cut off on the right.

- The image is given an actual width, which it maintains, regardless of the size of the window.

- The last button is unconstrained and grows and shrinks, matching the width of the window.

 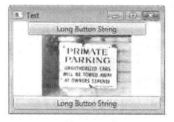 

```
<StackPanel>
    <Button MinWidth="125" MaxWidth="200">Long Button String</Button>
    <Image Width="150" Source="PrimateParking2.jpg"></Image>
    <Button>Long Button String</Button>
</StackPanel>
```

Figure 5-4. *The properties set on an element can set or constrain its size.*

Alignment

Setting an element's requested size is useful, but an element isn't an isolated entity. It is almost always associated with some sort of container that will place it in a particular slot in its layout.

If the slot is smaller than the element, then the element will generally be truncated to fit the slot. If the slot is larger than the element, you have some choices about how to size and place the element in the slot. With regard to size, you have three choices:

- You can give an explicit size to the element.

- You can have the container expand the element so that it fits the entire size of the slot.

- You can have the container size the element so that it snugly fits its content.

To set the alignment of where to place the element within the slot, you can assign to the HorizontalAlignment and VerticalAlignment properties. Each has a choice of four enumeration values to choose from:

- HorizontalAlignment: Left, Center, Right, or Stretch

- VerticalAlignment: Top, Center, Bottom, or Stretch

Figure 5-5 shows the markup used to set the properties, and the screenshots on the left show the resulting windows. The button elements fill the slots (represented by the dotted lines) in the StackPanel container. Don't worry about the details of the StackPanel container for right now, since we'll look at it shortly. But the first StackPanel stacks the buttons vertically, and the second one stacks them from the left to right.

```
<StackPanel>
    <Button HorizontalAlignment="Left">Left</Button>
    <Button HorizontalAlignment="Center">Center</Button>
    <Button HorizontalAlignment="Right">Right</Button>
    <Button HorizontalAlignment="Stretch">Stretch</Button>
</StackPanel>
```

HorizontalAlignment

```
<StackPanel Orientation="Horizontal">
    <Button VerticalAlignment="Top">Top</Button>
    <Button VerticalAlignment="Center">Center</Button>
    <Button VerticalAlignment="Bottom">Bottom</Button>
    <Button VerticalAlignment="Stretch">Stretch</Button>
</StackPanel>
```

VerticalAlignment

Figure 5-5. *HorizontalAlignment and VerticalAlignment*

Content Alignment

So far, all the content you've seen has been placed in the center of the element—the Button in our case. But you can also place the content on one end or the other, using the HorizontalContentAlignment or VerticalContentAlignment property. Figure 5-6 shows how to use these properties.

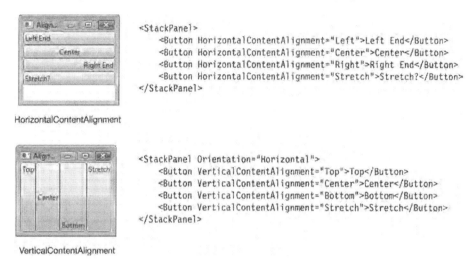

Figure 5-6. *You can specify the content alignment of elements.*

Visibility

You can control the visibility of an item using the `Visibility` property. There are three enumeration values that this property can take:

- `Visible`: This is the default value, and makes the element visible.

- `Hidden`: This value makes the element invisible—but the element still takes up the layout space in the container.

- `Collapsed`: This values also makes the element invisible—but in this case, the element is omitted from the layout and takes no space. Visibly, anyway, it appears not to exist.

Figure 5-7 shows two buttons where the `Visibility` property of Button 1 is set to different values.

- In the first case, both buttons are visible. The markup doesn't include the `Visibility` property because `Visible` is the default value.

- In the second case, the property is set to `Hidden`. The button is invisible, but you can see the space it's occupying.

- In the third case, the property is set to `Collapsed`. In this case, not only is the button invisible, but there is no visual evidence it even exists.

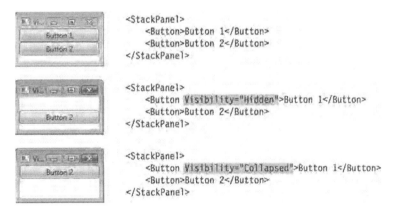

Figure 5-7. *The Visibility property controls different ways an object can be invisible.*

Padding and Margins

The padding and margins of a visual element refer to extra space added to the element's layout.

- *Padding* is extra space added *inside the element*, between the content and the element's outer border.

- Margins are amounts of extra space added around the outside of the element.

The following markup shows the XAML for two buttons with padding and margins. (Don't worry about the WrapPanel for now.) Figure 5-8 illustrates these buttons and shows the positions of padding and margins. The grayed areas are the visible buttons. The dotted line inside each button shows the size the button would be if it didn't have additional padding. The dotted line outside each button shows the extent of the margin around it.

```
<WrapPanel>
    <Button Padding="10" Margin="10">Button 1</Button>
    <Button Padding="10" Margin="10">Button 2</Button>

</WrapPanel>
                      ↑                ↑
             Set the Padding    Set the Margins
```

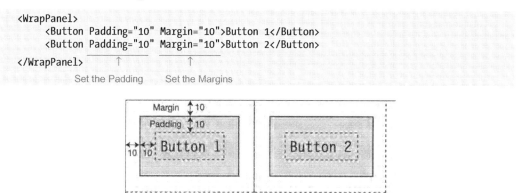

Figure 5-8. *The positions of content, padding, and margins in two buttons*

The buttons in the markup in Figure 5-8 have a padding value of 10 and margins of 10. Figure 5-9, on the bottom right, shows a screenshot of these buttons. The other three screenshots show other combinations of padding and margins.

Padding 0, Margin 0   Padding 0, Margin 10

Padding 10, Margin 0   Padding 10, Margin 10

Figure 5-9. *Two buttons with combinations of padding and margins*

There are three forms you can use in XAML to set the padding and margins. These consist of strings with one, two, or four comma-separated values. Figure 5-10 illustrates these forms for padding, but they apply to margins as well.

- *1 value*: If the parameter has a single value, that value is used on all four sides of the element.

- *2 values*: If the parameter has two values, the first is used for the left and right padding or margins, and the second is used for the top and bottom.

- *4 values*: If the parameter has four values, they correspond to the left, top, right, and bottom edges, respectively.

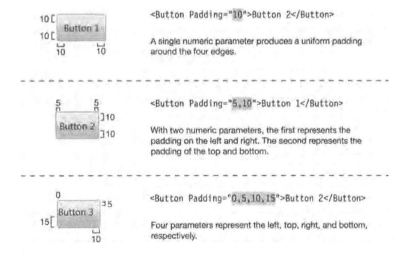

Figure 5-10. *Padding is the amount of extra space between the content of a visual element and the outside border of the element.*

Panels

Panels are containers for laying out visual elements. There are several classes of panels, each of which lays out its child elements in a different way. The most important types of panels, which I'll be covering for the rest of the chapter, are the following:

- StackPanel: StackPanels arrange their elements in stacks.

- WrapPanel: WrapPanels lay their elements next to each other, and when the line of elements reaches the edge of the panel, it wraps onto another line.

- DockPanel: The elements in a DockPanel cling to one of the four edges of the panel.

- Grid: The Grid is the most versatile panel and also the most complex. You start by defining the rows and columns of the grid and then place elements into the cells formed by the grid.

- Canvas: The Canvas is a panel on which you place elements relative to a particular corner. Using this panel is the most like layout methods from previous frameworks.

- UniformGrid: The UniformGrid is an extremely simple grid, where all the cells are the same size.

The StackPanel

The StackPanel arranges its contents next to each other in a stack. By default, the stack grows from the top of the panel toward the bottom.

The items can be stacked in one of three ways, as shown in Figure 5-11. The default is to stack the items starting at the top of the panel and progressing downward. To change the default behavior, you can set the Orientation and FlowDirection properties.

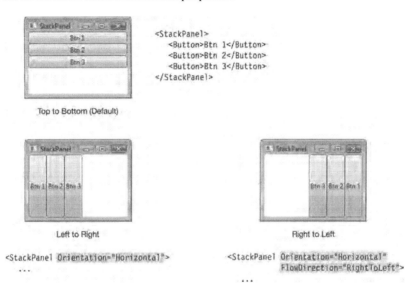

Figure 5-11. *StackPanels can stack their content items in one of three ways. The default is to stack from top to bottom.*

Several other important facts about the StackPanel are the following:

- You cannot stack items starting at the bottom and growing toward the top.

- The stack can grow without bounds, even if it grows beyond the visible edge of the StackPanel. The excess items continue to be stacked, even though they can't be seen.

The following is the markup for the first window in Figure 5-11:

```
<StackPanel>
    <Button>Btn 1</Button>
    <Button>Btn 2</Button>
    <Button>Btn 3</Button>
</StackPanel>
```

113

The WrapPanel

The WrapPanel places its elements next to each other, one after another, but unlike the StackPanel, when the elements get to the end of the WrapPanel, they start a new row or column.

By default, the WrapPanel starts at the top-left corner and places each succeeding element to the right of the previous one. But there are three other possibilities as well. Figure 5-12 shows the four variations.

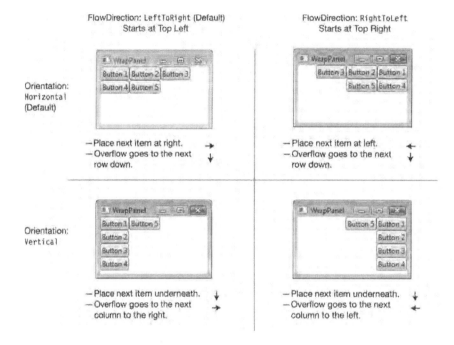

Figure 5-12. *The wrapping behavior of a WrapPanel depends on the values of the Orientation and FlowDirection properties.*

The following is the markup for the top-left WrapPanel in Figure 5-12. The Orientation and FlowDirection properties aren't actually necessary, since Horizontal and LeftToRight are the default values for those properties.

```
<WrapPanel Orientation="Horizontal" FlowDirection="LeftToRight">
    <Button>Button 1</Button>
    <Button>Button 2</Button>
    <Button>Button 3</Button>
    <Button>Button 4</Button>
    <Button>Button 5</Button>
</WrapPanel >
```

You can also set either the height of the rows or the width of the columns of a WrapPanel, using the ItemHeight or the ItemWidth properties.

- ItemHeight: The ItemHeight property sets the height of a row.
    - Items can request how they will be vertically aligned within that height.
    - Items too tall for the height will be truncated.
- ItemWidth: The ItemWidth property sets the width of the column. As with ItemHeight, items can request how they will be aligned, and items too wide will be truncated.

The following markup creates a WrapPanel with the height of the rows to be 90 device-independent units. Figure 5-13 shows the window produced by the WrapPanel.

```
<WrapPanel ItemHeight="90">
    <Button>Button 1</Button>
    <Button VerticalAlignment="Top">Button 2</Button>
    <Button VerticalAlignment="Center">Button 3</Button>
    <Button VerticalAlignment="Bottom">Button 4</Button>
    <Button VerticalAlignment="Stretch">Button 5</Button>
</WrapPanel>
```

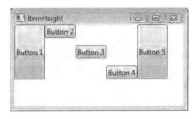

Figure 5-13. *The height of the rows of this WrapPanel are set to be 90 units high.*

115

The DockPanel

The DockPanel is a panel where each child element gravitates to one of the four edges.

- By default, elements in a DockPanel dock toward the left.

- By default, the last element placed in the panel is expanded to fill the remaining space. You can turn off this feature by setting the DockPanel's LastChildFill property to False.

Figure 5-14 shows three DockPanels with buttons docked in various arrangements. In the top row, the panels have the LastChildFill property set to False, producing a white, empty area.

The bottom row shows the same panels with the LastChildFill property set to the default value of True, causing the last button added to expand to fill the remaining space in the panel.

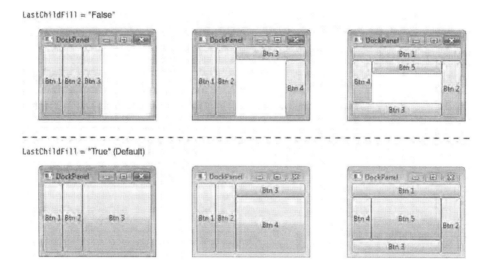

Figure 5-14. *The child elements of a DockPanel are docked to one of the four edges. By default, the final element is expanded to fill the remaining space in the panel.*

The following is the markup for producing the first DockPanel shown in Figure 5-14:

```
<DockPanel LastChildFill="False">
    <Button>Btn 1</Button>
    <Button>Btn 2</Button>
    <Button>Btn 3</Button>
</DockPanel >
```

To dock an item on an edge other than the left, you need to explicitly specify which edge to use. You do this using the DockPanel.Dock property. For example, to dock a button at the top edge, you would use the following syntax for the button:

```
<Button DockPanel.Dock="Top">Btn 3</Button>
                    ↑
            Set the Docking Edge
```

As another example, the following markup produces the window shown in the middle of the first row of Figure 5-14. Notice that buttons 3 and 4 are docked to the top and right, respectively.

```
<DockPanel LastChildFill="False">
    <Button>Btn 1</Button>                       Default Dock to Left
    <Button>Btn 2</Button>                       Default Dock to Left
    <Button DockPanel.Dock="Top">Btn 3</Button>  Dock to Top
    <Button DockPanel.Dock="Right">Btn 4</Button> Dock to Right
</DockPanel >
```

There are several things you should notice about setting the docking edge:

- The specification of which edge to use is placed in the child element—the buttons, in this example—not on the DockPanel itself.

- The edge specification is given in the form of an *attached property*.

Attached properties are explained in detail in Chapter 7, but as a preview, an attached property is a property that is used on objects of a class *other than the class on which it is declared!* In our example, the Dock property is a member of class DockPanel but is used on objects of class Button.

To use the Dock property, or any attached property, you must use its qualified name, which consists of its class name followed by a period followed by the property name. That is—DockPanel.Dock.

Another important concept about DockPanels is that their child items get space at a particular edge of the DockPanel in the order in which they are listed.

- Items placed later get space allocated from what is left over after the allocations of the previously placed items.

- For example, in Figure 5-15, only Btn 1 gets an entire edge to itself. Btn 2 and Btn 3 are each constrained on one end, and Btn 4 and Btn 5 are each constrained on two ends.

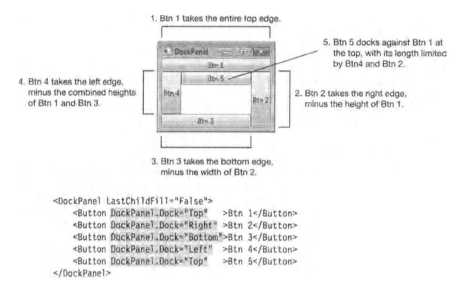

```
<DockPanel LastChildFill="False">
    <Button DockPanel.Dock="Top"    >Btn 1</Button>
    <Button DockPanel.Dock="Right"  >Btn 2</Button>
    <Button DockPanel.Dock="Bottom">Btn 3</Button>
    <Button DockPanel.Dock="Left"   >Btn 4</Button>
    <Button DockPanel.Dock="Top"    >Btn 5</Button>
</DockPanel>
```

Figure 5-15. *The child items of a DockPanel are allocated space on their chosen edge on a first-come, first-served basis. Space allocated for later items is taken from the remaining available space.*

The Grid

The Grid is a container that comprises cells, defined by rows and columns, as shown in Figure 5-16.

- A Grid can contain any number of rows and columns.

  – The row numbers and column numbers are 0-based, so the first row is row 0, and the first column is column 0.

  – By default the grid lines demarcating the cells aren't visible. You can make them visible, as in the left part of the figure, by setting the ShowGridLines property to True. Showing the grid lines can be useful during debugging so that you know exactly which content is in which cell.

  – By default, a Grid has one row and one column. So, even if you don't define any rows or columns, you still have row 0 and column 0.

- If you want to place an item in a cell other than row 0, column 0, then you must explicitly place it in that cell.

  – Generally, you'll place only a single item in a cell. That item, however, might itself be a container containing other items.

  – If a Grid item doesn't specify a row, it's placed in row 0. If it doesn't specify a column, it's placed in column 0.

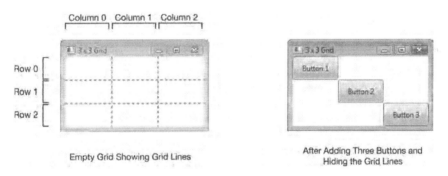

Figure 5-16. *A Grid comprises cells defined by rows and columns.*

Creating and populating a Grid is a three-step process:

1. Define the rows, by adding RowDefinition elements to a Grid.RowDefinitions property, using property element syntax. The following markup creates two rows:

```
<Grid.RowDefinitions>
    <RowDefinition></RowDefinition>
    <RowDefinition></RowDefinition>
</Grid.RowDefinitions>
```

2. Define the columns, by adding ColumnDefinition elements to a Grid.ColumnDefinitions property, using property element syntax. The following markup creates two columns:

```
<Grid.ColumnDefinitions>
    <ColumnDefinition></ColumnDefinition>
    <ColumnDefinition></ColumnDefinition>
</Grid.ColumnDefinitions>
```

3. Explicitly add the items to the cells by setting the Grid.Row and Grid.Column *attached properties* on the items. Again, Chapter 7 will explain the details of attached properties. The following markup shows how to add a button to the cell in the second row (row 1) and the third column (column 2):

```
                    Set the Row    Set the Column
                         ↓              ↓
<Button Grid.Row="1" Grid.Column="2">MyButton</Button>
```

Figure 5-17 shows the structure of the markup for creating a Grid object.

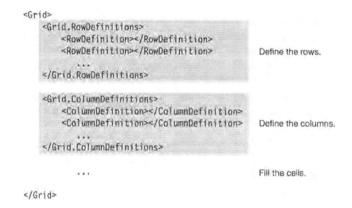

Figure 5-17. *Creating a Grid object is a three-step process. You must define the rows, define the columns, and then fill the cells.*

Figure 5-18 shows an example of creating a Grid with three buttons.

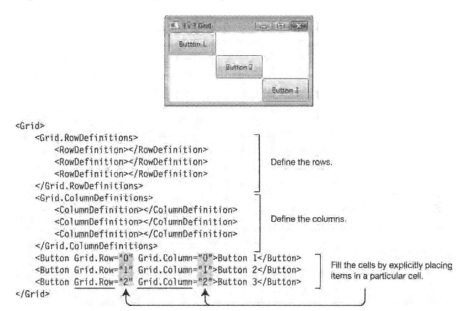

```
<Grid>
    <Grid.RowDefinitions>
        <RowDefinition></RowDefinition>              Define the rows.
        <RowDefinition></RowDefinition>
        <RowDefinition></RowDefinition>
    </Grid.RowDefinitions>
    <Grid.ColumnDefinitions>
        <ColumnDefinition></ColumnDefinition>
        <ColumnDefinition></ColumnDefinition>        Define the columns.
        <ColumnDefinition></ColumnDefinition>
    </Grid.ColumnDefinitions>
    <Button Grid.Row="0" Grid.Column="0">Button 1</Button>
    <Button Grid.Row="1" Grid.Column="1">Button 2</Button>    Fill the cells by explicitly placing
    <Button Grid.Row="2" Grid.Column="2">Button 3</Button>    items in a particular cell.
</Grid>
```

Figure 5-18. *Creating a Grid with Buttons in three cells*

Items Spanning Cells

When you place an element in a cell, you can also specify that the element use more than a single cell. Do this using one or both of the following attached properties:

- Grid.ColumnSpan is used to specify the number of columns an item should span.

- Grid.RowSpan is used to specify the number of rows an item should span.

Figure 5-19 shows how to use the Grid.ColumnSpan and Grid.RowSpan properties. The first three grids show the grid lines because they have the ShowGridLines property set to True. It's set to False in the fourth grid. Notice the following about spanning:

- Items can span rows, columns, or both.

- A Grid cell can contain more than a single item, as shown in the fourth grid.

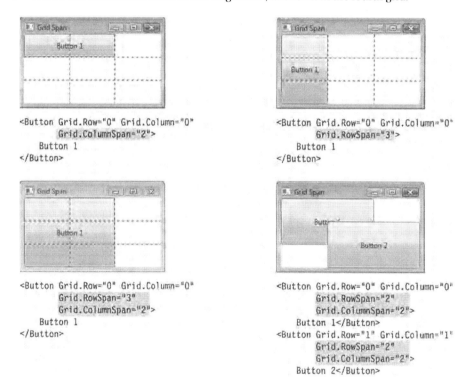

Figure 5-19. *Items can span multiple rows and columns.*

The window shown in Figure 5-20 contains a button that spans two columns. The annotated XAML listing produces this window.

Figure 5-20. *A button spanning two columns*

```
<Grid ShowGridLines="True">
    <Grid.RowDefinitions>
        <RowDefinition></RowDefinition>
        <RowDefinition></RowDefinition>
        <RowDefinition></RowDefinition>
    </Grid.RowDefinitions>
    <Grid.ColumnDefinitions>
        <ColumnDefinition></ColumnDefinition>
        <ColumnDefinition></ColumnDefinition>
        <ColumnDefinition></ColumnDefinition>
    </Grid.ColumnDefinitions>
    <Button Grid.Row="0" Grid.Column="0" Grid.ColumnSpan="2">Button 1</Button>
</Grid>
                    ↑              ↑                  ↑
              Set the Row    Set the Column    Span Two Columns
```

Sizing Rows and Columns

For your program to have an attractive visual layout on the screen, you must be able to control the widths of a grid's columns and the heights of its rows. The Grid provides three methods for controlling these sizes:

- *Absolute Sizing:* The rows and columns are given absolute sizes.

- *Automatic Sizing:* The rows and columns are sized automatically to match the size of the content.

- *Proportional Sizing:* The available space is split proportionally among the rows and columns.

Absolute Sizing

With absolute sizing, you specify the exact width of a column or the height of a row.

- The numeric value is given in device-independent units.

  - For a row, set the Height property in the row definition:

```
<RowDefinition Height="40"></RowDefinition>
```

  - For a column, set the Width property in the column definition:

```
<ColumnDefinition Width="40"></ColumnDefinition>
```

- Cells set with absolute sizing remain the same size regardless of whether the Grid changes size.

The following markup creates three row definitions and three column definitions. The first row is set with an absolute height of 60. The first two columns are set with widths of 35 and 150, respectively.

```
                                Set Absolute Height
<Grid.RowDefinitions>                 ↓
        <RowDefinition Height="60"></RowDefinition>
        <RowDefinition></RowDefinition>
        <RowDefinition></RowDefinition>
</Grid.RowDefinitions>
                                Set Absolute Width
<Grid.ColumnDefinitions>              ↓
        <ColumnDefinition Width="35"></ColumnDefinition>
        <ColumnDefinition Width="150"></ColumnDefinition>
        <ColumnDefinition></ColumnDefinition>
</Grid.ColumnDefinitions>
```

Figure 5-21 shows a window with a Grid containing the row and column structure of the previous code sample.

```
<Grid>
    <Grid.RowDefinitions>
        <RowDefinition Height="60"></RowDefinition>
        <RowDefinition></RowDefinition>
        <RowDefinition></RowDefinition>
    </Grid.RowDefinitions>
    <Grid.ColumnDefinitions>
        <ColumnDefinition Width="35"></ColumnDefinition>
        <ColumnDefinition Width="150"></ColumnDefinition>
        <ColumnDefinition></ColumnDefinition>
    </Grid.ColumnDefinitions>
    <Button Grid.Row="0" Grid.Column="0">Button 1</Button>
    <Button Grid.Row="1" Grid.Column="1">Button 2</Button>
</Grid>
```

Figure 5-21. *You can set the absolute sizes of Grid cells by setting the Height and Width properties of the rows and columns.*

When you change the size of the window containing this Grid, the three measurements set with absolute sizing don't change, regardless of the rest of the dimensions, as shown in Figure 5-22. Notice that the other dimensions, for example the height of Button 2, change with the window size.

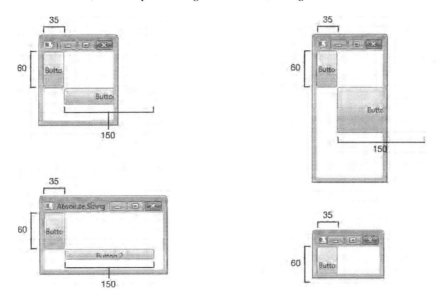

Figure 5-22. *Regardless of the size of the window, the height of the row and widths of the columns that are absolutely sized remain the same.*

125

Automatic Sizing

With automatic sizing, the width of a column or the height of a row is sized to fit the content of the cell. Figure 5-23 shows two windows with Grid panels.

- The Grid in the window on the left uses the default sizing of rows and columns. This uses all the space and allocates it proportionally among the rows and columns. In this case, there's a single row, with equal-width columns.

- The Grid in the window on the right uses automatic sizing. This creates rows and columns that are just large enough to hold the content.

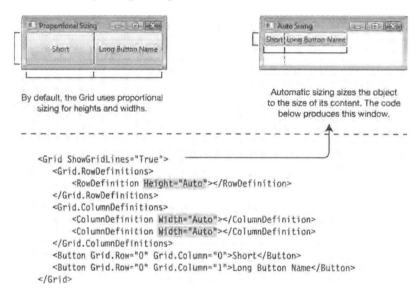

```
<Grid ShowGridLines="True">
    <Grid.RowDefinitions>
        <RowDefinition Height="Auto"></RowDefinition>
    </Grid.RowDefinitions>
    <Grid.ColumnDefinitions>
        <ColumnDefinition Width="Auto"></ColumnDefinition>
        <ColumnDefinition Width="Auto"></ColumnDefinition>
    </Grid.ColumnDefinitions>
    <Button Grid.Row="0" Grid.Column="0">Short</Button>
    <Button Grid.Row="0" Grid.Column="1">Long Button Name</Button>
</Grid>
```

Figure 5-23. *Autosized rows and columns produce cells that are sized to the content, as in the window on the right.*

Proportional Sizing

Proportional sizing means that the available space is divided among the proportionally sized rows and columns.

The following are some of the important things to know about proportional sizing:

- The width or height of proportionally sized rows or columns is represented by an asterisk (*). Hence, proportional sizing is also called *star sizing.*

- To use proportional sizing for a row or column, use the asterisk (*) in the RowDefinition or ColumnDefinition, as shown in the following line of code:

```
<ColumnDefintion Width="*"></ColumnDefinition>
```
                        ↑
                Set Proportional Width

- If the grid changes size, the calculations are redone, and all the proportionally sized rows and columns maintain their proportional layout, as shown in Figure 5-24.

The following markup defines a Grid with two rows and two columns that are all proportionally sized. The resulting Grid is shown in Figure 5-24. Note that when the window containing the Grid is resized, the widths and heights are adjusted automatically.

```
<Grid ShowGridLines="True">
    <Grid.RowDefinitions>
        <RowDefinition Height="*"></RowDefinition>
        <RowDefinition Height="*"></RowDefinition>
    </Grid.RowDefinitions>            ↑
                            Equal Heights
                            Equal Widths
    <Grid.ColumnDefinitions>          ↓
        <ColumnDefinition Width="*"></ColumnDefinition>
        <ColumnDefinition Width="*"></ColumnDefinition>
    </Grid.ColumnDefinitions>
    <Button Grid.Row="0" Grid.Column="0">Button 1</Button>
    <Button Grid.Row="1" Grid.Column="1">Button 2</Button>
</Grid>
```

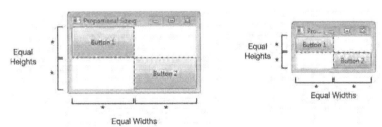

Figure 5-24. *The layout remains the same proportionally when you resize a Grid. The asterisk represents the unit of proportionality that is allocated to each row or column.*

Figure 5-25 shows how the remaining space in a row can be allocated among proportionally sized columns. The same principles also hold for rows.

- In the first example, there are no proportionally sized columns defined. The first column has an absolute width of 50, and the other three columns use automatic sizing, so they are sized to their content. This leaves a free area on the right.

- In the second example, the fourth column is set to proportional sizing, so it gets all the remaining space after the first three columns are sized.

- In the third example, both the third and fourth columns are proportionally sized, so after the first two columns are sized, the third and fourth columns split the remaining space.

- In the fourth example, the third and fourth columns are still proportionally sized, but one has a 2 in front of the * and the other has a 3 in front of the *. In this case, the space remaining after sizing the first two columns is divided by 5, and the third column gets 2/5 and the fourth column gets 3/5.

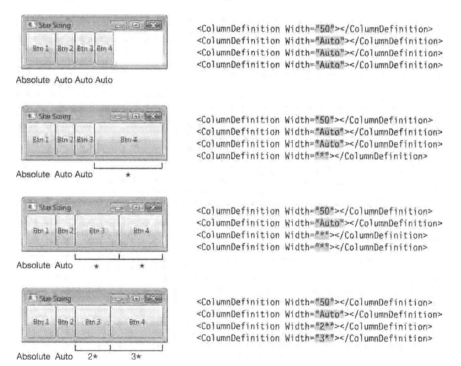

Figure 5-25. *A Grid with proportionally spaced columns or rows sizes its absolute and automatic columns and then takes whatever space is left over and divides it proportionally among the proportional rows and columns.*

Splitter Bars

A *splitter bar* is a vertical or horizontal line that divides a grid into two sections. The user can drag the splitter bar one way or the other to change the proportions of the two sides, as shown in Figure 5-26. You create a splitter bar using the GridSplitter control.

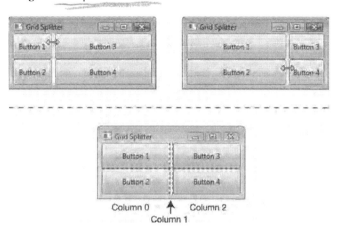

Figure 5-26. *A Grid with a vertical splitter bar*

Although it looks like the splitter bar is *between* cells, it's not. The GridSplitter control is placed inside a cell. In Figure 5-26, you can see that the splitter bar takes up column 1 of the grid. For the best results in creating a usable splitter bar, you should follow these guidelines:

- Allocate an entire row or column just for the splitter bar. This isn't actually required—it just makes life easier.

- To make the splitter bar more visible, do the following.

  - Set its width (or height, for a horizontal bar) to something visible, such as 5.

  - Set the GridSplitter's Background property to something more visible.

- Set the GridSplitter's VerticalAlignment and HorizontalAlignment properties.

  - *Vertical splitter.* Set the VerticalAlignment to Stretch so it spans the entire height. Set the HorizontalAlignment to Center to center it in the cells.

  - *Horizontal splitter.* Set the VerticalAlignment to Center to center it in the cells. Set the HorizontalAlignment to Stretch so it spans the entire width.

- Use Grid.RowSpan or Grid.ColumnSpan so that it spans the entire height or width of the grid.

A GridSplitter fits in a single cell, but you'll want to make sure it spans the entire height or width of the grid, or it's confusing to the user.

For example, the grid shown in Figure 5-27 shows the GridSplitter with its Background property set to make it visible, but it does not have the Grid.RowSpan property set. This grid splitter works normally except that the user can grab the splitter bar only on the visible part at the top. Once grabbed, however, the entire column acts as a normal splitter.

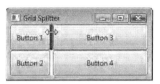

Figure 5-27. *A GridSplitter that does not span all the rows can be grabbed only in the visible portion, but it acts normally otherwise.*

Figure 5-28 shows the complete markup for a Grid using the GridSplitter.

```
<Window x:Class="GridSplitter2.Window1"
    xmlns="http://schemas.microsoft.com/winfx/2006/xaml/presentation"
    xmlns:x="http://schemas.microsoft.com/winfx/2006/xaml"
    Title="Grid Splitter" Height="120" Width="250">
    <Grid>
        <Grid.RowDefinitions>
            <RowDefinition></RowDefinition>                      Define two rows.
            <RowDefinition></RowDefinition>
        </Grid.RowDefinitions>
        <Grid.ColumnDefinitions>
            <ColumnDefinition></ColumnDefinition>
            <ColumnDefinition Width="Auto"></ColumnDefinition>   Define three columns.
            <ColumnDefinition></ColumnDefinition>
        </Grid.ColumnDefinitions>
        <Button Grid.Row="0" Grid.Column="0">Button 1</Button>   Place the left buttons.
        <Button Grid.Row="1" Grid.Column="0">Button 2</Button>
        <GridSplitter Grid.Row="0" Grid.Column="1"
                      Width="3"                                  Create the GridSplitter
                      Grid.RowSpan="2"                           in the center column.
                      Background="DarkGray"
                      HorizontalAlignment="Center"
                      VerticalAlignment="Stretch">
        </GridSplitter>
        <Button Grid.Row="0" Grid.Column="2">Button 3</Button>   Place the right buttons.
        <Button Grid.Row="1" Grid.Column="2">Button 4</Button>
    </Grid>
</Window>
```

Figure 5-28. *A simple Grid using the GridSplitter control*

Shared Size Groups

Several sections ago you saw that *autosized* columns are sized just wide enough for their content. Sometimes however, you want two autosized columns to always be the same width as each other, even if one or the other changes width. You can't do that by making them sized absolutely, because although they would be the same size, you couldn't change their size.

For example, in Figure 5-29, column 0 (containing the button with the *A* on it) and column 3 (containing the button with *Other Text* on it) are independently sized, "auto" columns. In the figure on the left, the column with the *A* button is much thinner than the column containing the *Other Text* button. In the figure on the right, as you drag the splitter to the right, the *A* column gets wider and the *Other Text* column remains the same width.

But what if you wanted the two columns to always be the same width as each other, regardless of one or the other changing width? You can do just that with *shared size groups*.

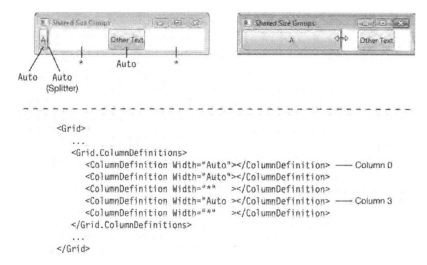

Figure 5-29. *By default, autosized columns are independently sized, as shown by columns 0 and 3. As the splitter bar is dragged to different positions, column 0 changes sizes, but column 3 doesn't.*

You can tie the widths of the two columns together by assigning them to the same shared size group. You do this by assigning a string to the SharedSizeGroup property of the column's ColumnDefinition element, as shown in the following line of markup:

```
<ColumnDefinition Width="Auto" SharedSizeGroup="Column0"></ColumnDefinition>
                                                ↑
                                    Name of SharedSizeGroup
```

The following are some of the important things to know about same shared size groups:

- The name of the same shared size group must be an alphanumeric string with no spaces. It can be any such string, but all the columns in the group must use the same string. The line of markup above uses the arbitrary string "Column0".

- You must activate the same shared size group functionality by assigning the Grid.IsSharedSizeScope attached property to True in some element that encloses the ColumnDefinitions of the columns.

- The SharedSizeGroup functionality works the same way for the height of rows as it does for the width of columns, except that it is, of course, set in the RowDefinition elements of the rows being tied together.

Figure 5-30 shows what happens when you place the column containing the *A* button and the column containing the *Other Text* button into the same shared size group. Now, when you move the slider, changing the width of the *A* button column also changes the width of the *Other Text* button column.

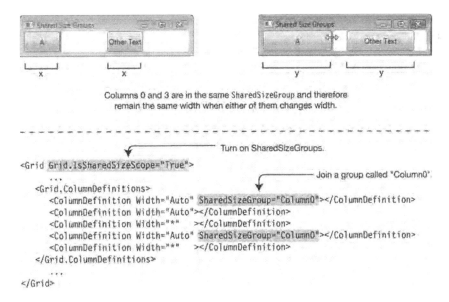

Columns 0 and 3 are in the same SharedSizeGroup and therefore remain the same width when either of them changes width.

```
                                        Turn on SharedSizeGroups.
<Grid Grid.IsSharedSizeScope="True">
    ...
                                                        Join a group called "Column0".
    <Grid.ColumnDefinitions>
        <ColumnDefinition Width="Auto" SharedSizeGroup="Column0"></ColumnDefinition>
        <ColumnDefinition Width="Auto"></ColumnDefinition>
        <ColumnDefinition Width="*"   ></ColumnDefinition>
        <ColumnDefinition Width="Auto" SharedSizeGroup="Column0"></ColumnDefinition>
        <ColumnDefinition Width="*"   ></ColumnDefinition>
    </Grid.ColumnDefinitions>
    ...
</Grid>
```

Figure 5-30. *Columns in the same SharedSizeGroup maintain the same width.*

133

The Canvas

The Canvas is a panel that's more like the panels and windows from previous development frameworks, in that you use coordinates to place elements where you want them.

In previous frameworks, however, the coordinates were always measured from the top-left corner. With the Canvas, you can choose any one of the four corners to be the reference point for an object.

- With the Canvas, you place every item in a particular place, using coordinates with respect to one of the four corners.

  – Set the horizontal reference with an assignment to either Canvas.Left or Canvas.Right. You cannot use both.

  – Set the vertical reference with an assignment to either Canvas.Top or Canvas.Bottom. Again, you cannot use both.

- When the Canvas is resized:

  – The items on the Canvas remain at their actual size; they are not resized to fit the new Canvas size.

  – An item changes position only if the corner with which it is associated moves. In that case, the item also moves so that it maintains the same position with regard to that corner.

The following markup shows a Canvas with two buttons. Both buttons are associated with the top-left corner. Figure 5-31 shows a window with this Canvas. Regardless of the size of the window, each button remains in the same position relative to the top-left corner. Notice that when the right edge of the window is moved to the left, Button 2 is cut off.

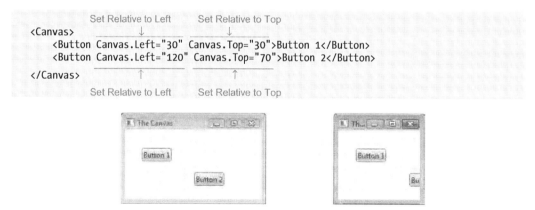

Figure 5-31. *Two buttons associated with the top-left corner of the Canvas*

Figure 5-32 shows the markup to produce a Canvas with four buttons. Each button is associated with a different corner. Above the markup are four screenshots of the running program. Notice that regardless of the size or shape of the Canvas in the window, each button remains a constant distance from the corner to which it is associated. (The numbers in the screenshots are annotations of the distances from the side—not output on the actual window.)

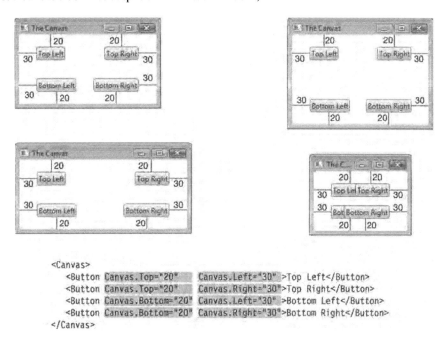

```
<Canvas>
    <Button Canvas.Top="20"    Canvas.Left="30" >Top Left</Button>
    <Button Canvas.Top="20"    Canvas.Right="30">Top Right</Button>
    <Button Canvas.Bottom="20" Canvas.Left="30" >Bottom Left</Button>
    <Button Canvas.Bottom="20" Canvas.Right="30">Bottom Right</Button>
</Canvas>
```

Figure 5-32. *You can think of items placed on a Canvas as being docked to one of the corners. Regardless of the size or shape of the Canvas, the items will retain their distance from their given corner.*

Z-Order on a Canvas

When elements of a Canvas overlap, the *z-order* is a way of specifying which element is in front and which element is behind. The z-order is determined by the value of the Canvas.ZIndex attached properties of the items. The following are some of the important things to know about the z-order:

- When two objects occupy the same area on a Canvas, two things determine which will be displayed in front and which will be behind:

  - If one has a Canvas.ZIndex property value higher than the other, it will be displayed in front.

  - If both have the same Canvas.ZIndex property value, then the one that was added to the Canvas last will be displayed in front.

- By default, any element on a Canvas has a Canvas.ZIndex value of 0.

- The absolute values of Canvas.ZIndex values are meaningless. The only thing that's important is which is higher when comparing two values.

For example, the following markup produces two buttons on the Canvas, as shown in Figure 5-33. The Top Left button is associated with the top, left corner of the Canvas. The Top Right button is associated with the top-right corner.

When the right edge of the window (and hence the Canvas) is moved to the left, the Top Right button moves with it and can partially cover the Top Left button, as shown in the second screenshot in the figure. This is because they both have the default Canvas.ZIndex value of 0, but the Top Right button was added after the Top Left button, so it's displayed in front.

```
<Canvas>
    <Button Canvas.Top="32" Canvas.Left="30">Top Left</Button>
    <Button Canvas.Top="20" Canvas.Right="30">Top Right</Button>
</Canvas>
```

Top Left: ZIndex = 0   Top Left: ZIndex = 5
Top Right: ZIndex = 0   Top Right: ZIndex = 0

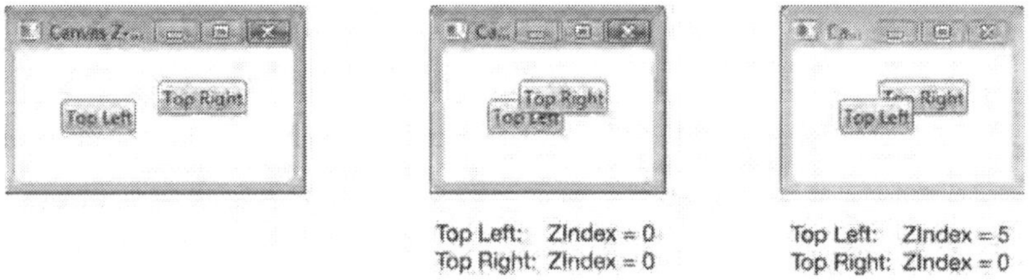

Figure 5-33. *The values of the Canvas.ZIndex properties can determine which is in front.*

If you set the Canvas.ZIndex value of the first button to a value greater than that of the second button, as shown in the following markup, *it* will be displayed in front, as shown in the third screenshot in Figure 5-33.

```
                                Increase the ZIndex
                                        ↓
<Canvas>
    <Button Canvas.Top="32" Canvas.Left="30" Canvas.ZIndex="5">Top Left</Button>
    <Button Canvas.Top="20" Canvas.Right="30">Top Right</Button>
</Canvas>
```

The UniformGrid

The UniformGrid is an extremely simple and limited version of a grid. The following are some of the important things to know about the UniformGrid:

- All the cells of a UniformGrid are always the same size as all the other cells, regardless of whether the UniformGrid changes size or shape.

- Each cell contains a single element.

- Elements are added to the cells in the order in which they are listed in listing.

- You create the cells by specifying the number of rows and columns in the UniformGrid element.

The following code creates a UniformGrid with two rows and two columns. It then populates each cell with a button.

```
       Set the Row Count     Set the Column Count
              ↓                     ↓
  <UniformGrid Rows="2" Columns="2">
     <Button>Button 1</Button>
     <Button>Button 2</Button>
     <Button>Button 3</Button>
     <Button>Button 4</Button>
  </UniformGrid>
```

This markup produces the UniformGrid shown in Figure 5-34.

Figure 5-34. All the cells is a UniformGrid are always the same size as all the other cells, regardless of how the size or shape of the UniformGrid changes.

Summary

In this chapter, you saw how to use the major layout panels and learned their characteristics:

- The StackPanel stacks its elements vertically or horizontally.
- The WrapPanel places its elements in rows or columns and wraps to a new row or column when the line reaches the end of the panel.
- The DockPanel allows its elements to select a side on which to adhere.
- The Grid comprises cells formed from rows and columns. This is the most powerful of the panels we covered.
- The Canvas allows you to associate elements with one of its corners.
- The UniformGrid produces a simple grid with cells that are all the same size.

CHAPTER 6

∎ ∎ ∎

Content and Controls

141

Liberating Content

WPF is a UI framework that excels in displaying visual content. In previous frameworks, different UI controls were specialized for particular purposes, and their visual presentations were more or less fixed. For example, a Label in the Windows Forms framework was a piece of static text. A Button was usually labeled with text but could also paint its background with an image.

But why should the content of your button be limited to either text or an image? Why shouldn't you be allowed to have video on your button—or an animation? Or why should it be so difficult to include images or individually colored backgrounds in the items of a list box?

In answer to these questions, the designers of WPF said—"it shouldn't." They decided to let the programmers and designers choose what the content of a button or list box item should be. They factored out the hard-coded restrictions so that you can include whatever kind of content might make sense in your application.

To create controls of this form, they created two major branches in the class hierarchy tree, from which the controls would derive. They are the following:

- The ContentControl class contains a property called Content that can hold a single element of whatever type of UI content is available in WPF.

- The ItemsControl class contains a property called Items, which is an ordered collection of whatever type of UI content is available in WPF.

The controls derived from these classes give you unprecedented freedom of design. An abridged version of the derivation hierarchy is shown in Figure 6-1. In this chapter, I'll cover the classes shown in the white boxes in the figure. The one class I'll cover that isn't derived from ContentControl or ItemsControl is Image.

Also, as a point of terminology, in WPF the term *control* has a more restricted meaning than in previous frameworks. In WPF, a *control* is a user interface element with which the user can interact. Previously, any UI element on the screen was called a control.

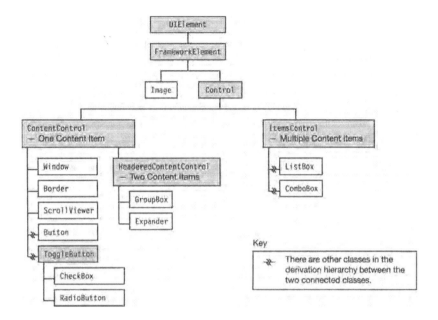

Figure 6-1. *An abridged derivation hierarchy of the major content controls*

Source Code Conventions

As described at the beginning of the previous chapter, the XAML samples shown throughout this chapter show only the content part of the Window element.

In this chapter, I'll be showing more C# code in addition to the XAML, so rather than repeat the boilerplate C# code, I'll show only the nonboilerplate code. To compile the code, place it inside the boilerplate code, as shown in Figure 6-2. This is a convention that I'll use throughout the rest of the book.

```
public partial class Window1 : Window
{
    public Window1()
    {
        InitializeComponent();
    }

    private void Button_Click( object sender, RoutedEventArgs e )
    {
        MessageBox.Show( Example.SelectionBoxItem.ToString(), "Selected");
    }
}
```
The Non-boilerplate Code

Figure 6-2. *The C# code throughout the chapter will contain only the nonboilerplate code of the Window1 class.*

143

The Image Element

The Image element (the only element I'll cover in this chapter that doesn't derive from ContentControl or ItemsControl) simply displays an image. Notice that it's called an *element*, rather than a control, because there's nothing for the user to interact with.

Some of the important things to know about the Image element are the following:

- There are two types of image an Image element can display. They are represented by the following two classes:

    - BitmapImage: This class handles images with the following file extensions—.jpg, .bmp, .png, .tiff, .wdp, and .ico.

    - DrawingImage: This class handles graphic images that are represented by objects of classes derived from the Drawing class, which I'll cover in Chapter 18.

- Using XAML, you can assign a picture to an Image element by assigning the picture's relative directory to the Source property, as shown in the following markup. In the example, the picture SweetieSleeping.jpg has the following characteristics:

    - The file must have been added to the project, with a Build Action type of Resource. Make sure you *don't* set it to Compiled Resource. We'll cover resources in detail in Chapter 11, but for now you just need to know that "compiled resources" are much more difficult to access.

    - This picture is in a subdirectory called Pictures. If the picture had been located in the same directory as the source files, the specification would not have included the Pictures/ part of the string.

Specify the location of the picture.
↓

```
<Image Source="Pictures/SweetieSleeping.jpg"/>
```

The following markup assumes that the file SweetieSleeping.jpg has been included as a project resource. It produces the window shown in Figure 6-3.

```
<Grid>
    <Image Source="SweetieSleeping.jpg"/>
</Grid>
```

Figure 6-3. *The Image element displays an image.*

Displaying an Image Using Code

Creating the Image element in markup is pretty simple, as you just saw in the previous section. Coding it by hand in C# is a bit more involved. The first things you need to understand are the relationships of the various class objects associated with an image. Figure 6-4 shows the relationship of these objects and an ordered description of the process.

An object of the Image class doesn't actually contain the image. Instead, its Source property refers to an object derived from the ImageSource class. In the case of bitmap images, it's the BitmapImage class.

The BitmapImage object doesn't contain the image either. Instead, it has a reference to a Uri object, which specifies where the actual image is located.

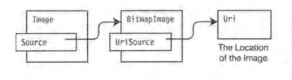

1. Create the Uri, assigning it the location of the picture.

2. Create the BitmapImage, with the reference to the Uri.

3. Create the Image object, with the reference to the BitmapImage.

Figure 6-4. *Creating an Image object requires the creation of supporting objects.*

When creating an Image object in C# code, you must create these three objects separately and connect them, as shown in the following code. The four lines following the InitializeComponent call perform that task. And, of course, you must also create the Grid containing the image and connect it to the Window.

```
public Window1()
{
    InitializeComponent();             Create the Uri for the location.
                                                    ↓
    Uri uri = new Uri( "Pictures/SweetieSleeping.jpg", UriKind.Relative);
    BitmapImage bitmap = new BitmapImage( uri );
    Image image = new Image();
    image.Source = bitmap;

    Grid grid = new Grid();            Create Grid
    grid.Children.Add( image );        Add Image to Grid
    Grid.SetRow( image, 0 );           Place Image in Row
    Grid.SetColumn( image, 0 );        Place Image in Column

    Content = grid;                    Add Grid to Window
}
```

The following is the markup for the program. (Image2 is the name of the namespace, which Visual Studio creates automatically if you create a solution named Image2.)

```
<Window x:Class="Image2.Window1"
    xmlns="http://schemas.microsoft.com/winfx/2006/xaml/presentation"
    xmlns:x="http://schemas.microsoft.com/winfx/2006/xaml"
    Title="Window1" Height="300" Width="300">
</Window>
```

The ContentControls

The ContentControls allow other WPF elements, controls, and panels as their content.

- The ContentControls allow only a single element of content (except the HeaderedContentControls, which I'll cover later in the chapter).

- The item of content is assigned to the Content property, which takes an item of type object.

Figure 6-5 shows a depiction of the Content property on the left, and the inheritance hierarchy of the ContentControl on the right.

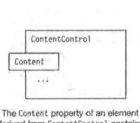

The Content property of an element derived from ContentControl contains a single element of content.

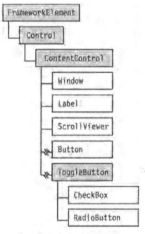

The Derivation Hierarcy of ContentControl

Figure 6-5. *The ContentControl inheritance hierarchy*

How the content is rendered depends on several factors:

- If the object assigned to the Content property is derived from UIElement, then WPF knows how to render it and renders it normally.

- If the object is not derived from UIElement, there are two possibilities:

  - If the object is a data object that has an associated data template, then the template is used to render it. I'll describe data templates in Chapter 15.

    — If the object doesn't have a template, then WPF calls the object's ToString method, which by default prints out the name of the class of which the object is an instantiation.

The Label Control

The Label is a simple element used primarily to statically display some content. Typically this content is text, but since this is a ContentControl, it can be any content, such as a picture or any other element derived from UIElement.

    The following markup creates a window with two Labels. The first has text as its content, and the second Label is an image. If the Label is text, you can set font characteristics such as FontFamily, FontWeight, FontSize, and FontStyle.

```
<StackPanel >
   <Label Content="Ocean Perch" FontWeight="Bold"/>
                      ↑                    ↑
   <Label>      Set the Content     Text Characteristics
      <Image Source="Images/OceanPerch.jpg"></Image>
   </Label>
</StackPanel>
```

This markup produces the window shown in Figure 6-6.

Figure 6-6. *A window with two Labels: a text Label and an image Label.*

A Label is useful in that it displays information to the user about some other element. You can make it even more useful by binding it to another element. I'll cover binding in detail in Chapter 8, but for our purposes here, if you bind a Label to another element, the user can use accelerator keys (also known as *access keys* or *keyboard shortcuts*) to go directly to the element to which it is bound.

To bind a Label to an element, you use a markup extension that assigns the bound element to the Label's Target property, as shown in the following line of markup. Notice the following about the sample markup:

- The markup binds the Label to some other element, named firstName.

- Placing the underscore before the F in the Content part assigns F as the accelerator key to bring the user to element firstName. When the user presses Alt+F, the cursor will go to element named firstName. (Under Vista, you need to first press the Alt key.)

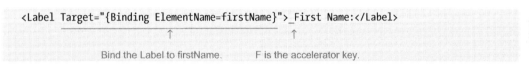

```
<Label Target="{Binding ElementName=firstName}">_First Name:</Label>
```
                 ↑   ↑
        Bind the Label to firstName.   F is the accelerator key.

The following markup creates two text Labels and binds each one to a TextBox (which I'll cover in Chapter 10). The first Label is bound to a TextBox named firstName, and the second is bound to a TextBox named lastName. The F and L keys are the respective accelerator keys for the TextBoxes. Figure 6-7 shows the window.

```
<StackPanel >
    <Label Target="{Binding ElementName=firstName}">_First Name:</Label>
    <TextBox Name="firstName"></TextBox>

    <Label Target="{Binding ElementName=lastName}">_Last Name:</Label>
    <TextBox Name="lastName"></TextBox>
</StackPanel>
```

Figure 6-7. *The Labels in the window are bound to the TextBoxes.*

The Button Control

As I'm sure you're aware, the Button is a visual object that a user can click to tell the program to take some action.

- When a button is clicked, the system raises an event associated with the button.

- To handle the event, you must have an event handler in the code-behind. The event handler performs whatever actions are represented by the button click.

- You can create the Button in either markup or the code-behind—but the event handler must be in the code-behind.

- Since a Button is a ContentControl, it can have any content.

Figure 6-8 shows the markup and code-behind for a simple button. When the button is clicked, the code-behind launches a message box. I'll cover the MessageBox class later in this chapter.

Figure 6-8. *A Button with an instantiation in XAML and the Click event handler in the code-behind*

The CheckBox and RadioButton Controls

A normal Button doesn't retain the information about whether or not it has been clicked before or whether any other Button has been clicked. The CheckBox and RadioButton controls, however, are special forms of buttons that maintain state.

- Every time the user clicks a CheckBox, it toggles between the checked and unchecked states by setting or unsetting its IsChecked property. It displays its state visually by showing a small box, either with or without a check mark.

- The RadioButton is like a CheckBox, except that it is designed to be a member of a group of RadioButtons. The group has the constraint that only one of the RadioButtons can be selected at any time. When a RadioButton is selected, any other RadioButton that might have been in the IsChecked state becomes unchecked.

- From the code-behind, you can check whether a particular CheckBox or RadioButton is selected by checking its IsChecked property.

- If a CheckBox or RadioButton has its IsThreeState property set to true, then the value of the IsChecked property can be true, false, or null.

Figure 6-9 shows a window with two CheckBoxes and three RadioButtons. The markup for the window is shown after the figure. I gave the controls Names so they could be manipulated from the code-behind. I gave them Margins so that they would look a little nicer, separated a bit from each other and from the window edges.

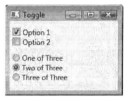

Figure 6-9. *CheckBoxes are independent, but only one RadioButton from a group can be selected.*

```
<StackPanel>
    <CheckBox     Name="cb1" Margin="5,10,0,0">Option 1</CheckBox>
    <CheckBox     Name="cb2" Margin="5,0,0,0">Option 2</CheckBox>
    <RadioButton Name="rb1" Margin="5,10,0,0">One of Three</RadioButton>
    <RadioButton Name="rb2" Margin="5,0,0,0">Two of Three</RadioButton>
    <RadioButton Name="rb3" Margin="5,0,0,0">Three of Three</RadioButton>
</StackPanel>
```

Grouping RadioButtons

Since RadioButtons are meant to be used in groups, it's important to know how to group them.

- By default, all RadioButtons in a parent element belong to the same group.

- You can explicitly create RadioButton groups by setting the GroupName properties of the buttons. For each RadioButton, you can set its GroupName property to a string. All the buttons with the same GroupName string belong to the same group.

For example, the following markup creates six RadioButtons, in three groups. The first two RadioButtons are, by default, grouped by the StackPanel, which contains them. The second two comprise a group called Group1, and the last two comprise a group called Group2.

```
<StackPanel>
    <RadioButton Margin="5,0,5,0">Default 1</RadioButton>
    <RadioButton Margin="5,0">Default 2</RadioButton>

    <RadioButton GroupName="Group1" Margin="5,7,5,0">Group1-1</RadioButton>
    <RadioButton GroupName="Group1" Margin="5,0">Group1-2</RadioButton>
                              ↑
                 Explicit Group Name
    <RadioButton GroupName="Group2" Margin="5,7,5,0">Group2-1</RadioButton>
    <RadioButton GroupName="Group2" Margin="5,0">Group2-2</RadioButton>
                              ↑
</StackPanel>      Explicit Group Name
```

Figure 6-10 shows the window produced by the markup.

Figure 6-10. *The window contains one default group and two explicit groups.*

The Window Class

The first class you studied, in Chapter 2, was the Window class. There you learned that most WPF programs consist of a Window object populated with other elements. You might be surprised, then, to learn that the Window class is derived from the ContentControl class.

Like all classes derived from ContentControl, this means that it can have only a single item as its content. Generally, that item is some sort of panel, which contains other items. In this section, I'll cover some of the other characteristics of the Window class.

As you probably remember, in order to create a window, you must create an object of type Window and then call that object's Show method. It's the second step that makes the window visible on the screen.

Table 6-1 describes some of the methods and properties that control a window's behavior.

Table 6-1. *Useful Methods and Properties of the Window Class*

Name	Method or Property	Purpose
Show	Method	Creates a visible window on the screen, representing the Window object. This method returns immediately after creating the window, without waiting for the window to close.
ShowDialog	Method	Creates a visible window on the screen and doesn't return until that window is closed.
Hide	Method	Makes a window invisible.
Topmost	Property	Specifies that the window should appear in front of all other windows in the application that are not marked as Topmost.
ShowInTaskBar	Property	Lists the window in the task bar.
WindowStartupLocation	Property	Specifies where the window should appear when it is created and made visible. Its value is one of the three members of the WindowStartupLocation enumeration—Manual, CenterScreen, or CenterOwner.

Window Ownership

A program can spawn multiple windows. These windows can be completely independent, or they can be owned by other windows.

- A window that is owned by another window is called a *child window*. Child windows are also called *modeless dialogs*.

- A child window minimizes, maximizes, and closes whenever its owner window is minimized, maximized, or closed.

- To make a window a child window, set its Owner property to the reference of the owner window.

The following markup and code show a program with a main window that contains a button. When the button is clicked, the program creates two new windows: an independent window and a child window.

```
<Grid>
    <Button Click="Button_Click" VerticalAlignment="Top">
        Create Other Windows
    </Button>
</Grid>
```

The following is the event handler in the code-behind:

```
private void Button_Click( object sender, RoutedEventArgs e )
{
    Window w1 = new Window();    w1.Background = Brushes.AliceBlue;
    w1.Title = "Win 1"; w1.Height = 120; w1.Width = 170;
    w1.Content = "Independent Window";
    w1.Show();

    Window w2 = new Window();    w2.Background = Brushes.PaleVioletRed;
    w2.Title = "Win 2"; w2.Height = 120; w2.Width = 170;
    w2.Content = "Child Window";
    w2.Owner = this;                  // Make this a child window.
    w2.Show();
}
```

Modal Dialog Boxes

A *modal dialog*, or *modal dialog box*, is a window that focuses on displaying a specific set of information or collecting information from the user. Usually the information collected from the user is information needed for the program to proceed.

Important information to know about modal dialogs includes the following:

- A window becomes a modal dialog when it is displayed by calling its ShowDialog method rather than its Show method, as shown in the following code:

```
MyDialog dlg = new MyDialog();      // Create the Window object.
bool? result = dlg.ShowDialog();    // Display it as a modal window.
                        ↑
    ...             Create modal dialog.
```

- The modal dialog disables user input to all other windows in the program; so while the dialog is visible, the user can only interact with the dialog.

- Normal operation resumes when the user closes the dialog window.

The Window class has a nullable bool property named DialogResult that, although it is a member of all windows, can be set only when a window is a modal dialog. Before the call to ShowDialog, it has a value of null. When the window closes, it has a value of either true or false. Figure 6-11 shows the life of a modal dialog and the states of DialogResult.

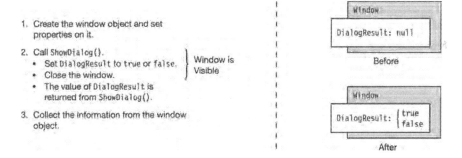

Figure 6-11. *The life cycle of a modal window and the states of property DialogResult*

There are several ways to set the value of DialogResult:

- In the modal window's logic, you can set the value to either true or false.

- If the user closes the window using the close icon in the window bar, the system sets the DialogResult value to false.

- You can set specially designated buttons on the dialog.

  - If you set a button's IsCancel property to true and the user clicks that button, the system will set DialogResult to false and close the window.

  - If you set a button's IsDefault property to true and the user clicks that button, the event handler for the button will be called. There, you have the opportunity to set the DialogResult value to true or false and close the window, using the Close method. Notice that you must provide the code to do these two things.

The windows shown in Figure 6-12 are produced by the code and markup shown next. The main window—Window1—contains a button that creates and displays the modal dialog—MyDialog.

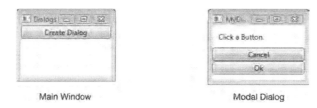

Figure 6-12. *The main window and the modal dialog produced by the example code*

The following is the markup and the code for the main window—Window1:

```
<Grid>
   <Button Click="Button_Click" VerticalAlignment="Top">
      Create Dialog
   </Button>
</Grid>
```

The following is the button's event handler in the code-behind:

```
private void Button_Click( object sender, RoutedEventArgs e )
{
   MyDialog dlg = new MyDialog();              // Create window object.
   string result = ( true == dlg.ShowDialog() )  // Make window modal.
                      ? "Ok Clicked."
                      : "Cancel";
   MessageBox.Show( result, "Result" );
}
```

The following is the markup and the code for the modal dialog—MyDialog:

```
<StackPanel>
    <TextBlock Padding="10">Click a Button.</TextBlock>
    <Button IsCancel="True">Cancel</Button>
    <Button IsDefault="True" Click="Button_Click">Ok</Button>
</StackPanel>
```
                                               ↑
                                   Set the event handler.

            Declare the event handler.
                     ↓
```
private void Button_Click( object sender, RoutedEventArgs e )
{
   DialogResult = true;          Set DialogResult.
   Close();                      Close the window.
}
```

The MessageBox Dialog Box

The MessageBox class creates preformatted modal dialog boxes to display messages, errors, or warnings to the user. Since the dialog box is modal, the user must address it before continuing with the program.

To display a message box, use the static Show method, giving it appropriate parameters. There are 12 overloads of the Show method, but for a simple informational dialog, you can use the two-parameter form, as shown in Figure 6-13.

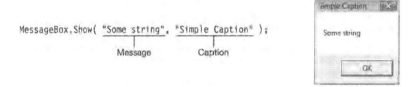

Figure 6-13. *The two-parameter Show method produces a simple informational message box.*

More generally, however, the message box has four areas that you can control, as shown in Figure 6-14. You control which set of buttons is shown and which image is shown by using the MessageBoxButton and MessageBoxImage enumerations, also listed in the figure. The following is an example of the syntax of the four-parameter form:

```
MessageBox.Show( "My Message", "Simple Caption",   // Message and Caption
                MessageBoxButton.OKCancel,         // Button Group
                MessageBoxImage.Information );      // Image
```

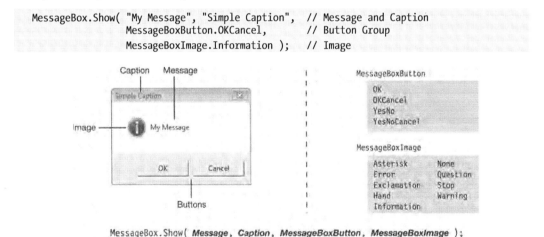

Figure 6-14. *There are four parts to a MessageBox. You specify which image and which buttons to show by using the MessageBoxButton and MessageBoxImage enumerations.*

When the user closes the message box, the Show method returns a value that specifies which button the user clicked, allowing you to take the appropriate action. The five possible values are those of the MessageBoxResult enumeration—Cancel, No, None, OK, and Yes.

The ScrollViewer

The ScrollViewer adds scroll bars to its Content element if the content is too large to be displayed in the allocated area.

For example, Figure 6-15 shows two windows with ScrollViewer controls. In the first case, there's not enough room to show all six buttons. In the second case, there's not enough room to show the entire image. In both cases, the ScrollViewer adds a scroll bar on the right.

Figure 6-15. *You can use the ScrollViewer to automatically put scroll bars on content that is too large for its container.*

The following is the markup for the ScrollViewer containing the Buttons:

```
<Grid>
   <ScrollViewer>
     <StackPanel>
        <Button>Button 1</Button>        <Button>Button 20</Button>
        <Button>Button 300</Button>      <Button>Button 4000</Button>
        <Button>Button 50000</Button>   <Button>Button 600000</Button>
     </StackPanel>
   </ScrollViewer>
</Grid>
```

The following is the markup for the ScrollViewer containing the Image:

```
<ScrollViewer>
   <Image   Source="ChurchSmall.jpg" />
</ScrollViewer>
```

The HeaderedContentControls

The HeaderedContentControl class derives from the ContentControl class, as shown in Figure 6-16. Instead of containing a single piece of data, however, classes derived from HeaderedContentControl contain two pieces of content— the Content and a Header. These are referenced by properties with those names, as shown on the left in the figure.

- The Content property holds the main content.

- The content in the Header property acts as the title for the main content.

There are three classes that derive from HeaderedContentControl. In the next sections, I'll cover the GroupBox and Expander elements. I'll postpone covering the TabItem element until Chapter 16, when I'll cover the TabControl.

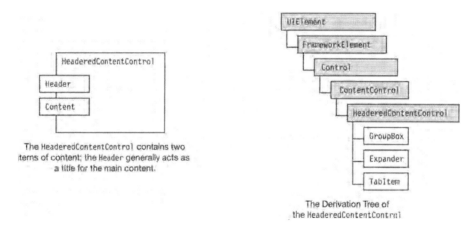

Figure 6-16. The HeaderedContentControl is a form of ContentControl that has two pieces of content rather than one. They are the Header and the Content.

The GroupBox Element

The GroupBox puts a border around its content and places the header in the border, at the top left. Some notable things about the GroupBox are the following:

- You can set the BorderThickness and the Background on a GroupBox.

- Although it usually consists of text, the Header itself can contain content.

The following markup includes a GroupBox that encloses an image and two buttons and gives the group the title Grouped Things. This markup produces the left window in Figure 6-17.

```
<GroupBox Header="Grouped Things" Margin="5">
    <StackPanel>
        <Image Margin="3" HorizontalAlignment="Left" Height="50"
            Source="Images/AL.jpg">
        </Image>
        <Button Margin="3">Btn 1</Button>
        <Button Margin="3">Btn 2</Button>
    </StackPanel>
</GroupBox>
```

GroupBox with Text Header   GroupBox with Image Header

Figure 6-17. *GroupBoxes with different Header content type*

The following markup moves the Image from being enclosed by the GroupBox to being the Header, as shown in the right window in Figure 6-17.

```
<GroupBox Margin="5">
    <GroupBox.Header>
        <Image Margin="3" HorizontalAlignment="Left" Height="50"
            Source="Images/AL.jpg">
        </Image>
    </GroupBox.Header>
    <StackPanel>
        <Button Margin="3">Btn 1</Button>
        <Button Margin="3">Btn 2</Button>
    </StackPanel>
</GroupBox>
```

161

The Expander Control

The Expander control is like a GroupBox that can show or hide its content by clicking a button.

- Like the GroupBox, it contains a Header and Content.

- Next to the Header, it also contains a circular button with a chevron pointing either up or down to indicate whether the content box should be dropped down (opened) or pulled up (closed).

- If there isn't enough room to display all the content when the Expander is expanded, the excess content is truncated. To fix this, you can use a ScrollViewer in the Content part so the user can scroll to all the content.

Figure 6-18 shows an Expander that contains a StackPanel with three buttons. In the left image, the Expander is closed, so you can't see its contents. In the right image, it's open.

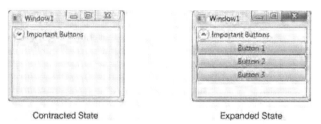

Figure 6-18. *An Expander in contracted and expanded states*

The following markup produces the Expander shown in Figure 6-18.

```
<Grid>
    <Expander Header="Important Buttons">
        <StackPanel>
            <Button>Button 1</Button>
            <Button>Button 2</Button>
            <Button>Button 3</Button>
        </StackPanel>
    </Expander>
</Grid>
```

ItemsControl Elements

While the ContentControl classes can have only a single item of content, the ItemsControl classes can have any number of content items.

- The content items are kept in an ordered collection, referenced by the Items property.

- The content items can be of the same or different types.

You can associate items with an element derived from ItemsControl in several ways. You can place the items in the element's Items collection, or you can bind the items from a data source to the ItemsSource property. Since I'll cover data binding in Chapter 8, I'll postpone the explanation of how to use the ItemsSource property until then.

Figure 6-19 shows the abridged derivation tree of the ItemsControl class.

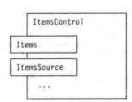

The elements contained in an ItemsControl element are members of its Items collection. Alternatively, an external collection can be bound to its ItemsSource property.

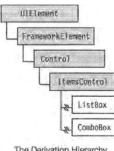

The Derivation Hierarchy of ItemsControl

Figure 6-19. *The ItemsControl derivation hierarchy*

The ListBox Control

A ListBox is a collection of items displayed to the user, from which he or she can select one or more items. The following are some important things to know about ListBoxes:

- As with all ItemsControls, the items in the ListBox can be of any type derived from the UIElement class, including Images and Buttons.

- By default, a ListBox sets its width to the width of its widest item.

There are two forms in which you can place items into a ListBox's Items collection—either by explicitly wrapping each item in a ListBoxItem element or by just placing them in the collection and letting the system implicitly wrap them.

- You can place items in the ListBox's Items collection by creating ListBoxItem elements and placing those elements in the content part of the ListBox, as shown in the following markup. This example inserts three strings into the ListBox. Figure 6-20 shows this window on the left.

```
<ListBox>
    <ListBoxItem>Sweetie</ListBoxItem>
    <ListBoxItem>Darwin</ListBoxItem>
    <ListBoxItem>Florence</ListBoxItem>
</ListBox>
```

- You can place items in the ListBox's Items collection, even without explicitly creating ListBoxItems for them, as shown in the following markup. Rather than creating explicit ListBoxItems, it inserts two TextBlocks and a Button. Figure 6-20 shows this window on the right.

```
<ListBox>
    <TextBlock>Sweetie</TextBlock>
    <TextBlock>Darwin</TextBlock>
    <Button>Florence</Button>
</ListBox>
```

 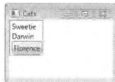

Figure 6-20. *The items in a ListBox can be added as ListBoxItems or as raw elements, in which case the system implicitly wraps them in ListBoxItems.*

Checking the Selection

When the user has selected an item in the list box, you can determine which item was selected by using the ListBox's SelectedItem property. This property returns an object reference to the first selected item, or null, if no item is selected. I'll cover multiple selections in the "Multiple Selections" section.

The markup and code-behind listed produce the window shown in Figure 6-21. In this example, the Button has an event handler, called Button_Click, which determines which item in the ListBox is selected, and displays that item.

Figure 6-21. *A ListBox with a button that determines which item is selected*

```
<StackPanel>
   <ListBox Name="lstbxCats" HorizontalAlignment="Left" Width="100">
      <ListBoxItem>Sweetie</ListBoxItem>
      <ListBoxItem>Darwin</ListBoxItem>
      <ListBoxItem>Florence</ListBoxItem>
   </ListBox>
   <Button Click="Button_Click" HorizontalAlignment="Left"
           Width="100" Padding="10,3" Margin="0,5">Enter</Button>
</StackPanel>
```

Notice in the following event handler that the reference returned is of type object, so it must be cast to the correct type before you can use it. Notice how the code does this by casting the reference to type ListBoxItem and then using the Content property of the result. The event handler must have the signature and return type shown in the code. Also, make sure to handle the case where a null value is returned.

```
private void Button_Click( object sender, RoutedEventArgs e )
{
                           Get the selected item.
                                 ↓
   object obj = lstbxCats.SelectedItem;
   string selected = ( obj == null )
                  ? "No item selected."
                  : (string) ( (ListBoxItem) obj ).Content;
                                              ↑
                  Cast to ListBoxItem and then use the Content.
   MessageBox.Show( selected, "Selected Item" );
}
```

Notification of Changed Selection

Whenever the selected item in the ListBox changes, the ListBox's SelectionChanged event is raised. If you create an event handler in the code-behind, you can assign the name of the event handler to the event, and when the event is raised, the event handler is called.

The markup and code-behind shown below create a window that shows a ListBox with the names of three dogs, as shown on the left in Figure 6-22. When the user selects one of the items in the ListBox, the event handler produces a dialog box showing the item selected, as shown on the right in Figure 6-22.

Figure 6-22. *A ListBox with three items. When the item selected changes, a dialog box shows the new selection.*

The following is the markup and code-behind of the window shown in Figure 6-22.

```
<StackPanel>
    <ListBox Name="lstbxDogs"
             HorizontalAlignment="Left" Width="100"
             SelectionChanged="lstbxDogs_SelectionChanged" >
                                   ↑
                     Assign the event handler to the event.
        <ListBoxItem>Princess</ListBoxItem>
        <ListBoxItem>Avonlea</ListBoxItem>
        <ListBoxItem>Brumby</ListBoxItem>
    </ListBox>
</StackPanel>
```

The code-behind contains a simple event handler named lstbxDogs_SelectionChanged, as shown here.

```
                        Event Handler
                             ↓
private void lstbxDogs_SelectionChanged( object sender, SelectionChangedEventArgs e )
{
    ListBox     lb = sender           as ListBox;
    ListBoxItem lbi = lb.SelectedItem as ListBoxItem;
    MessageBox.Show( lbi.Content.ToString(), "Dog Selected" );
}
```

Multiple Selections

By default, only a single item in a ListBox can be selected at any time. But there are several options allowing you to enable selection of multiple items from the ListBox. You set the selection mode with the SelectionMode property. The following are the possible values:

- Single: The user can select only a single item from the list. This is the default.

- Extended: The user can select multiple items from the list, but must hold down a special key to select items after the first one.

  - To select additional items after the first, the user must hold down the Ctrl key while selecting items.

  - To select a range of items, the user can select the first (or last) item and then, while holding down the Shift key, select the last (first) item. This selects all the items in between as well as the first and last items.

- Multiple: The user can select multiple items from the list by just clicking them, without having to press any special keys to allow the multiple selection.

In the code-behind, you can determine which items are selected by cycling through the list and checking the IsSelected property on each item.

For example, you could use the following Button event handler to display the cats selected in the cats ListBox example.

```
private void Button_Click( object sender, RoutedEventArgs e )
{
    foreach ( ListBoxItem item in lstbxCats.Items )
    {            Check to see whether it's selected.
                        ↓
        if ( item.IsSelected )
            MessageBox.Show( (string) item.Content, "Is Selected" );
    }
}
```

The markup would be the same, except for the addition of the assignment to the SelectionMode property, as shown here.

```
<ListBox Name="lstbxCats" HorizontalAlignment="Left" Width="100"
         SelectionMode="Multiple">
                        ↑
            Set the selection mode.
```

The ComboBox Control

The ComboBox is like a ListBox that only shows the one item that's selected. When the down arrow on the end is clicked, the list box drops down from the control, and the user can select a different item from the list.

The methods of setting the elements of the ComboBox's Items collection are similar to those of setting the collection in a ListBox. You can explicitly wrap the items in a ComboBoxItem or allow the system to wrap them implicitly. Or you can bind them to the ItemsSource property, which I'll cover in Chapter 8 when I talk about binding.

Figure 6-23 shows the windows produced by the markup and code-behind shown next.

ComboBox Closed   ComboBox Dropdown   MessageBox Displayed
                              Open   When the Button is Clicked

Figure 6-23. *By default a ComboBox shows only the currently selected item. Clicking the down arrow on the right of the ComboBox opens the drop-down, showing all the items available.*

```
<Canvas>
    <ComboBox Name="Example" SelectedIndex="0" Width="134">
        <ComboBoxItem>First Item</ComboBoxItem>
        <ComboBoxItem>Second Item</ComboBoxItem>
        <ComboBoxItem>Third Item</ComboBoxItem>
    </ComboBox>
    <Button Padding="10,3" Canvas.Right="5" Canvas.Bottom="5"
        HorizontalAlignment="Right" Click="Button_Click">Enter</Button>
</Canvas>
```

To get the selected item from the code-behind, use the SelectionBoxItem property, as shown in the following code.

```
private void Button_Click( object sender, RoutedEventArgs e )
{
    MessageBox.Show( Example.SelectionBoxItem.ToString(), "Selected");
}
```

Selecting and Entering Items

The ComboBox has a property named IsEditable, which is False by default. In this default state, when the ComboBox has the focus, it has the following characteristics:

- You can select an item by typing its string. It doesn't, however, recognize strings that aren't in the list of members.

- You can't perform copy or paste operations on the text in the ComboBox.

When the IsEditable property is set to True, the appearance of the ComboBox changes so that it looks like a text box. Figure 6-24 shows the difference in appearance between the two states.

IsEditable is False.

IsEditable is True.

Figure 6-24. *When the IsEditable property is True, the ComboBox looks like a text box.*

When IsEditable is true, the behavior of the text box depends on another property, named IsReadOnly. Table 6-2 summarizes this behavior.

Table 6-2. *The Relationship Between the IsEditable Property and the IsReadOnly Property*

IsReadOnly Is False	IsReadOnly Is True
You can enter a string into the text box even if it's not in the list.	You can only select entries from the drop-down list.
You can select, cut, copy, and paste the text in the text box.	You can select or copy text in the text box, but you cannot paste into it.
You can select an item by entering a string.	You cannot select an item by entering a string.

■ **Note** The ComboBox has a characteristic that sometimes seems odd. By default, its width readjusts to the size of the selected item. It can be a bit disconcerting to have the ComboBox changing width when you make a different selection. To avoid this behavior, you should set the Width property to an explicit value.

169

Summary

Rather than limiting most controls to containing only a single type content, as has been done in previous UI frameworks, the designers of WPF decided to allow the programmer and designer to select the type of content the individual controls and elements should display.

In this chapter, you learned about the most important elements designed for displaying content. The ones I covered were the following:

- The Image element, which simply displays an image

- The ContentControls, which hold a single element of content

- The HeaderedContentControls, which hold a single main element of content, and a second content item, which acts as a title or header for the main content

- The ItemsControls, which contain any number of content items

This freedom to determine the type of content to display has allowed unprecedented freedom to programmers and designers.

CHAPTER 7

■■■

Dependency Properties

Properties and a New Paradigm

You might have noticed by now that WPF uses properties extensively. The WPF classes have been specifically designed to use properties rather than methods, when possible, because properties are declarative, making them ideal for XAML's declarative syntax. But beyond just the *preference* for properties, WPF has produced a whole new way of *using* properties and a set of services to support that method.

Before looking at WPF's new paradigm for properties, however, let's review a bit about standard .NET properties in general. The following are some important things to remember about properties:

- A property is usually associated with a private field in the class and represents that field to other classes. The field is called the *backing field*.

- A property is a *functional member* of the class, which means it executes code.

    - When you assign a value to a property, that value is passed to the set accessor, which usually assigns it to the backing field.

    - When you read from a property, the get accessor usually just returns the value of the backing field.

Although this is the general paradigm, the get and set accessors aren't constrained to setting and returning the backing field; there doesn't even have to be a backing field. They can execute whatever code you choose to put in them. The only constraints are that the get accessor must return a value and the value must be of the correct type.

The following code gives an example of this standard .NET paradigm. The class declares a private int field called _myProp, and a public property called MyProp, which accesses it. As you would expect, at any given time, the value of a property is the value of the field.

```
class MyClass
{                    Backing Field
                          ↓
    private int _myProp;

    public int MyProp    ← Property
    {
        get { return _myProp; }
        set { _myProp = value; }
    }
}
```

WPF, however, introduces a new pattern that doesn't use a simple field, and adds a huge amount of functionality. The new type of property is called a *dependency property*. In contrast, regular .NET properties are called *CLR properties*. (CLR stands, of course, for Common Language Runtime.) The following are the important characteristics of dependency properties:

- The value of a dependency property isn't stored in a simple field, but is determined as needed.

- The value of a dependency property at any given time can depend on many things, including default values, data bindings, the values of other properties, user preferences, and a number of other factors.

  - The name *dependency property* comes from the fact that its value can *depend* on these other factors.

  - Because some of these factors can be changing, the value of a dependency property can change, even though the code hasn't assigned it a new value.

- There is an integrated set of services, called the *WPF property system*, whose job it is to keep track of all the factors and determine the values of these properties when they're called for.

- The syntax for using dependency properties in your code or markup is the same as that for using properties that are not dependency properties. As a matter of fact, most of the WPF properties you've seen since the beginning of this book have been dependency properties.

Figure 7-1 illustrates the difference between CLR properties and dependency properties. The diagram on the left shows a CLR property with a backing field. The diagram on the right illustrates the concept of a WPF dependency property. The dotted box labeled *InstanceDP* represents the instance of the dependency property, which is managed by the WPF property system. The box is dotted because a dependency property isn't really a memory location at all. It's far more, as you'll soon see.

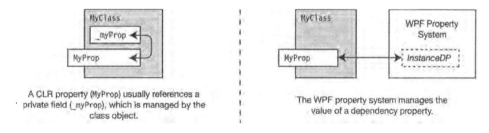

Figure 7-1. A CLR property and a dependency property

Dependency properties don't replace regular CLR properties. As a matter of fact, the vast majority of the properties you create in your own code will probably continue to be CLR properties.

Looking at an Example

As I stated earlier, most of the WPF properties you've seen throughout the book have been dependency properties. Although you've seen what the various properties do with respect to their classes, I haven't mentioned how the properties might affect each other.

Let's start by looking at an example using a simple GroupBox and see how the WPF property system orchestrates the values of a set of FontWeight dependency properties. The FontWeight dependency property has the dependency characteristic called *property value inheritance*, which I'll demonstrate in the example.

Figure 7-2 shows the markup of a GroupBox that contains a header and two buttons. The window produced by the markup is shown to the right of the markup.

```
<Window x:Class="InheritFont.Window1" ... >
    <GroupBox FontWeight="Bold">
        <GroupBox.Header>
            Buttons
        </GroupBox.Header>
        <StackPanel>
            <Button FontWeight="Medium">Button 1</Button>
            <Button>Button 2</Button>
        </StackPanel>
    </GroupBox>
</Window>
```

Figure 7-2. The value of the FontWeight property is set in the GroupBox, and is inherited by all the elements it contains, unless explicitly set locally.

If you look at the markup and the window, you'll see some interesting things:

- In the markup you see that the FontWeight property of the GroupBox is set to Bold, and the FontWeight property of the first button is set to Medium.

- In the window on the right, you see that the header and the second button are in bold font, and the first button is not.

The short explanation is that because the property is set at the GroupBox level, everything inside the GroupBox with a FontWeight property inherits the Bold value, except the element that explicitly sets its own value locally. Figure 7-3 shows the details about where the different FontWeight properties got their values. The figure shows the element tree on the left and the property values on the right along with the source of the value.

The element tree has five elements that have the FontWeight property. In this example, those five properties get their values from one of three sources: the default FontWeight value, an explicitly set value, or inheritance from an element higher in the element tree. Here's how each is set. The WPF properties system handles all the details.

- The FontWeight for the Window1 element isn't explicitly set in the markup; nor is there a FontWeight property higher up in the tree, since Window1 is at the top. Since neither of these is a source for the value of the property, the WPF property system looks up the registered default value and uses that. The default value is Normal.

- The FontWeight for the GroupBox element is set explicitly to Bold in the markup. Local assignment on an element has the highest priority, so it takes the assigned value. It also passes that value down to the FontWeight properties of the elements it encloses.

- The text of the Header is converted by the XAML parser to a TextBlock. Since the TextBlock isn't explicitly assigned a FontWeight value, and is enclosed by the GroupBox, its FontWeight property inherits the Bold value from the GroupBox.

- The first button is part of the GroupBox's Content and would therefore inherit the Bold value from the GroupBox. But since its value is explicitly assigned to Medium in the markup, that's the value it gets.

- The second button inherits the Bold value from the GroupBox.

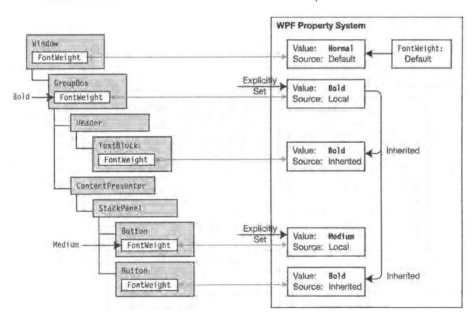

Figure 7-3. *The tree of elements showing the source of each value for FontWeight*

Determining the Value of a Property

Determining the value of a dependency property requires the WPF property system to evaluate a number of possible sources. I'm not going to cover all the aspects of how the value is calculated, but Figure 7-4 illustrates some of the major parts of the algorithm.

In particular, take a glance at the first column. I'll be covering styles, templates, and themes later in the text. Once I've covered these topics, you might want to refer back to this figure if the values of various properties aren't turning out to be what you expected.

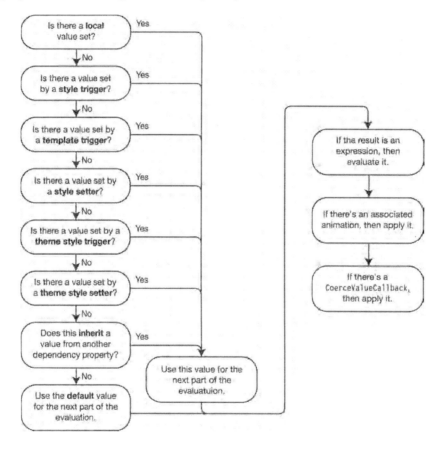

Figure 7-4. *Part of the algorithm used by the WPF property system to determine the value of any dependency property*

The Infrastructure of a Dependency Property

The dependency property architecture is based on the collaboration of two classes—DependencyProperty and DependencyObject—both of which depend on the services provided by the WPF property system.

- An instance of the DependencyProperty class is called a *dependency property identifier*, and it represents the *characteristics* of a particular dependency property. Notice that it doesn't represent the *value* of the property—but the *characteristics*, or metadata, about the property.

- An object of the DependencyObject class contains the infrastructure for interacting with the WPF property system to get and set the value of a particular dependency property.

Figure 7-5 illustrates the important relationships between the components. The following are some additional things to note about the figure:

- You can think of a dependency property as being held by the WPF property system. In the figure, this is represented by the dotted box labeled *InstanceDP*.

- The DependencyObject class has two methods—GetValue and SetValue—which your program uses to interact with the dependency property in the WPF property system.

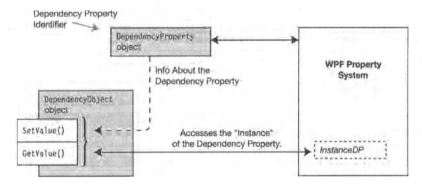

Figure 7-5. *A dependency property requires an object of the DependencyProperty class and an object of the DependencyObject class.*

▪ **Note** A DependencyProperty instance and a DependencyObject instance together map to a unique dependency property managed inside the WPF property system.

Creating a Custom Dependency Property

Most WPF programmers probably won't ever have to create a dependency property in a class unless they're creating custom controls. The process isn't difficult, however, so I've described the process in this section, and given an example in the next. It requires the following architectural characteristics of the class in which the dependency property is being created. Look carefully at the architecture illustrated in Figure 7-6.

- The class to which you want to add a dependency property must derive from the DependencyObject class. This sets up the required infrastructure inside the class for plugging it into the WPF property system. The DependencyObject's GetValue and SetValue methods will be used to get and set the value of the dependency property.

- The class must declare a field of type DependencyProperty, which will hold a reference to the dependency property identifier. The declaration looks like the following.

```
public static readonly DependencyProperty SidesProperty;
                              ↑                      ↑
                            Type               Field Name
```

- To get the dependency property identifier object, you must register the dependency property with the WPF property system. This informs the property system about the property's characteristics and how it should be managed—including its default value. The Register call returns a reference to the new dependency property identifier, which you then store in the field.

```
SidesProperty = DependencyProperty.Register(
                "Sides", typeof(int), typeof(Window1), metadata );
```

- Although your class could access the dependency property using the GetValue and SetValue methods inherited from DependencyObject, you should instead create a CLR property wrapper that calls these methods. Using and providing properties is more in the WPF programming paradigm than calling methods.

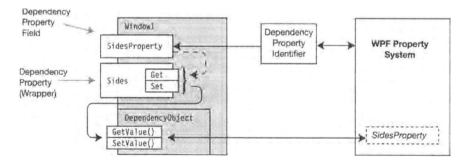

Figure 7-6. *The plumbing of a dependency property*

Now let's take a look at what these things look like in code. The following code shows the beginning of the `Window1` class declaration. These are some important things to notice about the code:

- The `Window` class derives from `DependencyObject`, so `Window1` is already set up to handle dependency properties.

- By convention, when you declare the dependency property field, the field name should end with the string *Property*. In the code, the dependency property name is `SidesProperty`. The property must be declared `public static readonly`.

- The CLR wrapper should have the same name as the dependency property field, but without the *Property* suffix.

  - Notice that the CLR wrapper does *not* get or set the value of the dependency property field. Instead, it calls the `GetValue` and `SetValue` methods of the `DependencyObject` base class to have the WPF property system get and set the values.

  - Internally, at runtime, WPF bypasses the CLR wrapper and calls the methods directly. So, to make sure that the wrapper and the runtime calls remain equivalent, your wrapper accessors shouldn't include any additional code other than the calls to the `GetValue` and `SetValue` methods.

Derives from DependencyObject
↓

```
public partial class Window1 : Window
{
    public static readonly DependencyProperty SidesProperty;        Always end
                                                                    w/ Property

                         The Dependency Property Field
    // The CLR property Wrapper
    public int Sides
    {
        get { return (int) GetValue( SidesProperty ); }      ] Does not
        set { SetValue( SidesProperty, value ); }              uses
    }                                                          get/set from
                                                               DependencyObject
    ...                                                          class.
```

179

I've now declared the dependency property field but haven't yet assigned an instance to it. Since the dependency property field is a static field, it must be assigned to in a static constructor of the Windows1 class.

That would be straightforward enough, except that there is no public constructor for the DependencyProperty class. Instead, to get an instance of the class, you must call the class's Register method. Registering a dependency property connects it to the WPF property system and tells the property system how to manage its value. This is usually a two-step process:

1. Create a FrameworkPropertyMetadata object for the dependency property and set the object's properties to describe how the dependency property should be managed. For example, the following code creates a FrameworkPropertyMetadata object and sets the property specifying that changing the dependency property can affect the arrange phase of the layout process.

```
FrameworkPropertyMetadata metadata = new FrameworkPropertyMetadata();
metadata.AffectsArrange = true;
```

2. Call the static DependencyProperty.Register method, giving the metadata object as its fourth parameter. The Register method returns a reference to a dependency property identifier.

Table 7-1 shows some of the properties you can set on a `FrameworkPropertyMetadata` object to specify the behavior of a dependency property.

Table 7-1. *Some Important FrameworkPropertyMetadata Properties*

Name	Type	Description
AffectsArrange	bool	Specifies whether the dependency property might affect the arrange phase of the layout process.
AffectsMeasure	bool	Specifies whether the dependency property might affect the measure phase of the layout process.
AffectsParentArrange	bool	Specifies whether the dependency property might affect the arrange phase of the parent element.
AffectsRender	bool	Specifies whether the dependency property might require a redraw of the element, for some reason other than standard arrange or measure issues.
BindsTwoWayByDefault	bool	Specifies whether the dependency property uses two-way binding when binding to data. (I'll cover data binding in Chapter 8.)
DefaultValue	object	Specifies the default value of the dependency property if no other factors set the property's value.
Inherits	bool	Specifies whether properties of this type can inherit values from properties of the same type, higher in the element tree.
PropertyChangedCallback	PropertyChangedCallback	Specifies a reference to a callback method to be called when the property changes.

The `Register` method creates a definition of the dependency property within the WPF property system, using the information in the metadata object to set the property's characteristics. There are several overloads of the `Register` method, allowing you to supply various pieces of information to the WPF property system. The following code shows a call to the `Register` method.

- The first parameter is a string that is the name of the dependency property field—without the *Property* suffix.

- The second parameter is the type represented by the dependency property, such as `bool`, `int`, and so forth. Clearly, the *field* is of type `DependencyProperty`, but it might *represent* an `int`.

- The third parameter gives the type of the class declaring the dependency property.

- The fourth parameter is a reference to the metadata object, which contains the rest of the data about the dependency property's characteristics.

```
Must Be Static Constructor
        ↓
  static Window1()
  {
     FrameworkPropertyMetadata metadata = new FrameworkPropertyMetadata();
     metadata.PropertyChangedCallback = OnSidesChanged;

     SidesProperty =
           DependencyProperty.Register(
                   "Sides",            // Dependency Property Field Name
                   typeof(int),        // Type of the Property
                   typeof(Window1),    // Type of Property Owner
                   metadata );         // Reference to Metadata
  }
```

Figure 7-7 puts the pieces together, showing the declaration of the dependency property field and how it is registered with the WPF property system.

```
                                          ┌ Derives from DependencyObject.
public partial class Window1 : Window ◄───┘
{
    public static readonly DependencyProperty SidesProperty;      } Declare the dependency
                                                                    property field.

    public int Sides
    {
        get { return (int) GetValue( SidesProperty ); }           } Wrap the calls referencing the depend-
        set { SetValue( SidesProperty, value ); }                   ency property inside a CLR property.
    }

    static Window1()
    {
        FrameworkPropertyMetadata md = new FrameworkPropertyMetadata();  } Create and set
        md.PropertyChangedCallback = OnSidesChanged;                       the metadata.

        SidesProperty = DependencyProperty.Register(              } Register the property with
                        "Sides", typeof(int), typeof(Window1), md );  the WPF property system.
    }

    static void OnSidesChanged( DependencyObject obj,
                         DependencyPropertyChangedEventArgs args)
    {
        Window1 win = obj as Window1;
        ...
```

Figure 7-7. *The parts of a dependency property in code*

183

Example: Creating a Dependency Property

So far, you've seen the architecture and the various pieces of Creating a Dependency Property (Advanced). This section shows a complete program that puts together all the pieces of creating and using a dependency property.

The example program creates a window, which consists of a text box at the top, and a Grid area underneath, which contains a polygon. The number of sides of the polygon is the same as the number entered in the text box. When the user enters an integer into the text box, the program automatically draws a polygon with the given number of sides, as shown in Figure 7-8.

 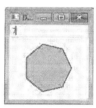

Figure 7-8. *When the user enters an integer in the text box, the program senses the change in the value of the text box and updates a dependency property representing the number of sides.*

To support this, the program creates a dependency property called Sides, of type int. Unlike a normal CLR int property, this dependency property is associated with a callback method called OnSidesChanged, which is called by WPF whenever the value of the dependency property changes. This method redraws the polygon with the number of sides currently returned by the Sides property.

Admittedly, I could have just put the code that draws the polygon inside the event handler (input_TextChanged) that's called when the content of the text box changes. That, however, wouldn't have demonstrated dependency properties. So, instead, the text box's event handler sets the value of the Sides dependency property, which in turn triggers the OnSidesChanged method to redraw the polygon.

So, the sequence of events triggering the redrawing of the polygon is the following:

1. The user enters an integer in the text box, which raises an event triggering its event handler input_TextChanged.

2. The input_TextChanged method interprets the string in the text box and sets the value of dependency property Sides.

3. Sides has an associated callback method called OnSidesChanged, which draws the polygon with the number of sides returned by the dependency property.

The following is the markup for the program. It declares a StackPanel that contains a TextBox and a Grid. The Grid, in turn, contains a Polygon.

```
<Window x:Class="DrawShape.Window1"
    xmlns="http://schemas.microsoft.com/winfx/2006/xaml/presentation"
    xmlns:x="http://schemas.microsoft.com/winfx/2006/xaml"
    Title="Dependency Prop" Height="160" Width="150">
    <StackPanel>
        <TextBox TextChanged="input_TextChanged" Name="input">
            0
        </TextBox>
        <Grid>
            <Polygon Name="poly" Stroke="Black" Fill="LightGray"/>
        </Grid>
    </StackPanel>
</Window>
```

The following is the code-behind for the program.

```
public partial class Window1 : Window
{
    public static readonly DependencyProperty SidesProperty;
                                            ↑
                            Dependency Property Field
    public int Sides    ← Dependency Property CLR Wrapper
    {
        get { return (int) GetValue( SidesProperty ); }
        set { SetValue( SidesProperty, value ); }
    }

    static Window1()                              // Static Constructor
    {
        FrameworkPropertyMetadata md = new FrameworkPropertyMetadata();
        md.PropertyChangedCallback = OnSidesChanged;  ← Set Callback.
        SidesProperty = DependencyProperty.Register(
                        "Sides", typeof(int), typeof(Window1), md );
    }

    public Window1() { InitializeComponent(); } // Instance Constructor

    private void input_TextChanged( object sender, TextChangedEventArgs e )
    {
        int sideCount;
        bool success = int.TryParse( input.Text, out sideCount );
        if( success && sideCount > 2 )
            Sides = sideCount;
    }
```

```
    static void OnSidesChanged( DependencyObject obj,
                      DependencyPropertyChangedEventArgs args)
    {
      Window1 win = obj as Window1;
      if ( win == null || win.poly == null ) return;

      const int xCenter = 65;  const int yCenter = 50;
      const int radius  = 40;
      double rads = Math.PI / win.Sides * 2;

      win.poly.Points.Clear();
      win.poly.Points.Add( new Point( xCenter + radius, yCenter ) );
      for ( double i=1; i <= win.Sides - 1; i++ )
      {
         double x = ( Math.Cos( rads * i ) * radius ) + xCenter;
         double y = ( Math.Sin( rads * i ) * radius ) + yCenter;
         win.poly.Points.Add( new Point( x, y ) );
      }
    }
}
```

Attached Properties

Attached properties are a special type of dependency property where the property is *declared in one class,* but is *used* on the object of a *different* class. The object on which it is used is called the *target object.* In Chapter 5 you saw attached properties used by several of the layout panels, such as DockPanel, Grid, and Canvas.

For example, the following markup shows the declaration of a DockPanel with two buttons in it. The first button is docked at the top, and the second is docked to the bottom. Each button element contains an attribute of the form DockPanel.Dock. The Dock property is declared in the DockPanel class, but is used by the Button element.

```
<DockPanel Name="MyDock" LastChildFill="False">
    <Button Name="btn1" DockPanel.Dock="Top">Click Me</Button>
    <Button Name="btn2" DockPanel.Dock="Bottom">Hi</Button>

</DockPanel>
```

Button is the target of the attached property.

Figure 7-9 illustrates the dependency property structure shown in the markup. The figure illustrates several notable structural differences between regular dependency properties and attached properties.

- Instead of a CLR property wrapper, the DockPanel class has two methods called GetDock and SetDock, which, like the CLR wrapper on a regular dependency property, call GetValue and SetValue.

- The major difference, though, is that the GetDock and SetDock methods call the GetValue and SetValue methods—*not of their own object*—but of the object *using* the attached property.

- This effectively attaches a DockProperty dependency property to each button. Later when the DockPanel is cycling through its list of children, it can call the GetValue method on each one to retrieve the value associated with the element.

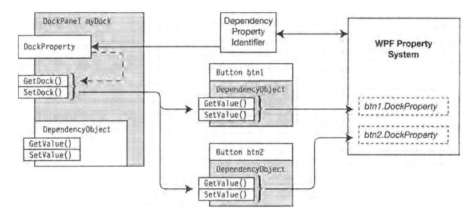

Figure 7-9. *The structure of the DockPanel's attached property Dock, when used by two buttons*

The Structure of an Attached Property

The major differences between attached properties and regular dependency properties are illustrated in Figure 7-10. The only major structural differences between regular dependency properties and attached properties are the following:

- Regular dependency properties have a CLR property wrapper around their calls to GetValue and SetValue.

- Attached properties have two static methods of the form Get*XXX* and Set*XXX*, where *XXX* is the name of the dependency property field, without the *Property* suffix.

  - These methods call the GetValue and SetValue methods of the target object.

  - The target object must be derived from DependencyObject, in order for the Get*XXX* and Set*XXX* methods to call its GetValue and SetValue methods.

Besides these differences, attached properties are registered with the static RegisterAttached method, rather than the Register method.

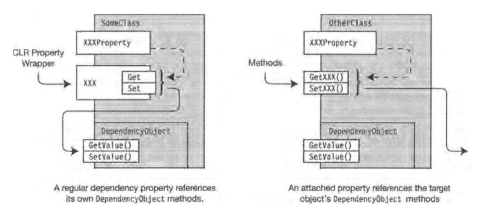

Figure 7-10. *Differences between regular dependency properties and attached properties*

189

Creating an Attached Property

This section shows a simple program that creates an attached property called CountProperty, which represents an object of type int. This property has no special dependency property characteristics beyond storing an int.

The target objects are objects of the following class called IntStorage. Notice that there's nothing in the class itself, other than what it inherits from DependencyObject (and all target objects must derive from DependencyObject).

```
public class IntStorage : DependencyObject
{
                                    ↑
}                    Must Derive from DependencyObject
```

The Window1 class sets up the structure for an attached property in the following manner:

- It declares the DependencyProperty CountProperty.

- The attached property is registered using the RegisterAttached method in the static constructor.

- The two access methods GetCount and SetCount are declared, and call the GetValue and SetValue methods on the instances of the objects *using* the attached method.

```
public partial class Window1 : Window
{
   public static readonly DependencyProperty CountProperty;

   static Window1()    // Static Constructor
   {
      CountProperty = DependencyProperty.RegisterAttached(
                         "Count", typeof( int ), typeof( Window1 ) );
   }

   public static int GetCount( IntStorage ints )
   {
      return (int) ints.GetValue( CountProperty );
   }

   public static void SetCount( IntStorage ints, int value )
   {
      ints.SetValue( CountProperty, value );
   }
      ...
```

With the structure in place, the window's instance constructor uses the attached property in the following way:

- It creates two instances of the target objects, called is1 and is2.

- It then calls the SetCount method on each one, assigning them the values 28 and 500, respectively. Remember that the SetCount method calls the SetValue method of the *target's* DependencyObject.

- Then, to see whether the values were successfully saved, the code calls the GetCount method on the targets.

- Finally, it displays the values in the window created with the markup. The markup is shown after the C# code.

```
public Window1()      // Instance Constructor
{
    InitializeComponent();

    IntStorage is1 = new IntStorage();    // Create Targets.
    IntStorage is2 = new IntStorage();

    SetCount( is1, 28 );                  // Store values.
    SetCount( is2, 500 );

    int i1 = GetCount( is1 );             // Retrieve the values.
    int i2 = GetCount( is2 );

    txt1.Text = i1.ToString();            // Display the values.
    txt2.Text = i2.ToString();
  z}
}
```

The following markup produces the window that shows the values retrieved from the two attached properties (Figure 7-11).

```
<Window x:Class="AttachedSimple.Window1" ... >
    <StackPanel>
        <TextBlock Name="txt1">Holder 1</TextBlock>
        <TextBlock Name="txt2">Holder 2</TextBlock>
    </StackPanel>
</Window>
```

Figure 7-11. *The window showing the values that were stored in attached properties and retrieved from them*

Figure 7-12 shows the structure of the objects in the program.

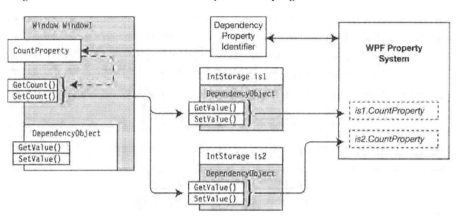

Figure 7-12. *The structure of the attached properties produced by the sample program*

Summary

In this chapter, you looked at dependency properties and the WPF property system. The following are the important topics we covered:

- WPF introduces a powerful new paradigm for using properties, as well as a new set of services to support the new paradigm.

  - The new type of properties are called *dependency properties*, because their values can depend on many factors.

  - The set of services supporting dependency properties is called the *WPF property system*.

- Some of the important terms are the following:

  - *Dependency property identifier*: This is an instance of the DependencyProperty class. In spite of its name, it doesn't hold a dependency property value; but instead, it holds the metadata about the dependency property.

  - *Dependency property field*: This is a public static readonly field that stores the dependency property identifier.

  - *Dependency property*: This is a CLR property wrapper that calls the methods that interact with the WPF property system to get and set the value of the class's dependency properties.

- A dependency property identifier and an instance of a DependencyObject map to a unique dependency property.

- Attached properties are a type of dependency property. They are designed to be declared on one class but used by other class objects. The affect is to attach a property of one class onto another class instance.

CHAPTER 8

■ ■ ■

Data Binding

What Is Data Binding?

Oftentimes a visual element displays the representation of some underlying data value. In this case, you usually want to ensure that the visual element stays up-to-date and changes when the underlying data value changes.

For example, consider a window that contains two elements—a TextBox at the top and a Slider control beneath it. You'd like to have the TextBox represent the value of the Slider such that when you move the Slider back and forth, the value in the TextBox changes to show the Slider's current value. This is illustrated in Figure 8-1, which shows the window in three different states.

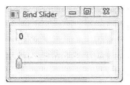  

Figure 8-1. *The value displayed in the TextBox is bound to the current value of the Slider.*

One way to achieve this is to write a simple event handler for the Slider such that whenever its position changes, the handler is called and updates the TextBox. This method is perfectly fine, but it requires you to write the handler code and associate it with the appropriate event. It would be even better if you could just associate the two controls, without having to write any additional code. This is the goal of *data binding*.

Data binding is the association of two objects, such that one of the objects is always kept up-to-date with the value of the other. With data binding, you can just create an association between the TextBox.Text property and the Slider.Value property, and WPF will take care of the updates automatically as they occur. This association is called a *binding*.

The window in Figure 8-1 uses this approach and was produced using the following markup. There isn't any additional code, including event handlers.

```
                                    Bind the Slider to the TextBox.Text.
                                                  ↓
<StackPanel>
    <TextBox Margin="10" Text="{Binding ElementName=sldrSlider, Path=Value}"/>
    <Slider Name="sldrSlider" TickPlacement="TopLeft"  Margin="10"/>
</StackPanel>
```

The following are some important things to know about bindings:

- You can create a binding in XAML, by using the Binding markup extension, or you can create a binding in the code-behind.

- The data elements being kept in sync must be properties. One property is called the *source property*, and the other is called the *target property*, as illustrated in Figure 8-2.

- The target property must always be a dependency property. As you'll soon see, this is because it is the WPF property system that monitors changes to the source and applies them to the target.

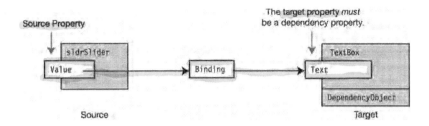

Figure 8-2. *A binding associates a source property with a target property.*

The following markup shows just the attribute being set by the Binding markup extension:

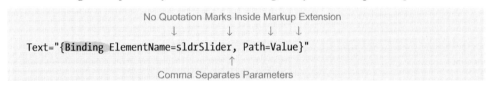

There are several important things you should notice about this syntax:

- The name of the markup extension class is Binding. In this instance, it has two parameters, which can be placed in either order.

  - The ElementName parameter specifies the source element containing the property to which you want to bind the target.

  - The Path parameter specifies the name of a public property inside the specified element. If the property is nested inside the main element, the path must be specified using dot-syntax notation.

- The entire markup extension is enclosed in double quotation marks, but there are no quotation marks inside the markup extension.

- As you learned in Chapter 4, the first string inside the markup extension—Binding, in this case—is the name of the class that will handle the assignment at runtime. The strings following that are parameters and must be separated by commas.

The Binding Object

Creating a binding in XAML is so easy that it obscures the details of what's actually happening. Although many WPF programmers go on to live useful and productive lives without ever understanding what a binding actually is, I think it's useful to understand what's going on underneath the covers. To see what's happening, let's take a look at how you would create a binding in the code-behind.

To do this, let's build the window shown in Figure 8-3. It contains a StackPanel with a Label at the top and a TextBox below it. Whatever text you type in the TextBox immediately shows in the Label above it, as well.

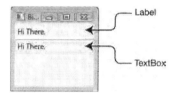

Figure 8-3. *The Label is bound to the TextBox such that whenever you change the content of the TextBox, the content of the Label is updated to match.*

The markup for the window is the following. It's very simple; it just specifies the creation of the Label and the TextBox and gives them names so they can be referenced from the code-behind. Figure 8-4 shows the objects before the binding is performed.

```
<StackPanel>
    <Label    Name="displayText"/>
    <TextBox Name="sourceInfo"/>
</StackPanel>
```

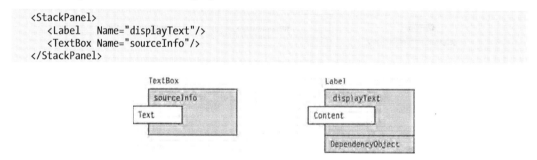

Figure 8-4. *The objects as produced by the markup, before binding the properties in the code-behind*

The code-behind is shown below. It performs the following tasks:

1. It creates the Binding object.

2. It sets the Source and Path values of the binding object.

   – The Source property contains a reference to the source object.

   – The source property can be nested inside objects that are inside the source object. The Path property specifies where to find the source property inside the source object.

3. It calls the SetBinding method on the target to create a BindingExpression, which connects the Binding object with the target dependency property.

```
public Window1()
{
    InitializeComponent();

    Binding myBinding = new Binding();              ← Create the Binding

    myBinding.Source  = sourceInfo;                 ← Set the Source
    myBinding.Path    = new PropertyPath( "Text" ); ← Set the Path

    // Connect the Source and the Target.
    displayText.SetBinding( Label.ContentProperty, myBinding );
}
```

Figure 8-5 shows the structure and connections of the binding object, as well as the process of creating it. The BindingExpression is shown inside the DependencyObject part of the target object because it is the WPF property system that manages the values and updates.

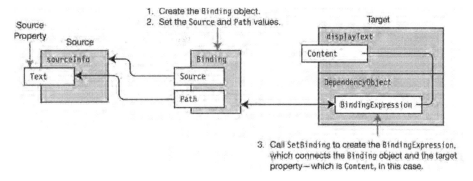

Figure 8-5. *The steps for creating a binding*

Binding Direction

In the previous example, the update data went in only one direction—from the TextBox to the Label—from the source to the target. There are several other options as well, including data going both directions and data going from the target to the source.

You set the direction of the data update by setting the Binding object's Mode property to one of the following values:

- OneWay: Updates the target when the source changes.

- TwoWay: Updates in both directions. Updates the target when the source changes and updates the source when the target changes.

- OneWayToSource: Updates the source when the target changes.

- OneTime: Updates the target property once, with the source's initial value. After that, the target isn't updated again.

- Default: Uses the default binding mode of the target.

Using the Mode setting, you can explicitly set a binding's update direction. If you don't, however, every UI element has a default mode that is either TwoWay or OneWay. You can also explicitly set the mode to the default mode of the target by assigning Default to the Mode.

For example, at the beginning of the chapter, you saw that when you bound the Slider to the TextBox, the update went from source to target, as you would expect. What I didn't point out at the time, though, was that if you were to enter a value in the TextBox and change the focus, the Slider would update appropriately—that is, updating from target to source.

The reason for this is that the default mode of a TextBox is the TwoWay mode. You can, of course, also set it explicitly, as shown in the following markup. Notice also that since there's an additional parameter, it must be separated from the others by a comma.

```
                                              Set the Mode
                                                   ↓
<TextBox Margin="10"
    Text="{Binding ElementName=sldrSlider, Path=Value, Mode=TwoWay}"/>
```

The following is the same markup but with the Mode set to OneWayToSource. In this case, if you enter a value in the TextBox and change focus, the slider is updated. But if you drag the slider, the TextBox is not updated.

```
                                                  Set the Mode
                                                       ↓
<TextBox Margin="10"
    Text="{Binding ElementName=sldrSlider, Path=Value, Mode=OneWayToSource}"/>
```

The OneWayToSource mode often seems odd to people. The question that's usually asked is, "Why not just put the binding on the other element?" One reason is that the source property might not be a dependency property. In that case, you can't switch them, because the *target* property must *always* be a dependency property.

Suppose, for example, that you had a TextBox that you wanted to bind to a property that was not a dependency property, and you wanted to update that property when the text in the TextBox changed. *Logically*, the TextBox is the source, and the other property is the target. But as you'll see later in the chapter, however, the plumbing of bindings relies on some of the features of the dependency property system and therefore requires that the target be a dependency property.

To get around this, you can reverse both the roles (target and source) and the direction of the updating, using OneWayToSource, as illustrated in Figure 8-6.

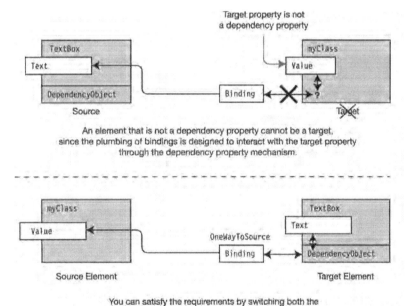

Figure 8-6. *The OneWayToSource mode is useful for updating elements that are not dependency properties.*

201

Triggers

Before continuing, let's review the behavior of the Slider/TextBox binding. When you change the position of the slider, the value in the TextBox is updated immediately. But when you change the value of the TextBox, the slider isn't updated until the focus in the window changes. The differences in their behavior depend on two factors—the direction of the update and the value of the Binding object's UpdateSourceTrigger.

The behavior for updating depends on the direction of the update, as follows:

- When the direction of the update is from the *source* to the *target*, the update always happens *immediately*.

- When the direction of the update is from the *target* to the *source*, then when the update occurs depends on the value of the UpdateSourceTrigger property of the Binding.

Figure 8-7 summarizes these points for the three major modes.

Mode	Direction of Update	Update When
OneWay	S ——▶ T	Immediate
TwoWay	S ——▶ T S ◀—— T	Immediate Depends on Value of UpdateSourceTrigger
OneWayToSource	S ◀—— T	Depends on Value of UpdateSourceTrigger

Figure 8-7. *Summary of the update behavior based on direction of the update*

For the TwoWay and OneWayToSource modes, you can specify the behavior of the update from the target to the source by setting the UpdateSourceTrigger property. The property can have one of three values shown in Table 8-1.

Table 8-1. *The Enum Values for Property UpdateSourceTrigger*

Value	When the Source Is Updated
PropertyChanged	The source is updated as soon as the target property is changed.
LostFocus	When the target property is changed, the source property is updated as soon the target loses the focus in the window.
Explicit	The source property is updated only when the code makes an explicit call to the UpdateSource method.

For example, if you set the value of UpdateSourceTrigger to PropertyChanged, as in the following markup, the slider will move immediately when you change the text in the TextBox, as long as the text is a valid number:

```
<StackPanel>
   <TextBox Margin="10" Text="{Binding ElementName=sldrSlider, Path=Value,
                    UpdateSourceTrigger=PropertyChanged}" />      ← Set the trigger.
   <Slider Name="sldrSlider" TickPlacement="TopLeft"  Margin="10"/>
</StackPanel>
```

Another option is illustrated by the window shown in Figure 8-8. In this case, the source is updated only when the Trigger button is clicked.

Figure 8-8. *Update the source explicitly when the Trigger button is clicked.*

To do that, you set the UpdateSourceTrigger to Explicit as shown in the following markup:

```
<StackPanel>
   <TextBox Margin="10" Name="tbValue"
            Text="{Binding ElementName=sldrSlider, Path=Value,
                    UpdateSourceTrigger=Explicit}" />      ← Set the trigger.
   <Slider Name="sldrSlider" TickPlacement="TopLeft"  Margin="10"/>
   <Button Click="Button_Click">Trigger</Button>
</StackPanel>
```

In the code-behind, you need to create an event handler for the button, to trigger the explicit update. You accomplish this by getting the BindingExpression for the target property and calling its UpdateSource method:

```
public partial class Window1 : Window
{
   public Window1() { InitializeComponent(); }

   private void Button_Click( object sender, RoutedEventArgs e )
   {
      BindingExpression be =
           tbValue.GetBindingExpression( TextBox.TextProperty );
      be.UpdateSource();
   }
}
```

In this case, the Slider (the source) will be updated to the value in the TextBox only when the button is clicked.

Data Converters

Having data binding automatically update an associated property can save a large amount of code. It's convenient and results in less code for there to be a bug in. Sometimes, however, the result isn't exactly what we would hope for. For example, the first two screenshots in Figure 8-9 show the window produced by a simple TwoWay binding.

In the first window, the value 2 in the TextBox looks a bit sparse, but when you drag the slider a bit to the right, the 14 decimal places seems a bit much. It would be nice if you could modify the data just a bit before it's placed in the TextBox, to produce, say, two decimal places, as shown in the last window in the figure.

Without a Data Converter   With a Data Converter

Figure 8-9. *Using a data converter allows you to manipulate the data between the source and the target*

Data converters allow you to do just that. A data converter is a special class you write that intercepts the data between the source and the target and that can manipulate it however you want. A data converter class must use the ValueConversion attribute and must implement the IValueConverter interface. The interface consists of two methods—Convert and ConvertBack. Figure 8-10 illustrates the structure of a data converter class.

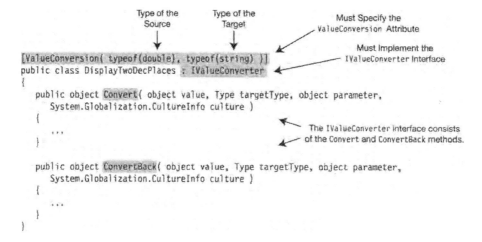

Figure 8-10. *The structure of a value conversion class*

As an example, the following markup and code implement a TextBox/Slider window where the TextBox always shows two decimal places, as shown in the third window of Figure 8-9. The following data converter class, called DisplayTwoDecPlaces, is in a separate file called DisplayTwoDecPlaces.cs. The namespace of my project, in this particular case, is TwoWayConverter.

```csharp
using System;
using System.Windows.Data;

namespace TwoWayConverter
{
    [ValueConversion( typeof( double ), typeof( string ) )]
    public class DisplayTwoDecPlaces : IValueConverter
    {
        public object Convert( object value, Type targetType,
            object parameter, System.Globalization.CultureInfo culture )
        {
            double dValue = (double) value;
            return dValue.ToString( "F2" );
        }

        public object ConvertBack( object value, Type targetType,
            object parameter,System.Globalization.CultureInfo culture )
        {
            double dValue;
            double.TryParse( (string) value, out dValue );
            return dValue;
        }
    }
}
```

The following is the markup for the program. Notice that you need to add the namespace of the project to use the data converter class and then associate the converter with the binding.

```xml
<Window x:Class="TwoWayConverter.Window1" ...
    xmlns:local="clr-namespace:TwoWayConverter">      ← Add Project Namespace
    <StackPanel>
        <TextBox Margin="10">
            <TextBox.Text>
                <Binding ElementName="sldrSlider" Path="Value">

                    <Binding.Converter>  ← Associate Converter with the Binding
                        <local:DisplayTwoDecPlaces/>
                    </Binding.Converter>

                </Binding>
            </TextBox.Text>
        </TextBox>
        <Slider Name="sldrSlider" TickPlacement="TopLeft"  Margin="10"/>
    </StackPanel>
</Window>
```

Multiple Bindings on an Element

Many visual elements have dozens of properties—most of which are dependency properties. Any number of these properties can be bound at the same time. An element with more than one of its properties bound is said to have *multiple bindings*.

For example, the window shown in Figure 8-11 contains a Label at the top and two ComboBoxes beneath it. The top ComboBox contains a list of font families and is bound to the FontFamily property of the Label. The second ComboBox contains a set of FontWeights and is bound to the FontWeight property of the Label. When a new selection is made in either of the ComboBoxes the text in the Label reflects the change.

Figure 8-11. *The FontFamily and FontWeight properties of the Label object are bound to two separate ComboBoxes.*

The following is the markup for this window. Notice that the process of binding multiple properties is the same as binding a single property. Figure 8-12 illustrates the structure.

```
<StackPanel>
    <Label Name="displayText" Margin="5" FontSize="16" Content="My Text"
           FontFamily="{Binding ElementName=fontBox, Path=Text}"
           FontWeight="{Binding ElementName=weightBox, Path=Text}"/>
    <ComboBox Name="fontBox" SelectedIndex="0" Margin="5,0,5,2">
        <ComboBoxItem>Arial</ComboBoxItem>
        <ComboBoxItem>Courier New</ComboBoxItem>
    </ComboBox>
    <ComboBox Name="weightBox" SelectedIndex="0" Margin="5,0,5,2">
        <ComboBoxItem>Normal</ComboBoxItem>
        <ComboBoxItem>Bold</ComboBoxItem>
    </ComboBox>
</StackPanel>
```

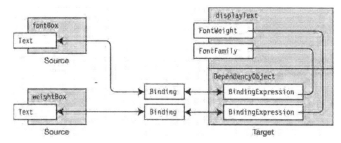

Figure 8-12. *The displayText Label has two bindings from two different sources.*

More Fun with Multiple Bindings

In the previous example, you saw that two separate source elements were bound to two separate target properties. To do this, you created two bindings and two BindingExpressions. You can also use a single Binding object with multiple BindingExpressions if multiple properties in the target share the same source property.

For example, Figure 8-13 shows a window with a TextBox and a Label. The TextBox is the source, and the Label is the target. But the Label has two properties bound to the text in the TextBox—the Content and the FontSize. This means that the Label shows the font size value as its content and also *uses* that font size for its display.

Figure 8-13. *The value entered in the TextBox is used by the Label as both its Content and its FontSize setting.*

Figure 8-14 shows the structure of the elements. Notice that there are two BindingExpressions using the same Binding object.

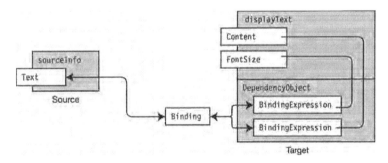

Figure 8-14. *In this example, both the Content and FontSize properties of the Label share the same source—the text of the TextBox.*

The following is the markup:

```
<StackPanel>
    <Label    Name="displayText" Margin="5"/>
    <TextBox Name="sourceInfo">10</TextBox>
</StackPanel>
```

The following is the code-behind. Notice that the code creates a single Binding object but binds it to two different properties—Content and FontSize.

```
public partial class Window1 : Window
{
    public Window1()
    {
        InitializeComponent();

        // Create the Binding object.
        Binding bindingShared = new Binding();

        // Set the source and path information.
        bindingShared.Source = sourceInfo;
        bindingShared.Path   = new PropertyPath( "Text" );
                                         Bind the Content Property
                                                    ↓
        displayText.SetBinding( Label.ContentProperty,  bindingShared );
        displayText.SetBinding( Label.FontSizeProperty, bindingShared );
    }                                              ↑
}                                       Set the FontSize Property
```

Of course, you could have just done it all in the markup, as shown in the following lines, but then the relationships wouldn't have been as clear. The following markup does the same thing, with no changes to the default code-behind supplied by Visual Studio.

```
<StackPanel>
    <Label Name="displayText" Margin="5"
           FontSize="{Binding ElementName=sourceInfo, Path=Text}"
           Content="{Binding ElementName=sourceInfo, Path=Text }"/>
    <TextBox Name="sourceInfo">10</TextBox>
</StackPanel>
```

Deleting Bindings

Using the ClearBinding or ClearAllBindings method, you can delete a single binding on a target, or you can delete them all. These are static methods on the BindingOperations class. Figure 8-15 illustrates the effects of these commands.

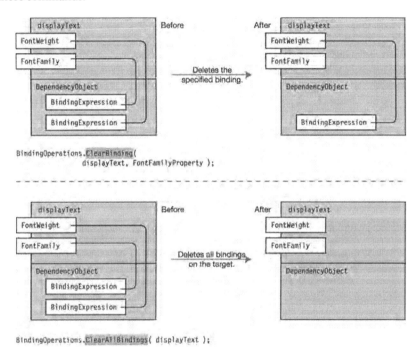

Figure 8-15. *Use the ClearBinding method to remove a specific binding from a target object. Use the ClearAllBindings method to remove all the bindings from a target object.*

The code on the following page implements a program that allows you to exercise these options to either clear the FontFamily binding or clear both bindings. Figure 8-16 shows the program's window.

Figure 8-16. *The Clear Bindings program*

209

The markup for the program is the following:

```
<Window x:Class="ClearBindings.Window1" ...
   Title="Clear Bindings" Height="152" Width="260">
   <StackPanel>
      <Label Name="displayText" Margin="5" FontSize="16"
         Content="My Text"
         FontFamily="{Binding ElementName=fontBox, Path=Text}"
         FontWeight="{Binding ElementName=weightBox, Path=Text}"/>

      <Grid>
         <Grid.ColumnDefinitions>
            <ColumnDefinition></ColumnDefinition>
            <ColumnDefinition></ColumnDefinition>
         </Grid.ColumnDefinitions>
         <StackPanel>

            <ComboBox Name="fontBox" SelectedIndex="0" Margin="5,0,5,2">
               <ComboBoxItem>Arial</ComboBoxItem>
               <ComboBoxItem>Courier New</ComboBoxItem>
            </ComboBox>

            <ComboBox Name="weightBox" SelectedIndex="0" Margin="5,0,5,2">
               <ComboBoxItem>Normal</ComboBoxItem>
               <ComboBoxItem>Bold</ComboBoxItem>
            </ComboBox>
         </StackPanel>

         <StackPanel Grid.Column="1">
            <Button Name="ClearFont" Margin="5,0,5,2"
                  Click="ClearFont_Click">Clear Font</Button>
            <Button Name="ClearAll" Margin="5,0,5,2"
                  Click="ClearAll_Click">Clear All</Button>
            <Button Name="CreateBindings" Margin="5,0,5,2"
                  Click="CreateBindings_Click">Create Bindings</Button>
         </StackPanel>
      </Grid>
   </StackPanel>
</Window>
```

The source for the code-behind is the following. It consists, essentially, of event handlers for the three buttons.

- The first handler clears the binding for just the FontFamily property.
- The second handler clears all the bindings associated with the displayText Label.
- The third handler creates the bindings again.

```
public partial class Window1 : Window
{
    public Window1() { InitializeComponent(); }

    // Clear the FontFamily binding.
    private void ClearFont_Click( object sender, RoutedEventArgs e )
    {
        BindingOperations.ClearBinding( displayText, FontFamilyProperty );
    }

    // Clear all the bindings.
    private void ClearAll_Click( object sender, RoutedEventArgs e )
    {
        BindingOperations.ClearAllBindings( displayText );
    }

    // Re-create the two bindings.
    private void CreateBindings_Click( object sender, RoutedEventArgs e )
    {
        // Create the FontFamily binding.
        Binding fontBinding = new Binding();
        fontBinding.Source = fontBox;
        fontBinding.Path = new PropertyPath( "Text" );
        fontBinding.Mode = BindingMode.OneWay;
        displayText.SetBinding( FontFamilyProperty, fontBinding );

        // Create the FontWeight binding.
        Binding weightBinding = new Binding();
        weightBinding.Source = weightBox;
        weightBinding.Path = new PropertyPath( "Text" );
        weightBinding.Mode = BindingMode.OneWay;
        displayText.SetBinding( FontWeightProperty, weightBinding );
    }
}
```

Binding to Nonelements

So far, all the source items for which you've created bindings have been WPF elements that derive from UIElement. But the source object can be any type of object. In this section, I'll show how to create a simple class and bind to several of its properties. Remember, however, that although the source object can be of any type, the Path must always point to a public property.

Start by defining a simple class called Person, as shown in the following code. This is in a file called Person.cs. The class consists of a constructor and three public properties, containing the first name, age, and favorite color of a person.

```
class Person
{
    public string FirstName    { get; set; }
    public int Age             { get; set; }
    public string FavoriteColor { get; set; }

    public Person( string fName, int age, string color )
    {
        FirstName     = fName;
        Age           = age;
        FavoriteColor = color;
    }
}
```

The markup is quite simple and consists of three Labels, each of which contains one of the pieces of data about a person.

```
<StackPanel Orientation="Horizontal">
    <Label Name="lblFName" FontWeight="Bold"/>
    <Label Name="lblAge/>
    <Label Name="lblColor"/>
</StackPanel>
```

The code-behind of the Window1 class is shown next. Notice the following about the code:

- The code creates a single Person object, which will be the source of the bindings.

- It then creates the bindings that connect each of the three properties in the Person object to a Label.

- The Binding constructor used here takes a single parameter, which sets the Binding object's Path property. Previously in the code samples, I've used the Binding constructor with no parameters and then set the Path explicitly. This just saves a line of code per Binding.

```
public Window1()
{
   InitializeComponent();

   Person p = new Person( "Shirley", 34, "Green" );    ← Create Person Object
                       Binding Constructor with Path Parameter
                                       ↓
   Binding nameBinding = new Binding( "FirstName" );
   nameBinding.Source  = p;
   lblFName.SetBinding( ContentProperty, nameBinding );

   Binding ageBinding = new Binding( "Age" );
   ageBinding.Source  = p;
   lblAgeSetBinding( ContentProperty, ageBinding );

   Binding colorBinding = new Binding( "FavoriteColor" );
   colorBinding.Source = p;
   lblColor.SetBinding( ContentProperty, colorBinding );
}
```

When this code is run, it produces the window shown in Figure 8-17.

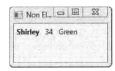

Figure 8-17. *The three Label elements are bound to three simple properties in a custom class.*

213

Data Contexts

In the code-behind of the previous example, each data binding required three lines of code: one to create the Binding object, one to set the source object, and one to create the BindingExpression. But all three bindings used the same source object, so for each binding, you set the Source property to the same source object.

When many binding use the same source object, you can designate a DataContext for the bindings. Every class derived from FrameworkElement has a DataContext property. The important things to know about using DataContexts are the following:

- You need to set the DataContext property of an element in the tree above the elements being bound and set it with a reference to the source object.

- Don't set the Source properties of the bindings unless you want to override the source for that particular binding.

- When the system finds a Binding object without a setting for the Source property, it starts searching up the element tree for an element with its DataContext property set. If it finds one, it uses that value as the source for the binding.

You can take advantage of this in the previous example by modifying the code in the following ways. In the markup, add a name to the StackPanel so you can reference it from the code-behind.

```
<StackPanel Orientation="Horizontal" Name="sp">
    ...
```

In the code-behind, you can set the DataContext of the StackPanel to a reference to the Person object. Then, below that, when setting up the bindings, you can eliminate the three lines that set the Source property of the bindings. At runtime, the system will find the source in the StackPanel's DataContext. The output of the program is the same as in the previous example.

```
Person p = new Person( "Shirley", 34, "Green" );
sp.DataContext = p;
           ↑
   Set the DataContext of the StackPanel
Binding nameBinding = new Binding( "FirstName" );
lblFName.SetBinding( ContentProperty, nameBinding );

Binding ageBinding = new Binding( "Age" );
lblAge.SetBinding( ContentProperty, ageBinding );

Binding colorBinding = new Binding( "FavoriteColor" );
lblColor.SetBinding( ContentProperty, colorBinding );
```

Bindings and ItemsControls

In the previous two examples, you bound the Label controls to a single Person object. A more common situation, however, is that you will want to bind the controls to one object at a time from a collection of objects.

Figure 8-18 shows an example. This program is similar to the example in the previous section, but with the addition of a ComboBox that contains the names of four people. When you select a person in the ComboBox, the program shows that person's information in the area at the top.

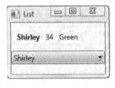  

Figure 8-18. *The area at the top of the window shows the details of the person selected in the ComboBox.*

Before I can explain how to bind the Labels to the information in the ComboBox, I'll review a bit about ItemsControls and then supply some additional information about how they store their data.

In Chapter 6, you saw that the controls derived from the ItemsControl class had two places to store their lists of data, as shown in Figure 8-19. In that chapter, you saw how the controls store and use items in the *internal* Items collection. In this section, you'll learn how they use the ItemsSource property to store and use *external* collections of items. An ItemsControl can use one source or the other, but not both.

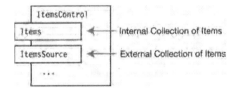

Figure 8-19. *The ItemsControl controls can store their collections of items in one or the other of the Items property or the ItemsSource property.*

Start by adding a ComboBox (which is an ItemsControl) to your simple Person-displayer window. The following is the markup:

```
<StackPanel>
   <StackPanel Orientation="Horizontal" Margin="5,10">
      <Label Name="lblFName" FontWeight="Bold"/>
      <Label Name="lblAge"/>
      <Label Name="lblColor"/>
   </StackPanel>
   <ComboBox Name="comboPeople" SelectedIndex="0"/>
</StackPanel>
```

The following is the code-behind. It creates an array of four Person objects and assigns the array to the ItemsSource property. The declaration of the Person class is the same as in the previous example.

```
public Window1()
{
   InitializeComponent();

   Person[] people = { new Person( "Shirley", 34, "Green" ),
                       new Person( "Roy", 36, "Blue" ),
                       new Person( "Isabel", 25, "Orange" ),
                       new Person( "Manuel", 27, "Red" ) };

   comboPeople.ItemsSource = people;          ← Assign to ItemsSource.
}
```

You now have the array of Person objects attached to the ItemsSource property of the ComboBox, as shown on the left in Figure 8-20. But when you run the program, the ComboBox contains only by the name of the type making up the array, as illustrated on the right in Figure 8-20. The problem is that the ComboBox doesn't know which of the objects' properties to display in the list.

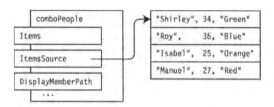 

Figure 8-20. *The ComboBox points to the external array but doesn't know which field to display in the output.*

To let the ComboBox know which property to use in the display, set the DisplayMemberPath to the name of the property. You can do this in either the markup or the code-behind. Putting it in the markup looks like the following:

```
<StackPanel>
    <StackPanel Orientation="Horizontal" Margin="5,10">
        <Label Name="lblFName" FontWeight="Bold"/>
        <Label Name="lblAge"/>
        <Label Name="lblColor"/>
    </StackPanel>
    <ComboBox Name="comboPeople" SelectedIndex="0"
            DisplayMemberPath="FirstName"/>
</StackPanel>
                        ↑
            Specify Which Property to Display
```

Figure 8-21 illustrates the state of the ComboBox now and shows that when it runs, it now displays appropriately.

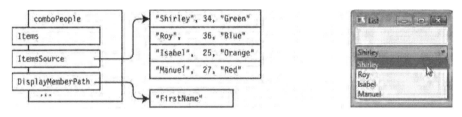

Figure 8-21. *Setting the DisplayMemberPath of the ComboBox tells it which property to display.*

Now that the ComboBox is hooked up and displaying the members correctly, it's time to bind the ComboBox to the line of display above the ComboBox so that the resulting window appears as in Figure 8-22.

Figure 8-22. *The display Labels are bound to the list in the ComboBox.*

First set the DataContext on the StackPanel that contains the three Labels that display the information. The markup is shown next.

- The source object is the ComboBox object, named comboPeople.

- The Path is whichever item is currently selected in the ComboBox, which is contained in the SelectedItem property.

```
<StackPanel>
    <StackPanel Orientation="Horizontal" Margin="5,10"
                DataContext=
                    "{Binding ElementName=comboPeople, Path=SelectedItem}">
                              ↑                            ↑
                         Set the Source Object        Set the Path

        <Label Name="lblFName" FontWeight="Bold"/>
        <Label Name="lblAge"/>
        <Label Name="lblColor"/>
    </StackPanel>
    <ComboBox Name="comboPeople" SelectedIndex="0"
              DisplayMemberPath="FirstName"/>
</StackPanel>
```

The bindings are the same as previously; only the DataContext has changed. Since no Source is set in the bindings, the system will start looking up the tree and find the DataContext in the StackPanel. The program now displays the information of the person chosen in the ComboBox.

```
public Window1()
{
    InitializeComponent();

    Person[] people = { new Person( "Shirley", 34, "Green"),
                         new Person( "Roy", 36, "Blue"),
                         new Person( "Isabel", 25, "Orange"),
                         new Person( "Manuel", 27, "Red")};

    comboPeople.ItemsSource = people;

    Binding nameBinding = new Binding( "FirstName" );
    lblFName.SetBinding( ContentProperty, nameBinding );

    Binding ageBinding = new Binding( "Age" );
    lblAge.SetBinding( ContentProperty, ageBinding );

    Binding colorBinding = new Binding( "FavoriteColor" );
    lblColor.SetBinding( ContentProperty, colorBinding );
}
```

Summary

In this chapter, I covered WPF's data binding feature. The following are the important things to remember:

- Data binding sets up an association between two properties, such that the value of one is kept in sync with the other. The association is called a *binding*.

  – One of the properties is the *source* property.

  – The other property is the *target* property. The target property *must* be a dependency property.

- You can create a binding in either the markup or the code-behind. To create a binding in the markup, you use the Binding markup extension.

- The direction of data update can be from the source to the target, from the target to the source, or both. Although elements have default directions, you can explicitly set a direction by setting the Mode property of the Binding object.

- Data updates going from the source to the target happen immediately. For data going from the target to the source, there are several conditions you can set as the trigger for the update.

- You can create data converters to manipulate the updates between the bound properties.

- An object can have multiple bindings.

- The source object of a binding can be of any type, including user-defined types.

- You can use the ItemsSource property of an ItemsControl to reference a collection of source objects.

Data binding is an extremely powerful feature, allowing you to associate properties with little or no additional code.

CHAPTER 9

■ ■ ■

Routing Events and Commands

What Is an Event?

Windows programming is *event driven*, which means that while a program is running, it can be interrupted at any time by user actions or system actions such as button clicks, key presses, or system timers. When this happens, the program needs to handle the event and then continue on its course. If you want your program to perform some set of tasks when a particular event occurs, you must write a method, called an *event handler*, to be called when the event occurs.

The mechanism the system uses for this process is called an *event*. An event is a .NET object that contains a list of references to the methods, the *event handlers*, associated with it. The system takes care of sensing when an event occurs. When the event occurs, all the event handlers associated with the event are invoked, sequentially.

You can specify in your XAML that an object should handle a particular event and give the name of the event handler for it. Since event handlers are methods, they must be written in imperative code, such as C#—not in XAML.

The Button class has more than 90 events associated with it. The following markup specifies that event handlers in the program will handle three of those events—Click, MouseEnter, and MouseLeave. The names of the event handler methods are assigned to each event.

```
<StackPanel>
    <Button Name="myButton" Padding="10"
            Click      ="myButton_Click"
            MouseEnter="myButton_MouseEnter"
            MouseLeave="myButton_MouseLeave">Click Me</Button>
</StackPanel>
```

Figure 9-1 illustrates the button's events and the event handlers attached to them. The up arrows following the event names in the figure indicate that the member is an event.

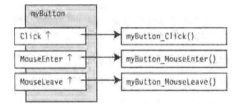

Figure 9-1. *A button that handles three events*

This program takes a particular action for each of these events. Figure 9-2 shows what the window looks like on each of these actions.

- When the mouse pointer enters the button area, the MouseEnter event is raised, which calls the myButton_MouseEnter event handler. This method changes the button text to "Mouse Over".

- When the mouse pointer leaves the button area, the MouseLeave event is raised, which calls the myButton_MouseLeave event handler. This method changes the button text back to "Click Me".

- When the button is clicked, the Click event is raised, which calls the myButton_Click event handler. This method sets the button text to either "Clicked" or "Clicked Again".

Figure 9-2. *The button changes its text whenever one of the three events is raised.*

The event handler code, shown here, simply changes the text of the button:

```csharp
private void myButton_MouseEnter( object sender, MouseEventArgs e )
{
    myButton.Content = "Mouse Over";
}

private void myButton_MouseLeave( object sender, MouseEventArgs e )
{
    myButton.Content = "Click Me";
}

private void myButton_Click( object sender, RoutedEventArgs e )
{
    string c = myButton.Content.ToString();
    myButton.Content = (c == "Clicked" || c == "Clicked Again")
        ? "Clicked Again"
        : "Clicked";
}
```

Event Handlers: Syntax and Semantics

The signature and return type for event handlers is fairly boilerplate—but not quite. The following code shows an example that uses a handler for an event generated by a mouse. Standard event handlers have the following characteristics:

- The return type must be void.

- The first parameter is a reference to the object that triggered the event. This is an object of type object and is usually named sender. Since the type of the parameter is object, you need to cast it back to the appropriate type if you want to access the object's members.

- The second parameter is an object that can contain additional information passed by the event. The type of this parameter is either EventArgs or a subclass of EventArgs.

   If you don't need to pass any additional information from the event into the event handler, you can use EventArgs for the type of the second parameter. Any standard event handler can use this type. If you want the event to pass event-specific information into the handler, you can use the argument type defined for that type of event. For example, the following handler is for a mouse event, and it uses the MouseEventArgs type, which contains additional mouse-specific information about the event.

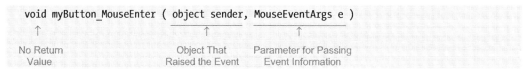

Attaching a Handler to an Event

You can attach an event handler to an event, using either XAML or C#. Attaching an event handler to an event is also called *subscribing* to the event.

   In XAML, you use attribute syntax, assigning the name of the event handler to the event, as shown in the following markup. This assigns method myButton_MouseEnter to the button's MouseEnter event.

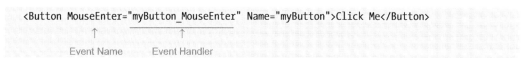

   To attach an event handler in the code-behind rather than in the markup, you use the C# += operator, as shown in the following line of code:

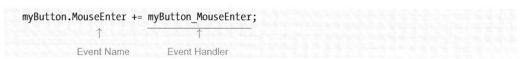

What Are Routed Events?

If you've provided an event handler and have attached it to an event, then when that event is raised, the handler is called. WPF, however, adds a new kind of event object called a *routed event*, which sends the event not just to the element to which the event handler is attached but also to other elements in the tree. The events built into the WPF controls and elements use this new type of event. To distinguish standard .NET events from routed events, standard events are called *CLR events*.

In this chapter, you'll learn how to use WPF's built-in routed events. You can also create your own custom routed events—but since most WPF programmers won't commonly do this, we won't cover that topic.

WPF uses three different routing strategies for its routed events:

- The *Direct* routing strategy is the most like standard CLR event behavior. When an event is raised on an element, WPF checks for an event handler only on the element that raised the event.

- The *Bubbling* routing strategy first checks the element on which the event was raised and then routes the event upward through the tree, all the way to the top element. On each successive element the event is raised, and if that element has a handler for it, the handler is invoked.

- The *Tunneling* routing strategy starts at the top of the tree and works its way down, raising the event on each element until it gets to the element on which the event was initially raised. By convention, the names of the built-in, WPF tunneling events start with the prefix Preview.

Any element involved in the tunneling or bubbling process can signal that the routing shouldn't go any further. We'll cover this topic shortly.

WPF's nested content model created the need for routed events. Consider, for example, the content of the window shown in Figure 9-3. It consists of an Image inside a Border inside another Border. If the user clicks the Image inside the window, which of the objects should handle the MouseLeftButtonUp event? Should it be handled by the Image, by one of the two Borders, or by the Window object? As you'll shortly see, the answer depends on the application and how the application conceptually groups the three components. Routed events add a great deal more built-in flexibility for handling events.

Figure 9-3. *A Window containing two Borders and an Image*

In many situations where WPF uses events, rather than raising a single routed event, it uses a pair of routed events—first raising the tunneling version of the event and then raising the bubbling version. The reason for this is that it gives you the opportunity to handle an event at a higher level, rather than at the level where the event is raised. Starting the routing at the top and tunneling down allows you to create a handler at the higher level, which takes over the event handling and halts it from going down further.

You can find out the routing strategy of any WPF built in event by checking its documentation page.

Handling Routed Events

Although you probably won't be creating routed events yourself, you'll probably be writing event handlers for WPF's built-in events. Event handlers for routed events are essentially the same as those for the CLR events. The signature and return type are as shown in the following code. Notice that although the first parameter is the same, the second is of type RoutedEventArgs or a subclass of RoutedEventArgs.

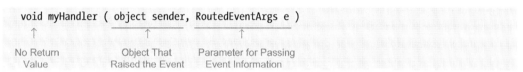

A RoutedEventArgs object has four properties that carry important information from the routed event:

- Source: This is a reference to the object that raised the event and might have information necessary for processing the event.

- OriginalSource: Elements, as programmers use them, are actually made up of subelements that we don't usually think about. For example, a Button with a text label consists of Chrome and TextBlock subelements. When you click a Button, you probably actually clicked one of these. A reference to the subelement you actually clicked is stored in OriginalSource. Mostly, however, we're interested in the Source.

- Handled: If you want to halt the routing of the event, you can set this property to true. By default its value is false.

- RoutedEvent: Often it's useful to have one event handler process multiple events. When this is the case, the code in the handler might need to know which event triggered it. It can get this information from the RoutedEvent property, which returns a reference to the original event that was raised.

Bubbling Example

In this section, we'll take a closer look at bubbling routed events by looking at an example program. This program creates a window with an area on the left and an area on the right. In the area on the left, we'll raise and handle events and see how they bubble through the elements. The output will go to the area on the right, allowing you to see which events are being raised, and in which order. There's also a button on the right side, to clear the results between different tries.

The area on the left consists of a StackPanel that contains a Border, which contains a Label, which contains an Image. The Image, the Label, and the Border have event handlers for the MouseUp event. Figure 9-4 shows the element tree.

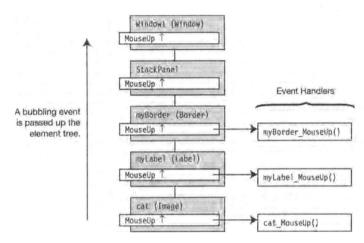

Figure 9-4. *When a bubbling event is raised at an element, it is passed up the tree, and any element with an event handler for the event will execute it.*

Figure 9-5 shows the output of the program when you click various parts of the left part of the window. You can see on the right side of each window that the event is handled first by the element clicked and then by the successive elements above it that have a handler.

Figure 9-5. *Event handling starts at the element clicked and progresses up the element tree.*

The following is the markup for the program. Notice that the Border, the Label, and the Image all set event handlers.

```
<StackPanel Orientation="Horizontal" >
    <Border Name="myBorder" BorderThickness="10" BorderBrush="BurlyWood"
            MouseUp="myBorder_MouseUp">
        <Label Name="myLabel" Padding="10"
                MouseUp="myLabel_MouseUp">
            <Image Name="cat" Source="DarwinFace.jpg" Stretch="None"
                    MouseUp="cat_MouseUp"/>
        </Label>
    </Border>
    <StackPanel>
        <Button Name="Clear" Padding="10,3" Click="Clear_Click">Clear</Button>
        <TextBlock Name="tb" Margin="5,5,0,0"></TextBlock>
    </StackPanel>
</StackPanel>
```

The following are the event handlers that are added to the Window1 class. The three MouseUp handlers just add text to the output window showing which event is being handled. The button Click handler clears the output.

Notice that for the first three handlers, the second parameter is MouseButtonEventArgs. This is a subclass of RoutedEventArgs that can carry addition information such as the states of the various mouse buttons when the event occurred.

```
private void cat_MouseUp( object sender, MouseButtonEventArgs e )
{
    tb.Text += "Image sees it.\r\n";
}

private void myLabel_MouseUp( object sender, MouseButtonEventArgs e )
{
    tb.Text += "Label sees it.\r\n";
}

private void myBorder_MouseUp( object sender, MouseButtonEventArgs e )
{
    tb.Text += "Border sees it.\r\n";
}

private void Clear_Click( object sender, RoutedEventArgs e )
{
    tb.Text = "";
}
```

Checking for Tunneling

When a user clicks most UI elements, WPF treats the MouseUp action as a tunneling/bubbling pair of events. In the previous section, you learned about the bubbling part of the action. The code in this section augments the previous code by adding event handlers for the tunneling event as well.
Figure 9-6 shows the output for various click positions.

Figure 9-6. *Tunneling and bubbling in the sample program*

The markup simply attaches handlers for the PreviewMouseUp event on the three elements you looked at before:

```
<StackPanel Orientation="Horizontal" >
   <Border Name="myBorder" BorderThickness="10" BorderBrush="BurlyWood"
          MouseUp="myBorder_MouseUp"
          PreviewMouseUp="myBorder_PreviewMouseUp">      ← Handle Tunneling
      <Label Name="myLabel" Padding="10"
             MouseUp="myLabel_MouseUp"
             PreviewMouseUp="myLabel_PreviewMouseUp">     ← Handle Tunneling
        <Image Name="cat" Source="DarwinFace.jpg" Stretch="None"
               MouseUp="cat_MouseUp"
               PreviewMouseUp="cat_PreviewMouseUp"/>      ← Handle Tunneling
      </Label>
   </Border>
   <StackPanel>
      <Button Name="Clear" Padding="10,3"
              Click="Clear_Click" FontWeight="Bold">Clear</Button>
      <TextBlock Name="tb" Margin="5,5,0,0"></TextBlock>
   </StackPanel>
</StackPanel>
```

The code-behind just adds the three tunneling handlers, which do exactly what the bubbling handlers do:

```csharp
private void cat_MouseUp( object sender, MouseButtonEventArgs e )
{
    tb.Text += "Bubbling: Image sees it.\r\n";
}

private void myLabel_MouseUp( object sender, MouseButtonEventArgs e )
{
    tb.Text += "Bubbling: Label sees it.\r\n";
}

private void myBorder_MouseUp( object sender, MouseButtonEventArgs e )
{
    tb.Text += "Bubbling: Border sees it.\r\n";
}

private void Clear_Click( object sender, RoutedEventArgs e )
{
    tb.Text = "";
}

private void cat_PreviewMouseUp( object sender, MouseButtonEventArgs e )
{
    tb.Text += "Tunneling: Image sees it.\r\n";
}

private void myLabel_PreviewMouseUp( object sender, MouseButtonEventArgs e )
{
    tb.Text += "Tunneling: Label sees it.\r\n";
}

private void myBorder_PreviewMouseUp( object sender, MouseButtonEventArgs e )
{
    tb.Text += "Tunneling: Border sees it.\r\n";
}
```

Commands

An event and its handler have a very simple relationship; when the event is raised, the handler code is executed. An example is a button's Click event and the code that handles it.

Suppose, however, that you also want to execute the button's Click handler when the user selects a particular menu item and also when the user executes a particular keyboard shortcut. An easy way to implement this is to assign the same handler to each of these events.

For example, the screenshots in Figure 9-7 show a simple program with a TextBox, a Button, and a menu item. (I'll cover menus in Chapter 10.) Whether the user clicks the button, selects the menu item, or uses the Ctrl+X keyboard shortcut, the program invokes the same event handler. The event handler cuts the text selected in the text box and places it on the system clipboard. Figure 9-8 shows the markup and code for the program.

No Text Selected   Text Selected   Text Cut

Figure 9-7. *A simple program that can cut text from a text box*

If you look at the first screenshot in the figure, you'll see that even though there is no text selected in the text box, both the button and the Cut menu item are enabled. Ideally, you'd like these to be enabled only when the text box has text selected. You could add this feature by creating an event handler that was called any time the text box changed. The event handler would check for selected text and enable the button and menu item when there was selected text and disable them if there wasn't.

If you analyze this program, you can see that several components are involved:

- There is the *action to be performed*. In this case, it consists of cutting the selected text.

- There is the *target of the action*, which in this case is the text box.

- There is the *source of the action*, which in this case can be the button, the menu item, or the keyboard shortcut, any of which can trigger the action. (The keyboard shortcut is also a form of *input gesture*. Input gestures are either mouse actions or keyboard shortcuts.)

- There is the set of conditions under which it is appropriate for the action to be available. In this case, this consists of the state where there is text selected in the text box.

Since many programs have this set of components in common, Microsoft has refactored this architecture and created the *command architecture*. This architecture adds an additional layer of abstraction on top of the routed events functionality.

```
<Window x:Class="SimpleCut.Window1" ... Height="133" Width="160">          SimpleCut.xaml
    <StackPanel>
        <Menu>
            <MenuItem Header="_Cut" Click="Button_Click"/>
        </Menu>
        <TextBox Name="txtBox" Margin="5" FontWeight="Bold"/>
        <Button Click="Button_Click" FontWeight="Bold" Margin="5">Cut Text</Button>
    </StackPanel>
</Window>
```

```
public partial class Window1 : Window                                      SimpleCut.xaml.cs
{
    public Window1() { InitializeComponent(); }

    private void Button_Click( object sender, RoutedEventArgs e )
    {
        if ( txtBox.SelectedText.Length <= 0 )
            return;
        Clipboard.SetData( DataFormats.Text, (object) txtBox.SelectedText );
        string pre  = txtBox.Text.Substring( 0, txtBox.SelectionStart );
        string post = txtBox.Text.Substring( txtBox.SelectionStart + txtBox.SelectionLength );
        txtBox.Text = txtBox.Text = pre + post;
    }
}
```

Figure 9-8. *Program to cut text from a TextBox and place it on the system clipboard*

The command architecture consists of the following components, as shown in Figure 9-9:

- A command *source* object triggers the execution of the command. Command sources are usually UI input elements such as Buttons or input gestures.

- The *command* object *represents* an action to be performed, including the conditions under which the action should be enabled, and the list of input gestures that represent the command. It doesn't, however, actually contain the code to execute the action!

- The command *target* is the object acted on by the command.

- The *command binding* connects the command with the target. It also binds the following code to the command architecture:

  − The handler code that should be invoked when the command is invoked

  − The code that determines whether the command can be invoked

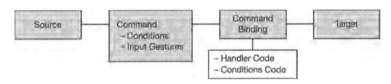

Figure 9-9. *The routed command architecture*

Built-in Commands and Support

WPF allows you to build your own commands, as you'll see shortly, or to use built-in commands that it provides. Also, many controls are designed to be used as command sources or command targets or both and have built-in support for these roles.

- Controls designed to be command sources have Command and CommandTarget properties that can hold references to the command object and the target object, respectively.

- Controls designed to be command targets have built-in bindings and built-in command handler code for WPF built-in commands.

Figure 9-10 shows the command architecture using the built-in commands and source and target elements with built-in support.

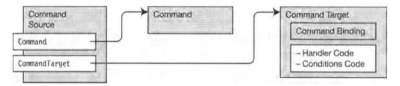

Figure 9-10. *The command architecture for a command target that has support for built-in commands*

WPF provides more than 100 built-in commands, contained in five different classes. These include the most common commands used in Windows applications for clipboard manipulation, text editing, navigation, and media control. These classes are listed in Table 9-1.

The predefined commands provide a huge amount of functionality, which you can easily plug into your own programs. Remember, however, that commands themselves don't include the handler code to actually perform anything on the target. They do, however include the common input gestures such as the keyboard shortcut Ctrl+X for the cut-to-clipboard command.

Table 9-1. *Classes for the Built-in Commands*

Class	Types of Commands
ApplicationCommands	These are common application commands, including the clipboard commands.
ComponentCommands	These commands represent moving around and selecting items in a program or component.
EditingCommands	These commands represent actions used in editing documents.
MediaCommands	These commands represent actions used in controlling media applications.
NavigationCommands	These commands represent actions used in moving around a document.

Before we build our own commands, we'll start by looking at a simple example program that uses two of the built-in clipboard commands—ApplicationCommands.Cut and ApplicationCommands.Paste.

The user interface for this program consists of a StackPanel containing two TextBoxes and two Buttons, as shown in Figure 9-11.

- The Cut button is the *source* for the Cut command, and the first TextBox is the *target* for the command.

- The Paste button is the *source* for the Paste command, and the second TextBox is the *target* for the command.

The figure also shows the stages of using the buttons.

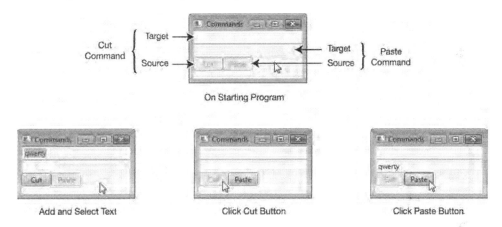

Figure 9-11. *Screenshots showing the different states of the sample program*

You can create this program entirely in XAML, without any additions to the code-behind. The markup is shown on the next page. Notice the following about the markup:

- Buttons have built-in support to be used as *command sources*, so the XAML sets the Command and CommandTarget properties of the two buttons. Notice that you use a Binding to set the CommandTarget.

- You don't need to do anything to the TextBoxes because they are designed to be command targets and have all that plumbing built-in. You only need to give them names so you can refer to them when setting the CommandTarget attributes of the buttons.

```
<StackPanel>
    <TextBox Name="cutFrom"></TextBox>          ← Name the TextBox
    <TextBox Name="pasteTo"></TextBox>          ← Name the TextBox

    <StackPanel Orientation="Horizontal">
        <Button Width="50"          ← The Cut Source
                Command="ApplicationCommands.Cut"
                CommandTarget="{Binding ElementName=cutFrom}">Cut</Button>
                       ↑                             ↑

                  Set the Target              The Cut Target


        <Button Width="50"          ← The Paste Source
                Command="ApplicationCommands.Paste"
                CommandTarget="{Binding ElementName=pasteTo}">Paste</Button>
    </StackPanel>           ↑                    ↑
</StackPanel>        Set the Target        The Paste Target
```

Figure 9-12 shows the structure of the Cut command architecture in this program. There's an analogous structure for the Paste command as well.

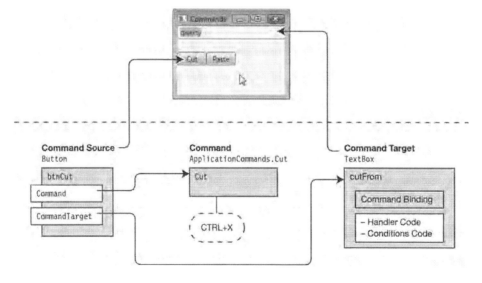

Figure 9-12. *The structure of the Cut command architecture in the sample program*

Alternatively, you could produce the same program by hooking up the commands in the code-behind rather than in the markup. The following is the XAML that does it:

```
<StackPanel>
    <TextBox Name="cutFrom"></TextBox>
    <TextBox Name="pasteTo"></TextBox>

    <StackPanel Orientation="Horizontal">

        <Button Name="btnCut"   Width="50">Cut</Button>
        <Button Name="btnPaste" Width="50">Paste</Button>

    </StackPanel>
</StackPanel>
```

The following is the code-behind:

```
public Window1()
{
    InitializeComponent();

    btnCut.Command = ApplicationCommands.Cut;
    btnCut.CommandTarget = cutFrom;

    btnPaste.Command = ApplicationCommands.Paste;
    btnPaste.CommandTarget = pasteTo;
}
```

There are several more interesting things to note about this program. The first is the automatic enabling and disabling of the buttons. The second is the availability of the keyboard shortcuts for the Cut and Paste commands. We'll look at these now.

Commands have, as part of their architecture, a way for the programmer to specify under what circumstances a command should be available and when it should not be available. You can see this in action in the buttons in the example program. Figure 9-13 shows that the buttons acting as the sources for the Cut and Paste commands are automatically enabled or disabled appropriately for their clipboard functions.

- In the first screenshot, neither of the buttons is enabled. This is because there is no selected text in the first TextBox for the Cut command to work on and no text on the system clipboard to be pasted by the Paste command.

- In the second screenshot, where there is selected text in the first TextBox, the Cut button has automatically become enabled.

- In the third screenshot, the Cut button has been clicked, deleting the text from the first TextBox and placing it on the system clipboard.

  - Since there's no longer any selected text in the first TextBox, the Cut button becomes disabled.

  - Since there's now text on the system clipboard, the Paste button automatically becomes enabled.

- Although you can't see it in the figure, the keyboard shortcuts also work as you'd expect.

  - When the Cut button is enabled *and the focus is on the first TextBox*, you can use the Ctrl+X keyboard shortcut to cut the text.

  - When the Paste button is enabled *and the focus is on the second TextBox*, you can use the Ctrl+V keyboard gesture to paste the text.

Notice that there is nothing explicitly in the code to create any of this behavior, and yet it does the right things. The reason these work is that this functionality was built in to the controls, to hook up with these predefined commands. The command architecture allows you to build similar functionality into your own custom commands.

Neither button is Enabled.

With selected text, the
Cut button becomes Enabled.

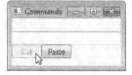
With text on the clipboard, the
Paste button becomes Enabled.

Figure 9-13. *The Cut and Paste buttons automatically become enabled or disabled appropriately for the conditions and their functions.*

The RoutedCommand Class

The key to the WPF command architecture is the RoutedCommand class. To create your own commands, you'll need to create an instance of this class, configure it, and bind it to the controls with which you want to use it, as you'll see in the next section.

You might be tempted to think that this class implements the actions that should be taken when the command is invoked. It doesn't. Its main job is to raise events that trigger actions. The RoutedCommand class has two major methods, Execute and CanExecute.

- The Execute method is called when the command is invoked as the result of the action of a command source.

    - The Execute method, however, *does not execute the code to implement the command!* Instead, it raises two routed events—PreviewExecuted and Executed.

    - These routed events traverse the tree to trigger the event handler that *actually* performs the implementation of the command.

- The CanExecute method is called when a source wants to find out whether it's appropriate to make the command available.

    - Like the Execute method, the CanExecute method also does not implement the action it represents. It also raises two routed commands—PreviewCanExecute and CanExecute.

    - These routed commands traverse the tree to find the event handler that can determine whether to make the command available.

There are also two other important members of the RoutedCommand class—CanExecuteChanged and InputGestures. Figure 9-14 shows the important members of these classes. The RoutedUICommand class derives from the RoutedCommand class and just adds a field named Text, which you can use to label controls or elements triggered by the command.

CanExecuteChanged is a RoutedEvent that is raised when there are changes that might affect whether the command should be available. These signal the command source that it should call the CanExecute method to determine whether it's appropriate to make the command available.

InputGestures is a property that returns the collection of input gestures associated with the command.

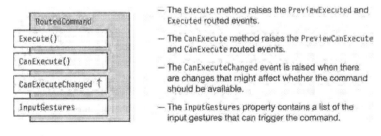

- The Execute method raises the PreviewExecuted and Executed routed events.

- The CanExecute method raises the PreviewCanExecute and CanExecute routed events.

- The CanExecuteChanged event is raised when there are changes that might affect whether the command should be available.

- The InputGestures property contains a list of the input gestures that can trigger the command.

Figure 9-14. *The important members of the RoutedCommand class*

Creating Custom Commands

The previous example showed how to use WPF's built-in commands with controls that have command support built in. This is very powerful and can be a huge time-saver. Sometimes, however, you might need to create your own custom commands. In this section, we'll create a small program that has a custom command called Reverse, which reverses a string in a TextBox.

Figure 9-15 illustrates the program and shows the states of the source and target. The Reverse button is the command source of the Reverse command. The TextBox is the command target. The other command source is the keyboard gesture Ctrl+R. When the command is executed, by either the button or the keyboard gesture, the text in the TextBox is reversed, as shown in the figure. If there's no text in the TextBox, then the button and the keyboard gesture are disabled.

Figure 9-15. *The window implementing the Reverse command*

Figure 9-16 shows the structure you'll need for implementing the Reverse command. You'll need to do the following things:

1. Create a new class that defines the command, including the input gestures.

2. Create the command handler methods to be invoked by the Executed and CanExecute events.

3. Create a command binding to connect the command with the command handler code

4. Connect the command source with the command.

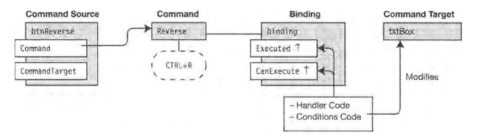

Figure 9-16. *The command structure for implementing the Reverse command*

First create the custom command inside a class called CommandReverse, which will create and supply the command through a property. Microsoft uses this pattern in its built-in commands. You'll place this code in a separate file called ReverseCommand.cs. The important things to notice are the following:

- The class creates a private variable called reverse, of type RoutedUICommand to hold the new command.

- The command is supplied to the outside through the read only Reverse property.

- The constructor creates a new KeyGesture object that represents the Ctrl+R keyboard shortcut, and adds it to an InputGesturesCollection, which will be associated with the new command.

- The constructor then creates a new RoutedUICommand and assigns it to the private variable.

```csharp
using System;
using System.Windows.Input;    // Required

namespace CommandReverse
{
    public class ReverseCommand
    {
        private static RoutedUICommand reverse;

        public static RoutedUICommand Reverse
        { get { return reverse; } }

        static ReverseCommand()
        {
            InputGestureCollection gestures = new InputGestureCollection();
            gestures.Add
                ( new KeyGesture(Key.R, ModifierKeys.Control, "Control-R"));

            reverse = new RoutedUICommand
                ( "Reverse", "Reverse", typeof(ReverseCommand), gestures);
        }
    }
}
```
       ↑   ↑   ↑   ↑
Description | Name of the Command | The Type Registering the Command | Collection of InputGestures

Next, create the markup, which is just used to create the source and target objects. All the other objects you'll create in the code-behind. This makes the markup very simple, as shown here—just a TextBox and a Button in a StackPanel:

```xml
<StackPanel>
    <TextBox Name="txtBox" Margin="10,10"
            FontWeight="Bold" Background="Aqua"/>
    <Button Name="btnReverse" HorizontalAlignment="Center" Padding="10,3"
            FontWeight="Bold" Margin="10,0"/>
</StackPanel>
```

In the code-behind, create the rest of the objects, and connect the plumbing.

- The first line after the InitializeComponent call assigns a reference to the command to the Reverse button command source.

- The next four lines create a new CommandBinding, initialize it with a reference to the command, and assign delegates of the event handlers to the Executed and CanExecute events.

- The command binding is then added to the window's collection of command bindings.

- Below that are the two command handler methods to be invoked when the Executed and CanExecute events are raised.

When you run the program, you can either click the button or use Ctrl+R to reverse the text in the TextBox.

```
using ...
using CommandReverse;

public Window1()
{
   InitializeComponent();

   btnReverse.Command = ReverseCommand.Reverse;

   CommandBinding binding = new CommandBinding();
   binding.Command    = ReverseCommand.Reverse;
   binding.Executed   += ReverseString_Executed;
   binding.CanExecute += ReverseString_CanExecute;

   CommandBindings.Add( binding );
}

// Reverses the string in txtBox.
public void ReverseString_Executed( object sender,
                          ExecutedRoutedEventArgs args )
{
   char[] temp = txtBox.Text.ToCharArray();
   Array.Reverse(temp);
   txtBox.Text = new string(temp);
}

// Checks whether there is a string in txtBox.
public void ReverseString_CanExecute( object sender,
                          CanExecuteRoutedEventArgs args )
{
   args.CanExecute = txtBox.Text.Length > 0;
}
```

Routing Commands

One thing you might have noticed in the code-behind was that you attached the code binding object to the CommandBindings collection of the Window1 object. This is perfectly fine and illustrates the *routed* part of routed commands.

When you click the Reverse button, this raises the Executed event. WPF checks the target to see whether it has a command binding for the command. If not, it routes the event up the element tree trying to find an element with a binding for the command. When it finds it, it invokes it. Figure 9-17 illustrates the routing.

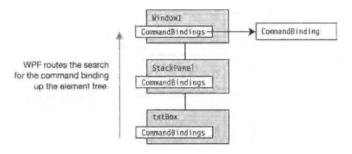

Figure 9-17. *Routed events are routed up the element tree.*

In determining where routing should start, WPF checks the command source to see whether there is a CommandTarget set. If so, it starts routing there. If not, it starts at the element that currently has the focus.

Figure 9-18 illustrates two situations where there are two TextBoxes at the same level, but the CommandBinding is set in different places in the tree. In both cases, the command source does not have a CommandTarget set. In one arrangement, both TextBoxes will always find the CommandBinding. In the other arrangement, one of the TextBoxes will not find it.

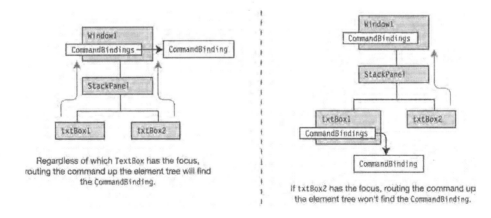

Figure 9-18. *The placing of the CommandBinding can affect the behavior.*

Summary

In this chapter, you saw that WPF has greatly expanded the definition of how events are handled. They no longer just go to the element that raised them but are routed up and down the element tree, as bubbling events and tunneling events.

You also saw that WPF provides a framework for creating and handling commands, giving a higher, more abstract model of processing events from different command sources such as buttons and input gestures.

CHAPTER 10

■ ■ ■

Other Controls and Elements

The TextBox Control

Menus

ContextMenus

ToolBars

StatusBars

ToolTips

Controls That Work with Ranges

Summary

The TextBox Control

In Chapter 6, you learned about many of the most important WPF controls that present content. In this chapter, you'll learn about other controls and elements you'll need to have a rich and smoothly functioning application. You'll start with the TextBox control and continue to menus, toolbars, and miscellaneous other elements.

The TextBox is designed for displaying small amounts of text to the user and allowing the user to enter small amounts of input text. Figure 10-1 shows a window where the user has entered his name into the TextBox.

Figure 10-1. *The TextBox is useful for retrieving small bits of text from the user.*

The following are some important things to know about the TextBox:

- The TextBox does not support formatted text.

- By default the TextBox doesn't wrap text, but you can change that by setting the TextWrapping property to true.

- The content of a TextBox is stored in the Text property.

The following is the markup that produces the content in the window shown in Figure 10-1. Notice the following about the markup:

- The TextBox is given a name so that it can be referenced in the code-behind, as well as in the Label's binding. (Chapter 6 describes how a Label can be bound to another element, namely, by setting an accelerator key for the element.)

- The button's callback method gets the text value from the TextBox and displays the string in a message box.

```
<StackPanel>
   <Label Target="{Binding ElementName=txtbxName}">_Enter Your Name</Label>
   <TextBox Name="txtbxName"/>
   <Button HorizontalAlignment="Right" Padding="10,3"
           Click="Button_Click">Enter</Button>
</StackPanel>
```

The code-behind is the following:

```
public partial class Window1 : Window
{
   public Window1()
   {
      InitializeComponent();
   }

   private void Button_Click( object sender, RoutedEventArgs e )
   {
      MessageBox.Show("You entered: " + txtbxName.Text, "TextBox Message");
   }                                            ↑
}                                    Get the text from the TextBox.
```

Menus

Menus are lists of options the user can choose from in order to execute commands or set options. WPF offers two types of menus: regular menus and context menus. Regular menus can be placed anywhere in a window, although they're usually docked at the top. A context menu, however, is associated with a particular element. I'll explain regular menus in this section and cover context menus shortly.

A menu consists of a single Menu object, containing a list of MenuItems, as shown in the markup shown next. Here are some things to notice about the markup:

- The list of MenuItems contained by the Menu object comprises the *top-level menu*, which is visible whenever the menu is visible.

- Each MenuItem object has a Header property that contains the string that labels the menu item.

- You can assign an event handler to a MenuItem's Click event, which will then execute the handler whenever the user clicks the menu item.

```
<Menu>
    <MenuItem  Header="First"   Click="MenuItemFirst_Click"/>
    <MenuItem  Header="Second"  Click="MenuItemSecond_Click"/>
    <MenuItem  Header="Third"   Click="MenuItemThird_Click"/>
</Menu>
                           ↑                    ↑
                   The Header contains    This assigns the
                    the menu label.        event handler.
```

On the left of Figure 10-2 is a screenshot that shows a window containing this menu. (The menu in the figure is inside a StackPanel, which constrains its size.) The drawing on the right of the figure shows the menu's structure.

Figure 10-2. *A menu consists of a single Menu object containing a list of MenuItem objects.*

As I stated earlier, the Menu object contains a set of MenuItem objects that comprise the top-level menu. MenuItems, however, can contain nested MenuItems, which act as submenus. The following markup shows two MenuItems contained in the content part of the first MenuItem:

```
<Menu>
    <MenuItem Header="File">
        <MenuItem Header="New Game"  Click="MenuItemNewGame_Click"/>
        <MenuItem Header="Exit"      Click="MenuItemExit_Click"/>
    </MenuItem>
    <MenuItem Header="Help"          Click="MenuItemHelp_Click"/>
</Menu>
```

Figure 10-3 shows, on the left, a window that contains this menu and, on the right, the nested structure of the menu.

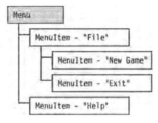

Figure 10-3. *"Submenus" are MenuItems nested in other MenuItems.*

The event handlers in this simple example just pop up message boxes. The following is the code-behind:

```
public partial class Window1 : Window
{
    public Window1()
    { InitializeComponent(); }

    private void MenuItemNewGame_Click( object sender, RoutedEventArgs e )
    { MessageBox.Show( "Clicked New Game", "Menu Info" ); }

    private void MenuItemExit_Click( object sender, RoutedEventArgs e )
    { MessageBox.Show( "Clicked Exit", "Menu Info" ); }

    private void MenuItemHelp_Click( object sender, RoutedEventArgs e )
    { MessageBox.Show( "Clicked Help", "Menu Info" ); }
}
```

▓ **Remember** Submenus are implemented as nested MenuItems—*not* as nested Menus.

Adorning the MenuItem

So far, the only thing you've seen on a menu is text. The area occupied by a MenuItem, however, has space for other useful information as well, as shown in Figure 10-4.

- You can set a check mark to the left of the menu label by setting the MenuItem's IsChecked property to true.

  - You can initialize this property in the markup to be either checked or unchecked and then change its value in the code-behind when appropriate.

  - Alternatively, you can have WPF automatically toggle the check mark on the MenuItem by setting the MenuItem's IsCheckable property to true. With this set, you don't have to programmatically set the value of IsChecked to true and false.

- You can set the Icon property to display an image. Despite the name of the property, it can be any type of image, not just an image of the icon type.

You can also add text to the right of the menu label by assigning it to the InputGestureText property. This is typically used to show keyboard shortcuts for the menu item. Setting this text, however, doesn't implement the functionality. You must still hook up the shortcut code to the menu item yourself, which is a bit of work unless you use commands. (You'll learn more about this in a moment.)

Figure 10-4. *You can set an image or a check mark to the left of the menu label and a string to the right of the label.*

The following is the markup for the menu in Figure 10-4:

```
<Menu>
    <MenuItem Header="File">
        <MenuItem Header="New Game" Click="MenuItemNewGame_Click"
                InputGestureText="Alt+N">              ← Set text on right.
            <MenuItem.Icon>
                <Image Source="Card.bmp"/>             ← Set image on left.
            </MenuItem.Icon>
        </MenuItem>
        <MenuItem Header="Shuffle Sound" Click="MenuItemExit_Click"
            IsChecked="True"  InputGestureText="Alt+S"/>  ← Set check and text.
    </MenuItem>
</Menu>
```

Other Content As the Menu Header

The menu labels you've seen so far have been text, but the Header property can be assigned an object of any class derived from UIElement. For example, Figure 10-5 shows a menu that uses bitmap images as the Header content.

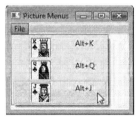

Figure 10-5. *You can use any UIElement-derived object as the menu label, including Images.*

The following markup produces the menu in Figure 10-5. Notice that to set the Header to an Image, you must use the property element syntax.

```
<Menu>
    <MenuItem Header="File">
        <MenuItem InputGestureText="Alt+K">
            <MenuItem.Header>                    ← Property Element Syntax
                <Image Source="kccard.bmp"/>     ← Set the Image.
            </MenuItem.Header>
        </MenuItem>
        <MenuItem InputGestureText="Alt+Q">
            <MenuItem.Header>
                <Image Source="qccard.bmp"/>     ← Set the Image.
            </MenuItem.Header>
        </MenuItem>
        <MenuItem InputGestureText="Alt+J">
            <MenuItem.Header>
                <Image Source="jccard.bmp"/>     ← Set the Image.
            </MenuItem.Header>
        </MenuItem>
    </MenuItem>
</Menu>
```

Attaching Commands to Menu Items

Hooking up the keyboard shortcuts to menu items by hand can be a chore. But hooking them up to a command is easy. (Commands were covered in Chapter 9.) All you have to do is assign the command to the MenuItem's Command property.

For example, the following markup attaches the two menu items to the built-in application commands New and Open:

```
<StackPanel>
    <Menu>
        <MenuItem Header="File">
            <MenuItem Command="ApplicationCommands.New" />
            <MenuItem Command="ApplicationCommands.Open"/>
        </MenuItem>
    </Menu>
</StackPanel>
```

Figure 10-6 shows the menu produced by the markup. WPF does several important things for you automatically when you attach a command to a menu item:

- It automatically sets the text of the Header to the text of the command name.

- It fills the keyboard shortcuts field with the appropriate string.

- Most important, it hooks up the command to the menu item so that the command is executed if the user either clicks the menu item or executes the keyboard shortcut. This assumes, of course, that you've bound the command correctly in the code-behind as you saw in Chapter 9.

Figure 10-6. *Menu items attached to built-in application commands*

I'm sure that, after having read Chapter 9, binding a command is now a snap for you; but just to refresh your memory, the code-behind for our little program is shown next. The code creates the bindings for the commands and declares the callback methods they require. These callbacks just show a message box.

```
public partial class Window1 : Window
{
    public Window1()
    {
        InitializeComponent();

        CommandBinding nBinding = new CommandBinding();        ← Binding for New
        nBinding.Command        = ApplicationCommands.New;
        nBinding.Executed      += DoNew_Executed;
        nBinding.CanExecute    += DoNew_CanExecute;

        CommandBinding oBinding = new CommandBinding();        ← Binding for Open
        oBinding.Command        = ApplicationCommands.Open;
        oBinding.Executed      += DoOpen_Executed;
        oBinding.CanExecute    += DoOpen_CanExecute;

        CommandBindings.Add( nBinding );        ← Add bindings to window.
        CommandBindings.Add( oBinding );
    }

    public void DoNew_Executed( object sender, ExecutedRoutedEventArgs e )
    {
        MessageBox.Show( "New Command Executed", "Command Info" );
    }

    public void DoNew_CanExecute( object sender, CanExecuteRoutedEventArgs e )
    {
        e.CanExecute = true;
    }

    public void DoOpen_Executed( object sender, ExecutedRoutedEventArgs e )
    {
        MessageBox.Show( "Open Command Executed", "Command Info" );
    }

    public void DoOpen_CanExecute( object sender, CanExecuteRoutedEventArgs e )
    {
        e.CanExecute = true;
    }
}
```

Context Menus

A *context menu* is a menu of actions associated with a particular element and contains actions relevant to that element only, in the given context. The context menu becomes visible when the user right-clicks the element.

The following are important things to know about context menus:

- The context menu is implemented by the ContextMenu class.

- An object of the ContextMenu class must be associated with the ContextMenu property of the element.

- Like the Menu class, a ContextMenu object contains a set of nested MenuItem objects that comprises the actual menu tree.

For example, Figure 10-7 shows a program window that contains an Image control that has a context menu with three menu items. The menu choices allow the user to flip the image on its vertical axis, to flip the image on its horizontal axis, or to return the image to its original configuration. When the user right-clicks anywhere on the image, the context menu appears at the position of the cursor.

Original

With Context Menu

Flipped on Vertical Axis

Figure 10-7. *Right-clicking the image brings up its context menu.*

The following markup shows how the context menu is created and associated with the ContextMenu property of the Image. Notice that you must define the context menu inside the content part of the Image.ContextMenu element using property element syntax.

```
<Grid>
    <Image Name="picture" Source="OceanPerchLeft.jpg">
        <Image.ContextMenu>                    ← Property Element Syntax
            <ContextMenu>                      ← Define Context Menu
                <MenuItem Header="Original" Click="Original_Click"/>
                <MenuItem Header="Flip on V Axis" Click="FlipVertical_Click"/>
                <MenuItem Header="Flip on H Axis" Click="FlipHorizontal_Click"/>
            </ContextMenu>
        </Image.ContextMenu>
    </Image>
</Grid>
```

The event handlers for the program are shown in the following code. As a sneak preview, these event handlers use the ScaleTransform to flip the image around either its vertical axis or its horizontal axis. I'll cover the 2D transforms in Chapter 18.

```
public partial class Window1 : Window
{
    public Window1()
    { InitializeComponent();  }

    private void FlipVertical_Click( object sender, RoutedEventArgs e )
    {
        picture.LayoutTransform = new ScaleTransform( -1, 1 );
    }

    private void FlipHorizontal_Click( object sender, RoutedEventArgs e )
    {
        picture.LayoutTransform = new ScaleTransform( 1, -1 );
    }

    private void Original_Click( object sender, RoutedEventArgs e )
    {
        picture.LayoutTransform = new ScaleTransform( 1, 1 );
    }
}
```

ToolBars

A *toolbar* is a container for a set of controls or elements. Typically it's docked at the top of the window and contains a set of buttons and ComboBoxes that allow the user to quickly access the program's most common functions.

Although toolbars are usually docked at the top of a window, in WPF you can place them anywhere in the window. Additionally, in WPF, you can insert any UIElement-derived object into a toolbar. In general, though, you should only insert controls that perform some action or set some setting. If you stick to this, your program will conform to what users expect, helping them avoid potential confusion.

To create and populate a toolbar, place the child elements inside the content area of the ToolBar element, as shown in the following markup:

```
<StackPanel>
    <ToolBar>
        <Menu>                                              ← Insert Menu.
            <MenuItem Header="File">
                <MenuItem Header="New Game"/>
                <MenuItem Header="Change Opponent"/>
            </MenuItem>
        </Menu>
        <Button Width="40">Bet</Button>                     ← Insert Button.
        <Button Width="40">Fold</Button>                    ← Insert Button.
        <ComboBox Width="70" SelectedIndex="0">             ← Insert ComboBox.
            <ComboBoxItem>Clubs</ComboBoxItem>
            <ComboBoxItem>Diamonds</ComboBoxItem>
            <ComboBoxItem>Hearts</ComboBoxItem>
            <ComboBoxItem>Spades</ComboBoxItem>
        </ComboBox>
    </ToolBar>
</StackPanel>
```

Figure 10-8 shows the window produced by the markup. The screenshots show the menu and the ComboBox being accessed, respectively.

Figure 10-8. *A toolbar can contain Buttons, Menus, ComboBoxes, and other UIElements*

Figure 10-9 shows the same window where the size is decreased so that it isn't large enough to show the whole toolbar. In this case, the toolbar displays a small down arrow on the right end that allows the user to access the *overflow toolbar*.

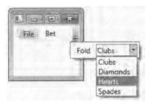

Figure 10-9. *If not all the elements can fit on the toolbar, it displays an overflow menu arrow, which the user can click to access the remaining elements.*

StatusBars

The StatusBar element is similar to the ToolBar element, except that the StatusBar isn't designed to be used for input from the user. Its purpose is to display information *to* the user. Status bars are usually docked to the bottom of a window, but they, like toolbars, can be placed anywhere in the window.

Figure 10-10 shows a window with a status bar that contains three items: a text message, a progress bar, and an image.

Figure 10-10. *Status bars display information to the user*

As with the ToolBar, to populate a StatusBar, place the child elements in the content part of the StatusBar element. The following markup produces the content of the window in the figure. Notice that the StatusBar is docked to the bottom of the DockPanel.

```
<DockPanel LastChildFill="False">
    <StatusBar DockPanel.Dock="Bottom">              ← Dock to Bottom
        <TextBlock>Backup In Progress</TextBlock>         ← Text Message
        <ProgressBar Height="20" Width="100" Value="65"/>   ← Progress Bar
        <Image Height="30" Source="kccard.bmp"/>          ← Image
    </StatusBar>
</DockPanel>
```

ToolTips

Tooltips are the small informative windows that automatically pop up when your mouse hovers over an element on the screen. These generally give terse descriptions of the object.

Tooltips are implemented by the ToolTip class and are assigned to the ToolTip property of the object they describe.

For example, the following markup assigns tooltips to a Button, a ComboBox, and each of the ComboBoxItems:

```
<StackPanel>
    <Button  ToolTip="Important Button">Start Game</Button>
    <ComboBox  ToolTip="Choose a Suit" SelectedIndex="0">
        <ComboBoxItem  ToolTip="Black Suit">Clubs</ComboBoxItem>
        <ComboBoxItem  ToolTip="Red Suit">Diamonds</ComboBoxItem>
        <ComboBoxItem  ToolTip="Red Suit">Hearts</ComboBoxItem>
        <ComboBoxItem  ToolTip="Black Suit">Spades</ComboBoxItem>
    </ComboBox>
</StackPanel>
```

The screenshots in Figure 10-11 show some of the tooltips as the mouse is over different objects. Notice that even the ComboBoxItems show tooltips.

Figure 10-11. *The tooltips pop up when the mouse has hovered over an element for a short amount of time.*

Since ToolTip is a ContentControl, it can contain any UIElement—not just text. It can't, however, gain focus, so it is useless to put it in something like a button, since the button won't be able to get focus and therefore won't be able to be clicked.

Controls That Work with Ranges

Several controls are based on a numeric range. Two of these are the ProgressBar and the Slider.

The range controls derive from the RangeBase class, which represents a numeric value that is constrained to be within a set range. Since the range controls inherit from the RangeBase class, the following are the important things you need to know about the RangeBase class:

- The numeric type represented by the range controls is of type double—not type int, as many people expect.

- The Minimum and Maximum properties of a range control contain the minimum and maximum values that the control can have.

- The Value property contains the current value of the control. If you attempt to set the Value either below or above the Minimum or Maximum, respectively, the Value property is set to the Minimum or the Maximum.

The ProgressBar

As mentioned, the ProgressBar derives from the RangeBase class. It is a simple visual element that shows the user that the program is making progress on a particular task—or is at least working on it. Figure 10-12 shows a progress bar indicating that a task is about 60 percent complete.

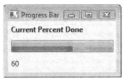

Figure 10-12. *A progress bar showing percentage completion*

The default range of the ProgressBar is 0.0 to 100.0, corresponding nicely with the definition of percentage. The following is the markup that produces the content of the window in the figure. Notice also how the text of the TextBlock at the bottom is bound to the value of the ProgressBar.

```
<StackPanel>
    <TextBlock Margin="5" FontWeight="Bold">Current Percent Done</TextBlock>
    <ProgressBar Name="pBar" Margin="5" Height="20" Value="60" />
    <TextBlock Text="{Binding ElementName=pBar, Path=Value}" Margin="5"/>
</StackPanel>
```

As an example, the following code shows a program that increments the ProgressBar by 10 percent whenever the user clicks the Next Step button. Figure 10-13 shows several screenshots from the program.

Figure 10-13. *You can manipulate the progress shown by the ProgressBar from the code-behind.*

The following is the markup for the program. Notice that the value is set to 0 in the markup.

```
<StackPanel>

    <ProgressBar Name="pBar" Value="0" Margin="5" Height="10" />

    <DockPanel HorizontalAlignment="Stretch" LastChildFill="False">
        <TextBlock Text="{Binding ElementName=pBar, Path=Value}" Margin="5"/>
        <Button DockPanel.Dock="Right" Margin="5" Click="Button_Click">
            Next Step
        </Button>
    </DockPanel>
</StackPanel>
```

The following is the code-behind. The button event handler simply increments the Value property of the ProgressBar.

```
public partial class Window1 : Window
{
    public Window1()
    { }

    private void Button_Click( object sender, RoutedEventArgs e )
    {
        pBar.Value += 10.0;
    }
}
```

You can also make a ProgressBar vertical by setting the Orientation property to Vertical, as shown in Figure 10-14 below.

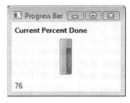

Figure 10-14. *A vertical ProgressBar*

The following is the markup producing the window in Figure 10-14:

```
<Grid>
    <Grid.RowDefinitions>
        <RowDefinition Height="*" />
        <RowDefinition Height="3*" />
        <RowDefinition Height="*" />
    </Grid.RowDefinitions>

    <TextBlock Grid.Row="0" Margin="5" FontWeight="Bold">
        Current Percent Done
    </TextBlock>

    <ProgressBar Orientation="Vertical" Grid.Row="1" Name="pBar"
                 Value="76" Margin="5" Width="20" />

    <TextBlock Text="{Binding ElementName=pBar, Path=Value}"
               Grid.Row="2" Margin="5"/>
</Grid>
```

There are also times when you can't determine the percentage of a process in progress, or for other reasons you might not want to update the progress bar with meaningful values. In these situations, you can set the mode of the ProgressBar so that it repeatedly progresses from left to right. To do this, set the IsIndeterminate property to true.

The Slider

The Slider control looks similar to the ProgressBar. Unlike the ProgressBar, however, the user can change the Slider's value by dragging a little "knob," called a *thumb*, back and forth on the control.

Figure 10-15 shows a slider control that goes from 0.0 to 10.0; it has tick marks showing the integer positions.

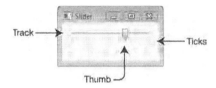

Figure 10-15. *The Slider control allows the user to set the value of the control by sliding the thumb back and forth on the track.*

For example, the following line of markup produces the Slider shown in Figure 10-15. The TickFrequency property specifies that there should be a tick mark every 1 unit. The value for the TickPlacement property is set to BottomRight. When the Slider is in the default horizontal position, this sets the ticks at the bottom of the Slider. Table 10-1 shows other values for TickPlacement.

```
<Slider TickFrequency="1" TickPlacement="BottomRight" Margin="10"/>
```

The following are other important things you should know about the slider:

- By default, the Slider's range is from 0.0 to 10.0.

- Like the ProgressBar, you can orient the Slider vertically rather than using the default horizontal orientation by setting the Orientation property to Vertical.

- You can have the thumb snap to the ticks by setting the IsSnapToTickEnabled to true.

Table 10-1. *The TickPlacement Enumeration Values*

Value	Meaning
None	No tick marks are shown.
TopLeft	If the Slider is horizontal, the tick marks are placed above the track. If the Slider is vertical, they are placed to the left of the track.
BottomRight	If the Slider is horizontal, the tick marks are place below the track. If the Slider is vertical, they are placed to the right of the track.
Both	Tick marks are placed on both sides of the track—either above and below or to the left and right.

263

You can also optionally display another range on the track. This additional range is called the *selection range*. The control doesn't do anything with the selection range other than display it—but the option is there if you have a use for it. For example, some streaming video viewers use the thumb to indicate the current position of the video, while displaying another range, on the same track, that shows how much of the video has been downloaded.

To use the selection range, set the IsSelectionRangeEnabled property to true, and set the SelectionStart and SelectionEnd properties to the values you want. Figure 10-16 illustrates a selection range from 2.0 to 7.0, on a primary range of 0.0 to 10.0.

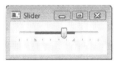

Figure 10-16. You can display a separate selection range on the track.

Summary

In this chapter, you looked at a number of controls and elements that aren't used primarily for displaying content, but for navigating and producing the standard graphical user interface. I covered the following elements:

- The TextBox is used for getting small amounts of text from the user.

- The Menu displays a set of options available to the user. Menus can be nested by nesting the MenuItem objects they contain.

- The ContextMenu is a menu attached to a particular element. It appears when the user right-clicks the element. A ContextMenu contains options valid for that element only.

- A ToolBar is a collection of UIElements allowing the user to quickly access the program's most common features.

- A StatusBar is a collection of UIElements that display information to the user about the status of the program.

- ToolTips are small windows with terse information about an element. They pop up when the mouse has hovered over the element for a threshold amount of time.

- The ProgressBar shows the user the progress that's being made on a particular task. It can also be used just to show that a task is currently being worked on.

- The Slider is a bar with a "thumb" that the user can slide back and forth within a range of values. The current position of the thumb sets the current value of the control.

CHAPTER 11

∎ ∎ ∎

Resources

Two Types of Resources

The ResourceDictionary

Assembly Resources

Accessing Assembly Resources from the Code

Two Types of Resources

WPF uses the term *resource* to refer to two different types of things:

- The first type of resource refers to items used by the program that aren't created by the program's source code. These include, for example, images or icons that are supplied from outside the code.

  - These are resources in the common sense of the term as it's been used since the beginning of Windows programming.

  - These are also called *assembly resources* or *binary resources* if they are compiled into the binary.

- WPF also uses the term in a new way, to describe .NET code objects that are stored in an object dictionary and then used at various places throughout the code.

  - These are usually associated with XAML markup but can also be used in the code-behind.

  - These are also called logical resources, object resources, or XAML resources.

The term *resource* is used for either of the two forms, with the meaning distinguished by the context. In this chapter, I'll cover both types of resources, starting with the new WPF meaning of the term.

The ResourceDictionary

General-purpose class libraries often provide classes called *dictionaries*, which you can use to store items you want to save and retrieve later. A dictionary is a container that stores *key-value pairs*, where the *value* is the object you want to store, and the *key* is the object you use to look it up, after it's stored.

WPF provides a dictionary class called the ResourceDictionary, which is the basis for WPF's logical resources.

- The ResourceDictionary class implements a dictionary into which you can place references to objects of any type, using keys of any type.

- The objects are always stored as references of type object, so after you retrieve them from the dictionary, you must cast them back to their original type.

The FrameworkElement class has a property called Resources, of the ResourceDictionary type. Since all the elements you've studied so far are derived from the FrameworkElement class, they all contain this built-in storage container. Figure 11-1 shows FrameworkElement's place in the inheritance hierarchy. From the figure you can see that all the controls inherit the Resources property. (The arrows in the figure point from a derived class to its base class.)

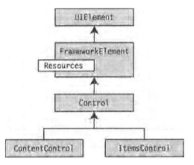

Figure 11-1. The controls inherit the Resources property from the FrameworkElement class, which derives from UIElement.

I'll start by showing how to store and retrieve a SolidColorBrush in a StackPanel's Resources property. It's easier to see exactly what's going on in the C# code than in markup, so first I'll cover how to do it in C# from the code-behind, and then later I'll show how to do it in XAML.

The following markup declares a button inside a StackPanel. I've given names to both the button and the StackPanel so that I can refer to them in the code-behind.

```
<StackPanel Name="sp">
    <Button Name="btn1">Button 1</Button>
</StackPanel>
```

If you did nothing in the code-behind, the button would have the default Button appearance. Instead, however, in the code-behind shown next, I've added two lines below the InitializeComponent() method call.

- The first line adds a silver Brush object to the Resources property of the StackPanel. The string "background" is the key that you'll use to look up the Brush object later.

- The second line uses the button's FindResource method to search for the resource and assign the result to the button's Background property. Notice that the result of the search must be cast back to the Brush type.

- The FindResource method starts at the current element and searches up the element tree querying each element's Resources property with the given key.

  - If it finds the resource, it returns its reference. Otherwise, it throws an exception.

  - Notice also that the call to the FindResource method is on btn1. That's because that's where you want the search up the tree to begin.

```
public Window1()
{
    InitializeComponent(); Key              Value
                           ↓                ↓
    sp.Resources.Add( "background", Brushes.Silver );
                      _____
                                ↑
            Add the key/value pair to the ResourceDictionary.
    btn1.Background = (Brush) btn1.FindResource("background");
                      ___↑_____↑_____
}                   Cast to the        Search for the resource.
                    Brush type.
```

In the screenshot on the left, Figure 11-2 shows the resulting button with the silver background. The drawing on the right shows the resulting element tree. Notice that the button doesn't create a new instance of the Brush object but shares it with the one in the StackPanel's ResourceDictionary.

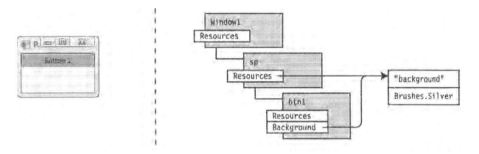

Figure 11-2. *This window places a Brush resource in the StackPanel and then uses it as the Background in the Button.*

As mentioned on the previous page, if the FindResource method doesn't find the resource, it throws an exception. This isn't generally what you want. To handle this situation more gracefully, you can use the TryFindResource method instead. This method returns null if it doesn't find the resource. For example, the following code sets the button Background to an AliceBlue brush if it doesn't find the resource:

```
                              Returns the resource or null.
                                         ↓
btn1.Background = (Brush) btn1.TryFindResource( "background" );

if ( btn1.Background == null )
   btn1.Background = Brushes.AliceBlue;
...
```

In this example, since you knew exactly where the resource was, you didn't actually have to use the FindResource method to search up the tree. You could have accessed the StackPanel's ResourceDictionary directly, using the indexer syntax, using square brackets, as shown in the following line of code:

```
btn1.Background = (Brush) sp.Resources ["background"];
                          ‾‾‾‾‾‾‾‾‾‾‾‾  ‾‾‾‾‾‾‾‾‾‾‾‾‾
                               ↑              ↑

                         Access the       Indexer
                      StackPanel directly.  Syntax
```

271

If the FindResource method or the TryFindResource methods get to the top of the element tree and haven't found the resource, they try two more places before giving up—the Application object and the system resources, as shown in Figure 11-3.

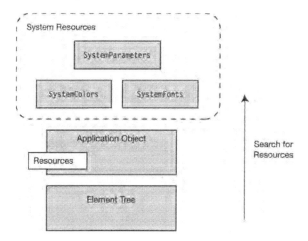

Figure 11-3. *The search for a resource extends beyond the application's UI element tree to the application object and then into the system resources.*

The following code shows how you can store a resource in the application object and use it just as if it had been stored in the UI element tree. Notice how you can get a reference to the Application object using the static Current method.

```
public Window1()
{   InitializeComponent();

    SolidColorBrush silverBrush = Brushes.Silver;

    App application = (App) Application.Current;        ← Get the Application Object.

    application.Resources.Add( "background", silverBrush );

    btn1.Background = (SolidColorBrush) btn1.FindResource( "background" );
}
```

You can also declare resources in the application markup file, as shown in the following markup. The following is the App.xaml file.

```
<Application x:Class="AppResources.App" ...>

    <Application.Resources>
      <SolidColorBrush x:Key="background" Color="Silver"/>
    </Application.Resources>

</Application>
```

So far, we've just used C# to handle resources, but you can also use XAML to store and retrieve the value of a resource. The following XAML shows how to do in markup what we did in the earlier example with the silver background button. There are several important things to notice about the markup:

- Elements added to a Resources property require more than a simple string, so you must use property element syntax, placing the declaration of each resource inside the content part of the construct.

- In each resource declaration, use the x:Key attribute to specify the key.

- To retrieve a reference to the resource, you must use a markup extension—either StaticResource, as shown below, or DynamicResource, which I'll discuss shortly—along with the resource's key.

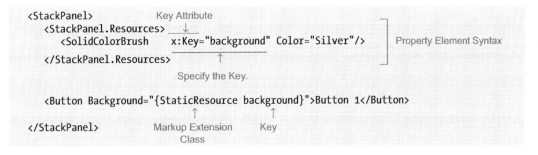

273

Now that you understand the basics, let's look at an example showing how useful this can be. The following markup produces a window with a StackPanel containing a TextBlock and two buttons, as shown on the left in Figure 11-4. The buttons' backgrounds are painted by a LinearGradientBrush, going from white to black. The brush is defined in both buttons. Notice how cluttered and difficult to read the markup has become. Imagine how difficult it would be if there were ten buttons instead of just two.

```
<StackPanel Name="sp">
    <TextBlock FontFamily="Arial Black" Margin="7">Some Buttons</TextBlock>
    <Button Height="40" Name="btn1" FontWeight="Bold">
        <Button.Background>                              ← Defining the Background
            <LinearGradientBrush StartPoint="0, 0" EndPoint="1,1">
                <GradientStop Color="White" Offset="0" />
                <GradientStop Color="Black" Offset="1"/>
            </LinearGradientBrush>
        </Button.Background>
        Button 1
    </Button>
    <Button Height="40" Name="btn2" FontWeight="Bold">
        <Button.Background>                              ← Defining the Background Again
            <LinearGradientBrush StartPoint="0, 0" EndPoint="1,1">
                <GradientStop Color="White" Offset="0" />
                <GradientStop Color="Black" Offset="1"/>
            </LinearGradientBrush>
        </Button.Background> Button 2
    </Button>
</StackPanel>
```

The drawing on the right of Figure 11-4 shows the structure of the element tree.

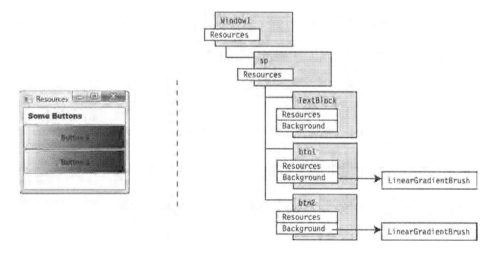

Figure 11-4. *A simple window with two gradient buttons*

Instead of defining the gradient brush in each button, a better strategy would be to define it once as a resource and store it higher up in the element tree—say, in the Window object. You can then retrieve it in the buttons. You can even go wild and set the Backgrounds of the TextBlock and the StackPanel to the same resource, as shown in the following markup:

```
<Window x:Class="GradientButtonsResource.Window1"... >
                        Define the Resource
    <Window.Resources>              ↓
        <LinearGradientBrush x:Key="gradBrush" StartPoint="0,0" EndPoint="1,1">
            <GradientStop Color="White" Offset="0" />
            <GradientStop Color="Black" Offset="1"/>
        </LinearGradientBrush>    Use StaticResource
    </Window.Resources>                       ↓
    <StackPanel Background="{StaticResource gradBrush}" Name="sp">
        <TextBlock FontFamily="Arial Black" Margin="7"
                    Background="{StaticResource gradBrush}">    ← StaticResource
                    Some Buttons</TextBlock>
        <Button Height="40" Name="btn1" FontWeight="Bold"
                Background="{StaticResource gradBrush}">

            Button 1</Button>                       ↑

                            Use StaticResource
        <Button Height="40" Name="btn2" FontWeight="Bold"
                Background="{StaticResource gradBrush}">

            Button 2</Button>                       ↑

    </StackPanel>                Use StaticResource
</Window>
```

Figure 11-5 shows the resulting window and the element tree. Although this particular window looks hideous, you can see how useful logical resources can be and how easy they are to use. Notice that all the elements share the same Brush object. If you want a particular element to have its own Brush object, you can set the x:Shared="False" property assignment.

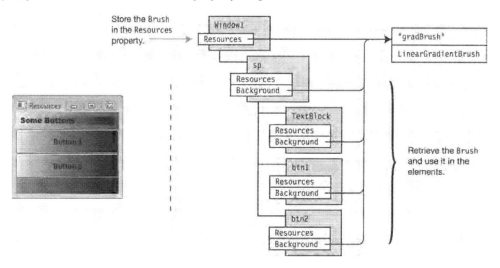

Figure 11-5. *A window with many elements using the same resource*

StaticResources and DynamicResources

When you assign a resource reference to a property, it's assigned as either a StaticResource or a DynamicResource. In spite of the nomenclature, it's not the resources themselves that are either static or dynamic; the same resource can be used as a StaticResource when assigned to one property and as a DynamicResource when assigned to another. The difference is in whether the reference in the ResourceDictionary is monitored for changes, which are then passed along to the property referencing the resource.

- When a StaticResource is read from the ResourceDictionary, its reference is assigned to the property once. If the reference in the resource library changes, the change doesn't propagate to the property holding the original reference.

- With a DynamicResource, if the resource in the library changes, the property holding the old reference is updated automatically, under the covers.

For example, suppose we use the markup from the previous example and make the following two changes:

- Of the four StaticResource markup extensions, let's change three of them to DynamicResource but leave btn1 using a StaticResource.

- Add another button below the others, labeled Change, and give it an event handler that assigns a new Brush to the gradBrush resource.

Here's the new markup:

```
<Window x:Class="DynamicResource.Window1" ... >
   <Window.Resources>
      <LinearGradientBrush x:Key="gradBrush" StartPoint="0,0" EndPoint="1,1">
         <GradientStop Color="White" Offset="0" />
         <GradientStop Color="Black" Offset="1"/>
      </LinearGradientBrush>
   </Window.Resources>              DynamicResource
                                         ↓
   <StackPanel Background="{DynamicResource gradBrush}" Name="sp">
      <TextBlock FontFamily="Arial Black" Margin="7"
            Background="{DynamicResource gradBrush}">     ← DynamicResource
            Some Buttons</TextBlock>
      <Button Height="40" Name="btn1" FontWeight="Bold"
            Background="{StaticResource gradBrush}">      ← Still StaticResource
         Button 1 </Button>
      <Button Height="40" Name="btn2" FontWeight="Bold"
            Background="{DynamicResource gradBrush}"> ← DynamicResource
         Button 2</Button>
      <Button HorizontalAlignment="Right" Click="Button_Click">Change</Button>
   </StackPanel>
</Window>
```

The following code is the code-behind for the window class. Notice that the event handler replaces the "gradBrush" entry in the ResourceDictionary with a silver SolidColorBrush.

```
public partial class Window1 : Window
{
    public Window1()
    { InitializeComponent(); }

    private void Button_Click( object sender, RoutedEventArgs e )
    {
        this.Resources["gradBrush"] = Brushes.Silver;
                        ↑
    }
}            Replace the resource.
```

Figure 11-6 shows the window before and after the Change button is clicked. Afterward, the three DynamicResource properties have been updated, but btn1.Background has not been updated with the new Brush.

Initial Appearance　　　　　After the Three DynamicResource
　　　　　　　　　　　　　Elements Are Updated

Figure 11-6. *The example program before and after the Change button changes the resource*

Figure 11-7 shows the structure of the element tree after the update. The StaticResource property is still referencing the initial LinearGradientBrush object.

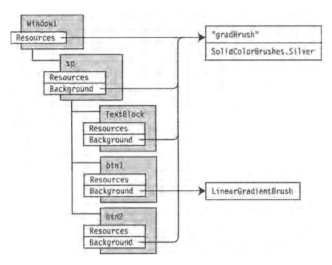

Figure 11-7. *After the update, the DynamicResource properties are referencing a new Brush, while the StaticResource property still references the original Brush.*

To set a DynamicResource in the code-behind, use the SetResourceReference method, as shown in the following code. Like FindResource, SetResourceReference searches up the element tree to find the resource with the given key. The SetResourceReference method takes two parameters:

- The first parameter is the name of the dependency property to which the resource is to be assigned. You must use the name of the dependency property, and not the name of the CLR wrapper property. So in this case, you must use BackgroundProperty and not Background.

- The second parameter is the resource key.

```
btn2.SetResourceReference(BackgroundProperty, "gradBrush" );
                                   ↑                 ↑
                            Dependency         Resource Key
                          Property Name
```

To review, suppose you have the markup shown on the left of Figure 11-8. Then the following code shows the three different forms for retrieving resources in C# code: first, the direct assignment, second the FindResource method, and third, the SetResourceReference method for assigning a DynamicResource. The first button uses the default Button properties, and the last three buttons set their Background properties using the resource.

```
public Window1()
{   InitializeComponent();
    sp.Resources.Add( "background", Brushes.Aqua );
    btn2.Background = (Brush) sp.Resources["background"];
    btn3.Background = (Brush) btn3.FindResource( "background" );
    btn4.SetResourceReference( BackgroundProperty, "background" );
}
```

Figure 11-8 shows a screenshot of the results on the right.

```
<StackPanel Name="sp">
    <Button Name="btn1">Button 1</Button>
    <Button Name="btn2">Button 2</Button>
    <Button Name="btn3">Button 3</Button>
    <Button Name="btn4">Button 4</Button>
</StackPanel>
```

Figure 11-8. *The output and the XAML of the sample program*

One last difference between StaticResources and DynamicResources is that StaticResources don't allow forward references in the XAML. This means that in the text of the XAML, a resource must be defined before you can assign it to a property. DynamicResources don't have this restriction.

Assembly Resources

As I stated at the beginning of the chapter, assembly resources are digital objects, such as images, that aren't generated by the source code. You got a preview of using images as assembly resources in Chapter 6, when I covered the Image control. In this chapter, I'll go into the subject in a bit more detail.

Assembly resources can be embedded in the executable, or you can supply them to the executable as separate files, also called *loose files*. Figure 11-9 shows the two forms. In the drawing on the left, the two JPG files are embedded in the executable. In the drawing on the right, the two JPG resources are separate from the executable; one is in the same directory, and the other is in a subdirectory called Images.

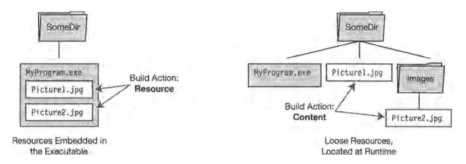

Figure 11-9. *Assembly resources can be embedded in the executable or supplied as loose files at runtime.*

To embed a resource in the executable, first add the resource to the Visual Studio project. The easiest way to do this is by right-clicking the project name in the Solution Explorer, selecting the Add ➤ Existing Item... menu selection, and navigating to the item. Visual Studio then adds to the project the item you selected.

Next you need to tell Visual Studio to embed the resource in the executable in the form that WPF uses. You do this by setting the Build Action property in the Properties window. To show the Properties window, right-click the resource name (which is now visible in the Solution Explorer), and select the Properties menu item. In the Properties window, select Resource—*not* Embedded Resource—for the Build Action.

■ **Note** Although it sounds like exactly what you want, make sure you don't choose Embedded Resource. This option stores the resource in a different part of the assembly that is used by the Windows Forms framework, but it is much more difficult to access from WPF.

For resources that you don't want embedded in the executable, you don't have to do anything in Visual Studio as long as you deploy the resource files along with the executable and make sure they're located where your code thinks they are, which I'll explain in the next several sections.

Visual Studio, however, can manage that process for you and save you trouble. To take advantage of this, you need to add the resource to the project, as you did to embed the resource and then set the Build Action property to Content. The Content setting tells Visual Studio not to embed the resource. Finally, you need to set the Copy to Output Directory property to either "Copy always" or "Copy if newer."

Accessing Assembly Resources from the Code

Using assembly resources from XAML is easy—you just specify the name of the resource file as a string and assign it to the property where you want to use it.

For example, the following line of markup hooks up the Balloons.jpg to the Source property of the Image element:

```
<Image Source="Balloons.jpg"/>
```

Specifying locations in the code-behind is a bit uglier but not difficult. You do it using an object of the Uri class. A Uri object represents a *universal resource identifier*, which specifies the location of a resource. You can create either absolute Uris, which give the fully qualified location of a resource, or relative Uris, which give the relative location.

For a relative Uri, the path is relative to one of two places. At compile time, the compiler looks for the file using the path relative to the location of the project file, which has the .csproj extension. If it finds it, the compiler embeds the resource into the executable and includes an encoding of the resource's path.

To retrieve the resource at runtime, the program does the following:

- It checks its executable file to see whether there is a resource with that encoded path—if so, it uses that resource.

- If it doesn't find the resource in the executable file, it checks the path relative to the location of the executable file.

The following lines of code show the two most common overloaded forms of the Uri constructors. The constructor with a single string parameter assumes the string is an absolute path to the resource. In the second form, the second parameter specifies whether the path is absolute or relative. For an absolute path, you would use the UriKind.Absolute enum member.

```
Uri uri2 = new Uri( "C:/Pictures/HotAirBalloons.jpg" );
Uri uri1 = new Uri( "/DogInSnow.jpg", UriKind.Relative );
```

For example, the following code shows the use of Uris in the code-behind of a simple window that contains two Images in a StackPanel named sp, which is declared in the markup:

```
Uri uri1 = new Uri( "/Balloons.jpg", UriKind.Relative );
Uri uri2 = new Uri( "C:/Pictures/DogInSnow.jpg" );
BitmapImage bi1 = new BitmapImage( uri1 );
Image balloons = new Image();
balloons.Source = bi1;

BitmapImage bi2 = new BitmapImage( uri2 );
Image dogInSnow = new Image();
dogInSnow.Source = bi2;

sp.Children.Add( balloons );
sp.Children.Add( dogInSnow );
```

Pack URIs

The URI forms you saw in the previous section are shorthand of a form called a *pack URI*, which you might sometimes see in programs that access resources from other assemblies and locations. Most of the time, however, you won't need more than you learned in the previous section.

From a practical standpoint, although the syntax of pack URIs is ugly, most of the time it's pretty boilerplate. Take, for example, the following two pack URI specifications. If you remove the first 22 characters of each, you'll see the form we've been using throughout the book.

```
"pack://application:,,,/DogInSnow.jpg"
"pack://application:,,,/Images/CatsOnTheBed.jpg"
            ↑                        ↑
    Scheme and Authority           Path
```

For example, the following code uses a pack URI to specify the source used for an Image. Just as with the shorthand form, from the specification you can't tell whether the JPG it references is embedded in the executable or is a loose file.

```
public Window1()
{
   InitializeComponent();

   Uri uri = new Uri("pack://application:,,,/DogInSnow.jpg");

   BitmapImage bi = new BitmapImage( uri );
   Image dogInSnow = new Image();
   dogInSnow.Source = bi;

   sp.Children.Add( dogInSnow );   // Add to StackPanel, named "sp".
}
```

One situation where you might need to use a full pack URI is if you need to reference a resource in a different assembly. In that case, you need to add a bit to the middle of the pack URI syntax. The augmented syntax looks like the following, where ImagesLibrary is the name of the external assembly that contains the picture. The word component is a *constant part of the syntax* and must always be included. It specifies that the assembly named just before it, ImagesLibrary, in this case, is being referenced by the current program.

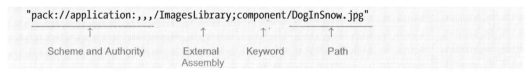

The following code is an example of the code getting the JPG resource out of an assembly called ImagesLibrary. The result is shown in the following illustration.

```
Uri dogUri = new Uri
        ( "pack://application:,,,/ImagesLibrary;component/DogInSnow.jpg" );

BitmapImage bmi = new BitmapImage( dogUri );
Image img = new Image();
img.Source = bmi;
sp.Children.Add( img );
```

Summary

WPF documentation uses the term *resource* to refer to two different types of things—*logical resources* and *binary resources.*

Logical resources are objects that are created by the program and stored in an object dictionary for use by elements in the XAML tree. This is particularly useful when you want a number of different elements to use the same object. Rather than redefining the object multiple times, you can create the object once and store it as a resource that the other elements can access.

The following are some of the important characteristics of logical resources:

- Logical resources are usually defined in the markup at a high level in the element tree.

- The elements that need to use a logical resource can search up the tree to find it.

- A logical resource can be attached to an element as either a static resource or a dynamic resource.

  - If a resource is attached as a static resource, the system looks up the resource once and associates the resource with the element.

  - If a resource is attached as a dynamic resource and that resource object changes after it's been associated with an element, then the system updates the element's reference to the new version of the resource.

Assembly resources are objects that aren't created by the program's markup or C# code, such as bitmap images or icons. These are generally created outside the program and associated in Visual Studio with the program's project file. These are what have traditionally been called *resources* in Windows programming.

Assembly resources can be embedded in program's executable, or they can be accessed at runtime as loose files.

CHAPTER 12

■ ■ ■

Styles

What Are Styles?

Named Styles

Targeted Styles

Comparing Named and Targeted Styles

EventSetters

The Collections in a Style

Property Triggers

MultiTriggers

Other Types of Triggers

Summary

What Are Styles?

In the previous chapter, you saw how to declare and save the value of a dependency property as a logical resource in a resource collection. Once the resource is declared, you can then use it anywhere below the declaration in the element tree, without having to re-define it each time. Also, if you need to change the value of the property, you can do it in just one place, and the change is reflected in all the locations that use it.

Logical resources are very useful, as far as they go—but their limitation is that each resource corresponds to a single property. Most of the time when you're setting the look and feel of a UI, you want to set the values of a *group* of properties. Ideally, you want to define the values of the properties only once and then apply that group of property settings to a number of different elements. In HTML, you can do this with *Cascading Style Sheets* (CSS). In WPF, you do it with *styles*.

For example, Figure 12-1 shows two screenshots of a window. In the screenshot on the left, the buttons have their default appearance. In the screenshot on the right, the buttons have had a style applied. The style defines the values of the four button properties listed to the right of the figure.

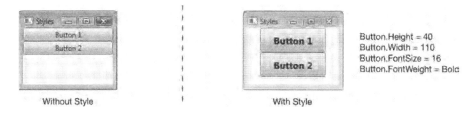

Figure 12-1. *In WPF you can collect a group of property settings into a style and then apply that style to many different elements.*

The following are some of the important things to know about styles:

- Styles are declared as resources, as shown in the following code. As such, they can be applied to elements below them in the element tree.

```
<Window.Resources>
   <Style ...>
      ...
   </Style>
</Window.Resources
```

- There are two ways to define and apply styles—*named styles* and *targeted styles*.

  – With *named styles*, you give the style a name when you declare it. You then use the style's name to explicitly apply it to selected elements.

  – With *targeted styles*, you give the style a target type when you declare it. The style is then automatically applied to elements of that type.

- Setting a property locally on an object overrides any Style setting that might be on that property.

Named Styles

We'll start with an example of named styles. The following code shows the syntax for the declaration of a style that sets the four properties shown in Figure 12-1:

```
            Key        Style Name Suffix
             ↓              ↓
<Style x:Key="buttonStyle">
    <Setter Property="Button.Height"      Value="40"   />
    <Setter Property="Button.Width"       Value="110"  />
    <Setter Property="Button.FontSize"    Value="16"   />
    <Setter Property="Button.FontWeight"  Value="Bold" />

</Style>           ↑            ↑                 ↑
              Property    Setters for a Named    Value
              Attribute   Style Must Include a   Attribute
                              Class Name
```

The following are important things to notice about the code:

- Use the x:Key attribute to name a style.

    - As with any resource, the key can be of any type—but it is usually a string.

    - By convention, the names of styles should end with the suffix *Style*.

- The property values of a Style are set using elements called Setters. Setters require two attributes—a Property and a Value.

- The Property attribute specifies which property of the target element should be set.

    - The property specified must be a dependency property.

    - For named styles, when assigning to the Property attribute of the Setter, it's not sufficient to give just the property name—*you must also include a class name as well.*

- The Value attribute specifies the value with which to set the target property. The values in the example code are simple, but for complex values you'll need to use the attribute element syntax.

Since styles are declared as resources; you apply a named style to an element the same way you would apply the simple resources you saw in the previous chapter—using a markup extension of the StaticResource type.

For example, the following markup applies the style declared above, to a button.

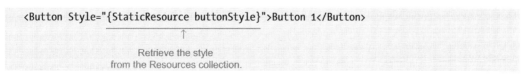

```
<Button Style="{StaticResource buttonStyle}">Button 1</Button>
                            ↑
                  Retrieve the style
              from the Resources collection.
```

Figure 12-2 shows the full markup for the window shown on the right of Figure 12-1 at the beginning of the chapter.

```
<Window x:Class="ButtonStyle.Window1"
    xmlns="http://schemas.microsoft.com/winfx/2006/xaml/presentation"
    xmlns:x="http://schemas.microsoft.com/winfx/2006/xaml"
    Title="Styles" Height="130" Width="170">

    <Window.Resources>
        <Style x:Key="buttonStyle">
            <Setter Property="Button.Height"      Value="40"  />
            <Setter Property="Button.Width"       Value="110" />
            <Setter Property="Button.FontSize"    Value="16"  />
            <Setter Property="Button.FontWeight"  Value="Bold"/>
        </Style>
    </Window.Resources>

    <StackPanel>
        <Button Style="{StaticResource buttonStyle}">Button 1</Button>
        <Button Style="{StaticResource buttonStyle}">Button 2</Button>
    </StackPanel>
</Window>
```

Style
Definition

Resources

Figure 12-2. *Styles are retrieved from the Resources collection and applied to the Style property of the elements that use the style.*

Figure 12-3 shows the element tree produced by the markup.

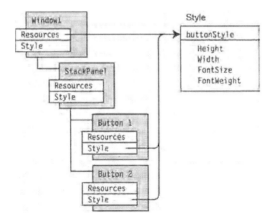

Figure 12-3. *The element tree produced by the markup in Figure 12-2*

I mentioned earlier that in the `Setters` of a named style you must use a class name with the property name. The class name, however, doesn't have to be the exact class of the target element; it can also be that of a class from which the target element derives—for example `Control` or `ButtonBase`.

```
<Setter Property="Control.FontWeight" Value="Bold" />
```

Setters for named styles
must include a class name.

Using the class name of a class higher in the derivation tree allows you to apply the style to any type of element derived from that base class. If, for example, you used `Control` as your base class, you could apply the style to `Buttons`, `Labels`, `Windows`, and anything else derived from `Control`.

If the target doesn't include some of the properties set by a style—those style properties are ignored, and only the relevant properties are applied.

The following markup shows an example of using a style on more than one target type. In this example, the `Setter` uses `Control` as the property class. It then sets the style on a `GroupBox` and two `Buttons`.

```
<Window.Resources>
   <Style x:Key="buttonStyle">
      <Setter Property="Control.FontSize"    Value="16" />
      <Setter Property="Control.FontWeight" Value="Bold"/>
   </Style>                          ↑
</Window.Resources>       Base Class

<GroupBox Header="Some Buttons" BorderBrush="Black" Margin="5"
          Style="{StaticResource buttonStyle}">           ← Apply Style
   <StackPanel Margin="5">
      <Button Style="{StaticResource buttonStyle}">Button 1</Button>
      <Button Style="{StaticResource buttonStyle}">Button 2</Button>

   </StackPanel>                        ↑
</GroupBox>                     Apply Style
```

Figure 12-4 shows the window produced by the markup.

Figure 12-4. *The Buttons and the header of the GroupBox display the font settings set by the style.*

Targeted Styles

Targeted styles are designed to be used on exactly one type of target element. The style is automatically applied to all elements of that type in the tree below the declaration. These are also called *typed styles*.

The markup shown next shows a style that is applied to Button objects. Notice the following differences between this markup and that of the named styles in the previous example.

- In the style declaration:

    - Set the TargetType attribute to the exact type of the elements on which to apply the style. The style will not be applied to elements of types *derived* from the specified type.

    - Do *not* set the x:Key attribute. Setting the x:Key attribute inhibits the targeted style from being applied automatically.

    - The Setters do not require a class name with the property name. If you supply one, it must be the same as the TargetType.

- In the target elements, the styles are applied automatically, so there is nothing to add to their declarations.

```
<Window.Resources>
              Set the target type.
                      ↓
    <Style TargetType="Button">
        <Setter Property="FontSize"   Value="16" />
        <Setter Property="FontWeight" Value="Bold"/>
    </Style>                    ↑
                        No Class Name
</Window.Resources>
<GroupBox Header="Some Buttons" BorderBrush="Black" Margin="5">
    <StackPanel>
        <Button>Button 1</Button>        ← No Explicit Application of the Style
        <Button>Button 2</Button>        ← No Explicit Application of the Style
    </StackPanel>
</GroupBox>
```

Figure 12-5 shows the output of the previous markup. Notice that the Buttons have had the style applied, but the header of the GroupBox is unaffected.

Figure 12-5. *The targeted style is automatically applied to just the Button elements.*

Comparing Named and Targeted Styles

Figure 12-6 summarizes the syntactic differences between named styles and targeted styles. The important points are the following.

Named styles have the following characteristics, as shown in the figure.

- The declaration of a named style uses the x:Key attribute to name the style.

  - A named style can be applied to more than one type of element.

  - The Setters require a class name, which must be a base class of any types to which the style will be applied.

- You apply the named style explicitly by using the StaticResource markup extension to the Style attribute of the element it is being applied to.

Targeted styles have the following characteristics:

- The declaration of a targeted style has the following characteristics:

  - It uses the TargetType attribute, giving the *exact* type to which the style should be applied.

  - The style must not use the x:Key attribute.

  - Setters do not require a class name.

- The style is applied automatically to every element of the given type below it in the element tree.

```
                                                                    Declaration
Named Styles    <Window.Resources>
                    <Style x:Key="buttonStyle">
                        <Setter Property="Control.FontSize" ... >

                                                                    Application
                <StackPanel>
                    <Button Style="{StaticResource buttonStyle}">Button 1</Button>
```

```
                                                                    Declaration
Targeted Styles <Window.Resources>
                    <Style TargetType="Button">
                        <Setter Property="FontSize" ... >

                                                                    Application
                <StackPanel>
                    <Button>Button 1</Button>
```

Figure 12-6. *Comparing named and targeted styles*

EventSetters

Each Setter in the Setters collection of the Style can set the value of one dependency property. As you've seen, this is extremely useful. There are times, however, when you might need to do more than just set properties; you need to execute procedural code from the code-behind. For this situation, WPF provides the EventSetter element.

EventSetters allow you to attach event handlers to a style. If the element on which the style is applied receives the given event, it calls the given event handler. The EventSetter element has two attributes, Event and Handler, to which you assign the name of the event and the name of the event handler.

The following markup declares an EventSetter in a style that targets Buttons. The EventSetter specifies that when the button receives the MouseEnter event, it will call the ChangeValue_OnEnter event handler in the code-behind.

```
<Window.Resources>

   <Style TargetType="Button">
      <EventSetter Event="MouseEnter" Handler="ChangeValue_OnEnter"/>
   </Style>
                           ↑                        ↑
                        Set Event                Set Handler
</Window.Resources>
<StackPanel>
   <Button Width="75" Height="40">0</Button>
</StackPanel>
```

The following code is the event handler in the window's code-behind. The handler retrieves the number displayed by the button and increments it. The result is that the number displayed by the Button is the number of times the mouse has entered the Button area.

```
private void ChangeValue_OnEnter( object sender, RoutedEventArgs e )
{
   Button btn = (Button) sender;
   int value;
   if ( int.TryParse( (string) btn.Content, out value ) )
   {
      value++;
      btn.Content = value.ToString();
   }
}
```

Figure 12-7 shows a sequence of screenshots of the program. Every time the mouse enters the Button area the number increments by one.

Figure 12-7. *The Button displays the number of times its area has been entered by the mouse.*

The Collections in a Style

You've seen that a `Style`'s `Setters` are used to affect the elements on which the `Style` is applied. The `Setters` are stored in the `Setters` property, which is a collection of `Setter` objects. There are, however, several other important collections in a `Style` object, as illustrated in Figure 12-8.

- The `Triggers` property is a collection of `Trigger` objects. These are "conditional" styles, which we'll look at in the next section.

- You can use the `Resources` property to store logical resources used by the `Setters` and `Triggers`.

Setters and Triggers affect the properties of the object on which they are applied. The resources are used internally by the `Setters` and `Triggers`.

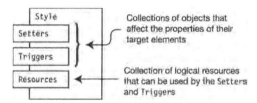

Figure 12-8. *The Style class contains three important collection properties.*

The `Setters` property is the default property of the `Style` object, which is why you can use the shortcut of listing the `Setters` directly inside the `Style` element declaration. The fully qualified form is to list them inside the `Style.Setters` tags, as shown in the following markup. Triggers and resources must always use their fully qualified forms, as shown.

```
<Style TargetType="Button">
   <Style.Setters>                                        ← Fully Qualified Tag
     <Setter Property="FontStyle" Value="Italic"></Setter>
     <Setter Property="FontWeight" Value="Bold"></Setter>
     <Setter Property="FontSize" Value="14"></Setter>
   </Style.Setters>

   <Style.Triggers>                  ← Fully Qualified Tag
     <Trigger ...> ... </Trigger>
     <Trigger ...> ... </Trigger>
   </Style.Triggers>

   <Style.Resources>                 ← Fully Qualified Tag
     ...
   </Style.Resources>
</Style>
```

Property Triggers

You can think of a *property trigger*, or just *trigger*, as a "conditional style," where the condition is based on the value of a particular dependency property. When (and while) that property has a certain value, the style is applied. If the property ceases to have that value, the style immediately ceases to apply, and the element reverts to its "nontriggered" appearance.

The markup shown next shows the syntax of a `Trigger` element. It consists of the following components:

- A dependency property (`Property`) that is monitored for a particular value (`Value`).

- A collection of `Setter`s that are applied when the property being watched has the specified value.

```
                Property to            Value Being
                 Monitor               Watched For
                     ↓                      ↓
<Trigger Property="IsMouseOver" Value="True">
    <Setter Property="FontWeight" Value="Bold"/>    ← Setter
    <Setter Property="FontSize" Value="20"/>        ← Setter
</Trigger>
```

The following markup declares a style that sets the `FontStyle` of a `Button` to `Italic`. It also has a `Trigger` that monitors the `IsMouseOver` property of the button. When the mouse cursor is over the button, the property becomes true, and the `Trigger`'s `Setter`s are activated, changing the size of the font to 20 and changing the `FontWeight` to Bold.

```
<Window.Resources>
    <Style TargetType="Button">      ← Type Targeted Style

        <Setter Property="FontStyle" Value="Italic"/>        ← Style Setter

        <Style.Triggers>                                     ← Trigger Collection
            <Trigger Property="IsMouseOver" Value="True">        ← Trigger
                <Setter Property="FontWeight" Value="Bold"/>     ← Trigger Setter
                <Setter Property="FontSize" Value="20"/>         ← Trigger Setter
            </Trigger>
        </Style.Triggers>

    </Style>

</Window.Resources>

<StackPanel>
    <Button>Button 1</Button>
    <Button>Button 2</Button>
</StackPanel>
```

Figure 12-9 shows the triggered and untriggered states of the buttons. Note that in the untriggered state, the FontStyle is Italic. When the Trigger is applied, the FontStyle property isn't affected, so the triggered font has a size of 20 and is bold and italic.

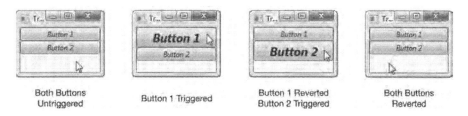

Both Buttons   Button 1 Triggered   Button 1 Reverted   Both Buttons
Untriggered   Button 2 Triggered   Reverted

Figure 12-9. *The states of Buttons with a Trigger*

The example markup shown earlier has only a single Trigger in its Triggers collection, but there can be any number of Triggers—all watching different properties of the buttons.

MultiTriggers

Simple Triggers monitor one condition—the value of a single dependency property. If you want your Trigger to fire only if all the conditions in a set are true, you can use the MultiTrigger element.

The code in Figure 12-10 shows an example of a MultiTrigger that fires only when both the IsMouseOver and the IsFocused properties are true. Each condition is specified by a Condition element, and the Condition elements are contained in the Conditions collection.

Figure 12-10. *A MultiTrigger contains a collection of conditions, all of which must be true for the collection of Setters to take effect.*

Other Types of Triggers

Triggers and MultiTriggers are *property triggers*, because their Setters are triggered by the values of properties. There are also three other types of triggers—EventTriggers, DataTriggers, and MultiDataTriggers. Table 12-1 summarizes the uses of these triggers.

Table 12-1. *Summary of the Style Trigger Types*

Name	Usage
Trigger	A simple Trigger applies its Setters when, and for as long as, the value of a certain dependency property has a particular value.
MultiTrigger	A MultiTrigger applies its Setters when, and for as long as, all the values of its collection of conditions is met.
EventTrigger	An EventTrigger is activated when the element on which it is applied receives a particular event. These are commonly used in animation, which is covered in Chapter 19.
DataTrigger	A DataTrigger is activated when the value of some property has a particular value. Like a simple Trigger, the property can be a dependency property. Unlike a simple Trigger, however, it can also be a .NET property that is *not* a dependency property, if the data property is bound to an element.
MultiDataTrigger	A MultiDataTrigger is a DataTrigger that has multiple data value conditions that must be satisfied before it is activated.

Summary

The following are some of the important things to remember about Styles:

- WPF Styles provide a convenient way to encapsulate the settings of a set of properties, so they can be applied to a number of elements. They perform a function similar to Cascading Style Sheets styles in HTML.

- Styles are declared as logical resources at a level in the element tree above where they will be applied.

- There are two types of Styles—named styles and targeted styles.

  - Named styles are applied explicitly to selected elements and can be applied to more than one type of element.

  - Targeted styles are applied automatically to only the exact target element type.

- Setters are elements in a Style that allow you to specify a property and a value with which to set the property.

- EventSetters are elements in a Style that allow you to attach an event handler to the Style. This allows you to execute procedural code, rather than just setting properties.

- Triggers are "conditional" styles, which apply only when a certain condition is met. There are five types of Triggers: simple Triggers, MultiTriggers, EventTriggers, DataTriggers, and MultiDataTriggers.

CHAPTER 13

■ ■ ■

Control Templates

Separating Appearance from Behavior

One of the major features of WPF is that it allows you unprecedented control of the way your applications looks. This extends even to the appearance of the standard controls.

So far, you've seen that you can change some of the basic characteristics of controls, such as their content, background colors, and margin characteristics. But it goes much deeper than that. You can change the entire look of a control—without changing its fundamental behavior.

The reason for this is that the appearance of a control isn't hard-coded into the control itself, as it has been in previous frameworks. In previous frameworks, the control classes were implemented as wrappers around the controls built into Win32. Since they were built in to Win32, you couldn't change them.

WPF, however, implements controls from scratch and separates the behavior of a control from its appearance. You might, for example, think of a Button as a visual object. Actually, however, it's a set of behaviors *represented* by an appearance.

The appearance of a particular button, for example, might be rectangular, circular, or even irregularly shaped; but when you click it, its behavior should be that of a button, which is to execute its event handler. In WPF, you specify a control's *behavior* by setting properties in its class object.

The *appearance* of a control is determined by an object of the ControlTemplate class. The ControlTemplate object specifies the visual elements that comprise a control's display.

When WPF creates an instance of a control, it performs the following two tasks:

- It creates an object of the class, which contains the specification of the control's behavior. This object is called the *templated parent*.

- It instantiates a tree of visual objects as specified by the control's ControlTemplate. This tree is called the control's *visual tree*. A control stores a reference to its ControlTemplate object in its Template property.

Figure 13-1 illustrates these concepts.

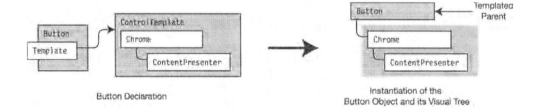

Figure 13-1. *When WPF creates a control, it creates an instance of the control class (the templated parent) and then instantiates the control's visual tree, as specified by its ControlTemplate.*

The standard WPF controls all come with default templates that produce the default control appearances. You can, however, replace those templates with ones of your own design, giving the controls an entirely different appearance. Because the behavior and the appearance are separate, changing the appearance of a control doesn't change its behavior.

Except for a short introduction in Chapter 3, throughout this book I've been showing you the *logical trees* associated with the example UIs. These are the tree structures formed by the element objects. If you're going to create your own ControlTemplates, however, you'll need to look at the program's visual tree, which is the tree comprising the templated parents, as well as their visual trees.

For example, the following markup creates a Window object that contains a Button object, which contains the text "Click Me". This simple markup produces a simple logical tree. The visual tree, however, consists of many additional elements, as shown in Figure13-2.

```
<Window x:Class="Junk.Window1" ... >
    <Button>
        Click Me
    </Button>
</Window>
```

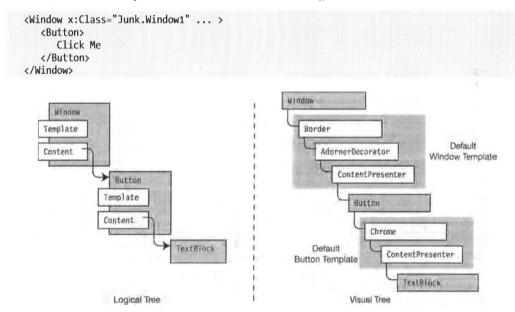

Figure 13-2. *The visual tree is an expanded view of the logical tree, including all the visual subcomponents that produce the appearance of the control.*

Developing a Simple Control Template

To illustrate these concepts, I'll start with a simple button that uses the default Button template and then replace its control template. The following is the markup that produces a standard button, as you've seen throughout the book:

```
<StackPanel>
    <Button FontWeight="Bold" Click="myButton_Click" Name="myButton">
        Click Me</Button>
</StackPanel>
```

In the code-behind, I've added a simple event handler for the button's Click event. When the button is clicked, the event handler simply displays a MessageBox.

```
private void myButton_Click( object sender, RoutedEventArgs e )
{
    MessageBox.Show( "Button Clicked", "Button Message" );
}
```

Figure 13-3 shows the button produced by the program, before I replace the default Button template.

Figure 13-3. *A Button with its default control template*

The next thing I want to do is to create a control template and substitute it for the default Button template. The appearance I want for the button consists of a Border containing a TextBlock, as shown in Figure 13-4. Although control templates can be quite fancy and elaborate, I'll use a simple one in order to keep the markup as simple as possible, allowing you to focus on the template fundamentals.

Figure 13-4. *The goal appearance for buttons using the template*

Figure 13-5 shows the markup producing this button. Rather than creating the template at the individual button level, I've placed the new button template in the Resources collection of the Window object. This allows me to use the same template for all the buttons in the program. Figure 13-6 shows this architecture.

There are several important things to notice about the markup in Figure 13-5:

- Because the control template is stored in the Resources collection, it must have an x:Key attribute so you can refer to it later when you apply it to the button.

- When assigning the template to the button's Template property, you must use the StaticResource markup extension.

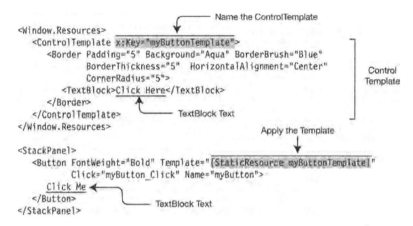

Figure 13-5. *Use the StaticResource markup extension to assign the new template to the button.*

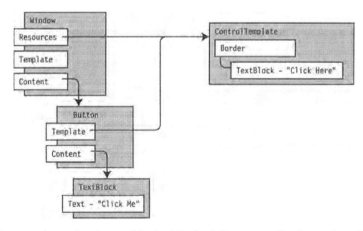

Figure 13-6. *The control template is stored in the Window's Resource collection and used by the Button object.*

305

The ContentPresenter Class

There's another important thing to notice about the markup in Figure 13-5; there are two different messages for the text of the button—the one in the template that says "Click Here" and the one in the button declaration that says "Click Me." Which of the two messages will be displayed? The answer is that it's the message in the template that will be displayed.

For example, if you were to create three buttons using this template, their text would all use the "Click Here" message for all three, regardless of the Content value in the button declarations. Figure 13-7 illustrates this with three buttons using the template. In the markup you can see that each button declaration has a different text label as its Content. In spite of that, the screenshot on the right shows that the template gives them all the same string label.

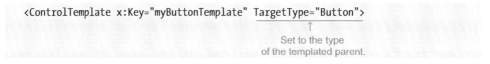

```
<StackPanel>
    <Button FontWeight="Bold" Template="{StaticResource myButtonTemplate}"
            Name="myButton">Click Me</Button>

    <Button FontWeight="Bold" Template="{StaticResource myButtonTemplate}"
            Name="myButton1">Button 2</Button>

    <Button FontWeight="Bold" Template="{StaticResource myButtonTemplate}"
            Name="myButton2">Button 3</Button>
</StackPanel>
```

Figure 13-7. *Three buttons using the same template all use the template text rather than the buttons'*
content text.

Although there might be times when this behavior is exactly what you want, most of the time you'll probably want to display the content specified in the controls' declarations. For example, in the markup in Figure 13-7, what I really wanted was to have the buttons display "Click Me", "Button 2" and "Button 3", as specified in their respective declarations—not to have them all display the "Click Here" text.

To accomplish this, I need to use an object that can retrieve the Content from the templated parent and display *that* content. The class designed to do this is the ContentPresenter class. To use this, I needed to make two changes to the template declaration.

- Set the TargetType attribute of the ControlTemplate to Button, as shown in the following markup line:

  ```
  <ControlTemplate x:Key="myButtonTemplate" TargetType="Button">
  ```
                                                         ↑
                               Set to the type
                         of the templated parent.

- Replace the TextBlock object, which produces the specific output string, with a ContentPresenter object.

Objects of the ContentPresenter class do just what their name suggests; they generate the presentation of content to the user interface. As a matter of fact, it's not just your custom ControlTemplates that require ContentPresenter objects to display the content; the default template of every ContentControl class also contains a ContentPresenter object.

The following are some important things to know about the ContentPresenter class:

- The ContentPresenter object acts as a placeholder inside the template to specify where the content should be placed.

- By default, the ContentPresenter gets the actual content from the templated parent and binds it to its own Content property. As a matter of fact, the ContentPresenter doesn't event *allow* direct content of its own.

- To use a ContentPresenter, you must set the TargetType attribute of the ControlTemplate to the type of the templated parent.

The following markup shows the updated ControlTemplate, along with the button declarations:

```
                                              Set the TargetType.
                                                      ↓
<Window.Resources>
    <ControlTemplate x:Key="myButtonTemplate" TargetType="Button">
        <Border Padding="5" Background="Aqua" BorderBrush="Blue" CornerRadius="5"
                BorderThickness="5"  HorizontalAlignment="Center">
          <ContentPresenter />          ← Display the content from the templated parent.

    </Border></ControlTemplate></Window.Resources>

<StackPanel>
    <Button FontWeight="Bold" Template="{StaticResource myButtonTemplate}"
            Name="myButton">Click Me</Button>
    <Button FontWeight="Bold" Template="{StaticResource myButtonTemplate}"
            Name="myButton1">Button 2</Button>
    <Button FontWeight="Bold" Template="{StaticResource myButtonTemplate}"
            Name="myButton2">Button 3</Button>
</StackPanel>
```

This time when you run the program, the ContentPresenter uses the content specified by each of the button declarations—giving them their own text.

Figure 13-8. *Using the ContentPresenter inside the ControlTemplate labels the buttons with the content specified by the button declarations.*

Template Binding

As you've just seen, the ContentPresenter always retrieves the content from the templated parent. There are times, however, when you might want the ContentPresenter to use additional properties from the templated parent. The TemplateBinding class is a special type of binding designed for this purpose.

For example, suppose you want to add some space around the ContentPresenter to space it out a bit from the control containing it. Since in most content controls you would accomplish this by setting the Padding property, you might be tempted to set the Padding property of the ContentPresenter object.

The ContentPresenter class, however, doesn't include the Padding property. This actually makes sense when you remember that the Padding property specifies the thickness a control should add around its content, separating it from the outside of the control. But in this case the ContentPresenter represents the content itself. So, what looks like Padding to the control, corresponds to a Margin around the ContentPresenter.

So, what we'd like is to set up the ControlTemplate such that if the programmer specifies a Padding value on the templated parent, the ContentPresenter uses that value as its Margin property. We can accomplish this by using the TemplateBinding markup extension to bind the templated parent's Padding property to the ContentPresenter's Margin property, as shown in the following markup:

```
<ContentPresenter Margin="{TemplateBinding Padding}"/>
```

Use the value of the Padding
property from the templated parent.

For example, the markup in Figure 13-9 creates a Button template where the visible shape of the button is an ellipse with an aqua fill color, and the Padding property of the templated parent is mapped to the Margin property of the ContentPresenter. The window contains two buttons that use the template. The first button declaration doesn't set a Padding value, and the resulting button looks crowded. The second button sets a Padding value, which the ContentPresenter maps to its Margin property.

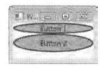

```
<Window.Resources>
    <ControlTemplate x:Key="btnTemplate" TargetType="Button">
        <Grid>
            <Ellipse Fill="Aqua" Stroke="Blue" StrokeThickness="2"/>
            <ContentPresenter HorizontalAlignment="Center"
                              VerticalAlignment="Center"
                              Margin="{TemplateBinding Padding}"/>
        </Grid>
    </ControlTemplate>
</Window.Resources>

<StackPanel>
    <Button Template="{StaticResource btnTemplate}">
                    Button 1</Button>
    <Button Template="{StaticResource btnTemplate}"
            Padding="7">Button 2</Button>
</StackPanel>
```

Figure 13-9. *A Button ControlTemplate that maps the Padding property of the templated parent to the ControlTemplate's Margin property*

ControlTemplate Triggers

A normal button, with the default `ControlTemplate`, has several visual states. The exact appearance of these states depends on the operating system and the theme. In Vista's Aero Glass theme, the background of a button is a light blue when the mouse is over the button. When the mouse *isn't* over the button, its background is a light gray. When the button is clicked, the background becomes a darker blue, and the border darkens.

In contrast, the button appearances you've created with the templates so far in this chapter have been completely static. They always look the same regardless of what you do with them.

In Chapter 12, I explained `Styles`, and you saw that `Styles` can have `Triggers`, which change the appearance of the element depending on the values of certain properties. `ControlTemplates` can also have `Triggers`.

`Triggers` in `ControlTemplates` work the same way as those in `Styles`. They define the *dynamic* visual characteristics of the control to which the template is attached. The following are some important things to remember from Chapter 12 about `Triggers`:

- A `Trigger` consists of a property name, a value, and a group of `Setters`. A `Setter` assigns a certain value to a property.

- When a `Trigger`'s named property has the specified value, each `Setter` does its job—assigning its value to its property.

- When the `Trigger`'s property no longer has the specified value—the properties set by the `Setters` revert to their previous values.

In comparison with the `ControlTemplate Triggers`, however, `Style Triggers` are a bit simpler. Their `Setters` work on a property of the control. `ControlTemplates`, however, can be made up of many elements, and each `Setter` must know to which element it must be applied. To meet this requirement, you must do two things:

- Assign a name to each element in the `ControlTemplate` that is acted on by one of its `Triggers`.

- In each `Setter`, assign to its `TargetName` attribute the name of the element on which it is to act.

The result of this is that `Setters` in `ControlTemplate Triggers` assign to three attributes rather than two. They are `TargetName`, `Property`, and `Value`.

For example, Figure 13-10 shows a ControlTemplate with a Trigger. The following are the important things to notice about the syntax and semantics of ControlTemplate Triggers:

- The Triggers must be inside a property element syntax node named ControlTemplate.Triggers.

- The Triggers collection can have any number of Triggers.

- Each Setter of a Trigger must be targeted at one of the elements within the template, by assigning the target's name to the TargetName attribute.

- A Trigger can have any number of Setters.

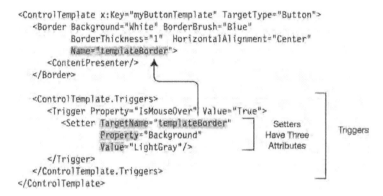

Figure 13-10. *Triggers in a ControlTemplate*

To make the buttons more exciting and bring them more into line with the way buttons are expected to appear dynamically, I've added two Triggers to the template. The first one fires when the mouse is over the button. The second one fires when the button is clicked.

The resulting button has the states shown in Figure 13-11. When the mouse isn't over the button, its background is white. When the mouse is over the button, its background is light gray. When the button is clicked, the border gets thicker, and the Padding gets correspondingly smaller.

Figure 13-11. *We can add dynamic visual states to the button template by adding Triggers.*

The following markup shows the updated template and the button that uses it:

```
<Window.Resources>

    <ControlTemplate x:Key="myButtonTemplate" TargetType="Button">
        <Border Padding="5" Background="White"
                BorderBrush="Blue" CornerRadius="5"
                BorderThickness="5"  HorizontalAlignment="Center"
                Name="templateBorder">                    ← Name the element.
            <ContentPresenter/>
        </Border>

        <ControlTemplate.Triggers>
            <Trigger Property="IsMouseOver" Value="True">
                <Setter TargetName="templateBorder"
                        Property="Background" Value="LightGray"/>
            </Trigger>
            <Trigger Property="IsPressed" Value="True">
                <Setter TargetName="templateBorder"       ← Use the element name.
                        Property="Padding" Value="2"/>
                <Setter TargetName="templateBorder"       ← Use the element name.
                        Property="BorderThickness" Value="8"/>
            </Trigger>
        </ControlTemplate.Triggers>
    </ControlTemplate>

</Window.Resources>
<StackPanel>

    <Button FontWeight="Bold" Template="{StaticResource myButtonTemplate}"
            Click="myButton_Click" Name="myButton">
        Click Me
    </Button>

</StackPanel>
```

Summary

As part of its arsenal of ways to allow you to make attractive and customized user interfaces, WPF allows you to completely change the appearance of even the standard controls. It does this by separating the specification of the appearance of the control from the specification of its behavior. It does this by using control templates.

- The appearance of every control is determined by a ControlTemplate object, which specifies the tree of visual elements to be displayed to represent the control.

- The control object represented by its visual tree is called the *templated parent*.

- The *visual tree* of a program consists of the tree comprising the templated parents and their visual trees.

- Inside a ControlTemplate, you can use a ContentPresenter object to display the Content property of the templated parent.

- You can use a template binding to read and use other dependency property values from the templated parent.

- You can specify dynamic changes to the appearance of a control by using control template Triggers. These Triggers are mostly the same as those available in Styles.

CHAPTER 14

■■■

Page Navigation Programs

Types of Navigation

Navigating Programmatically

XAML Browser Applications

Types of Navigation

Most normal Windows programs start by showing the user a single main window. The user can then click buttons on the window or select menu items, and the program opens additional windows, which present the user with additional options or data.

In contrast to a standard Windows application, a web browser offers a very different paradigm for navigating an application. The major differences are the following:

- A web browser presents only a single page at a time.

- A web browser offers Back and Forward buttons and hyperlinks to navigate from site to site or between pages within a site.

This simple, intuitive model has proved to be very powerful for a broad range of web applications, even for people with limited computer skills. Because of this, WPF provides the tools for producing desktop applications with the same navigation paradigm.

There are two forms these programs can take—stand-alone navigation programs and browser-hosted navigation programs.

- Stand-alone navigation programs are Windows programs where some, or all, of the program uses the page navigation paradigm.

- Browser-hosted navigation programs are also Windows programs but are hosted by a browser, such as Internet Explorer or Firefox. These types of applications are called *XBAPs* (pronounced "EX-bap"), which stands for *XAML Browser APplications*.

Although these types of programs can look like web applications—especially XBAPs—both types of applications are Windows applications and require .NET 3.0 or above on the target machine. Both types use the same WPF components in their construction.

Figure 14-1 shows screenshots of both types. Notice that the stand-alone program has a navigation bar with a Forward and Back button, inside the window frame, whereas an XBAP uses the browser's navigation buttons.

Stand-Alone Page
Navigation Program

XBAP Program

Figure 14-1. *Stand-alone page navigation application and an XBAP application*

In standard Windows programs, Window is the class that contains most of the content you want to present. In navigation programs, the Page class contains the items your program displays.

Rather than start by looking at the characteristics of the Page class, in this chapter you'll start by creating a simple stand-alone page navigation program that contains just a single page. You'll then expand it by adding pages and using the navigation features. After the example, you'll look more closely at the Page class and the other components of a navigation program.

Figure 14-2 shows the output of the example program. Notice in the figure that the Forward and Back buttons on the navigation bar are both grayed since this program contains only a single page and therefore hasn't navigated anywhere.

Figure 14-2. *A single-page stand-alone page navigation program*

To duplicate this program, create a new solution called SimpleApp in Visual Studio using the standard *WPF Application* template. Then modify the XAML and code-behind files as shown in Figure 14-3. Besides adding the StackPanel content, this involves making the following changes to the files:

1. Change the visual tree root element from type Window to type Page, in both the XAML *and code-behind* files.

2. Remove the Height and Width properties from the Page element, and change the Title attribute to the WindowTitle attribute.

```
<Page x:Class="SimpleApp.Window1"
    xmlns="http://schemas.microsoft.com/winfx/2006/xaml/presentation"
    xmlns:x="http://schemas.microsoft.com/winfx/2006/xaml"
    WindowTitle="Simple Page 1" >
    <StackPanel>
        <TextBlock>                      ← No Width or Height
            This is Page 1.
        </TextBlock>
    </StackPanel>
</Page>
```
XAML File

```
public partial class Window1 : Page
{
    public Window1() { InitializeComponent(); }
}
```
Code-Behind File

Figure 14-3. *A simple stand-alone page navigation program with a single page*

When you compile and run the program, it looks like Figure 14-2.

A page navigation program with only a single page isn't very interesting, so let's add two more Pages and several HyperLink objects for navigation.

A Hyperlink object is rendered like an HTML hyperlink and functions just like it. For a basic Hyperlink, you need to include at least two things: the hyperlink content to display and the URI to navigate to when the user clicks it.

- You can either place the content between the Hyperlink element's tags, as shown in the following markup, or assign it to the Content attribute.

- Set the NavigateUri property to the URI of the destination Page.

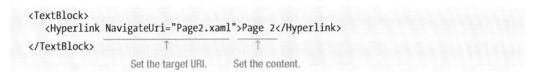

```
<TextBlock>
    <Hyperlink NavigateUri="Page2.xaml">Page 2</Hyperlink>
</TextBlock>
```

                        Set the target URI.   Set the content.

⬛ **Note** The Hyperlink class isn't a control and can't be placed arbitrarily where controls can be placed. Instead, it can be placed only in TextBlocks. The Hyperlink class is derived from the TextElement class, which I'll cover in Chapter 17.

To extend the program, do the following:

1. In Visual Studio, click the Project menu at the top, and select the Add Page menu item.

2. In the Name text box, change Page1.xaml to Page2.xaml. Repeat the process to add a Page called Page3.xaml.

3. Change the markup for the three XAML pages, adding TextBlocks and Hyperlinks to match the markup shown in Figure 14-4.

Figure 14-4 shows the changes to the XAML files. Notice the `Hyperlink`s in `Window1` and `Page2`.

```
<Page x:Class="SimpleApp.Window1" ... WindowTitle="Page 1">
   <Grid>
      <TextBlock>This is Page 1. Go to
         <Hyperlink NavigateUri="Page2.xaml">Page 2</Hyperlink>.
      </TextBlock>
   </Grid>
</Page>
                                                    Window1.xaml
```

```
<Page x:Class="SimpleApp.Page2" ... WindowTitle="Page 2">
   <Grid>
      <TextBlock>This is Page 2. Go to
         <Hyperlink NavigateUri="Page3.xaml">Page 3</Hyperlink>.
      </TextBlock>
   </Grid>
</Page>
                                                      Page2.xaml
```

```
<Page x:Class="SimpleApp.Page3" ... WindowTitle="Page 3">
   <Grid>
      <TextBlock>This is Page 3.</TextBlock>
   </Grid>
</Page>
                                                      Page3.xaml
```

Figure 14-4. *Markup with Hyperlinks added*

When you compile and run the program, you can use the `Hyperlink`s to move to Page 2 and Page 3, and then you can use the Forward and Back buttons to navigate between them.

The screenshots in Figure 14-5 show the sequence of navigating from Page 1 to Page 3 by clicking the hyperlinks and then back to Page 2 using the Back button. Notice that you can build a fully navigable program using simple `Page`s and `Hyperlink`s.

Figure 14-5. *Navigation between the pages*

The Components of a Navigation Program

Now that you've seen how to create a navigation program using Hyperlinks, let's take a closer look at the components that make up a navigation program. At the highest level, these include the Page objects and a *navigation host*, as shown in Figure 14-6.

- The Page contains the content displayed to the user. The Page class is similar to the Window class but is a bit simpler. Page objects are designed to be used, or *hosted*, inside a navigation host.

- The *navigation host* implements and coordinates the navigation features. It has two main subcomponents.

  - The NavigationService takes care of locating and loading the next page to display—the target page.

  - The *journal* keeps track of the navigation history for the Forward and Back buttons.

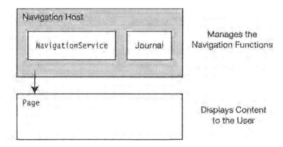

Figure 14-6. *The components of the page navigation architecture*

Figure 14-7 shows the visual relationship between the navigation host and the Page object; the Page is inside the navigation host. The navigation host in this case is an object of the NavigationWindow class.

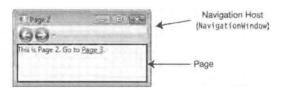

Figure 14-7. *A Page inside a NavigationWindow*

Figure 14-8 illustrates the NavigationService class. The NavigationService object of a navigation host performs the tasks of locating and loading the navigation target.

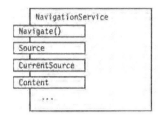

— The Navigate method locates and downloads the navigation target.

— The Source property is the URI of the navigation target.

— The CurrentSource property is the URI of the current object being displayed.

— The Content property contains a reference to the current object.

Figure 14-8. *The NavigationService object*

The journal keeps track of the navigation history. It consists of two stacks—the Back stack and the Forward stack—and the logic that governs them, as illustrated in Figure 14-9. The stacks contain *journal entries,* which are items that contain a set of information about the Pages or items that have been visited.

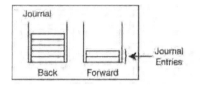

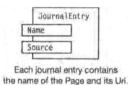

Each journal entry contains the name of the Page and its Uri.

Figure 14-9. *The journal stacks hold JournalEntry objects.*

When the user navigates from one page to another, the journal keeps track of the process by manipulating the stacks as shown in Figure 14-10.

- *New page:* A journal entry for the previous page is placed on the Back stack; the new page is loaded as the current page, and the Forward stack is emptied.

- *Backward:* A journal entry for the current page is pushed onto the Forward stack, and the top journal entry of the Back stack is popped to become the current page.

- *Forward:* A journal entry for the current page is pushed onto the Back stack, and the top journal entry in the Forward stack is popped to become the current page.

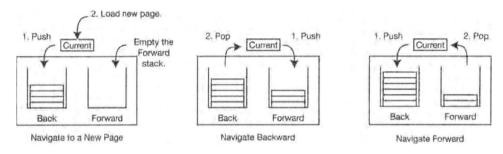

Figure 14-10. *The states of the journal*

For stand-alone navigation programs, there are two classes that can act as navigation hosts. They are the NavigationWindow class and the Frame class.

- The NavigationWindow class is derived from the Window class.

    - If you use a NavigationWindow, it must always be the top-level element of its element tree. It acts like a browser.

    - If the compiler sees that the startupUri of a program is a Page, it creates a NavigationWindow to host it. This is why in the previous examples you haven't had to specify the navigation host.

- The Frame class is a ContentControl and is designed to provide navigation inside other Windows or other ContentControls.

Frames

Unlike NavigationWindow, Frame objects can't be used as the top-level navigation host. The following are some other important things to know about Frames:

- Since Frame is derived from the ContentControl class, you can place Frames wherever you can place a control, including inside other Frame objects.

- A Frame object can handle its own navigation by producing its own navigation bar. By default it will do this only if it's not inside an enclosing NavigationWindow or Frame.

For example, the screenshots shown in Figure 14-11 show a Frame with a black border inside a normal Window object. There are several important things to note about the screenshots:

- Initially the Frame does not have a navigation bar, because no navigation has taken place.

- When the user clicks the "Page 2" hyperlink and is taken to Page 2, a navigation bar automatically appears in the Frame itself. After that, the navigation bar remains visible and active.

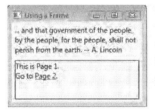 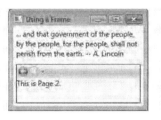 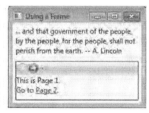

Figure 14-11. *A Frame can supply its own navigation bar.*

Figure 14-12 shows the markup to produce this program. The following are some important things to notice about the markup:

- The Frame is placed in a standard Window object and is used to navigate between two Page objects.

- The initial URI of the Frame is set by assigning it to the Source attribute.

```
<Window x:Class="NavFrame.Window1" ...                          Window1.xaml
    Title="Using a Frame" Height="168" Width="237">
  <Grid>
    <Grid.RowDefinitions>
      <RowDefinition Height="Auto"/>
      <RowDefinition Height="*"   />
    </Grid.RowDefinitions>
    <TextBlock Grid.Row="0" TextWrapping="Wrap" Margin="5">
      ... and that government of the people, by the people, for
      the people, shall not perish from the earth. -- A. Lincoln
    </TextBlock>

    <Frame Grid.Row="1" Source="Page1.xaml" Margin="5"
        BorderBrush="Black" BorderThickness="1">
    </Frame>

  </Grid>
</Window>
```

```
<Page x:Class="NavFrame.Page1" ... Title="Page1">           Page1.xaml
  <Grid>
    <TextBlock>This is Page 1.<LineBreak/>Go to
      <Hyperlink NavigateUri="Page2.xaml">Page 2</Hyperlink>.
    </TextBlock>
  </Grid>
</Page>
```

```
<Page x:Class="NavFrame.Page2" ... Title="Page2">          Page2.xaml
  <Grid>
    <TextBlock>This is Page 2.</TextBlock>
  </Grid>
</Page>
```

Figure 14-12. *The markup for the three files that produce the navigation Frame inside a Window*

Journal Options in Frames

In the previous example, you saw that once the user moved from the initial Page, the Frame produced its own navigation bar. This indicates that it's using its own journal. In other situations, however, a Frame's navigation history might be handled by the journal of an enclosing navigation host.

The different cases are the following:

- By default, if a Frame is enclosed by a NavigationWindow or by another Frame with an active journal, its navigation is merged with, and handled by, the enclosing navigation host's journal.

- If there is no active journal of an enclosing navigation host, the Frame activates its own journal.

- You can explicitly set the journaling behavior by setting the JournalOwnership property of the Frame to one of the three values shown in Table 14-1.

Table 14-1. *The Enum Values for a Frame's JournalOwnership Property*

Enum Value	Description
Automatic	If there's no enclosing navigation host with an active journal, the Frame uses its own journal. This is the default value.
OwnsJournal	The Frame uses its own journal, regardless of enclosing navigation hosts.
UsesParentJournal	If there is an enclosing navigation host with an active journal, the Frame's navigation history is maintained by that host's journal. Otherwise, *no* navigation history is kept for the Frame.

In contrast to the different options for journal ownership for the Frame class, a NavigationWindow always has a journal.

Navigating Programmatically

Using Hyperlinks to navigate through a sequence of pages is a powerful method for simple navigation. Sometimes, however, you might want to take programmatic control of navigation in the code-behind. You can do this by getting an instance of a NavigationService object and calling its Navigate method.

- To get an instance of a NavigationService for the current page, call the static GetNavigationService method, passing a reference to the current page as the parameter.

- To use the NavigationService object's Navigate method, you can pass it one of two things:

  - An object of the page to which you want to navigate

  - The URI of the target page, if the target page is HTML

The following lines of code illustrate the process, passing an object of the destination page to the Navigate method:

```
                               Get an instance of a NavigationService object.
NavigationService navService =      ↓
       NavigationService.GetNavigationService( this );

PagePortrait pp = new PagePortrait();  ← Create a destination Page object.
navService.Navigate( pp );             ← Navigate to the page.
```

For example, Figure 14-13 shows screenshots of a program that has an initial page with a ListBox and a Button. The user first selects either Landscape or Portrait, from the ListBox. When the user clicks the button, the button's message handler determines which item is selected in the ListBox and programmatically navigates to one of two pages: one with text on the bottom and the other with text on the right side.

Initial Screen with ListBox and Button

With Landscape Selected

With Portrait Selected

Figure 14-13. *A program with programmatic navigation, depending on the item selected in the ListBox*

Figure 14-14 shows the code for this program.

```xml
<Page x:Class="ProgramaticNav.Window1" ... >
    <StackPanel>
        <ListBox Name="lbxSelection" BorderBrush="Black" Margin="2"
                Padding="3" SelectedIndex="0"  HorizontalAlignment="Left">
            <ListBoxItem>Landscape</ListBoxItem>
            <ListBoxItem>Portrait </ListBoxItem></ListBox>
        <Button HorizontalAlignment="Left" Margin="2"
                Padding="4" Click="Button_Click">Show Picture</Button>
    </StackPanel>
</Page>
```
Window1.xaml

```csharp
public partial class Window1 : Page
{
    public Window1() { InitializeComponent(); }

    private void Button_Click( object sender, RoutedEventArgs e )
    {
        NavigationService navService = NavigationService.GetNavigationService(this);
        string selString = ((ListBoxItem) lbxSelection.SelectedItem).Content.ToString();
        if ( selString == "Portrait" )
        {
            PagePortrait pp = new PagePortrait();
            navService.Navigate( pp );
        }
        else
        {
            PageLandscape pl = new PageLandscape();
            navService.Navigate( pl );
        }
    }
}
```
Window1.xaml.cs

```xml
<Page x:Class="ProgramaticNav.PageLandscape" ... Title="PageLandscape">
    <Grid>
        <Grid.RowDefinitions>
            <RowDefinition Height="*"   />
            <RowDefinition Height="Auto"/>
        </Grid.RowDefinitions>
        <Image Margin="5" Grid.Row="0" Source="DogInSnow.jpg"></Image>
        <TextBlock Margin="5" FontWeight="Bold" Grid.Row="1">
            Avonlea playing in the Snow</TextBlock>
    </Grid>
</Page>
```
PageLandscape.xaml

```xml
<Page x:Class="ProgramaticNav.PagePortrait" ... >
    <Grid>
        <Grid.ColumnDefinitions>
            <ColumnDefinition Width="*"   />
            <ColumnDefinition Width="Auto"/>
        </Grid.ColumnDefinitions>
        <Image Margin="5" Grid.Column="0" Source="DogInSnow.jpg"></Image>
        <TextBlock Margin="5" FontWeight="Bold" TextWrapping="Wrap" Grid.Column="1">
            Avonlea<LineBreak/>playing<LineBreak/>in the<LineBreak/>Snow</TextBlock>
    </Grid>
</Page>
```
PagePortrait.xaml

Figure 14-14. *Programmatically navigating*

Passing Data to a Page

If your program navigates programmatically, there are times you might want to pass data into the destination page. You can do this in several ways.

The most common way is to create a nondefault constructor for the target Page class and call that constructor to create the Page object, which you then send in to the Navigate method, as shown in the following code. This code assumes that you've created a constructor for the Page1 class that takes a string as the single parameter.

```
Page1 p1 = new Page1("This too shall pass.");
                          ↑
                Use the custom constructor.
NavigationService ns = NavigationService.GetNavigationService( this );
ns.Navigate( p1 );
```

Figure 14-15 shows a complete program using this method.

```
<Page x:Class="CustomConstructor.Window1"... >                    Window1.xaml
    <Grid>
        <Button Click="Button_Click">Click Me</Button>
    </Grid>
</Page>
```

```
public partial class Window1 : Page                              Window1.xaml.cs
{
    public Window1() { InitializeComponent(); }

    private void Button_Click( object sender, RoutedEventArgs e )
    {
        Page1 p1 = new Page1( "This too shall pass." );
        NavigationService ns = NavigationService.GetNavigationService( this );
        ns.Navigate( p1 );
    }
}
```

```
<Page x:Class="CustomConstructor.Page1" ... Title="Page1">        Page1.xaml
    <Grid>
        <TextBlock Name="tb"></TextBlock>
    </Grid>
</Page>
```

```
public partial class Page1 : Page                                Page1.xaml.cs
{
    public Page1() { InitializeComponent(); }

    public Page1( string inputString)             Custom
    {                                             Constructor
        InitializeComponent();
        tb.Text = inputString;
    }
}
```

Figure 14-15. *You can use a custom constructor to pass data to a Page.*

Figure 14-16 shows screenshots of the running program produced by the code. The string "This too shall pass." was passed to Page1 in the constructor.

Figure 14-16. *The program using the custom constructor for the Page*

■ **Note** If you create a custom constructor for your Page class, make sure the first thing it does is call the InitializeComponent method, which is what the default constructor does.

A second way to pass data to the target page is to use the overloaded form of the Navigate method shown here. Instead of taking just a reference to the target page object, it also takes a second parameter of type object. You can use this to pass in whatever custom data structure you want.

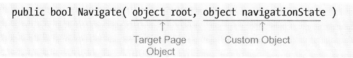

On the other end, to use the custom data object you've passed in, you must implement an event handler for the LoadCompleted event.

Getting Data Back from a Page

You've now seen how to pass data to a Page. Sometimes, however, you need to get data back from a Page. WPF has a special type of Page designed just for that—called a PageFunction.

The PageFunction class is a generic class, where you specify the type of the object it should return. If you're not completely comfortable with C# generics, don't worry; the Visual Studio template takes care of most of the details. (You also might want to pick up a copy of *Illustrated C# 2010*, also published by Apress.)

To add a PageFunction to your project using Visual Studio, do the following:

- Click the Project menu, and select the Add Page menu item. This brings up the Add New Item dialog box.

- From the Templates section of this dialog box, select the Page Function (WPF) template.

- Enter a name for your PageFunction in the Name text box.

- Click the Add button, which adds the new PageFunction class to your project.

A PageFunction must return a value of a specific type. By default, the Visual Studio Page Function template sets the return type of the newly created PageFunction to String. (String is the .NET type name for the C# string type. They're the same class.) It does this by assigning the value String to the TypeArguments attribute. The String class is in the System namespace, which is declared as the sys prefix.

Figure 14-17 shows the parts of the markup file and the code-behind that set the return type. If you want your PageFunction to use a different return type, you must change it in these two places and fix up the namespace declaration accordingly.

```
<PageFunction ...
    x:Class="UsingPageFunction.UserInputPageFunction"
    xmlns:sys="clr-namespace:System;assembly=mscorlib"   ←——— The Type's Namespace
    x:TypeArguments="sys:String">
    ...
</PageFunction>                    The Type to
                                   Be Returned
```

```
public partial class UserInputPageFunction : PageFunction<String>
{
    public UserInputPageFunction() { InitializeComponent(); }
    ...                                               The Type to
}                                                     Be Returned
```

Figure 14-17. *The declaration of the PageFunction*

The PageFunction must also have code that returns a value of the given type. To return a value, you must use the PageMethod's OnReturn method to return an object of the ReturnEventArgs<T> type, where T is the type of the object returned by the PageFunction. For example, the following line of code returns a string:

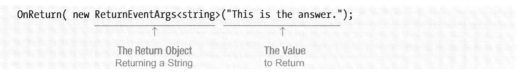

Once you have the PageFunction class set up, you need to do several things in the page from which you're going to navigate. Since the Navigate method is asynchronous, you need to write and register an event handler that will be called when the PageFunction returns its value. The second parameter of the event handler is a bit different from you've seen previously.

- The second parameter must be of type ReturnEventArgs<T>, again, where T is the type being returned.

- The actual value returned is in the Result property of the second parameter.

```
private void handleInput( object sender, ReturnEventArgs<string> e )
{                                                              ↑
                                                          The Generic Type
    string stringReturned = (string) e.Result;
                                       ↑
                               The Returned Value
```

To navigate to the page, you must do the following three things, as shown in the code shown next. This code assumes that the name of your PageFunction class is UserInputPageFunction.

1. Create an instance of your PageFunction class.

2. Attach the event handler to the Return event of the class instance so that when that event is raised, the handler will be called.

3. Call the Navigate method of the NavigationService that is managing the navigation for the current page from which you're navigating.

```
UserInputPageFunction uiPageFunction = new UserInputPageFunction();
uiPageFunction.Return += handleInput;
this.NavigationService.Navigate( uiPageFunction );
```

Figure 14-18 shows screenshots of the running program, and the code in Figure 14-19 puts together all the pieces.

Figure 14-18. *Navigating to a PageFunction that returns a string to the calling page*

```
<Page x:Class="UsingPageFunction.Window1" ...
    WindowTitle="PageFunction" WindowHeight="140" WindowWidth="200">
    <StackPanel>
        <Button Click="Button_Click" Margin="5">Get Data From Page</Button>
        <TextBox Name="textBox" Margin="5"></TextBox>
    </StackPanel>
</Page>
```
                                                                    Window1.xaml

```
public partial class Window1 : Page
{
    public Window1() { InitializeComponent(); }

    private void Button_Click( object sender, RoutedEventArgs e )          Create and Call
    {                                                                      the PageFunction
        UserInputPageFunction uiPageFunction = new UserInputPageFunction();
        uiPageFunction.Return += handlePageFunctionInput;
        this.NavigationService.Navigate( uiPageFunction );
    }

    private void handlePageFunctionInput( object sender, ReturnEventArgs<string> e )
    {
        string stringReturned = (string) e.Result;
        if ( stringReturned != null )                      Use the Generic
            textBox.Text = stringReturned;              ReturnEventArgs Parameter
    }
}                       Get the Value from
                        the Result Member                  Window1.xaml.cs
```

```
<PageFunction ...
    x:Class="UsingPageFunction.UserInputPageFunction"
    xmlns:sys="clr-namespace:System;assembly=mscorlib"      The Type to
    x:TypeArguments="sys:String"                            Be Returned
    Title="UserInputPageFunction">
    <StackPanel>
        <TextBox Name="pfTextBox" Margin="5"></TextBox>
        <Button Margin="5" Click="Button_Click">Return Data</Button>
    </StackPanel>
</PageFunction>
```
                                                        UserInputPageFunction.xaml

```
public partial class UserInputPageFunction : PageFunction<String>
{
    public UserInputPageFunction() { InitializeComponent(); }
                                                                PageFunction Is
    private void Button_Click( object sender, RoutedEventArgs e )   a Generic Type
    {
        string returnValue = pfTextBox.Text;
        OnReturn( new ReturnEventArgs<string>( returnValue ) );
    }
}
```
                                                        UserInputPageFunction.xaml.cs

Figure 14-19. *Code implementing and navigating to a PageFunction*

XAML Browser Applications

At the beginning of the chapter I introduced XAML browser applications. As you probably remember, these applications, also called *XBAPs*, don't run as their own stand-alone executable programs. Instead, they must be run (*hosted*) inside a web browser, such as Internet Explorer or Firefox.

The following are some of the important characteristics of XBAPs:

- Like the stand-alone navigation programs, they offer a simple navigation paradigm that's easy and intuitive. This can be ideal for people who aren't comfortable running computer programs but know how to surf the Web.

- XBAPs run in Internet Explorer and Firefox. However, they are *Windows programs*, not web applications, so they must be run on a Windows computer running .NET 3.0 or above.

- From a developer's standpoint, the navigation API for XBAPs is the same API we've been using throughout this chapter.

- XBAPs are easier to deploy than standard Windows programs—using a technology called ClickOnce deployment.

- XBAPs run in partial trust mode and hence have their functionality limited for security reasons. This means that not all the API calls that are valid in a stand-alone page navigation program can run in an XBAP!

Creating an XBAP Application

Visual Studio provides a standard template for XBAPs. It's called the WPF Browser Application template. To create an XBAP project, do the following:

1. In Visual Studio click on File ➤ New ➤ Project, which pops up the New Project window.

2. In the Project Types panel of the New Project window, select Windows.

3. In the Templates panel, select WPF Browser Application, and fill in the Name text box. (Use the name FirstXBAP if you want to create and run the next example.)

4. Click the OK button, and Visual Studio prepares the project for you.

From here, you can use the API you have been using throughout this chapter. When you compile your program, the compiler produces three files in the output directory, which together make up the program. All three are required to run the application.

If, for example, you created an XBAP program called *FirstXBAP*, the names of the three files would be the following:

- FirstXBAP.exe: This file has the CIL code for the application. (CIL code is the *Common Intermediate Language* code that makes up .NET executables.)

- FirstXBAP.exe.manifest: This file has metadata about the application.

- FirstXBAP.xbap: This file contains the application deployment information.

Deploying and Running

With XBAPs, you don't need to perform a standard installation of your program. Instead, you "publish" the application to a location where the user will browse to it. When the user points his or her browser at the XBAP file at that location, the browser downloads the application into its cache and displays its first page. This process is much more user friendly than the standard program installation procedure.

To try this for yourself, do the following:

1. Create a program called FirstXBAP as described in the previous steps.

2. Add two new pages—Page2.xaml and Page3.xaml.

3. Duplicate the first Hyperlink example program of the chapter into the three pages in the FirstXBAP project.

When you compile and run the project from the IDE, Visual Studio opens a new browser window and starts up the application in it.

Running the application from Visual Studio, however, isn't the way your end users are going to be running the program. Instead, most likely you'll publish the program to a network share or to a virtual directory. The users will then use their browsers and browse to that location.

As a simple example, publish the program to a location on your hard drive by doing the following:

1. Create a folder such as C:\Temp\Test on your hard drive.

2. In Visual Studio click Build ➤ Publish FirstXBAP.

3. In the Publish Wizard window, click the Browse button to browse to the folder you created, and click the Finish button.

Now that the program is published, start a web browser, and browse to the application by putting the address of the XBAP file into the address line of your browser: `C:\Temp\Test\FirstXBAP.xbap`. Make sure you point at the file with the `.xbap` extension, and not one of the other files. The browser will automatically load the application and run it. Figure 14-20 shows screenshots of the results.

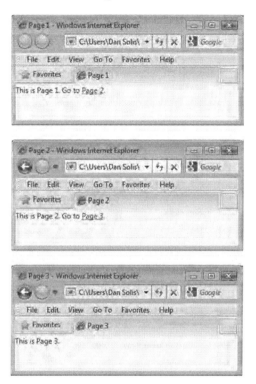

Figure 14-20. *The FirstXBAP program*

Summary

Web browsers use a different navigation paradigm than standard Windows programs have traditionally used. The browser paradigm is characterized by three things: the user is always on a single page, the user can move to another page using hyperlinks, and the user can use the browser's Back and Forward buttons to move backward and forward through the sequence of pages they've visited.

WPF introduces this browser navigation paradigm, called *page navigation*, to Windows programs in two forms. One form consists of a stand-alone, executable program with built-in Back and Forward buttons, and the other, called an XBAP, must be hosted by a browser.

The following are some important things to remember about these page navigation programs:

- Both types of program must be run on a Windows machine with .NET 3.0 or higher installed.

- Although XBAPs must be run on a Windows machine, they can be hosted by major web browsers such as Internet Explorer and Firefox.

- The WPF programming API is the same for both forms of program.

- XBAPs are distributed using the ClickOnce deployment technology, which makes them very simple for users to install.

- As with HTML programming, page navigation programs allow you to pass information from the current page to the next page.

Page navigation programs are ideal for programs that need a simple, familiar interface. In particular, XBAPs are especially well suited for nontechnical audiences, since they don't require the user to perform an explicit multistep installation process.

CHAPTER 15

∎∎∎

More Data Binding

Data Templates

In Chapter 8 you saw how to bind a control to a collection of data objects. In Chapter 13 you saw how to replace the default appearance of a control with an appearance of your own design. In this chapter, I'll combine and extend these two concepts and show you how to specify the appearance of *data* you've mapped to a control.

In the example at the end of Chapter 8, I mapped a set of data about four people, to a ComboBox control. For the first example in this chapter, I've modified that program so that the ComboBox is a now ListBox and is at the left of the window, as shown in Figure 15-1.

When the user selects an item in the ListBox, the panel to the right of the ListBox displays the information about that person. The following are some things to notice about the ListBox:

- I didn't change the template for the ListBox, so it uses the default ListBox ControlTemplate, as illustrated in the drawing at the right of the figure. The default template simply produces a rectangle around the elements in the list.

- The elements in the ListBox consist of the FirstName strings corresponding to the four elements in the collection bound to the ListBox.

Figure 15-1. *A ListBox with a set of data bound to it*

The following is the markup for the program:

```
<StackPanel Orientation="Horizontal">
    <ListBox Name="listPeople" SelectedIndex="0" Margin="5" Padding="8"
            DisplayMemberPath="FirstName" Width="80"/>

                        The Data to Display
    <StackPanel Name="sp" Margin="10, 5" DataContext=
                "{Binding ElementName=listPeople, Path=SelectedItem}">
        <Label Name="lblFName" FontWeight="Bold"/>
        <Label Name="lblAge"/>
        <Label Name="lblColor"/>
    </StackPanel>
</StackPanel>
```

You can make the appearance of the ListBox a bit more interesting by replacing the default ListBox control template with one of your own, as shown in Figure 15-2. In this case, the ListBox has a thick blue border, enclosing a thin white border, and the Background is set to pink. The drawing at the right of the figure illustrates the new custom template.

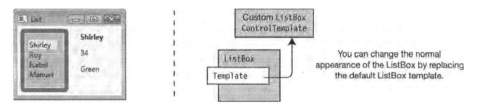

Figure 15-2. *The ListBox with a fancier appearance*

The following is the markup for this modified program. It declares a ControlTemplate called ListTemplate, which is applied to the ListBox control. The Binding in the StackPanel at the bottom binds the Labels at the right of the window to the selected item in the ListBox. You can ignore those, since there's nothing new about them; in this chapter you're concentrating on binding the data to controls.

```
                        Declare the Control Template
                                    ↓
<Window.Resources>
   <ControlTemplate x:Key="ListTemplate">
      <Border BorderBrush="SteelBlue" BorderThickness="7"
              CornerRadius="3" Background="Pink">
         <Border BorderBrush="White" BorderThickness="1" Padding="5,10,10,10">
            <Grid>
                <ItemsPresenter TextBlock.Foreground="Black"/>
            </Grid>
         </Border>
      </Border>
   </ControlTemplate>
</Window.Resources>
<StackPanel Orientation="Horizontal">

   <ListBox Name="listPeople" SelectedIndex="0" Margin="5" Padding="8"
            DisplayMemberPath="FirstName" Width="80"
            Template="{StaticResource ListTemplate}"/>
                                    ↑
                        Apply the Custom Template

   <StackPanel Name="sp" Margin="10, 5" DataContext=
               "{Binding ElementName=listPeople, Path=SelectedItem}">
      <Label Name="lblFName" FontWeight="Bold"/>
      <Label Name="lblAge"/>
      <Label Name="lblColor"/>
   </StackPanel>
</StackPanel>
```

Figure 15-3 shows the C# code for these two programs. There's nothing new so far, so if it's not sounding familiar, you might want to review Chapter 8.

- The Person class represents the information about a single person. You can place this class in a separate file or place it in the Window1.xaml.cs file.

- The Window1 class performs the following actions:

  - It creates the collection of Person objects.

  - It binds the array of Person objects to the Listbox by assigning to the ListBox's ItemsSource property.

  - It sets the bindings to the three Labels at the right of the ListBox.

The DataContext is set on the StackPanel in the markup file. Since the Binding statements don't include a Source setting, the system searches up the tree at runtime and finds the DataContext in the StackPanel.

```
class Person
{
   public string FirstName    { get; set; }
   public int    Age          { get; set; }
   public string FavoriteColor { get; set; }

   public Person( string fName, int age, string color )
   {
      FirstName     = fName;
      Age           = age;
      FavoriteColor = color;
   }
}

public partial class Window1 : Window
{
   public Window1()
   {
      InitializeComponent();

      Person[] people = { new Person( "Shirley", 34, "Green" ),
                           new Person( "Roy",     36, "Blue"  ),
                           new Person( "Isabel",  25, "Orange"),
                           new Person( "Manuel",  27, "Red"   ) };

      listPeople.ItemsSource = people;

      Binding nameBinding = new Binding( "FirstName" );
      lblFName.SetBinding( ContentProperty, nameBinding );
      Binding ageBinding = new Binding( "Age" );
      lblAge.SetBinding( ContentProperty, ageBinding );
      Binding colorBinding = new Binding( "FavoriteColor" );
      lblColor.SetBinding( ContentProperty, colorBinding );
   }
}
```

Create an array of Person objects.

Bind the array to the ListBox.

Bind the DataContext to the three Labels at the right of the ListBox.

Figure 15-3. *The C# code for the program with the ListBox*

In the modified program, I made the control a bit fancier by replacing the ControlTemplate, but the data listed in the ListBox is still just plain strings. There's another type of template, however, called a DataTemplate, which you can use to specify the appearance of the data displayed by a control. Some important things to know about data templates are the following:

- Like control templates, data templates are usually declared as resources higher in the element tree.

- You can apply data templates to ContentControls or ItemsControls. The name of the property to which you assign a DataTemplate depends on whether the control is a ContentControl or an ItemsControl. Figure 15-4 Illustrates these properties.

  – For ContentControls: Assign a DataTemplate to the ContentTemplate property.

  – For ItemsControls: Assign a DataTemplate to the ItemTemplate property.

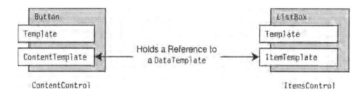

Figure 15-4. *In ContentControls, a DataTemplate is assigned to the ContentTemplate property. In ItemsControls, they're assigned to the ItemsTemplate property.*

You can use data templates to make the items in the ListBox a bit fancier and more informative. In the screenshot in Figure 15-5, I've gone back to the default ListBox ControlTemplate, so it no longer has the thick border around the ListBox, but more noticeable than that, I've added a DataTemplate that enhances the display of the items in the ListBox. This DataTemplate formats the item content in the following ways:

- It surrounds the data item with a blue Border.

- Inside the Border it creates a 2 ×2 Grid. The person's name is placed in the first row in the first column. Their age is placed in the second row in the first column. The person's favorite color fills a rectangle spanning both rows of the second column.

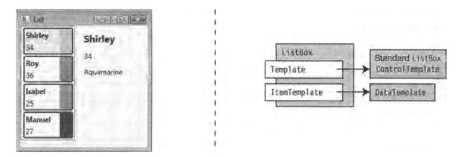

Figure 15-5. *The ListBox with a DataTemplate that enhances the appearance of the ListBox items*

To declare a DataTemplate in a Resources section, do the following:

1. Insert a DataTemplate element, giving it a Key, just as you would do with a ControlTemplate.

```
<Window.Resources>
    <DataTemplate x:Key="NiceFormat">
                        ↑
                    Lookup Key

        ...
    </DataTemplate>
</Window.Resources>
```

2. Include the layout code between the DataTemplate element tags.

3. Use the Binding markup extension to bind layout elements in the DataTemplate to fields in the DataContext.

```
<TextBlock FontWeight="Bold" Grid.Row="0" Grid.Column="0"
        Text="{Binding FirstName}" Padding="2"/>
                  ↑
        Bind to a field in the DataContext.
```

The following is the markup for the new version:

```
                            Declare the control template.
<Window.Resources> _____↓_____
    <DataTemplate   x:Key="NiceFormat">
        <Border Margin="1" BorderBrush="Blue"
                BorderThickness="2" CornerRadius="2">
          <Grid>
            <Grid.RowDefinitions>
                <RowDefinition/><RowDefinition/>
            </Grid.RowDefinitions>
            <Grid.ColumnDefinitions>
                <ColumnDefinition Width="60"/><ColumnDefinition Width="20"/>
            </Grid.ColumnDefinitions>
            <TextBlock FontWeight="Bold" Grid.Row="0" Grid.Column="0"
                       Text="{Binding FirstName}" Padding="2"/>
                       _____
                                  ↑
                       Bind to a field in the DataContext.
            <Rectangle Grid.Row="0" Grid.Column="1" Grid.RowSpan="2"
                       Fill="{Binding FavoriteColor}"/>
                       _____
                                  ↑
                       Bind to a field in the DataContext.
            <TextBlock Padding="2" Grid.Row="1" Grid.Column="0"
                       Text="{Binding Age}"/>
                       _____
                                  ↑
                       Bind to a field in the DataContext.
          </Grid>
        </Border>
    </DataTemplate>
</Window.Resources>

<StackPanel Orientation="Horizontal">
    <ListBox Name="listPeople" SelectedIndex="0" VerticalAlignment="Top"
             ItemTemplate="{StaticResource NiceFormat}"/>
             _____
                                  ↑
                      Apply the data template.
    <StackPanel Orientation="Vertical" Name="sp" Margin="10, 5"
                DataContext="{Binding ElementName=listPeople, Path=SelectedItem}">
        <Label Name="lblFName" FontWeight="Bold" FontSize="16"/>
        <Label Name="lblAge"/>
        <Label Name="lblColor"/>
    </StackPanel>
</StackPanel>
```

For comparison, Figure 15-6 shows the various permutations of the ListBox template and the content template in the example.

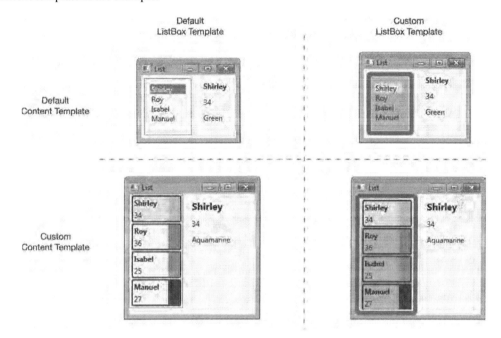

Figure 15-6. *The combinations of the ListBox template and the content template used in the examples*

Views

When you create a binding, WPF creates an object called a *view*, which represents the collection of objects, and presents that collection to the target control. A view is an object of the CollectionView class, and it manages the logical representation of the data. It can perform the following functions:

- Keep track of which item is the "current" item in the collection

- Perform filtering—*logically* eliminating some data members, based on some criterion

- Sort the data objects based on the values of specified properties

- Partition the data objects into different groups

Figure 15-7 illustrates the view's position in the binding, between the source and the target.

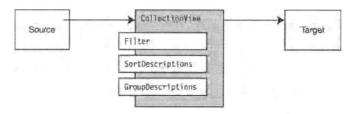

Figure 15-7. *A view is between the source and the target in a binding.*

By default, the view doesn't perform any filtering, sorting, or partitioning of the data. If you want the view to perform these tasks, you must retrieve a reference to the view attached to the binding. To do this, use the static CollectionViewSource.GetDefaultView method, as shown in the following code. Notice that you need to cast the result to the CollectionView type.

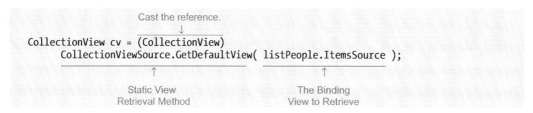

Filtering in a View

By default, the view always gets all the data objects from the source. To have it filter out certain objects from the collection, and pass only the nonfiltered items to the target, you must attach a *predicate method* to the view's Filter property, as shown in Figure 15-8.

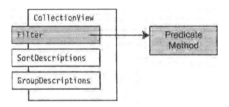

Figure 15-8. *The predicate method is applied to the view by assigning it to the view's Filter property.*

A *predicate method* is a Boolean method that determines whether a particular item is a member of a group. From mathematics, a *predicate* is a Boolean function that returns true if an element is a member of a particular set and false otherwise. (In mathematics it's also known as a *characteristic function*.)

- For a view to perform filtering, you must provide it with a predicate method that specifies whether a particular data object should be included or excluded.

- The predicate method must take a single parameter, of type object.

The following code shows a predicate that takes as a parameter an object of type Person and returns true if the age of the person is less than 30. Otherwise, it returns false.

```
                         Must Be of Type Object
                                  ↓
private bool IsLessThan30( object obj )
{
    return (obj as Person).Age < 30;
}              ↑
        Cast to the actual type.
```

To attach the predicate to the view, assign it to the view's Filter property, as shown in the following code. The first statement retrieves a reference to the view, and the second assigns the predicate.

```
CollectionView cv = (CollectionView)
    CollectionViewSource.GetDefaultView( listPeople.ItemsSource );

cv.Filter = IsLessThan30;
              ↑
Assign the predicate to the view.
```

Figure 15-9 shows screenshots of a program that can apply two filters to the data objects. The Less Than 30 button has the view filter out objects with an Age property greater than 30. The Greater Than 30 button filters out objects with an Age value not greater than or equal to 30. (There are two Roy objects—one with an age of 19 and the other with an age of 36.) The button labeled Default removes filtering and shows all five data items.

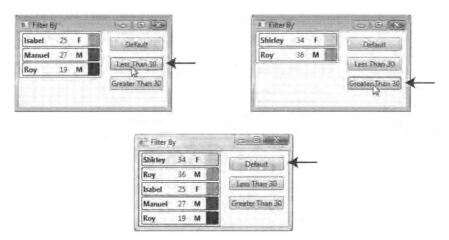

Figure 15-9. *The view can selectively pass objects to the target by filtering out those that don't meet the predicate's criteria.*

The code for this program consists of the usual files plus the code for the Person class. The code for the Person class is the following. Notice that I've added a property called Sex to the Person class. I'll use this new version of the class through the next few sections.

```
class Person
{
    public string FirstName    { get; set; }
    public int     Age         { get; set; }
    public string FavoriteColor { get; set; }
    public string Sex          { get; set; }      ← New Property

    public Person( string fName, int age, string color, string sex )
    {
        FirstName     = fName;
        Age           = age;
        FavoriteColor = color;
        Sex           = sex;
    }
}
```

The code-behind for the program is the following. The two predicates are at the bottom of the listing.

```
public partial class Window1 : Window
{
    CollectionView cv;          // Store the view.

    public Window1()
    {
        InitializeComponent();

        Person[] people = { new Person( "Shirley", 34, "Aquamarine", "F"),
                             new Person( "Roy",    36, "GoldenRod",  "M"),
                             new Person( "Isabel", 25, "DarkGray",   "F"),
                             new Person( "Manuel", 27, "Red",        "M"),
                             new Person( "Roy",    19, "Blue",       "M") };

        listPeople.ItemsSource = people;
        cv = (CollectionView)
                CollectionViewSource.GetDefaultView( listPeople.ItemsSource );
    }

    private void Default_Click( object sender, RoutedEventArgs e )
    {
        cv.Filter = null;
    }

    private void AgeLessThanThirty_Click( object sender, RoutedEventArgs e )
    {
        cv.Filter = IsLessThan30;
    }

    private void AgeGreaterThanThirty_Click( object sender, RoutedEventArgs e )
    {
        cv.Filter = IsGreaterThan30;
    }

    private bool IsLessThan30( object obj )              // Predicate
    {
        return (obj as Person).Age < 30;
    }

    private bool IsGreaterThan30( object obj )           // Predicate
    {
        return (obj as Person).Age >= 30;
    }
}
```

The following XAML is the program's markup. Most of this XAML will remain the same throughout the next few examples. Only the marked section will change.

```xaml
<Window x:Class="PersonList.Window1"
    xmlns="http://schemas.microsoft.com/winfx/2006/xaml/presentation"
    xmlns:x="http://schemas.microsoft.com/winfx/2006/xaml"
    Title="Filter By" Height="160" Width="270">
    <Window.Resources>

        <DataTemplate x:Key="NiceFormat">
            <Border Margin="1" BorderBrush="Blue"
                    BorderThickness="1" CornerRadius="2">
                <Grid>
                    <Grid.RowDefinitions><RowDefinition/></Grid.RowDefinitions>
                    <Grid.ColumnDefinitions>
                        <ColumnDefinition Width="60"/>
                        <ColumnDefinition Width="20"/>
                        <ColumnDefinition Width="30"/>
                        <ColumnDefinition Width="20"/>
                    </Grid.ColumnDefinitions>
                    <TextBlock Grid.Column="0" FontWeight="Bold" Padding="2"
                                Text="{Binding FirstName}"/>
                    <TextBlock Grid.Column="1" Padding="2"
                                Text="{Binding Age}"/>
                    <TextBlock Grid.Column="2" Padding="2"
                                HorizontalAlignment="Center"
                                Text="{Binding Sex}" FontWeight="Bold"/>
                    <Rectangle Grid.Column="3"
                                Fill="{Binding FavoriteColor}"/>
                </Grid>
            </Border>
        </DataTemplate>

    </Window.Resources>
    <StackPanel Orientation="Horizontal">

        <ListBox Name="listPeople" SelectedIndex="0"
                VerticalAlignment="Top"
                ItemTemplate="{StaticResource NiceFormat}"/>
        <StackPanel Orientation="Vertical" Name="sp" Margin="10, 5">
            <Button Click="Default_Click" Margin="5">Default</Button>
            <Button Click="AgeLessThanThirty_Click"
                    Margin="5">Less Than 30</Button>
            <Button Click="AgeGreaterThanThirty_Click"
                    Margin="5">Greater Than 30</Button>
        </StackPanel>

    </StackPanel>
</Window>
```

The Part That Will Change in the Upcoming Examples

Sorting in a View

A view can also sort the data objects based on the values of the fields. To do this, you create
SortDescription objects and add them to the SortDescriptions property of the view, as illustrated in
Figure 15-10.

Each SortDescription object specifies a property on which to sort, and the direction in which to
sort—i.e., ascending or descending. The view then presents the objects to the target control in the
specified sort order.

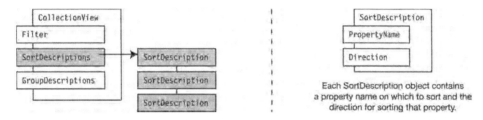

Figure 15-10. *The SortDescriptions property is a list of SortDescription objects.*

Figure 15-11 shows screenshots of the modified example program, which allows you to sort on
Name, Age, or Sex and Age.

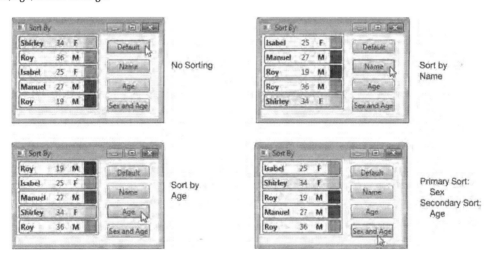

Figure 15-11. *Various sortings of the data objects*

The following is the portion of the markup that is different for this example:

```xml
<StackPanel Orientation="Horizontal">
    <ListBox Name="listPeople" SelectedIndex="0" VerticalAlignment="Top"
             ItemTemplate="{StaticResource NiceFormat}"/>
    <StackPanel Orientation="Vertical"  Name="sp" Margin="10, 5">
        <Button Click="Default_Click"     Margin="5">Default</Button>
        <Button Click="SortByName_Click" Margin="5">Name</Button>
        <Button Click="SortByAge_Click"  Margin="5">Age</Button>
        <Button Click="SortBySexAndAge_Click"  Margin="5">Sex and Age</Button>
    </StackPanel>
</StackPanel>
```

The code-behind for the program is the following. Notice that to sort by Sex and Age, I added two SortDescription objects to the SortDescriptions property.

```
using System.ComponentModel;  // Need this.

public partial class Window1 : Window
{
    CollectionView cv;          // Store the view.
    public Window1()
    {
        InitializeComponent();
        Person[] people = { new Person( "Shirley", 34, "Aquamarine", "F"),
                            new Person( "Roy",     36, "GoldenRod",  "M"),
                            new Person( "Isabel",  25, "DarkGray",   "F"),
                            new Person( "Manuel",  27, "Red",        "M"),
                            new Person( "Roy",     19, "Blue",       "M") };
        listPeople.ItemsSource = people;
        cv = (CollectionView)
                CollectionViewSource.GetDefaultView( listPeople.ItemsSource );
    }

    private void Default_Click( object sender, RoutedEventArgs e )
    { cv.SortDescriptions.Clear();  }

    private void SortByName_Click( object sender, RoutedEventArgs e )
    {
        cv.SortDescriptions.Clear();
        SortDescription sd =
            new SortDescription( "FirstName", ListSortDirection.Ascending );
        cv.SortDescriptions.Add( sd );
    }

    private void SortByAge_Click( object sender, RoutedEventArgs e )
    {
        cv.SortDescriptions.Clear();
        SortDescription sd =
            new SortDescription( "Age", ListSortDirection.Ascending );
        cv.SortDescriptions.Add( sd );
    }

    private void SortBySexAndAge_Click( object sender, RoutedEventArgs e )
    {
        cv.SortDescriptions.Clear();
        SortDescription sd1 =
                new SortDescription( "Sex", ListSortDirection.Ascending );
        SortDescription sd2 =
                new SortDescription( "Age", ListSortDirection.Ascending );
        cv.SortDescriptions.Add( sd1 );        ← Sort by Sex.
        cv.SortDescriptions.Add( sd2 );        ← Sort by Age.
    }
}
```

Grouping in a View

You can also have views group the data into logical groups, based on the values of properties. To specify how to group the data items, you add PropertyGroupDescriptor objects to the view's GroupDescriptions property, as shown in Figure 15-12.

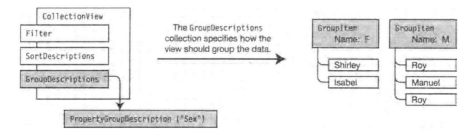

Figure 15-12. *The view can partition the data items into groups, according to the PropertyGroupDescription objects attached to its GroupDescription property.*

For example, the following code groups the data according to the Sex property of a Person item:

```
PropertyGroupDescription pgd = new PropertyGroupDescription( "Sex" );
cv.GroupDescriptions.Add( pgd );
```

The view then collects into a group, the data items with the same value for that property.

- Each group is assigned a GroupItem object.

- The Name property of each GroupItem object contains the value shared by all the members of the group.

For example, Figure 15-12 shows a view where the grouping is specified to be on the Sex property of the Person objects. The result is two groups, named F and M, since these are the two values that the data has for this field.

Setting the GroupDescriptions property of the view, however, isn't the only thing you need to do to display the groupings. Getting groupings to show up in the target requires an additional step.

The view can organize the data objects into groups, but the target container must know what to do with these groups and how to display them. For that, you need to set the GroupStyle property of the target control. The GroupStyle property allows you to specify such things as headers for groups and whether to hide a group if it has no members.

Figure 15-13 shows the structure of this architecture.

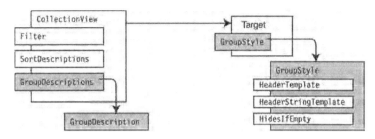

Figure 15-13. *The GroupStyle object attached to the target's GroupStyle property specifies how to display the group headers.*

When the program combines the GroupDescriptions in the view and the GroupStyle settings in the target, it produces headers for each group, as shown in Figure 15-14.

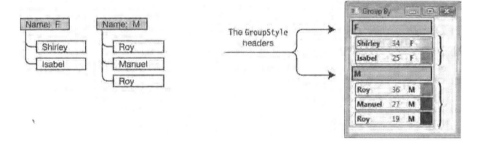

Figure 15-14. *The members of the groupings are displayed under the headers.*

Usually you'll add the GroupStyle specification in the markup rather than the code-behind and specify it as a DataTemplate, as shown in the following markup. Notice that it's listed inside the ListBox element. It's *very* important to notice in this markup that you must bind to the Name property of the GroupItem to get the text that's common to all the elements in group.

```
<ListBox Name="listPeople" SelectedIndex="0" VerticalAlignment="Top"
         ItemTemplate="{StaticResource NiceFormat}">
    <ListBox.GroupStyle>
        <GroupStyle>
            <GroupStyle.HeaderTemplate>
                <DataTemplate>
                    <Border BorderBrush="Blue" BorderThickness="2"
                            Background="LightGray" Margin="2">
                        <TextBlock Margin="2" FontSize="12" FontWeight="Bold"
                                   Text="{Binding Path=Name}"/>

                    </Border>

                </DataTemplate>                         Bind to the Name
            </GroupStyle.HeaderTemplate>         Property of the GroupItem
        </GroupStyle>
    </ListBox.GroupStyle>
</ListBox>
```

The following is the code-behind for the program:

```
public partial class Window1 : Window
{
    CollectionView cv;          // Store the view.

    public Window1()
    {
        InitializeComponent();

        Person[] people = { new Person( "Shirley", 34, "Aquamarine", "F"),
                            new Person( "Roy",     36, "GoldenRod",  "M"),
                            new Person( "Isabel",  25, "DarkGray",   "F"),
                            new Person( "Manuel",  27, "Red",        "M"),
                            new Person( "Roy",     19, "Blue",       "M")
                          };

        listPeople.ItemsSource = people;

        cv = (CollectionView)
                CollectionViewSource.GetDefaultView( listPeople.ItemsSource );

        PropertyGroupDescription pgd = new PropertyGroupDescription( "Sex" );
        cv.GroupDescriptions.Add( pgd );
    }
}
```

You can attach multiple `PropertyGroupDescription` objects to the view's `GroupDescriptions` property. The first one is the primary grouping, and each successive one is a subsidiary grouping of the ones above it.

For example, the following code adds more `Person` objects and adds another `PropertyGroupDescription` object, which specifies grouping by the favorite color. The primary grouping is on the `Sex` property, and those groups are subgrouped on the `FavoriteColor` property.

```
Person[] people = {
    new Person( "Shirley",34,"Red","F"),  new Person( "Roy",36,"Blue","M"),
    new Person( "Frank",25,"Yellow","M"), new Person( "Manuel",21,"Red","M"),
    new Person( "Amy",29,"Blue","F"),      new Person( "Roy",42,"Yellow","M"),
    new Person( "Isabel",30,"Red","F"),    new Person( "Sam",27,"Blue","M"),
    new Person( "Tom",19,"Yellow","M")  };

listPeople.ItemsSource = people;
cv = (CollectionView)
        CollectionViewSource.GetDefaultView( listPeople.ItemsSource );

PropertyGroupDescription pgd = new PropertyGroupDescription( "Sex" );
cv.GroupDescriptions.Add( pgd );
pgd = new PropertyGroupDescription( "FavoriteColor" );
cv.GroupDescriptions.Add( pgd );
```

Figure 15-15 shows screenshots of the data grouped on Sex and then on both Sex and FavoriteColor. The second list is longer because it contains the headers for the color groupings.

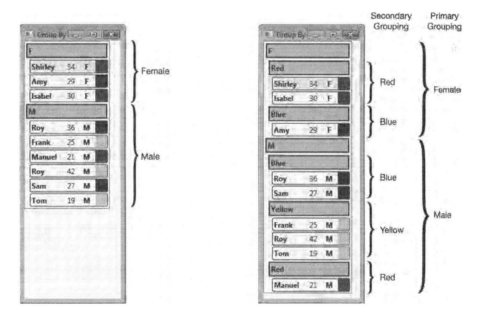

Figure 15-15. *Grouping on a single property and grouping on two properties*

Summary

Previously you learned about simple data binding, which allows you to bind data to a control. You also looked at control templates, which allow you to specify the appearance of a control. In this chapter, however, you saw how to specify the appearance of the *data* that is bound to a control using data templates.

In this chapter you also looked at view objects, which represent the data to the target control. Views allow a simple yet powerful way to do the following:

- You can filter the bound data objects so that only a subset of the items is presented to the target control.

- You can sort the objects based on any number of fields and present the resulting sequence to the target control.

- You can group the objects based on any number of fields and specify the format of the headers representing each group.

CHAPTER 16

■ ■ ■

Trees, Tabs, and Other Controls

The TreeView Control

The HierarchicalDataTemplate

Using Event Handlers with TreeViews

Binding Other Controls to a TreeView

The TabControl

The Calendar Control

The DatePicker Control

The DataGrid Control

In this chapter, I'll cover two important controls that weren't covered in the previous chapters: TreeView and TabControl. I'll also cover the three new controls included in WPF 4.0, which is scheduled for release shortly after the release of this text.

These new controls are the Calendar, DatePicker, and DataGrid classes. They were previously part of the WPF Toolkit, which is a downloadable collection of controls that Microsoft made available between the releases of WPF. The descriptions of these new controls is based on the Beta 1 release of WPF 4.0, which is quite stable, so there shouldn't be any differences between the descriptions given here and the final release versions.

The TreeView Control

The TreeView control is designed to represent hierarchical collections of data. Figure 16-1 shows an example of a TreeView control that has three top-level nodes and seven subnodes.

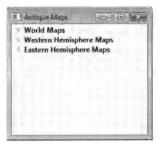 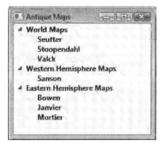

Figure 16-1. *The screenshots show an example of a two-level TreeView control. In the first screenshot, the top-level nodes are contracted. In the second screenshot, they're expanded.*

The two main classes for creating a tree view are the TreeView class and the TreeViewItem class, as shown in Figure 16-2.

- A tree control consists of a single TreeView object, which represents the tree.

- The nodes of the tree are represented by TreeViewItem objects, which are attached to the TreeView's Items property.

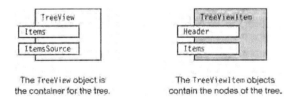

Figure 16-2. *The classes required for building a populated a tree are the TreeView class and the TreeViewItem class.*

The following are some important things to know about the TreeView and TreeViewItem classes:

- The TreeView object is a container that manages and displays a tree consisting of TreeViewItem objects. A TreeView object never represents a node or a subtree.

- The TreeView class is derived from ItemsControl and therefore gets its contents from either its Items property or its ItemsSource property. As you'll probably remember from Chapter 6, these properties have the following characteristics:

  - The Items property is a collection, internal to the TreeView, that contains the list of the top-level nodes of the tree. This is the default property, so when you place elements in the content part of the TreeView element, they're added to its Items property.

  - The ItemsSource property can contain a reference to an external collection of objects used to populate the tree. The collection must implement IEnumerable.

- TreeViewItem objects represent the nodes of the tree. Every node of the tree is represented by a TreeViewItem object, which can itself reference a list of TreeViewItem objects representing a subtree, and so forth.

- The TreeViewItem class is derived from HeaderedItemsControl and therefore, as you no doubt remember, has two important properties.

  - The Header contains a reference to the single item of content displayed by the node.

  - The Items property contains a list of the items to be used as a subtree. This is the default property, so when you place elements in the content part of a TreeViewItem element, they are added to the Items property. This is where you place TreeViewItems that represent subnodes or subtrees.

■ **Note** Remember that every TreeView tree has only a single TreeView element. Often people are initially confused by thinking that each subtree is itself a tree and should therefore be represented by another TreeView. Although this makes perfect sense, it's just not the way it's done in this case. Instead, all *subtrees* and *leaves* are represented by TreeViewItem objects.

In the simplest case, where you know the structure of your tree beforehand, you can create the tree explicitly, in the XAML. You do this by inserting a TreeView element and then adding the TreeViewItem elements to it, as shown in the markup in Figure 16-3. Notice the following about the markup:

- There is a single TreeView object, which contains the three TreeViewItem objects that make up the highest level of the tree. The TreeView has the FontWeight property set to Bold, which is inherited by all the nodes in the TreeView.

- The Header properties of the TreeViewItems contain the text displayed by the nodes in the TreeView.

- The Content part of the second TreeViewItem contains another TreeViewItem, which becomes its subnode.

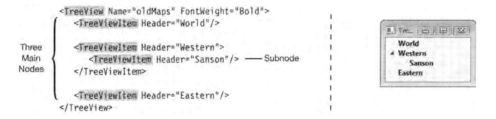

Figure 16-3. *A simple TreeView with three main nodes and a subnode*

Figure 16-4 represents the tree whose output is shown in Figure 16-1. Notice that it consists of one TreeView object and ten TreeViewItem objects.

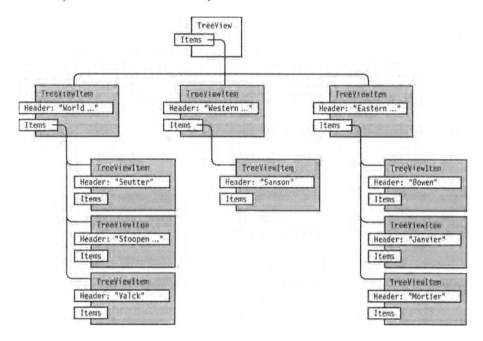

Figure 16-4. *A TreeView control contains a hierarchy of TreeViewItem objects.*

The HierarchicalDataTemplate

In the TreeViews you've seen so far, the structure of the tree was known beforehand and was specified explicitly in the XAML. When this is the case, the items are placed in the TreeView's Items collection.

Another way to build a TreeView, however, is to assign a collection of data objects to its ItemsSource property. When WPF renders the tree, it goes through each item in the list and creates a top-level node for it.

For example, Figure 16-5 shows the structure of a TreeView where a List<> of three objects of type WorldRegion (which I'll define shortly) is assigned to the ItemsSource property of the TreeView.

- Each WorldRegion object contains a string property with the name of a region of the world. It also has a property called Maps, which is a List<> of MapInfo objects.

- Each MapInfo object contains the information about a particular antique map.

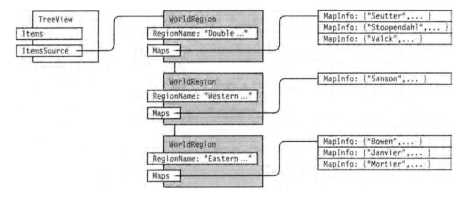

Figure 16-5. *A data structure attached to the ItemsSource property of the TreeView*

For this program's markup, I'll start simple, with just the TreeView inside a Grid, as shown in the following lines:

```
<Grid >
    <TreeView Name="oldMaps" Grid.Column="0" FontWeight="Bold"/>
</Grid>
```

The following is the code for the WorldRegion and MapInfo classes. To re-create the program, do the following:

1. Create this class in a separate file called MapInfo.cs.

2. Change the namespace name from TreeBound to whatever namespace is used in your Window1.xaml.cs file for this project.

MapInfo class objects store the information about a particular map. WorldRegion objects consist of a RegionName property and a Maps property, which is a reference to a list of MapInfo objects.

```
namespace TreeBound
{
    class WorldRegion
    {
        public string RegionName  { get; set; }
        public List<MapInfo> Maps { get; set; }

        public WorldRegion( string name )
        {
            Maps = new List<MapInfo>();
            RegionName = name;
        }
    }

    class MapInfo
    {
        public string LastName    { get; set; }
        public string FirstName   { get; set; }
        public string Title       { get; set; }
        public string Year        { get; set; }
        public string Description { get; set; }
        public Uri Picture        { get; set; }

        public MapInfo( string ln, string fn, string title, string year,
                        string desc, string pictUri )
        {
            LastName    = ln;
            FirstName   = fn;
            Title       = title;
            Year        = year;
            Description = desc;

            string uriString = string.Format( "Images/{0}", pictUri );
            Picture = new Uri( uriString, UriKind.Relative );
        }
    }
}
```

The following is the code-behind for this example. The constructor first creates a new, empty list of WorldRegion objects. It then calls the CreateMapsDataStructure method, which creates and populates the array of WorldRegion objects stored in the class's mapRegions field.

```
public partial class Window1 : Window
{
    List<WorldRegion> mapRegions;

    public Window1()
    {
        InitializeComponent();

        mapRegions = new List<WorldRegion>();
        CreateMapsDataStructure();
        oldMaps.ItemsSource = mapRegions;
    }

    private void CreateMapsDataStructure()
    {
        WorldRegion region = new WorldRegion( "Double Hemisphere" );
        region.Maps.Add( new MapInfo( "Seutter", "Mattheus",
                "Diversi Globi Terr-Aquei",
                "c. 1730", "Double hemisphere", "Seutter.jpg" ) );
        region.Maps.Add( new MapInfo( "Stoopendahl", "Daniel", "Orbis Terrarum",
                "c. 1680", "Double hemisphere", "Stoopendahl.jpg" ) );
        region.Maps.Add( new MapInfo( "Valck", "Gerard", "Mappe Monde",
                "c. 1700", "Double Hemisphere", "Valck.jpg" ) );
        mapRegions.Add( region );

        region = new WorldRegion(     "Western Hemisphere" );
        region.Maps.Add( new MapInfo( "Sanson", "Nicholas",
                "California as an Island",
                "c. 1657", "Calif. as an island", "Sanson.jpg" ) );
        mapRegions.Add( region );

        region = new WorldRegion(     "Eastern Hemisphere" );
        region.Maps.Add( new MapInfo( "Bowen", "Emanuel", "Spain and Portugal",
                "c. 1752", "Spain and Portugal", "Stoopendahl.jpg" ) );
        region.Maps.Add( new MapInfo( "Janvier", "Jean",
                "Les Isles Britanniques",
                "c. 1762", "The British Isles", "Janvier.jpg" ) );
        region.Maps.Add( new MapInfo( "Mortier", "Pierre",
                "Les Isles Britanniques",
                "c. 1738", "The British Isles", "Stoopendahl.jpg" ) );
        mapRegions.Add( region );
    }
}
```

Figure 16-6 shows the output from this program. As you can see, there are two problems with this output. The first problem is that instead of printing the names of the regions, it prints the class name of the elements in the collection. The second problem is that it doesn't appear to be aware that these three nodes contain subnodes.

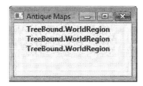

Figure 16-6. *The TreeView doesn't know how to display WorldRegion objects, so it just displays their class name.*

The reason for the first problem is that, although the TreeView knows it has a list of three WorldRegion objects, it doesn't know how to display them. When this happens, the default action is to call the object's ToString method. In this case, the ToString method just returns the class name.

In Chapter 15, you learned that DataTemplates are templates where you can specify how a certain data type should be displayed. This seems like an ideal place to use one, since you can define a DataTemplate for the WorldRegion type, thereby telling the program how to display objects of this type.

The following markup adds a DataTemplate that specifies that a WorldRegion object should be displayed as a TextBlock bound to the RegionName property of the WorldRegion object. Since WorldRegion is a type defined in the local project, you need to declare a prefix for the local namespace. In my project, the name of the namespace is TreeBound—so that's what the local prefix is bound to. You should use whatever is the name of your project's namespace.

```
<Window x:Class="TreeBound.Window1" ...
        xmlns:local="clr-namespace:TreeBound">
                              ↑
                      Project's Namespace
<Window.Resources>
    <DataTemplate DataType="{x:Type local:WorldRegion}">
        <TextBlock Text="{Binding Path=RegionName}" Foreground="Gray"/>
    </DataTemplate>
</Window.Resources>
<Grid>
    <TreeView Name="oldMaps" Grid.Column="0" FontWeight="Bold"/></Grid>
</Window>
```

Figure 16-7 shows the output from the modified program. This is an improvement, in that it now shows the top-level nodes—but it's still not aware of the subnodes.

Figure 16-7. *The tree displaying the top-level nodes but not the subnodes*

To address this issue, WPF provides a special type of data template called a HierarchicalDataTemplate, which has the following characteristics:

- Like a regular DataTemplate, the HierarchicalDataTemplate specifies how to display elements of a particular data type.

- Additionally, however, it has its own ItemsSource attribute, which you use to specify *where to find the next level of items*.

For example, to fix the first problem in the sample program, you can replace the DataTemplate with a HierarchicalDataTemplate, as shown in the following markup. Notice the following about the markup:

- The template is set to be applied to objects of type WorldRegion. As in the previous section of markup, the XAML uses the local prefix to specify the project's namespace.

- The binding to ItemsSource specifies that the next level of nodes for a WorldRegion object is in its Maps property.

- The TextBlock displays the name of the region by binding it to the RegionName property. In this example, it also displays the Foreground as Gray.

```
                              Apply HierarchicalDataTemplate
                                  to the local data type.
                                           ↓
<Window.Resources>
  <HierarchicalDataTemplate DataType="{x:Type local:WorldRegion}"
        ItemsSource="{Binding Path=Maps}">
                        ↑
              Specify the path to the next level of nodes.

    <TextBlock Text="{Binding Path=RegionName}" Foreground="Gray"/>
                        ↑
              Bind to the RegionName property.

  </HierarchicalDataTemplate>
</Window.Resources>
```

If you run the program now, it produces the output shown on the left of Figure 16-8. It shows the names of the tree's top-level nodes and the class names of the subnodes. It still doesn't know how to display the MapInfo elements in the list.

To solve this, you have to create a HierarchicalDataTemplate for the MapInfo type as well. Since MapInfo doesn't reference any lower-level nodes, you don't have to assign anything to its ItemsSource property. The result is shown on the right in the figure.

Figure 16-8. *The program on the left includes a HierarchicalDataTemplate for type WorldRegion, but not for type MapInfo. The program on the right includes both.*

The following is the final markup for the program. It includes HierarchicalDataTemplates for both WorldRegion and MapInfo.

```
<Window x:Class="TreeBound.Window1"
    xmlns="http://schemas.microsoft.com/winfx/2006/xaml/presentation"
    xmlns:x="http://schemas.microsoft.com/winfx/2006/xaml"
    xmlns:local="clr-namespace:TreeBound"
    Title="Antique Maps" Height="220" Width="200">

    <Window.Resources>

        <HierarchicalDataTemplate
                DataType="{x:Type local:WorldRegion}"
                ItemsSource="{Binding Path=Maps}">
            <TextBlock Text="{Binding Path=RegionName}" Foreground="Gray"/>
        </HierarchicalDataTemplate>

        <HierarchicalDataTemplate DataType="{x:Type local:MapInfo}">
            <TextBlock Text="{Binding Path=LastName}"/>
        </HierarchicalDataTemplate>

    </Window.Resources>

    <Grid>
        <TreeView Name="oldMaps" Grid.Column="0" FontWeight="Bold"/>
    </Grid>
</Window>
```

Using Event Handlers with TreeViews

The example program now shows all the tree's nodes and subnodes, and you can expand and collapse the nodes, but there's no data associated with the leaves. It would be more useful if, when you selected a leaf node, the program displayed information about the selected map in the section to the right, as shown in Figure 16-9.

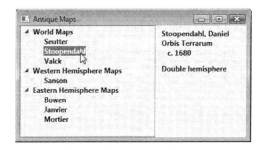

Figure 16-9. *A program using a handler for the SelectedItemChanged event, which displays detailed information about the selected item*

To accomplish this, you need to do the following:

- Add controls in the markup, to the right of the TreeView, that will contain the information about the selected item.

- Create an event handler called oldMaps_SelectedItemChanged in the code-behind.

- Connect the event handler to the TreeView object in the markup.

The following is the markup for the program. Again, you should set the `clr-namespace` to the namespace name used in your project.

```xml
<Window x:Class="TreeBound.Window1"
    xmlns="http://schemas.microsoft.com/winfx/2006/xaml/presentation"
    xmlns:x="http://schemas.microsoft.com/winfx/2006/xaml"
    xmlns:local="clr-namespace:TreeBound"
    Title="Antique Maps" Height="220" Width="400">
    <Window.Resources>
        <HierarchicalDataTemplate DataType="{x:Type local:WorldRegion}"
                ItemsSource="{Binding Path=Maps}">
            <TextBlock Text="{Binding Path=RegionName}" Foreground="Gray"/>
        </HierarchicalDataTemplate>

        <HierarchicalDataTemplate DataType="{x:Type local:MapInfo}">
            <TextBlock Text="{Binding Path=LastName}"/>
        </HierarchicalDataTemplate>

    </Window.Resources>
    <Grid>
        <Grid.ColumnDefinitions>
            <ColumnDefinition Width="3*"/>
            <ColumnDefinition Width="2*"/>
        </Grid.ColumnDefinitions>
                                    Set the event handler.
                                         ↓
        <TreeView SelectedItemChanged="oldMaps_SelectedItemChanged"
                Name="oldMaps" Grid.Column="0"  FontWeight="Bold"/>

        <StackPanel Grid.Column="1" TextBlock.FontWeight="Bold">
            <TextBlock Name="name"  Margin="10, 5, 0, 0"/>   ⌐
            <TextBlock Name="title" Margin="10, 0, 0, 0"/>     Controls to
            <TextBlock Name="date"  Margin="20, 0, 0, 0"/>     Show Map Details
            <TextBlock Name="desc"  Margin="10, 10, 0, 0"/>  ⌐
        </StackPanel>
    </Grid>
</Window>
```

The following is the code-behind. It's the same as before but with the addition of the event handler.

```
public partial class Window1 : Window
{
   List<WorldRegion> mapRegions;

   public Window1()
   {
      InitializeComponent();

      mapRegions = new List<WorldRegion>();
      CreateMapsDataStructure();
      oldMaps.ItemsSource = mapRegions;
   }

   private void CreateMapsDataStructure()
   {
      WorldRegion region = new WorldRegion( "Double Hemisphere" );

         ...      Same As Previous Listing

   }

   private void oldMaps_SelectedItemChanged( object sender,
                     RoutedPropertyChangedEventArgs<object> e )
   {
      MapInfo map = oldMaps.SelectedItem as MapInfo;
      if ( map == null )
         return;

      name.Text  = map.LastName + ", " + map.FirstName;
      title.Text = map.Title;
      date.Text  = map.Year;
      desc.Text  = map.Description;
   }
}
```

Binding Other Controls to a TreeView

In the previous section, you saw how to use event handlers to display the specific information about a leaf element in the TreeView. Data binding, however, is much more elegant and is easy to use implement.

For example, the following markup creates a binding between a TextBlock and the selected item in the TreeView. Binding to the TreeView requires two parameters, the ElementName and the Path. To create the binding, do the following:

- Assign the name of the TreeView element to the ElementName parameter.

- For the Path, use the TreeView's SelectedItem property, suffixed with a dot and the property of the object you want to reference. In the markup, the binding of the Path is to the FirstName property of the selected item represented by the node.

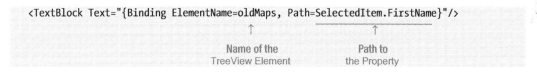

For example, you can modify the example program so that the elements to the right of the TreeView bind to its nodes, rather than using event handlers. You can also expand the program to display an image of the selected map, as shown in Figure 16-10.

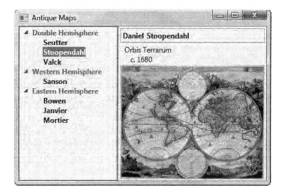

Figure 16-10. *Program binding the elements on right of the TreeView to the selected node in the TreeView*

This program uses a Grid with three columns. The TreeView is in the left column. There's a GridSplitter in the center column, and the detailed information about the selected map is in a DockPanel in the right column.

The following is the markup for the program. It binds to four TextBlocks and an Image.

```
<Window.Resources>
    <HierarchicalDataTemplate DataType="{x:Type local:WorldRegion}"
                              ItemsSource="{Binding Path=Maps}">
        <TextBlock Text="{Binding Path=RegionName}" Foreground="Gray"/>
    </HierarchicalDataTemplate>
    <HierarchicalDataTemplate DataType="{x:Type local:MapInfo}">
        <TextBlock Text="{Binding Path=LastName}"/>
    </HierarchicalDataTemplate>
</Window.Resources>

<Grid >
    <Grid.ColumnDefinitions>
        <ColumnDefinition Width="2*"/>
        <ColumnDefinition Width="Auto"/>
        <ColumnDefinition Width="3*"/>
    </Grid.ColumnDefinitions>

    <TreeView Name="oldMaps" Grid.Column="0" FontWeight="Bold"/>

    <GridSplitter Grid.Column="1" Width="2" Background="DarkGray"
                  VerticalAlignment="Stretch"
                  HorizontalAlignment="Center"/>

    <DockPanel Grid.Column="2">
    <StackPanel DockPanel.Dock="Top">
        <Border BorderBrush="DarkGray" BorderThickness="1"
                Margin="3" Padding="3">
            <StackPanel Orientation="Horizontal" TextBlock.FontWeight="Bold">
                                                    Bind TextBlock to FirstName.
                                                              ↓
                <TextBlock Text=
                    "{Binding ElementName=oldMaps, Path=SelectedItem.FirstName}"/>
                                                    Bind TextBlock to LastName.
                                                              ↓
                <TextBlock Text=
                    "{Binding ElementName=oldMaps, Path=SelectedItem.LastName}"
                              Margin="5,0,0,0"/>
            </StackPanel>
        </Border>
        <TextBlock Text="{Binding ElementName=oldMaps, Path=SelectedItem.Title}"
                   Margin="10, 0, 0, 0"/>
        <TextBlock Text="{Binding ElementName=oldMaps, Path=SelectedItem.Year}"
                   Margin="20, 0, 0, 0"/>
    </StackPanel>
        <Viewbox Stretch="Uniform" Margin="2">          Bind Image to Picture.
                                                              ↓
            <Image Source=
                   "{Binding ElementName=oldMaps, Path=SelectedItem.Picture}"/>
        </Viewbox>
    </DockPanel>
</Grid>
```

The code-behind is the same as the previous version, except that this time there's no event handler:

```
public partial class Window1 : Window
{
    List<WorldRegion> mapRegions;
    public Window1()
    {
        InitializeComponent();

        mapRegions = new List<WorldRegion>();
        CreateMapsDataStructure();
        oldMaps.ItemsSource = mapRegions;
    }

    private void CreateMapsDataStructure()
    {
        WorldRegion region = new WorldRegion( "Double Hemisphere" );

        ...          Same As Previous Listing

    }
}
```

The TabControl

The TabControl is a panel that looks like a set of file folders with labeled tabs. Each tab represents a different set of content that is displayed on the panel when the tab is selected. These tabs are implemented as TabItem objects.

Figure 16-11 shows an example. The screenshots show a TabControl with three TabItems. Selecting a tab shows the content of the selected TabItem.

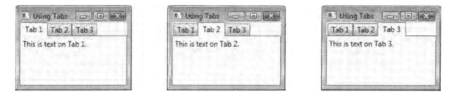

Figure 16-11. *A TabControl with three TabItems*

Figure 16-12 shows the markup to produce this simple tab control program. The illustration on the right shows the architecture of the example. The TabControl's Items property is a collection of the TabControl's TabItems.

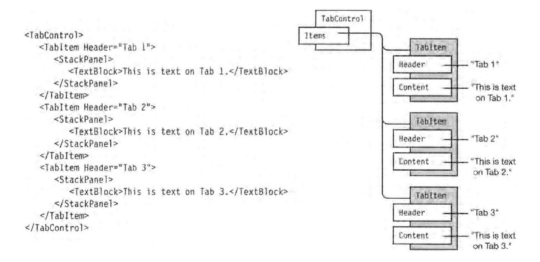

```
<TabControl>
   <TabItem Header="Tab 1">
      <StackPanel>
         <TextBlock>This is text on Tab 1.</TextBlock>
      </StackPanel>
   </TabItem>
   <TabItem Header="Tab 2">
      <StackPanel>
         <TextBlock>This is text on Tab 2.</TextBlock>
      </StackPanel>
   </TabItem>
   <TabItem Header="Tab 3">
      <StackPanel>
         <TextBlock>This is text on Tab 3.</TextBlock>
      </StackPanel>
   </TabItem>
</TabControl>
```

Figure 16-12. *The markup for the simple TabControl with three TabItems*

You can also populate a TabControl dynamically from the code-behind. This is ideal when you don't know what tabs should be created until runtime.

The following markup and code show an example. Notice that the TabControl is declared in the markup, and the TabItems are added at runtime. The output is the same as that shown in Figure 16-11.

```
<Grid>
    <TabControl Name="simpleTabs"></TabControl>
</Grid>
```

The following is the code-behind:

```
public Window1()
{
    InitializeComponent();

    TabItem ti1 = new TabItem();
    ti1.Header = "Tab 1";
    ti1.Content = "This is text on Tab 1.";
    simpleTabs.Items.Add( ti1 );

    TabItem ti2 = new TabItem();
    ti2.Header = "Tab 2";
    ti2.Content = "This is text on Tab 2.";
    simpleTabs.Items.Add( ti2 );

    TabItem ti3 = new TabItem();
    ti3.Header = "Tab 3";
    ti3.Content = "This is text on Tab 3.";
    simpleTabs.Items.Add( ti3 );
}
```

The Calendar Control

The Calendar control displays a graphic calendar that allows the user to select dates. In the code-behind, you can pick up the dates the user has selected. Calendar is new in WPF 4.0.

The following are some of the important things to know about the Calendar control:

- Calendar has three display modes, Month, Year, and Decade, which determine the granularity displayed by the calendar.

- You can set the range of dates displayed by the calendar, as well as mark blackout days, which can't be selected by the user.

- You can allow the user to select multiple contiguous or noncontiguous dates from the calendar.

Figure 16-13 shows three screenshots of the Calendar control with various numbers of date ranges selected. In the example, the bottom TextBlock is bound to the Calendar control's SelectedDate property. In the second two screenshots, the date listed in the TextBlock remains unchanged even though the user has selected additional ranges of dates.

Single Date Selected   Multiple Dates Selected   Multiple Date Ranges Selected

Figure 16-13. *The Calendar control*

The following is the markup to produce the Calendar control in the screenshots in Figure 16-13:

```
<StackPanel>
    <Calendar Name="cal" SelectionMode="MultipleRange" />
    <TextBlock Text="Selected Date" FontWeight="Bold" Margin="5,5,5,2"/>
    <TextBlock Margin="20,0"
               Text="{Binding ElementName=cal, Path=SelectedDate}"  />
</StackPanel>
```

The Calendar control also allows you to specify blackout ranges, which are ranges of dates that the user can't select. You can also specify a range of dates to display by giving a start date and an end date. Figure 16-14 shows two Calendar controls demonstrating these options.

Using the
BlackoutDates Property

Using the DisplayDateStart
and DisplayDateEnd Properties

Figure 16-14. *You can set blockout date ranges and starting and ending display dates.*

The following is the markup for the Calendar control shown on the left in the figure. Notice that there are two blackout ranges specified. These are shown in the display with light gray *X*s over the given dates.

```
<Calendar Name="cal" SelectionMode="MultipleRange">
   <Calendar.BlackoutDates>
      <CalendarDateRange Start="11/8/2009"  End="11/10/2009"/>   ← First Range
      <CalendarDateRange Start="11/18/2009" End="11/22/2009"/>   ← Second Range
   </Calendar.BlackoutDates>
</Calendar>
```

The following is the markup for the Calendar control shown on the right in Figure 16-14, that shows only the dates between November 10, 2009, and November 26, 2009:

```
<Calendar Name="cal" SelectionMode="MultipleRange"
          DisplayDateStart="11/10/2009"            ← Start Date
          DisplayDateEnd ="11/26/2009"  />         ← End Date
```

Figure 16-15 shows the important properties of the Calendar control.

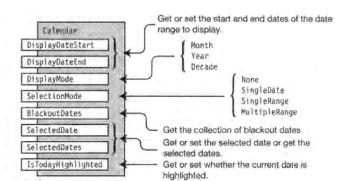

Figure 16-15. *The important properties of the Calendar control*

The DatePicker Control

The DatePicker control allows the user to enter a date either by typing the text in a text box or by using the DatePicker's built-in Calendar control. Like the Calendar control, the DatePicker control is included in WPF 4.0. Figure 16-16 shows screenshots of the DatePicker control.

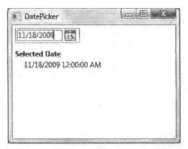

The user can enter the date by typing it directly into the control, and then pressing Enter.

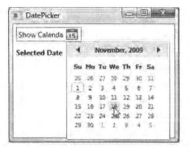

The user can enter a date by clicking the calendar icon, which brings up the built-in Calendar.

Figure 16-16. *The DatePicker control allows the user two ways to enter a date.*

The following is the markup for the DatePicker control shown in Figure 16-16:

```
<StackPanel>
    <DatePicker Name="datePicker" HorizontalAlignment="Left" Width="110"/>
    <TextBlock Text="Selected Date" FontWeight="Bold" Margin="5,5,5,2"/>
    <TextBlock Margin="20,0"
               Text="{Binding ElementName=datePicker, Path=SelectedDate}" />
</StackPanel>
```

Most of DatePicker's important properties are for interacting with its built-in Calendar control and behave the same way. These properties include DisplayDateStart, DisplayDateEnd, BlackoutDates, and SelectedDate. For example, Figure 16-17 shows a DatePicker with the DisplayDateStart and DisplayDateEnd properties set.

```
<StackPanel>
    <DatePicker Name="datePicker" HorizontalAlignment="Left"
        Width="110" Margin="5"
        DisplayDateStart="5/10/2009"
        DisplayDateEnd  ="5/30/2009"/>

    <TextBlock Text="Selected Date" FontWeight="Bold"
        Margin="5,5,5,2"/>
    <TextBlock Margin="20,0" Text=
        "{Binding ElementName=datePicker, Path=SelectedDate}"/>
</StackPanel>
```

Figure 16-17. *The DatePicker control uses many of the same properties as the Calendar control.*

The DataGrid Control

The DataGrid control, introduced in WPF 4.0, displays a two-dimensional grid of data, as shown in Figure 16-18. Although the screenshots in the figure show a very plain grid, the DataGrid gives you extensive control over many aspects of its appearance.

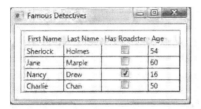
Initial Display

Sorted on Age

Figure 16-18. *By default, the user can sort a DataGrid on any column.*

The DataGrid is a powerful control, with a large number of features. The following are some of the most important:

- *Sorting*: You can programmatically sort the rows on a particular column. The user can sort on a column by clicking its header.

- *Column headers*: You can display just column headers, just row headers, or both.

- *Rearrange columns*: You can rearrange the columns programmatically, or the user can rearrange them by dragging the headers left or right.

- *Specialized cell types*: The grid supplies specialized column types for text, Buttons, CheckBoxes, ComboBoxes, and Hyperlinks.

- *Customized appearance*: You can attach Styles and Templates to the DataGrid, as well as to most of its components. This gives you a large number of options for customizing the grid's appearance.

Because of the DataGrid's large number of features, an exhaustive description is beyond the scope of this text. Using the DataGrid, however, is fairly simple, once you have the basics. The three basic things you need to do when creating a DataGrid are the following:

- Create the column descriptions.

- Attach the data.

- Customize the various parts of the grid with Styles, Templates, and Brushes.

Figure 16-19 illustrates the structure of the DataGrid and the four properties for defining the columns and attaching the data.

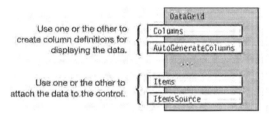

Figure 16-19. *The DataGrid requires column definitions and data. The sample program defines four columns and attaches a List of Person objects to the ItemsSource property.*

If the AutoGenerateColumns property is set to True (which is the default value), then WPF inspects the data and creates columns automatically based on the data. When you use this method, however, you don't have control of the appearance of the data in the grid.

Although automatically generating the columns can be useful as an initial pass, or for a quick prototype, generally you'll want to create a set of column definitions that specify how to display the data in the column. To do this, set AutoGenerateColumns to False, and define each column in the DataGrid's Columns property, as shown in the following markup. This markup defines two text columns. The first is bound to a property called FirstName, and the second is bound to a property called LastName.

```
<DataGrid Name="dg" AutoGenerateColumns="False">    ← Explicitly turn off autogeneration.
   <DataGrid.Columns>
      <DataGridTextColumn Binding="{Binding FirstName}" Header="First Name"/>
      <DataGridTextColumn Binding="{Binding LastName}"  Header="Last Name"/>
```
         ↑   ↑   ↑
  Use the correct type of colum.   Bind to the data field.   Set the text of the header.

There are four predefined DataGrid column types: DataGridTextColumn, DataGridCheckBoxColumn, DataGridHyperlinkColumn, and DataGridComboBoxColumn. There is also the DataGridTemplateColumn, which allows you to specify your own column types.

Since the DataGrid is derived from ItemsControl (through several intermediate classes), you can attach data to a DataGrid using either its Items property or its ItemsSource property.

The following is the markup that produces the DataGrid shown in Figure 16-18. Notice the Width attributes in the last two column definitions. The first one is set to SizeToHeader, and the last one is set to *.

The Width property of a DataGrid column can have a numerical value as you've seen with Widths throughout the text. Beyond that, however, it can have several other interesting values, which are the following:

- Auto: This is the standard automatic sizing mode, which determines the size necessary to fit all the content.

- SizeToCells: This determines the size necessary to display the content of the data cells, regardless of the size of the header.

- SizeToHeader: This determines the size necessary to display the header, regardless of the size of the content of the data cells.

- *: "Star" sizing specifies that this column should take up the remaining width of the DataGrid or split the remaining width among the other "star-sized" columns.

```
<StackPanel>
    <DataGrid Name="dg" AutoGenerateColumns="False" Margin="10">
        <DataGrid.Columns>
            <DataGridTextColumn Binding="{Binding FirstName}"
                                Header="First Name"/>
            <DataGridTextColumn Binding="{Binding LastName}"
                                Header="Last Name"/>
            <DataGridCheckBoxColumn Binding="{Binding HasRoadster}"
                                Header="Has Roadster"
                                Width="SizeToHeader"/>          ← Width
            <DataGridTextColumn Binding="{Binding Age}"
                                Header="Age"
                                Width="*"/>                     ← Width
        </DataGrid.Columns>
    </DataGrid>
</StackPanel>
```

Figure 16-20 illustrates the structure of the example program. The DataGrid defines four columns, and the data is taken from a List<> of Person objects.

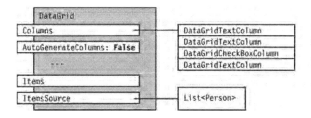

Figure 16-20. *The structure of the example program*

The following is the code-behind for the program. The Person class, with four properties, is declared at the top of the file. The Window class, declared at the bottom, creates a List of four Person objects and assigns the List to the DataGrid's ItemsSource property.

```
class Person
{
    public string FirstName   { get; set; }
    public string LastName    { get; set; }
    public int    Age         { get; set; }
    public bool   HasRoadster { get; set; }

    public Person(string fName, string lName, int age, bool hasRoadster)
    {
        FirstName   = fName;
        LastName    = lName;
        Age         = age;
        HasRoadster = hasRoadster;
    }
}

public partial class Window1 : Window
{
    List<Person> _people = new List<Person>();

    public Window1()
    {   InitializeComponent();

        _people.Add(new Person("Sherlock", "Holmes", 54, false));
        _people.Add(new Person("Jane",     "Marple", 60, false));
        _people.Add(new Person("Nancy",    "Drew",   16, true));
        _people.Add(new Person("Charlie",  "Chan",   50, false));

        dg.ItemsSource = _people;
    }
}
```

Figure 16-21 illustrates additional properties of the DataGrid control that allow you to customize its appearance. You can use Brushes, Styles, and Templates to control the appearances of most of the DataGrid's parts.

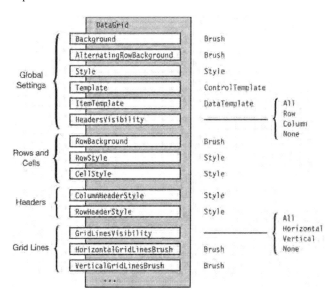

Figure 16-21. *Some of the important properties available for formatting the DataGrid control*

Figure 16-22 illustrates properties of the DataGrid associated with rows or cells the user selects.

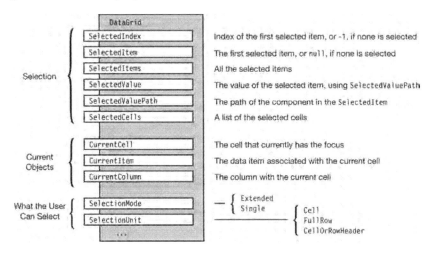

Figure 16-22. *Properties of the DataGrid control that deal with selected rows and items*

Summary

In this chapter, I covered controls that didn't fit into categories earlier in the text and also three controls introduced in WPF 4.0.

- The TreeView control is ideal for representing hierarchical collections. It consists of a set of nodes, where each node can have subnodes, down to arbitrary depth.

- The TabControl is a panel that acts like a file folder, where every tab contains a different set of content.

- The Calendar control presents the visual display of a calendar, and the user can select dates on the calendar. You can programmatically restrict the calendar to show only ranges of dates or to include "blackout" dates, which the user can't select. Calendar is new with WPF 4.0.

- The DatePicker control presents a text box for the user to enter a date. At the right of the text box is an icon that can display the Calendar control, from which the user can select a date. DatePicker is new with WPF 4.0.

- The DataGrid control is a powerful grid control for displaying data. DataGrid is new with WPF 4.0.

■ ■ ■

CHAPTER 17

Text and Documents

Text in WPF

WPF allows programmers to design programs with amazing graphic content with unprecedented ease. Text, however, still plays an important part in most programs and can even be the dominant component of some. Programs can use different amounts of text and use it in very different ways. In this chapter, you'll learn some of the ways WPF provides for presenting text.

Generally, programs use small amounts of text to label parts of the UI so the user knows what controls and elements are used for. This is text *about* the program and is often implemented using the Label element you saw in Chapter 6. In this case, the text is just an incidental part of the program.

Sometimes, however, the text isn't about the program; instead, the purpose of the program is to present the text. For example, you might want to build an application that allows the user to access a set of documentation. WPF supplies the following ways of presenting this type of text:

- *Fixed documents*: These are documents where the text is laid out in a fixed format. The user can page through the document, but regardless of the size of the window, the pagination and formatting of the document remain unchanged. This is similar to an Adobe PDF file. I won't be covering this type of document.

- *Flow documents*: These documents behave in a manner similar to HTML pages. When the user changes the size of the window, the hosting program (the browser in the case of HTML) readjusts the layout of the text to fit the new size and shape of the window.

- *TextBlock elements*: These are advanced versions of the TextBox element that allow you to format the text.

Fixed documents and flow documents are generally used for large amounts of text that span multiple pages. The TextBlock element is used for small amounts of text that need to be formatted.

An Overview of Flow Documents

Before I cover the details of creating flow documents, I'll show you what they look like and how they behave. The following are the major points about flow documents:

- The text is automatically paginated to fit the size of the window.

- The text is automatically placed into columns for easy viewing. If the window is narrow enough that columns would be distracting, WPF places the text in a single column.

- The text is hosted in a container, which provides built-in tools for navigating and viewing the document.

Figure 17-1 shows a flow document with text that takes up four screens. The built-in tools provided by the hosting element are at the bottom of the window. These tools are the following:

- A search box for searching the document for words or phrases

- Page navigation controls for moving back and forth through the document

- Viewing mode controls, which allow the user to select between single-page mode, two-page mode, and scrolling

- The zoom controls, which allow the user to change the size of the content

All these tools are built-in to the hosting element *without any additional work* required by the programmer.

Figure 17-1. *The flow document reader adds powerful built-in tools for displaying flow documents.*

The application's built-in tools are simple and intuitive to use. The first tool on the left is a search box that allows the user to search for words or phrases. To make the search box visible, the user clicks the magnifying glass icon and can then type the text into the text box. Figure 17-2 shows the search text box.

Figure 17-2. *The user can click the magnifying glass to make the search text box visible.*

Immediately to the right of the search box are the page navigation controls, which include a left arrow, a right arrow, and text. The text part of the navigation control shows which page is currently being displayed, as well as the total number of pages. The right and left arrow buttons allow the user to move forward and backward through the text.

To the right of the page navigation controls are three icons that represent different ways of viewing the document. The first icon represents the default form, which consists of a page occupying the entire window. The page might be displayed in columns, but it is still a single page. This is the form shown in Figure 17-2.

The second icon represents a "two page at a time" view, where the first page is on the left of the window and the second page is shown on the right. Each "page" is contained in a bounding box. Figure 17-3 shows this form of display. Notice that the display is almost the same as that in Figure 17-2, except for the addition of the bounding boxes, and the change in the text in the navigation controls, which now lists eight pages, rather than four.

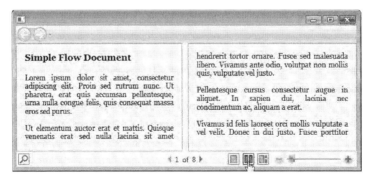

Figure 17-3. *Two page a time mode*

The third icon represents the scrolling viewing mode. In this mode, the text isn't paginated but is instead scrolled in the window. Figure 17-4 shows this mode. Notice that the page navigation tools have been removed, and a scroll bar has been placed at the right of the window. This is very similar to the way HTML is displayed.

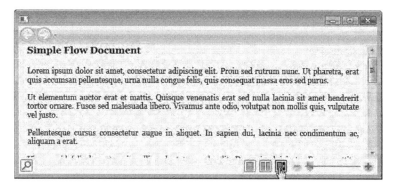

Figure 17-4. *Scrolling mode removes the page navigation controls and places a scroll bar at the right of the window.*

To the right of the viewing mode icons are the sizing controls. These proportionally control the size of the contents of the window. These controls consist of a plus button, a minus button and a slider. Figure 17-5 shows the window when the slider has been dragged to the right to increase the size of the window content.

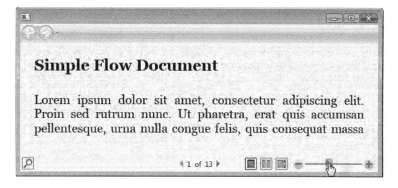

Figure 17-5. *The size controls comprise a plus button a minus button and a slider control.*

The Components of a Flow Document

The structure of a flow document application consists of three major parts—the hosting control, the FlowDocument element, and the actual contents of the document.

- The *hosting control* determines the viewing mode or modes available to the application using it. It also determines which built-in tools are available at the bottom of the window. I'll explain the three possible types of hosting control shortly.

- The FlowDocument element is the container that holds the content of the document.

- The content of the flow document consists of a number of containers that hold and manage the actual content of the document.

The illustration on the left of Figure 17-6 shows the structure of these major components. The hosting control contains the FlowDocument element, which contains the actual contents of the document. The illustration on the right of the figure shows an example of that structure. (Don't worry about the details of the content in the example, because I'll be covering these components shortly.)

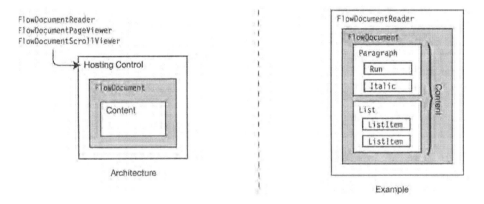

Figure 17-6. *The three major components of a flow document*

The Hosting Controls

There are three hosting controls for flow documents—the FlowDocumentReader, the FlowPageViewer, and the FlowScrollViewer. The first control allows the user to switch between paging and scrolling. The second two display the text in either paging or scrolling mode. Figure 17-7 shows screenshots of programs using the second and third hosting controls.

- The FlowDocumentReader is the one you've seen throughout this chapter. It presents the three view icons, allowing the user to switch between the three different views—one page at a time, two pages at a time, or scrolling.

- The FlowDocumentPageViewer element shows the text only in paging mode.

- The FlowDocumentScrollViewer element shows the text only in scrolling mode.

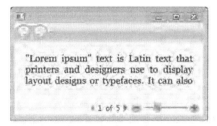
Using the FlowDocumentPageViewer

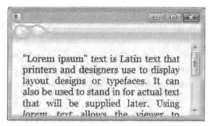
Using the FlowDocumentScrollViewer

Figure 17-7. *The FlowDocumentPageViewer and the FlowDocumentScrollViewer hosting elements don't allow the user to select the viewing mode.*

The following markup shows an example of using the FlowDocumentReader hosting control:

```
                   The Hosting Control
                          ↓
<FlowDocumentReader x:Class="SimpleFlowDocument.Window1"
    xmlns="http://schemas.microsoft.com/winfx/2006/xaml/presentation"
    xmlns:x="http://schemas.microsoft.com/winfx/2006/xaml">
    <FlowDocument>
        <Paragraph FontSize="20" FontWeight="Bold">              The Flow
            <Run>Simple Flow Document</Run>                      Document
        </Paragraph>
    </FlowDocument>
</FlowDocumentReader>
```

In this example, the FlowDocumentReader is at the root of the element tree, so in the code-behind you'll have to change the type of the class from Window to FlowDocumentReader, as shown in the following code fragment:

```
public partial class Window1 : FlowDocumentReader
{ ...
```

The Content of a Flow Document

All three of the hosting elements you saw in the previous section require as their content a single FlowDocument element. The FlowDocument is the container for the content.

A FlowDocument element can contain any number of elements derived from the Block class. These include the Paragraph, Section, List, Table, and BlockUIContainer classes. Figure 17-8 shows the part of the object derivation tree containing the classes used in flow documents. Notice that there are two main branches.

- The Block-derived classes are containers. They can contain any number of the following:

  – Other Block-derived class objects

  – Inline-derived class objects

- The Inline-derived classes contain presentation content such as text or UIElement objects. (The oddly named Run class contains text.)

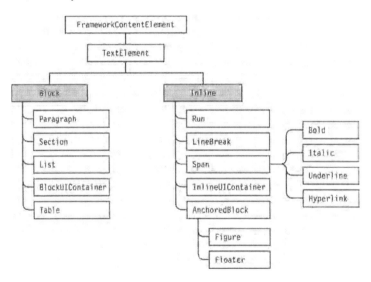

Figure 17-8. *The Block-derived classes are containers for organizing content. The Inline-derived classes contain actual content such as text or UIElement objects.*

For example, Figure 17-9 shows the markup for a simple flow document application. The figure on the right shows the structure of the application. Notice the following about the markup:

- The FlowDocument contains two Paragraph objects.

- Each Paragraph object contains Inline-derived objects containing text.

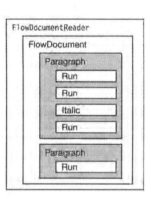

```
<FlowDocumentReader x:Class="Containment.Window1" ... >
   <FlowDocument>
      <Paragraph>
         <Run>"Lorem ipsum" text is Latin text that printers
               and designers use to display layout designs or
               typefaces. It can also be used to stand in
               for actual text that will be supplied later.</Run>
         <Run>Using</Run>
         <Italic>lorem text</Italic>
         <Run>allows the viewer to concentrate on the
               layout or typeface rather than the content.</Run>
      </Paragraph>
      <Paragraph>
         <Run>
            The text is based on a passage from Cicero, but
            is not a direct quotation. It was used by early
            printers starting in the 1500's or early 1600's.
         </Run>
      </Paragraph>
   </FlowDocument>
</FlowDocumentReader>
```

Figure 17-9. *A simple flow document and its structure*

Figure 17-10 shows a screenshot of the program shown in Figure 17-9.

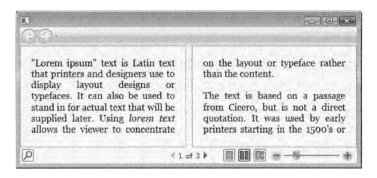

Figure 17-10. *The FlowDocumentReader hosting element lays out the content of the FlowDocument.*

Creating a flow document consists, essentially, of mixing, matching, and embedding the elements of different types. Table 17-1 lists the different element types and their roles.

Table 17-1. *The Block-Derived Elements Used in a FlowDocument*

Name	Description
BlockUIContainer	Hosts, at the Block level, a UIElement such as a Button.
List	Contains a formatted set of list item elements.
Paragraph	Represents a paragraph. It groups sets of Inline elements.
Section	Represents a section. It groups sets of other Block-derived elements.
Table	Represents a table containing a set of rows.

Table 17-2. *The Inline-Derived Classes Used in a FlowDocument*

Name	Description
Bold	Formats the enclosed text in bold font.
Figure	Hosts a figure or other element. You can specify the placement of a Figure in relation to the flow of the text. A Figure is sizeable and can span more than a single column.
Floater	Hosts a figure or other element. The placement of a Floater can't be specified explicitly, and it is placed wherever the FlowDocument determines there is space for it.
Hyperlink	Formats the enclosed text as a hyperlink.
InlineUIContainer	Hosts, at the Inline level, a UIElement such as a Button.
Italic	Italicizes the enclosed text.
LineBreak	Forces a new line in the run of the text.
Run	Contains plain text. In markup, text that isn't inside an Inline-derived element is assumed by WPF to be a Run element.
Span	Groups other Inline-derived elements. You can use this to apply formatting to a contiguous set of inline elements.
Underline	Underlines the enclosed text.

Not all elements, however, can be arbitrarily embedded in any other type of element. Figure 17-11 shows the types of elements that can be embedded in various types of elements. For example, a Paragraph element can contain Runs, LineBreaks, Spans, and so on. Sections, Figures, and Floaters can contain Paragraphs, Sections, BlockUIContainers, and so on.

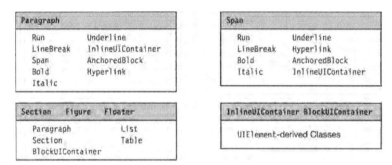

Figure 17-11. *The containment relationships allowed for various element types*

The markup in Figure 17-12 illustrates some of these relationships. Some important things to notice about the markup are the following:

- Titles are created by using a Paragraph element with bold font of a larger size.

- Inline elements such as Bold and Underline can be nested.

```
<FlowDocument>
   <Paragraph FontSize="22" FontWeight="Bold">
      Simple Flow Document
   </Paragraph>
   <Section>
      <Paragraph FontSize="18">
         <Bold>First Section</Bold>
      </Paragraph>
      <Paragraph>
         Lorem ipsum dolor sit amet, ... consequat massa eros sed purus.
      </Paragraph>
      <Paragraph>
         Ut elementum auctor erat et mattis. Quisque ... malesuada libero.
         <Bold><Underline>Vivamus ante odio</Underline></Bold>,
         volutpat non mollis quis, vulputate vel justo.
      </Paragraph>
   </Section>
   <Section>
      <Paragraph FontSize="18">
         <Bold>Second Section</Bold>
      </Paragraph>
      <Paragraph>
         Pellentesque cursus consectetur augue in ...
            ...
   </Section>
</FlowDocument>
```

Figure 17-12. *A simple flow document*

Figure 17-13 shows the resulting flow document. Notice the titles, and the underlined, bold text. Notice also that this is a single page with two columns. The `FlowDocument` automatically lays out the text in columns when the container window gets wide enough.

Figure 17-13. *The appearance of the simple flow document*

Tables and Lists

You can include tables and formatted lists in a flow document by using the Table and List elements. These elements are Block-derived classes and can be used wherever a Block-derived class is legal.

Figure 17-14 shows the containment relationships between Table and its subelements and List and its subelements. Notice that at the innermost level, the content is contained in a Block-derived element—which of course contains an Inline-derived element.

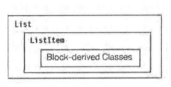 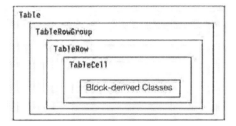

Figure 17-14. *The containment relationships of the Table and List classes*

Figure 17-15 shows an example of a simple list in a flow document.

Figure 17-15. *A simple list and a simple table in flow documents*

The following markup produces the simple list.

```
<FlowDocument>
    <Paragraph>This is a simple list.</Paragraph>
    <List>
        <ListItem>
            <Paragraph>Lorem ipsum dolor sit amet ...</Paragraph>
        </ListItem>
        <ListItem>
            <Paragraph>Nemo enim ipsam voluptatem quia voluptas ...</Paragraph>
        </ListItem>
        <ListItem>
            <Paragraph>Neque porro quisquam est, qui ...</Paragraph>
        </ListItem>
    </List>
</FlowDocument>
```

The following markup produces the simple table shown in Figure 17-16:

```
<FlowDocument>
    <Paragraph>The following is a table of information about
            several antique maps.</Paragraph>
    <Table>
        <Table.Columns>
            <TableColumn Width="150"/><TableColumn Width="60"/>
            <TableColumn Width="200"/>
        </Table.Columns>
        <TableRowGroup >
            <TableRow FontSize="18" FontWeight="Bold">
                <TableCell><Paragraph>Cartographer</Paragraph></TableCell>
                <TableCell><Paragraph>Year</Paragraph></TableCell>
                <TableCell><Paragraph>Name</Paragraph></TableCell>
            </TableRow>
            <TableRow>
                <TableCell><Paragraph>Seutter</Paragraph></TableCell>
                <TableCell><Paragraph>1730</Paragraph></TableCell>
                <TableCell>
                    <Paragraph><Italic>Diversi Globi Terr-Aquei</Italic></Paragraph>
                </TableCell>
            </TableRow>
            <TableRow>
                <TableCell><Paragraph>Stoopendahl</Paragraph></TableCell>
                <TableCell><Paragraph>1680</Paragraph></TableCell>
                <TableCell>
                    <Paragraph><Italic>Orbis Terrarum</Italic></Paragraph>
                </TableCell>
            </TableRow>
            <TableRow>
                <TableCell><Paragraph>Valck</Paragraph></TableCell>
                <TableCell><Paragraph>1700</Paragraph></TableCell>
                <TableCell>
                    <Paragraph><Italic>Mappe Monde</Italic></Paragraph>
                </TableCell>
            </TableRow>
        </TableRowGroup>
    </Table>
</FlowDocument>
```

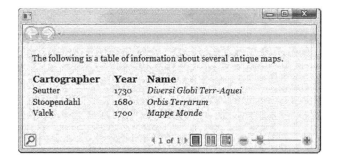

Figure 17-16. *A simple table*

Embedded Flow Documents

All the flow documents you've seen so far have been at the root of the element tree in place of the `Window` class. But they don't need to be at that level. They can also be embedded as content.

For example, Figure 17-17 shows a window that contains a `Grid` with two columns. In the left column is a `StackPanel` with three buttons. In the right column is a `Border`, containing a flow document.

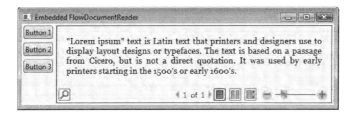

Figure 17-17. *An embedded flow document in the right column of a Grid*

The following is the markup that produces the window:

```
<Window x:Class="EmbeddedFlowDocument.Window1" ...
    Title="Embedded FlowDocumentReader" Height="205" Width="520">
    <Grid>
        <Grid.ColumnDefinitions>
            <ColumnDefinition Width="auto"/>
            <ColumnDefinition Width="*"/>
        </Grid.ColumnDefinitions>
        <StackPanel Grid.Column="0">
            <Button VerticalAlignment="Top" Margin="3">Button 1</Button>
            <Button VerticalAlignment="Top" Margin="3">Button 2</Button>
            <Button VerticalAlignment="Top" Margin="3">Button 3</Button>
        </StackPanel>
        <Border Grid.Column="1" BorderBrush="Black"
                BorderThickness="1" Margin="3">
            <FlowDocumentReader>
                <FlowDocument>
                    <Paragraph>
                        <Run>"Lorem ipsum" text is Latin text that printers
                            and designers use to display layout designs or
                            typefaces. The text is based on a passage from
                            Cicero, but is not a direct quotation. It was
                            used by early printers starting in the 1500's
                            or early 1600's.</Run>
                    </Paragraph>
                </FlowDocument>
            </FlowDocumentReader>
        </Border>
    </Grid>
</Window>
```

The TextBlock Element

The features you've been looking at so far in this chapter have been aimed at presenting medium to large amounts of text. The TextBlock, on the other hand, is a simple way to display small amounts of text.

- The TextBlock is a small, lightweight element designed for displaying text. It doesn't accept user input.

- Text in the TextBlock can wrap from one line to the next. By default, text doesn't wrap, but you can enable wrapping by setting the TextWrapping property to true.

The following markup shows a simple use of the TextBlock. Figure 17-18 shows the window produced by this code.

```
                       Set text wrapping.
                              ↓
<StackPanel>
    <TextBlock TextWrapping="Wrap">
        I know you believe you understand what you think I said. But what
        you fail to realize is that what you heard is not what I meant.
    </TextBlock>
</StackPanel>
```

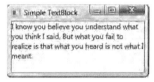

Figure 17-18. *A simple use of the TextBox*

The TextBlock is easy to use in its simplest form, but it also allows extensive formatting. You can apply formatting characteristics to the entire element by setting the attributes in the start tag of the TextBlock.

- You can set text characteristics such as FontFamily, FontSize, and FontStyle.

- You can set alignment to the left, right, or center using the HorizontalAlignment property.

Different portions of text in a TextBlock can have different formatting characteristics. Inside a TextBlock you can modify the text characteristics or text flow using the appropriate elements. For example, you can use the following elements:

- Bold and Italic elements apply the given style to the enclosed text.

- The LineBreak tag starts a new line.

- The Span tag encloses text set aside for special processing.

407

For example, the following markup illustrates these simple but powerful formatting capabilities. The code shows a StackPanel containing four TextBlock elements.

- The first TextBlock uses the Bold and Italic tags inline and a combination of both at the end.

- The last three TextBlock elements show horizontal positioning. The last one also demonstrates the use of the LineBreak tag.

```
<StackPanel>
    <TextBlock Margin="10" TextWrapping="Wrap">
        <Italic>I know you believe you understand         Italic
        what you think I said.</Italic> But what you
        <Bold>fail to realize</Bold> is that what you heard is   Bold
        <Italic><Bold>not what I meant</Bold></Italic>.      Both
    </TextBlock>
    <TextBlock HorizontalAlignment="Left" FontSize="15" Margin="10,0">
        Push 'em to the left.
    </TextBlock>
    <TextBlock HorizontalAlignment="Right"  FontSize="15" Margin="10,0">
        Push 'em to the right.
    </TextBlock>
    <TextBlock HorizontalAlignment="Center"  FontSize="15">
        Stand up. sit down.<LineBreak/><Italic>Fight, fight, fight!</Italic>
    </TextBlock>
</StackPanel>
```

Figure 17-19 shows the window produced by this markup.

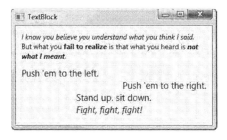

Figure 17-19. *Four TextBlocks with simple formatting*

Besides this simple formatting, the TextBlock is capable of far more than I can cover in this chapter, so I'll let you explore that on your own. The markup shown next, however, gives you just a sample. Figure 17-20 shows the window it produces. The following are several things to notice about this markup:

- The first TextBlock uses a drop shadow bitmap effect on its text.

- The second TextBlock uses the Span tag to set different font families on selected portions of text.

- The third TextBlock includes controls. Before using this feature, however, you might want to think about whether it's actually wise to do so. Depending on the situation—it might or might not be the best design.

```xml
<StackPanel>
    <TextBlock FontSize="20" FontWeight="Bold" HorizontalAlignment="Center">
        <TextBlock.BitmapEffect>
            <DropShadowBitmapEffect Color="Black"
                ShadowDepth="4" Direction="330"
                Opacity="0.5" Softness="0.25" />
        </TextBlock.BitmapEffect>
        Drop Shadow Text
    </TextBlock>
    <TextBlock TextWrapping="Wrap" Margin="10">
        Below is a <Span FontFamily="Courier New">TextBlock</Span>
        containing a <Span FontFamily="Courier New">CheckBox</Span>
        and a <Span FontFamily="Courier New">ToolBar</Span>
        with two <Span FontFamily="Courier New">Button</Span>s.
    </TextBlock>
    <TextBlock>
        <CheckBox></CheckBox>
        <ToolBar>
            <Button>Button 1</Button>
            <Button>Button 2</Button>
        </ToolBar>
    </TextBlock>
</StackPanel>
```

Figure 17-20. *A window with three TextBlocks showing more advanced features*

Summary

WPF provides several ways of presenting formatted text. In this chapter, I covered the FlowDocument element its associated elements as well as the TextBlock element.

Flow documents allow you to present large amounts of text in an elegant way. Flow documents have the following characteristics:

- The text is laid out and paginated automatically according to the size and shape of the container.

- The documents include built-in tools that allow the user to do the following things:

    - Search the text for a string

    - Page through the document

    - Increase or decrease the size of the displayed content

- The flow document classes allow a great deal of control over the formatting of the content, including allowing the display of UIElements, tables, and lists.

- Flow documents can be embedded in the UI tree.

In contrast to flow documents, which are generally used with medium to large amounts of content, the TextBlock element is a lightweight but powerful class for presenting small amounts of text. It allows extensive formatting capabilities, as well as allowing bitmap effects.

CHAPTER 18

Graphics in WPF

Graphics in WPF

As you've seen throughout this text, WPF is a much more graphics-oriented framework than any previous Windows development framework. So far, I've covered graphics piecemeal, in the context of whatever topic I was covering at the time. In this chapter, I'll cover graphics from a higher perspective and show how various graphics features apply across WPF as a whole.

In this chapter, I'll be covering five areas of graphics that are used in various ways. These topics fall into three categories:

- The first two topics, transforms and bitmap effects, cover several ways in which you can modify the visual presentation of an element.

- Next I'll cover brushes, which you can use to paint areas of elements.

- Finally I'll describe shapes, geometries, and drawings, which allow you to create and use two-dimensional graphics.

Figure 18-1 lists the topics I'll be covering in this chapter and how they fit into the scheme of WPF.

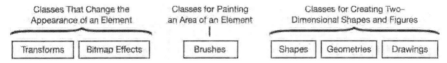

Figure 18-1. *The major areas of graphics in WPF*

The first two topics I'll cover are Transforms and BitmapEffects. These topics are applicable to all elements derived from the UIElement and FrameworkElement classes, which includes most of WPF's visual elements. As you can see in Figure 18-2, these classes define properties that allow you to apply Transforms and BitmapEffects to any objects derived from these classes. In the next several sections, I'll explain what Transforms and BitmapEffects are.

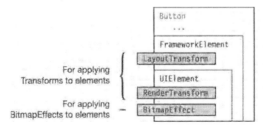

Figure 18-2. *The three properties allowing you to apply Transforms and BitmapEffects are defined in the UIElement and FrameworkElement classes.*

Transforms

Transforms allow you to modify the appearance of an element in specific ways. There are six classes that derive from the base class Transform, and they fall into the following three categories. Figure 18-3 illustrates the classes and their categories.

- There are four predefined Transforms: RotateTransform, ScaleTransform, SkewTransform, and TranslateTransform. Respectively, these allow you to rotate an element, change its size, skew its angles, and move it.

- The generalized Transform class, called MatrixTransform, allows you to manipulate all the parameters of a transformation individually. The four predefined classes are specialized versions of the MatrixTransform class.

- The TransformGroup is a collection of Transforms. TransformGroup derives from the base class Transform, so it can be used anywhere one of the other Transform objects is used. When a TransformGroup is applied to an element, each of the Transforms in the collection is applied to the element.

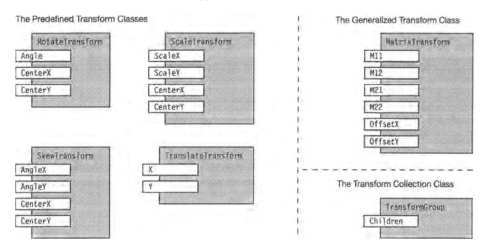

Figure 18-3. *The six Transform classes fall into three categories.*

You apply a Transform to an element by assigning it to one of the element's two Transform properties—LayoutTransform or RenderTransform. If you assign it to the LayoutTransform property, the transformation is performed when WPF is calculating the layout of the element. If you assign it to the RenderTransform property, WPF delays applying the transform until the rendering phase of the display. I'll address this in more detail shortly.

The RotateTransform

The RotateTransform rotates the element at a specified angle around a pivot point. By default the pivot point is the top-left corner of the element's bounding box.

Figure 18-4 shows a button rotated around the default pivot point, which is marked by a dot.

Button Without
RotateTransform

Button with
RotateTransform at 45°.

Figure 18-4. *The RotateTransform rotates an object around a point.*

You rotate an element by setting the Angle property of the Transform property, as shown in the following markup. This markup produces the rotated button shown in the previous figure. The Ellipse at the bottom of the markup creates the dot at the rotation point.

```
<Canvas>
    <Button Canvas.Left="30" Canvas.Top="20">

        <Button.RenderTransform>
            <RotateTransform    Angle="45"/>
        </Button.RenderTransform>         ↑

                                    Set the angle.
        Rotate Me
    </Button>
    <Ellipse Canvas.Left="27.5" Canvas.Top="17.5" Height="5" Width="5"
             Fill="Red"/>
</Canvas>
```

Figure 18-5 illustrates the structure of the `RotateTransform` class. In it you see two other important properties besides the `Angle` property. They are the `CenterX` and `CenterY` properties. These specify the pivot point of the rotation. By default these values are each 0.

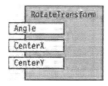

Figure 18-5. *The most important properties of the RotateTransform class*

Figure 18-6 shows the result of changing the pivot point. In each case, the third button in the `StackPanel` is rotated around one of its four corners.

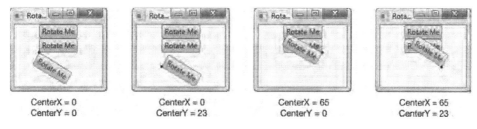

Figure 18-6. *The bottom button shown being rotated around each of its four corner positions*

The following is the markup producing the fourth screenshot in the figure:

```
<StackPanel HorizontalAlignment="Center">
    <Button Width="65" Height="23">Rotate Me</Button>
    <Button Width="65" Height="23">Rotate Me</Button>

    <Button Width="65" Height="23">
        <Button.RenderTransform>
            <RotateTransform Angle="30" CenterX="65" CenterY="23" />
                                       ‾‾‾‾‾‾‾‾‾‾‾‾‾‾‾‾‾‾‾‾‾‾‾‾‾
        </Button.RenderTransform>                  ↑
        Rotate Me                          Set the Pivot Point
    </Button>

</StackPanel>
```

Using LayoutTransform vs. RenderTransform

As I mentioned earlier, you can apply a Transform to either the LayoutTransform property or the RenderTransform property. Figure 18-7 shows the architecture.

- If you apply the Transform to the LayoutTransform property, then the WPF layout engine applies the Transform when it is laying out the page and determining the positions of all the elements. In this case, the result of the Transform is taken into account when laying out the other elements.

- If you apply the Transform to the RenderTransform property, then the Transform isn't applied until the "last minute," when the screen is being rendered and after all the other elements have been laid out. Therefore, the transformed appearance isn't taken into account in the layout.

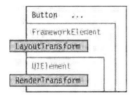

Figure 18-7. *Elements derived from FrameworkElement have both the LayoutTransform property and the RenderTransform property.*

Figure 18-8 illustrates the difference between applying the transform at layout time and applying it at render time. The UI consists of three buttons in a StackPanel.

- The screenshot on the left shows the button rotated at layout time. In this case, the button is rotated, and the layout engine determines the new dimensions of the button's bounding box and accounts for it before laying out the third button.

- In the screenshot on the right, the button isn't rotated until render time. By this time, the third button has already been assigned its position by the layout engine, so the rotated second button is rotated underneath the third button.

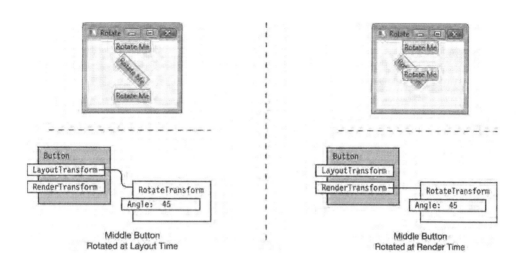

Figure 18-8. *A transform performed at layout time is figured into the layout. A transform performed at render time is perfomed heedless of other elements.*

The markup for the screenshot on the left is shown below. The markup for the screenshot on the right is the same, except that RenderTransform is substituted for LayoutTransform in the opening and closing Transform tags.

```
<StackPanel HorizontalAlignment="Center">
   <Button>Rotate Me</Button>

   <Button>
      <Button.LayoutTransform>
         <RotateTransform Angle="45"/>
      </Button.LayoutTransform>
      Rotate Me
   </Button>

   <Button>Rotate Me</Button>
</StackPanel>
```

The TranslateTransform

The TranslateTransform moves an element to a different position. For example, Figure 18-9 shows three buttons in a StackPanel. The middle button has been moved to the right by 30 units and down by 10.

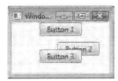

Figure 18-9. *A TranslateTransform applied to the middle button*

Figure 18-10 shows the structure of the TranslateTransform class. The TranslateTransform class has two important properties. Use the X property to set the right or left offset for the object and the Y property for the down and up offset.

Figure 18-10. *The TranslateTransform class contains an x offset and a y offset.*

The following markup produces the buttons shown in Figure 18-9:

```
<StackPanel HorizontalAlignment="Center">
    <Button Width="70">Button 1</Button>
    <Button Width="70">
                                    Move Right 30
                                          ↓
        <Button.RenderTransform>
            <TranslateTransform     X="30" Y="10"/>

        </Button.RenderTransform>          ↑

                                    Move Down 10

        Button 2
    </Button>
    <Button Width="70">Button 3</Button>
</StackPanel>
```

The SkewTransform

The SkewTransform skews an element at an angle. You can skew the X coordinates, the Y coordinates, or both.

Figure 18-11 shows examples of Button 2 being skewed in various ways. In the left set of screenshots, the X coordinates are skewed. In the center screenshots, the Y coordinates are skewed. In the one on the right, both X and Y coordinates are skewed.

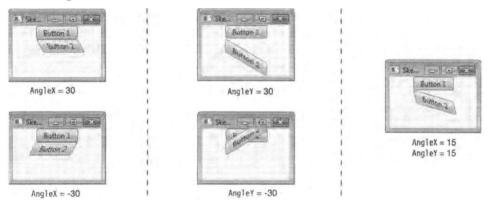

Figure 18-11. *The second button with various SkewTransform values applied*

Figure 18-12 illustrates several important properties of the SkewTransform class.

- The AngleX property skews the X coordinates of the element. A positive value for this property represents a counterclockwise angle from the y-axis.

- The AngleY property skews the *y* coordinates of the element. A positive value for this property represents a clockwise angle from the x-axis.

- The default position of the center of skewing is 0, 0. You can change that, however, by assigning values to the CenterX and CenterY properties.

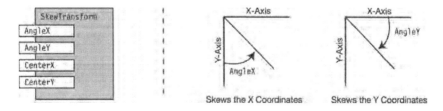

Figure 18-12. *The SkewTransform class allows you to skew the X coordinates, the Y coordinates, or both.*

419

Figure 18-13 shows a StackPanel with three buttons—two of which are skewed. The second button has its X values skewed, and the third button has its Y values skewed. The following markup produces the buttons:

```
<StackPanel HorizontalAlignment="Center">

    <Button Width="90" FontWeight="Bold" Margin="2">No Skew</Button>

    <Button Width="90" FontWeight="Bold" Margin="2">
        <Button.RenderTransform>
            <SkewTransform AngleX="30"/>
        </Button.RenderTransform>
        AngleX="30"
    </Button>

    <Button Width="90" FontWeight="Bold" Margin="2">
        <Button.RenderTransform>
            <SkewTransform AngleY="30"/>
        </Button.RenderTransform>
        AngleY="30"
    </Button>

</StackPanel>
```

This markup produces the window shown in Figure 18-13.

Figure 18-13. *The second button is skewed on it X coordinates, and the third button is skewed on its Y coordinates.*

The ScaleTransform

The scale transform changes the size of an element. You can choose whether the element should be scaled in the X direction, the Y direction, or both.

Figure 18-14 illustrates the important properties of the ScaleTransform class.

- The ScaleX and ScaleY properties set the scale values of the two dimensions. The default values are 1.0.

- The CenterX and CenterY properties set the point from which to scale the element.

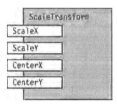

Figure 18-14. *The ScaleTransform class*

Figure 18-15 shows an example of a button that has been scaled in both directions. In the first screenshot, the button was scaled in the layout phase, and in the second it was scaled at the render phase.

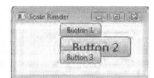

ScaleTransform at Layout

ScaleTransform at Render

Figure 18-15. *Screenshots of the ScaleTransform applied to Button 2 at layout and at render*

The following is the markup that produces the first screenshot in Figure 18-15:

```
<StackPanel HorizontalAlignment="Center">
   <Button Width="70">Button 1</Button>
   <Button Width="70">
      <Button.LayoutTransform>
         <ScaleTransform ScaleX="1.75" ScaleY="1.5"/>
      </Button.LayoutTransform>
      Button 2
   </Button>
   <Button Width="70">Button 3</Button>
</StackPanel>
```

BitmapEffects

The BitmapEffects feature is the second graphics feature that allows you to modify the appearance of an element. The BitmapEffects feature allows you to apply one of five different filters to an element's appearance.

Figure 18-16 illustrates the five effects applied to five Button objects. Remember, however, that the BitmapEffect property is declared down in the UIElement base class, so it is applicable to most visual elements. (Whether or not it's a good thing to use it on a particular element is another question.)

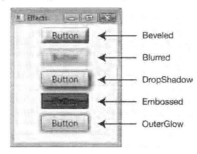

Figure 18-16. *Five buttons with the five different BitmapEffects applied*

The following is the markup for producing the button with the drop shadow effect—the third one down. Table 18-1 describes the five BitmapEffects.

```
<Button Content="Button">
    <Button.BitmapEffect><DropShadowBitmapEffect/></Button.BitmapEffect>
</Button>
```

Table 18-1. *Built-in BitmapEffects*

Name	Description
BevelBitmapEffect	Creates a beveled effect such that the interior looks raised and the edges look lowered
BlurBitmapEffect	Creates a blurred effect.
DropShadowBitmapEffect	Creates an effect that looks like the object is casting a shadow from a light source
EmbossBitmapEffect	Creates an effect that makes the object look like it is embossed.
OuterGlowBitmapEffect	Creates an effect that looks like a glow around the outer edge of the object.

The following is the markup that produces the window shown in Figure 18-16. In the markup, I've refactored all the properties of the buttons into a Button Style so that you can more easily see the BitmapEffect assignments. (The default color of the OuterGlowBitmapEffect is yellow, which didn't show up very well in the black-and-white screenshot, so I've changed the color to Gray.)

```xml
<Window.Resources>
    <Style TargetType="Button">
        <Setter Property="TextBlock.FontSize" Value="15"/>
        <Setter Property="TextBlock.Margin" Value="5"/>
        <Setter Property="TextBlock.Padding" Value="3"/>
        <Setter Property="TextBlock.Width" Value="80"/>
        <Setter Property="TextBlock.HorizontalAlignment" Value="Center"/>
        <Setter Property="TextBlock.VerticalAlignment" Value="Center"/>
    </Style>
</Window.Resources>
<StackPanel>

    <Button Content="Button">
        <Button.BitmapEffect><BevelBitmapEffect/></Button.BitmapEffect>
    </Button>

    <Button Content="Button">
        <Button.BitmapEffect><BlurBitmapEffect/></Button.BitmapEffect>
    </Button>

    <Button Content="Button">
        <Button.BitmapEffect><DropShadowBitmapEffect/></Button.BitmapEffect>
    </Button>

    <Button Content="Button">
        <Button.BitmapEffect><EmbossBitmapEffect/></Button.BitmapEffect>
    </Button>

    <Button Content="Button">
        <Button.BitmapEffect><OuterGlowBitmapEffect GlowColor="Gray"/>
        </Button.BitmapEffect>
    </Button>

</StackPanel>
```

Brushes

Brushes are used for painting an area with a color or graphic. Figure 18-17 illustrates the inheritance tree of the three categories of brushes—SolidColorBrushes, GradientBrushes, and TileBrushes. The white, dashed boxes represent abstract classes.

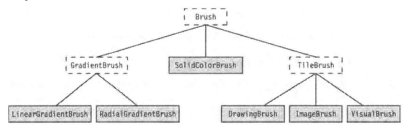

Figure 18-17. *The abstract Brush class and the classes derived from it*

In Chapter 3, I introduced SolidColorBrushes and GradientBrushes. In this chapter, I'll expand that coverage by going into more detail on LinearGradientBrushes and then covering the DrawingBrush and ImageBrush classes at the end of the chapter.

When I introduced brushes in Chapter 3, I hadn't yet covered XAML, so you only saw brushes created and used in the C# code (although you've seen them in many markup samples throughout the book). So for completeness, the first thing I want to show is that you can create Brushes using markup. For example, the following markup uses many different brushes assigned to the various Background, Foreground, and BorderBrush properties. The following markup produces the window shown in Figure 18-18:

```
<StackPanel Background="Yellow">
    <GroupBox Header="Buttons" Background="AliceBlue" BorderBrush="Blue"
            BorderThickness="3" Padding="10">
        <StackPanel>
            <Button Width="100" FontWeight="Bold" Background="Coral"
                    Foreground="White">Button 1</Button>
            <Button Width="100" FontWeight="Bold" Background="Coral"
                    Foreground="White">Button 2</Button>
            <Button Width="100" FontWeight="Bold" Background="Coral"
                    Foreground="White">Button 3</Button>
        </StackPanel>
    </GroupBox>
</StackPanel>
```

Figure 18-18. *A window using many brushes*

LinearGradientBrushes

As you saw in Chapter 3, a LinearGradientBrush paints an area with a changing line of color that starts as one color and ends as another. In Chapter 3, however, I only mentioned the StartPoint, the EndPoint, and the beginning and ending colors.

The LinearGradientBrush, however, also allows you to have multiple color points along the gradient's path. The graphic on the left of Figure 18-19 illustrates the important properties of the LinearGradientBrush class. They are the following:

- StartPoint and EndPoint hold points that define the vector that defines the path of the linear gradient.

- The GradientStops property is a collection of GradientStop objects—each of which defines the color at a position along the vector. The graphic at the right of the figure shows the structure of the GradientStop class objects that make up this collection.

- The SpreadMethod property specifies how WPF should render the area before the StartPoint and after the EndPoint.

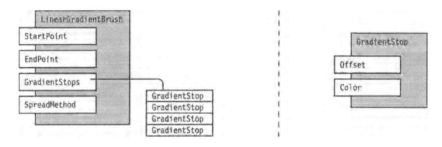

Figure 18-19. *The important members of the LinearGradientBrush and the GradientStop classes*

As you learned in Chapter 3, when you use a Brush to paint an area of an object, the dimensions of the object are always considered to range from position (0,0) in the top-left corner to (1,1) in the bottom-right corner, *regardless of the actual dimensions of object.*

By default, the vector defining the gradient path travels this path from (0,0) to (1,1). But you can set a different StartPoint and EndPoint for the vector. Figure 18-20 shows six buttons (with no text) painted with LinearGradientBrushes with various StartPoint and EndPoint values.

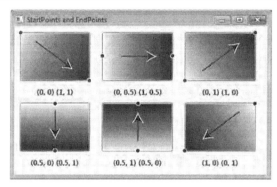

Figure 18-20. *StartPoints and EndPoints of a LinearGradientBrush*

The StartPoint and EndPoint values used in Figure 18-20 are all on the edges of the buttons, but they don't have to be. For example, the graphic on the right in Figure 18-21 shows the vector defined from (0.25, 0.25) to (0.75, 0.75).

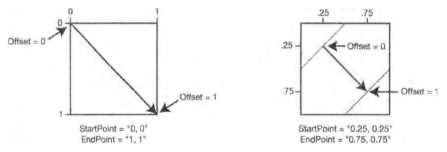

Figure 18-21. *The StartPoint and EndPoint represent the extent of the vector representing the LinearGradientBrush. Each GradientStop has an Offset position along the vector.*

Along the vector defined by the linear gradient, you can place any number of GradientStop objects.

- Each GradientStop object specifies a color and can be placed anywhere along the vector.

- The positions along the vector are specified as offsets—where the beginning of the vector has an offset of 0.0 and the end of the vector has an offset of 1.0.

- Between each GradientStop and the next, WPF gradually changes the color from that of the first one to that of the second one.

For example, the following markup specifies a LinearGradientBrush that paints the Background of a Button. The LinearGradientBrush has five GradientStops, including the start point and the end point.

```
<StackPanel>
    <Button Height="200" Width="230" Margin="10">
        <Button.Background>

            <LinearGradientBrush StartPoint="0,0" EndPoint="1,1">
                <GradientStop Offset="0"   Color="Red"/>
                <GradientStop Offset=".25" Color="Orange"/>
                <GradientStop Offset=".5"  Color="Green"/>
                <GradientStop Offset=".75" Color="Blue"/>
                <GradientStop Offset="1"   Color="Violet"/>
            </LinearGradientBrush>

        </Button.Background>
    </Button>
    <TextBlock HorizontalAlignment="Center" FontWeight="Bold">
        (0, 0) (1, 1)</TextBlock>
</StackPanel>
```

Figure 18-22 shows the window produced by this markup. Although it's difficult to see in black and white, the colors progress from red at the top-left corner to orange at the 0.25 offset along the vector, all the way to violet at the bottom-right corner.

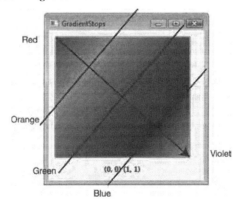

Figure 18-22. *A LinearGradientBrush with five GradientStops, going from red to violet and passing through orange, green, and blue*

In the examples so far, we've been using vectors that go from one corner to the other, or on the edges. But what if we specified the StartPoint and EndPoint at positions in the interior? If you look back at Figure 18-21, the graphic on the right shows the vector of a LinearGradientBrush that goes from (0.25, 0.25) to (0.75, 0.75). Notice that the top-left corner and the bottom-right corner are not included in the span of the vector. How should WPF render these areas?

You can specify how to render these areas by setting the LinearGradientBrush's SpreadMethod property. The enumeration for this property has three possible values.

- Pad: This value specifies that the area before the StartPoint should be painted with the color used at the StartPoint and that the area after the EndPoint should be painted with the color set at the EndPoint.

- Reflect: This value specifies that the area before the StartPoint should be painted as a *reflection* of the colors along the vector. That is, the colors are in the opposite order, starting at the StartPoint and going in the opposite direction of the brush's vector. The same is true at the EndPoint, where the area beyond the Endpoint is a reflection of the end of the vector.

- Repeat: This value specifies that the coloring of the vector repeats after the EndPoint and before the StartPoint. That is, it is just a repeating pattern of colors gradients.

Figure 18-23 shows three versions of a LinearGradientBrush that are identical except for the values of their SpreadMethod properties.

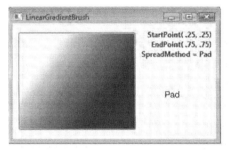
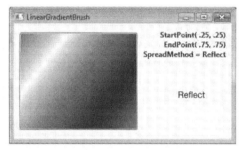
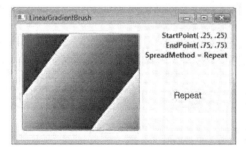

Figure 18-23. *The SpreadMethod property of a LinearGradientBrush specifies the appearance before the StartPoint and after the EndPoint.*

Shapes

WPF provides six shape elements you can use into your UI. The following are some important things to know about the shapes:

- There are five simple shape classes and a shape class called Path, which allows you to define arbitrary shapes.

- The shape classes are derived from the abstract Shape class, which contains the properties for setting the line stroke and the fill of the shape.

- The shapes are elements and can therefore be placed directly into your UI.

Figure 18-24 illustrates some of the important properties of the six Shape classes.

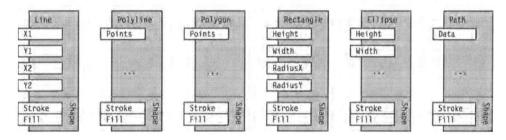

Figure 18-24. *WPF provides five simple shapes and a complex Path shape.*

Figure 18-25 shows examples of the five simple shapes.

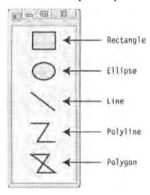

Figure 18-25. *Examples of the five simple shapes*

The following markup produces the shapes in the window shown in Figure 18-25:

```
<StackPanel Orientation="Vertical" HorizontalAlignment="Center">
    <Rectangle Stroke="Black" StrokeThickness="2" Margin="10"
               Height="30" Width="40" Fill="AliceBlue"/>

    <Ellipse   Stroke="Black" StrokeThickness="2" Margin="10"
               Height="30" Width="40" Fill="AliceBlue"/>

    <Line      Stroke="Black" StrokeThickness="2" Margin="10"
               X1="0" Y1="0" X2="40" Y2="30"/>

    <Polyline  Stroke="Black" StrokeThickness="2" Margin="10"
               Points="0,0 30,0 10,30 40,30"/>

    <Polygon   Stroke="Black" StrokeThickness="2" Margin="10"
               Points="0,0 30,0 10,30 40,30"/>
</StackPanel>
```

The remaining shape class is the Path class, which allows you to produce arbitrary two-dimensional shapes. You do this by creating an object derived from the Geometry class and assigning it to the Data property of the shape object. I'll explain the Geometry-derived classes in the next section. Figure 18-26 illustrates the six shape types.

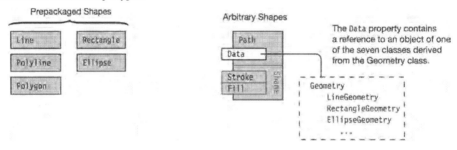

Figure 18-26. *The Path shape draws whatever shape is defined by the Geometry object assigned to its Data property.*

The Geometry Classes

The Geometry classes allow you to define two-dimensional shapes and paths. Geometry objects themselves aren't visible. Instead, you use them to specify a shape to paint, to specify a hit test region, or to specify a path along which to animate an object.

There are eight Geometry classes in the System.Windows.Media namespace. Figure 18-27 shows a categorization of the classes. The following are the important things to know about the Geometry classes:

- The Geometry class is the base class for the other classes. It's an abstract class and therefore can't be instantiated. Instead, you'll use the seven derived classes.

- The Geometry classes are not designed to render themselves. Their function is to *define* a shape—not to *draw* a shape. To render a Geometry, you assign it to a Path shape, which performs the rendering.

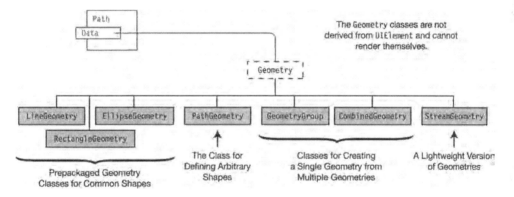

Figure 18-27. *The Geometry classes*

The following markup shows an example of using a Path shape to render an EllipseGeometry. The Path object takes care of applying the Black stroke and filling the interior with the LightBlue color.

```
<Path Stroke="Black" Fill="LightBlue" StrokeThickness="2">
   <Path.Data>
      <EllipseGeometry RadiusX="20" RadiusY="15" Center="30,25"/>
   </Path.Data>
</Path>
```

In the following sections, I'll describe the various Geometry classes.

The Simple Geometry Classes

The LineGeometry, RectangleGeometry, and EllipseGeometry classes are simple prepackaged geometries corresponding, as you probably guessed, to the line, rectangle, and ellipse. Figure 18-28 shows a window with an instance of each of these class objects.

Figure 18-28. *Examples of the simple Geometry classes*

Figure 18-29 illustrates the structures of the three simple Geometry classes. Although most of the properties are pretty straightforward, some require a bit of explanation.

- The Rect property of the RectangleGeometry is of type System.Windows.Rect. It takes four numeric parameters, which are the following:

    - X: The X coordinate of the left of the rectangle.

    - Y: The Y coordinate of the top of the rectangle.

    - The last two numbers are the Width and Height of the rectangle, respectively— *not the X and Y coordinates of the bottom-right corner!*

- The RadiusX and RadiusY properties are used in both the RectangleGeometry and EllipseGeometry classes. In the RectangleGeometry class they allow you to round the corners of the rectangle. In the EllipseGeometry class they determine the shape of the ellipse.

- All three classes derive from the Geometry class, which contains a property called Transform. You can use this property to attach to the Geometry object one of the Transform objects you looked at earlier in the chapter.

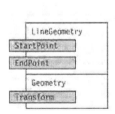 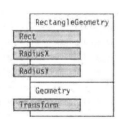 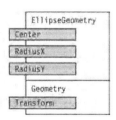

Figure 18-29. *Architecture of the simple Geometry classes*

The following is the markup that produces the shapes shown in Figure 18-28:

```
<StackPanel Orientation="Horizontal">
    <Path Stroke="Black" StrokeThickness="2">
        <Path.Data>
            <LineGeometry StartPoint="10,10" EndPoint="50, 40"/>
        </Path.Data>
    </Path>

    <Path Stroke="Black" Fill="LightBlue" StrokeThickness="2">
        <Path.Data>
            <RectangleGeometry Rect="10,10  40,30"/>
                                      ↑      ↑
        </Path.Data>
    </Path>                      Position  Size

    <Path Stroke="Black" Fill="LightBlue" StrokeThickness="2">
        <Path.Data>
            <EllipseGeometry RadiusX="20" RadiusY="15" Center="30,25"/>
        </Path.Data>
    </Path>
</StackPanel>
```

The PathGeometry Class

The PathGeometry class allows you to specify arbitrarily complex paths, comprising combinations of lines, arcs, and Bezier ("BEH-zee-ay") curves. Figure 18-30 shows an example of a path with a PathGeometry consisting of several line segments and an arc segment.

Like all the Geometry classes, a PathGeometry doesn't actually draw anything on the screen; it just specifies a path. The drawing is performed by the Path object that contains it.

Figure 18-30. *An example of a simple PathGeometry object*

The architecture of a PathGeometry object consists of three types of class objects:

- The PathGeometry object itself contains a property called Figures, which is a collection of PathFigure objects.

- Each PathFigure object has a property called Segments, which is a collection of path segment definitions.

- The path segments are the objects that actually describe positions, arcs, and paths. There are seven types of path segments, which include the LineSegment, the ArcSegment, and five types of Bezier segments.

Figure 18-31 shows an example of the structure of a PathGeometry object.

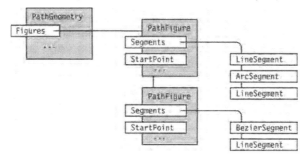

Figure 18-31. *A PathGeometry can contain any number of PathFigures, and each PathFigure can contain any number of segments.*

Figure 18-32 shows the most important properties of the classes associated with a
PathGeometry. In the following sections, I'll cover the various types of path segments in more detail.

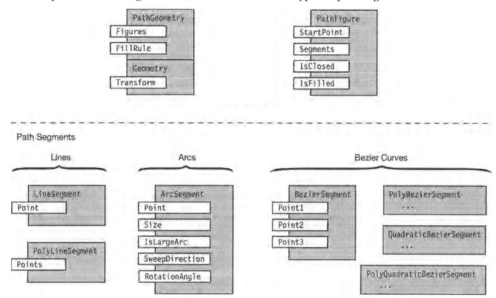

Figure 18-32. *The classes associated with a PathGeometry*

The LineSegment and the PolyLineSegment

The LineSegment class allows you to specify a single line. The PolyLineSegment class allows you to specify a sequence of lines, where the beginning point of each line is the end point of the previous line.

Figure 18-33 illustrates the structures of the two classes. The following are several important things to notice about these classes:

- The LineSegment class has only a single Point property. This specifies the *end point* of the line segment. The starting point of the line segment is wherever the previous segment in the PathFigure ended.

- Although the PolyLineSegment contains a collection of points in its Points property, like the LineSegment, its starting point is the end point of the previous segment in the PathFigure.

Figure 18-33. *The LineSegment and PolyLineSegment classes*

Figure 18-34 shows markup for two paths that draw the same shape. The first path uses three LineSegment objects. The second path uses a single PolyLineSegment object. Notice that in both cases the starting point is set in the PathFigure element. The screenshot at the right of the figure shows the resulting output.

```
<StackPanel>
    <Path Stroke="Black" StrokeThickness="3">
        <Path.Data>
            <PathGeometry>
                <PathFigure StartPoint="10, 10">
                    <LineSegment Point="100, 10"/>
                    <LineSegment Point="100, 40"/>
                    <LineSegment Point="70, 40"/>
                </PathFigure>
            </PathGeometry>
        </Path.Data>
    </Path>
    <Path Stroke="Black" StrokeThickness="3">
        <Path.Data>
            <PathGeometry>
                <PathFigure StartPoint="10, 10">
                    <PolyLineSegment Points="100,10 100,40 70,40"/>
                </PathFigure>
            </PathGeometry>
        </Path.Data>
    </Path>
</StackPanel>
```

Figure 18-34. *Examples of PathGeometry objects using the LineSegment and the PolyLineSegment*

The ArcSegment

An *elliptical arc* is a segment of an ellipse. The ArcSegment class allows you to specify elliptical arcs of various sizes and shapes.

The screenshots in Figure 18-35 show four elliptical arcs (drawn with solid lines) on top of the ellipses (drawn with a dashed line) of which they are segments. The following are some of the important things to notice about the arcs:

- Each arc has a start point and an end point on the path of the ellipse. In the two screenshots on the top, the start point and end point are on the bottom part of the ellipse. In the bottom two, they're on the top.

- Given a particular ellipse and the start and end points of the desired arc, you can create either a small arc or a large arc, depending on whether you sweep clockwise or counterclockwise along the arc. The top two screenshots show large arcs. The bottom two show small arcs.

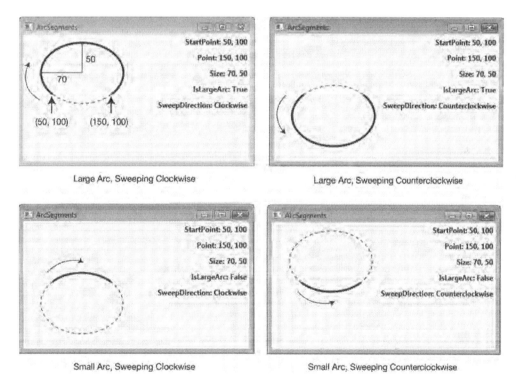

Figure 18-35. *Given a start point, an end point, and a size, there are four different arcs that can be produced.*

Figure 18-36 shows the most important properties of the ArcSegment class. These properties can produce any elliptical arc. The following are important things to know about ArcSegment:

- The Point property specifies the end point of the arc. There is no start point specified in the class, because the start point is the end point of the previous segment in the figure or the StartPoint set in the containing object. The default value is (0, 0).

- The Size property consists of the radius of the width of the reference ellipse and the radius of the height of the reference ellipse. Notice that these are radii, *not diameters*. The default value is (0, 0), which is a Width (radius) of 0 and a Height (radius) of 0.

- The IsLargeArc property specifies whether to produce the large arc or the small arc on the reference ellipse. The default value is false.

- The SweepDirection property specifies whether the arc is drawn clockwise or counterclockwise around the ellipse from the start point to the end point. The default value is CounterClockwise.

- The RotationAngle property specifies the amount, in degrees, that the ellipse is rotated around the x-axis. The default value is 0.

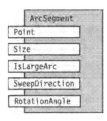

Figure 18-36. *The properties of ArcSegment (plus a start point) determine a unique arc.*

The following markup produces the arc shown in the screenshot at the top left of Figure 18-35:

```
<Grid>
   <Path Stroke="Black" StrokeThickness="3">
      <Path.Data>  <PathGeometry>
            <PathFigure StartPoint="50,100">
               <ArcSegment Point="150,100" Size="70,50"
                            IsLargeArc="True"  SweepDirection="Clockwise"/>
            </PathFigure>
         </PathGeometry>
      </Path.Data>
   </Path>
</Grid>
```

Combining Geometries

There are two ways in which you can combine several Geometry objects:

- The GeometryGroup class can contain a collection of Geometry objects that are treated as a single object. You can use a GeometryGroup object wherever you can use a single Geometry object.

- The CombinedGeometry class takes two Geometry objects and combines them into a single Geometry object that has a different path than either of the two separate objects. There are four operations you can use to combine the objects—Union, Intersection, Exclude, and Xor.

Figure 18-37 shows an example of a GeometryGroup with two ellipses. The Data property of the Path class requires a reference to a single Geometry object, so we can't place two EllipseGeometry objects directly into the Data property. To solve that problem, you can place the ellipses inside a GeometryGroup and assign *that* to the Data property.

```
<Grid>
    <Path Stroke="Black" StrokeThickness="2" Fill="LightGray">
        <Path.Data>
            <GeometryGroup FillRule="Nonzero">
                <EllipseGeometry Center="60,50"
                                 RadiusX="40" RadiusY="30"/>
                <EllipseGeometry Center="100,50"
                                 RadiusX="40" RadiusY="30"/>
            </GeometryGroup>
        </Path.Data>
    </Path>
</Grid>
```

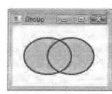

Figure 18-37. A GeometryGroup is a collection of Geometry objects that can be used anywhere a single Geometry object can be used.

Unlike the GeometryGroup class, which is a just a collection of Geometry objects, the CombinedGeometry class combines parts of exactly two Geometry objects into a single object that is unlike either of the two original objects. Figure 18-38 shows the results of combining two overlapping ellipses, using the four available combining operations.

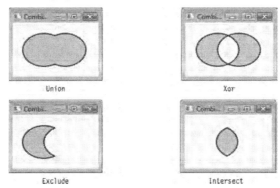

Figure 18-38. *The CombinedGeometry class allows you to combine two Geometry objects, yielding a new path different from either of the two initial Geometries.*

Figure 18-39 shows the important properties of the CombinedGeometry class. Notice that it takes exactly two Geometry objects and a mode for combining them.

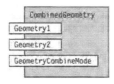

Figure 18-39. *The CombinedGeometry class*

The following is the markup of the top-right screen in Figure 18-38:

```
<Path Stroke="Black" StrokeThickness="2" Fill="LightGray">
   <Path.Data>
      <CombinedGeometry GeometryCombineMode="Xor">

         <CombinedGeometry.Geometry1>
            <EllipseGeometry Center="60,50" RadiusX="40" RadiusY="30"/>
         </CombinedGeometry.Geometry1>
         <CombinedGeometry.Geometry2>
            <EllipseGeometry Center="100,50" RadiusX="40" RadiusY="30"/>
         </CombinedGeometry.Geometry2>

      </CombinedGeometry>
   </Path.Data>
</Path>
```

Path Markup Syntax

From the previous examples, you can see that the markup for the PathFigures in a PathGeometry object can be quite extensive, even to describe simple paths. To remedy this, WPF provides the *path markup syntax*, which allows you to significantly abbreviate the markup.

To use the path markup syntax, you assign a string to the Figures property of the PathGeometry. The string contains shorthand for describing the path. The following are some important things to know about the path markup syntax:

- The syntax consists of single-letter commands followed by sets of numeric parameters. The meanings of the numeric parameters depend on the command.

- There are three types of commands.

  - *The move command*: This command sets the start point of the figure. This command is either an uppercase M or lowercase m.

  - *The draw commands*: There are a number of different draw commands, depending on the path to be drawn.

  - *The close command*: This command is optional and is either an uppercase Z or a lowercase z.

- The numeric parameters can be separated by either commas or whitespace. (Although the parser doesn't care, I find it significantly easier to read the X and Y coordinate pairs when they're separated by commas.)

For example, the following PathGeometry uses the path markup syntax to describe the first of the two paths from the previous example. Notice the following about the markup:

- The first command is an uppercase M. This is the move command, which, in this case, sets the starting point of the figure to position 10, 10. The fact that the command is uppercase means that the position is an *absolute* position. A lowercase m, by comparison, means "relative to the previous position."

- The second command is the uppercase L. This is the "line to" command, which means that the series of coordinate positions following the command are points in the path. As with the M command, uppercase means that the points specify absolute positions, and lowercase means that each point is relative to the previous point.

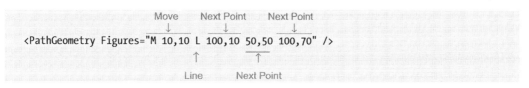

The following markup uses path markup syntax to describe two multi-segment paths:

```
<Grid>
    <Path Stroke="Black" StrokeThickness="3">
        <Path.Data>
            <PathGeometry Figures="M 10,10 L 100,10 50,50 100,70
                                   M 10,50 L 10,90 100,90" />
        </Path.Data>
    </Path>
</Grid>
```

Table 18-2 summarizes the path markup syntax commands.

Table 18-2. *Summary of the Path Markup Syntax Draw Commands*

Syntax	Parameters	Description
L	points	The Line command. Draws a line or a sequence of lines from the current position to an endpoint.
H	x	The Horizontal command. Draws a horizontal line from the current position to the given X coordinate position. The Y coordinate remains the same as that of the start position.
V	y	The Vertical command. Draws a vertical line from the current position to the given Y coordinate position. The X coordinate remains the same as that of the start position.
A	size, rotation angle, isLargeArcFlag, sweepDirectionFlag, endpoint	The Arc command. Draws an elliptical arc.
C, Q, S, T	Various control points and end points	These represent the four Bezier curve commands: cubic Bezier, quadratic Bezier, smooth cubic Bezier, and smooth quadratic Bezier. We won't be covering the Bezier curves in detail.

Filling Geometries

As you've seen, Geometry objects *define* paths or shapes. Geometry objects, however, are not elements and therefore aren't directly rendered in your layout. Instead, they must be hosted in an element, such as Path, that draws them. The Path element allows you to apply a Stroke and a Fill to a Geometry object.

- The Stroke contains a reference to a Brush object that is used to paint the path of the Geometry.

- The Fill contains a reference to a Brush used to paint the interior of the object.

- The IsClosed property is a bool value specifying whether to automatically add a line from the end point of the path to the starting point.

- The IsFilled property is a bool value specifying whether to paint the interior of the path with the Fill brush.

When paths become complex, however, it can be confusing as to which regions should be considered interior regions and filled and which regions should be considered exterior regions and not filled. I'll start with the simple path shown in Figure 18-40. This path is a simple closed ArcSegment filled with the LightGray brush. The result is pretty straightforward.

```xml
<Grid>
    <Path Stroke="Black" StrokeThickness="2" Fill="LightGray">
        <Path.Data>

            <PathGeometry FillRule="EvenOdd">
                <PathFigure StartPoint="60,110" IsClosed="True">
                    <ArcSegment Point="120,110" Size="50,40"
                                IsLargeArc="True"
                                SweepDirection="Clockwise"/>
                </PathFigure>
            </PathGeometry>

        </Path.Data>
    </Path>
</Grid>
```

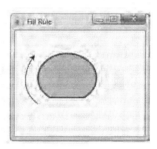

Figure 18-40. *Simple filled path*

If, however, you add an identical ArcSegment, offset to the right and up a bit, you get the result shown in Figure 18-41. In this case, the overlapping region is considered outside the path and is therefore not filled. Clearly, I need to cover the rules for determining which regions are interior and which are exterior.

```
<Grid>
    <Path Stroke="Black" StrokeThickness="2" Fill="LightGray">
        <Path.Data>
            <PathGeometry FillRule="EvenOdd">
                <PathFigure StartPoint="60,110" IsClosed="True">
                    <ArcSegment Point="120,110" Size="50,40"
                                IsLargeArc="True"
                                SweepDirection="Clockwise"/>
                </PathFigure>
                <PathFigure StartPoint="100,80" IsClosed="True">
                    <ArcSegment Point="160,80" Size="50,40"
                                IsLargeArc="True"
                                SweepDirection="Clockwise"/>
                </PathFigure>
            </PathGeometry>
        </Path.Data>
    </Path>
</Grid>
```

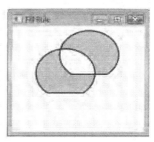

Figure 18-41. *An exterior region inside a path*

There are two rules by which many vector graphics programs (not just WPF) determine whether a region is interior or exterior. You can choose one or the other of these two rules for a particular path. They're called the *EvenOdd* rule and the *Nonzero* rule.

To determine whether a region is considered interior or exterior, start by doing the following. Select a point in the region, and draw a line from that point, in any direction, until you're outside of the figure.

- Using the EvenOdd rule—count the number of times the line crosses the path.

    - If the count is *odd*, the region is considered an *interior* region.

    - If the count is *even*, the region is considered an *exterior* region.

- Using the Nonzero rule, you must know the sweep direction of each path the line crosses.

    - Each time the line crosses the path, where the path is being drawn in one direction, add 1 to the count.

    - Each time the line crosses the path, where the path is being drawn in the other direction, subtract 1 from the count.

    - If, at the end, the total is 0, then the region is considered *exterior*. If the total is not 0, then the region is considered *interior*.

You can specify which rule to use by setting the FillRule attribute of the PathGeometry object. Figure 18-42 illustrates the different rules being applied to two different configurations.

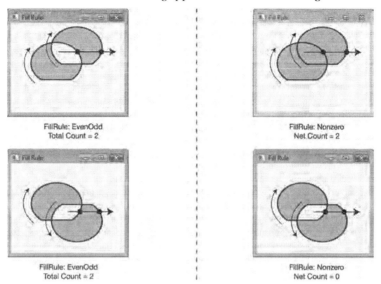

Figure 18-42. *Determining whether a region is interior or exterior using the EvenOdd rule and the Nonzero rule*

The markup for the first window shown at the top left of Figure 18-42 is shown next. Notice that the FillRule property of the PathGeometry object is set to EvenOdd.

```
<Grid>
    <Path Stroke="Black" StrokeThickness="2" Fill="LightGray">
        <Path.Data>                    Set the FillRule.
                                            ↓
            <PathGeometry FillRule="EvenOdd">
                <PathFigure StartPoint="60,110" IsClosed="True">
                    <ArcSegment Point="120,110" Size="50,40"
                                IsLargeArc="True" SweepDirection="Clockwise"/>
                </PathFigure>
                <PathFigure StartPoint="100,80" IsClosed="True">
                    <ArcSegment Point="160,80" Size="50,40"
                                IsLargeArc="True" SweepDirection="Clockwise"/>
                </PathFigure>
            </PathGeometry>

        </Path.Data>
    </Path>
</Grid>
```

445

Drawings

WPF allows you to use many type of graphics objects, and you can use them in various ways. WPF supplies two sets of classes that allow you to use graphics for different purposes. Figure 18-43 illustrates these sets of classes.

- There are three classes, used to package graphics for a particular use. The names of these classes begin with the word Drawing (the Drawing*XXX* classes). These classes are the following:

    - DrawingImage: This class packages graphics to be used as images.

    - DrawingBrush: This class packages graphics to be used as Brushes.

    - DrawingVisual: This class packages graphics to be used as graphic objects called Visuals.

- There are four classes (the *XXX*Drawing classes) derived from the abstract Drawing class that are used for packaging various types of graphics so they can be used by any of the three Drawing*XXX* classes.

- There's also a fifth class derived from Drawing, called DrawingGroup, that serves as a collection of *XXX*Drawing objects.

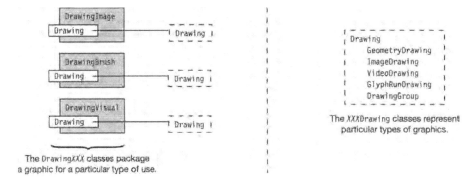

Figure 18-43. *The DrawingXXX classes and the XXXDrawing classes*

These classes together allow you to do amazing things with graphics. Figure 18-44 shows the important properties of both sets of classes.

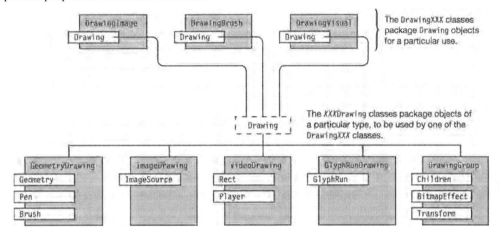

Figure 18-44. The three DrawingXXX classes each take a reference to an object derived from the Drawing class and wrap it for a particular use.

▓ **Note** The names of the *XXX*Drawing classes describe the type of graphic they package, in other words, Geometry, Image, and Video, but what about GlyphRun? A GlyphRun is a sequential set of characters or symbols sharing the same typeface and font size. It contains all the information needed to produce a visual representation of each character or symbol.

The DrawingImage Class

The DrawingImage class allows you to use a graphic as an image. Figure 18-45 shows a DrawingImage packaging a GeometryDrawing and presented in an Image element.

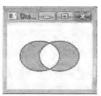

Figure 18-45. *An Image element using a DrawingImage as its Source*

Figure 18-46 shows the markup used to produce the screenshot in Figure 18-45. Notice that the Image's Source property is set with a DrawingImage, which packages a GeometryDrawing, which packages a CombinedGeometry object.

```
<Grid>
    <Image Width="100" Height="60">
        <Image.Source>

            <DrawingImage>
                <DrawingImage.Drawing>

                    <GeometryDrawing Brush="Aqua">
                        <GeometryDrawing.Pen>
                            <Pen Thickness="1" Brush="Black"/>
                        </GeometryDrawing.Pen>
                        <GeometryDrawing.Geometry>
                            <CombinedGeometry GeometryCombineMode="Xor">
                                <CombinedGeometry.Geometry1>
                                    <EllipseGeometry Center="60,50"
                                                     RadiusX="40" RadiusY="30"/>
                                </CombinedGeometry.Geometry1>
                                <CombinedGeometry.Geometry2>
                                    <EllipseGeometry Center="100,50"
                                                     RadiusX="40" RadiusY="30"/>
                                </CombinedGeometry.Geometry2>
                            </CombinedGeometry>
                        </GeometryDrawing.Geometry>
                    </GeometryDrawing>

                </DrawingImage.Drawing>
            </DrawingImage>

        </Image.Source>
    </Image>
</Grid>
```

Figure 18-46. *The markup for the shapes in Figure 18-45*

The DrawingBrush Class

The DrawingBrush class allows you to package a graphic to be used as a Brush. For example, Figure 18-47 shows the same CombinedGeometry object as in the previous example, but this time it's being used as a Brush to paint the Background of a Button.

Figure 18-47. *A Button using a DrawingBrush to paint its Background*

The following is the markup that produces this button. In this case, the Button's Background property is assigned a DrawingBrush, which wraps a GeometryDrawing, which wraps the CombinedGeometry object.

```
<Grid>
    <Button Height="50" Width="100" FontWeight="Bold" Content="My Button">
        <Button.Background>

            <DrawingBrush>
                <DrawingBrush.Drawing>

                    <GeometryDrawing Brush="Aqua">
                        <GeometryDrawing.Pen>
                            <Pen Thickness="1" Brush="Black"/>
                        </GeometryDrawing.Pen>
                        <GeometryDrawing.Geometry>
                            <CombinedGeometry GeometryCombineMode="Xor">
                                <CombinedGeometry.Geometry1>
                                    <EllipseGeometry Center="60,50"
                                                     RadiusX="40" RadiusY="30"/>
                                </CombinedGeometry.Geometry1>
                                <CombinedGeometry.Geometry2>
                                    <EllipseGeometry Center="100,50"
                                                     RadiusX="40" RadiusY="30"/>
                                </CombinedGeometry.Geometry2>
                            </CombinedGeometry>
                        </GeometryDrawing.Geometry>
                    </GeometryDrawing>

                </DrawingBrush.Drawing>
            </DrawingBrush>

        </Button.Background>
    </Button>
</Grid>
```

As an example that's a bit more interesting, notice that one of the *XXX*Drawing classes is VideoDrawing. This means that you should be able to package a video object to be used by a DrawingBrush to paint a surface. Although I won't cover video until Chapter 20, I'll give you a preview by using a video to paint the Background of a Button. Figure 18-48 shows the screenshot. (I realize it's not very impressive since you can't see it playing on the printed page, but you can copy the code and try it yourself.)

Figure 18-48. *A Button Background being painted by a video*

For reasons you'll understand when you get to Chapter 20, you can't do this all in markup. The video player I'm using must be created and manipulated in the code-behind. The following is the markup:

```
<Grid>
    <Button Height="70" Width="100" Foreground ="White" Content="My Button">
        <Button.Background>
            <DrawingBrush x:Name="lakeBrush"/>
        </Button.Background>
    </Button>
</Grid>
```

The following is the code-behind. This code assumes you have a video file called Lake.wmv as a Content object in your project and that it is copied to the output folder on compilation.

```
public Window1()
{
    InitializeComponent();

    MediaPlayer player = new MediaPlayer();
    player.Open( new Uri( "Lake.wmv", UriKind.Relative ) );

    VideoDrawing videoDrawing = new VideoDrawing();
    videoDrawing.Rect = new Rect( 0, 0, 50, 50 );
    videoDrawing.Player = player;

    lakeBrush.Drawing = videoDrawing;
    player.Play();
}
```

Summary

In this chapter, you saw six of WPF's features for creating and modifying visual effects. These features allow you to create visually rich programs with relatively little effort. The features I covered in this chapter fall into three major categories. These categories are classes that modify the appearance of an element, classes used for painting an area, and classes for creating two-dimensional shapes and figures.

The classes that change the appearance of an element can be summarized as follows:

- *Transforms*: The six Transform classes allow you to modify the appearance of most visual elements.

  - You can use transforms to do the following to an element: rotate it, change its size, skew it, or move it. You can also combine any number of these features.

  - You can apply transforms during the layout phase of construction or during the render phase of construction.

- *BitmapEffects*: The five BitmapEffect classes are filters you can apply to the rendering of an element. Each filter produces a different visual effect. The five effects are the following: bevel, blur, drop shadow, emboss, and outer glow.

The brush classes paint an area. These consist of the solid color brushes, gradient brushes, and tile brushes.

The categories of classes for creating two-dimensional shapes and figures are the following:

- *Shapes*: These classes are visual elements that produce shaped objects. There are five classes that produce simple shapes, and the Path class, which can produce arbitrarily complex shapes. The simple shapes are lines, multiple lines, polygons, rectangles, and ellipses.

- *Geometries*: The Geometry classes are not, in themselves, visual objects. Instead, they define shapes. You can render Geometry objects by assigning them to a Path shape. You can also use them for defining regions or specifying a path along which to animate an object (Chapter 19).

- *Drawings*: These classes allow you to take a particular type of graphic element and package it to be used as an image, as a brush, or as an object called a *visual*.

CHAPTER 19

■ ■ ■

Animation

What Is Animation?

A graphic animation, such as an animated cartoon, is a sequence of frames, where the objects in each frame are moved just a small bit from where they were in the previous frame. When the frames are shown in rapid succession, the objects in the frames appear to be moving.

In WPF, the term *animation* has a more restricted meaning. It refers to the process of having WPF sequentially change the value of a dependency property from one value to another in extremely small increments over a period of time. You can use this to give objects the appearance of movement.

For example, you could have WPF animate the FontSize property of a button from 12.0 to 22.0 over a period of one second. Figure 19-1 illustrates this animation. The three screenshots at the top of the figure show the text at different sizes as it grows. The illustration below each screenshot shows the value of the FontSize property at that moment in time.

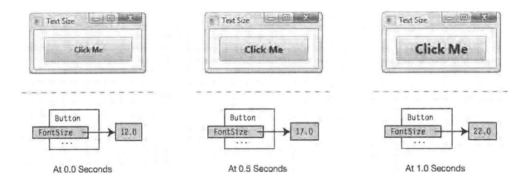

Figure 19-1. *The button's FontSize property is animated to grow from 12.0 points to 22.0 points.*

The following are some important things to know about animation:

- An animation always works on a *single* dependency property. There can, however, be many animations in progress simultaneously, as you'll see shortly.

- Only dependency properties can be animated.

- Support for WPF animation is in the System.Windows.Media.Animation namespace.

- Animation can't change the structure of the visual tree. That is, it can't add or delete elements. It can, however, make objects appear or disappear by animating the object's Opacity property.

- The speed of an animation is independent of the speed of the hardware executing it. That is, a particular animation performed on a fast processor will take the same amount of time as when it's performed on a slow machine. When performed on the faster machine, however, the animation appears smoother.

The following is the markup for the previous example. It simply creates a button named myButton.

```
<Grid>
  <Button Name="myButton" FontWeight="Bold" Height="40" Width="150">
    Click Me</Button>
</Grid>
```

The code-behind, shown next, contains the code for creating the animation. Notice the following about the code:

- You must create an *animation object* for the property you want to animate. In this case, the program is animating the FontSize property.

  - Since the FontSize property is of type double, you must use the DoubleAnimation type.

  - Set the From, To, and Duration property values of the animation object. These specify the beginning and ending values to be used by the animation, as well as the duration over which to animate.

- Attach the animation object to the target object using the BeginAnimation method on the target object.

  - The BeginAnimation method connects the property and the animation object and starts the animation.

  - Notice that in the BeginAnimation method, you must use not the name of the property's CLR wrapper but the name of the backing dependency property, which includes the Property suffix. In this case, therefore, you must use FontSizeProperty, rather than just FontSize.

```
...
using System.Windows.Media.Animation;          ← Must use this namespace.

public Window1()
{ InitializeComponent();                   Create the animation object.
                                                      ↓
  DoubleAnimation animateFontSize = new DoubleAnimation();

  animateFontSize.From = 12.0;                          ← Set the start value.
  animateFontSize.To   = 22.0;                          ← Set the end value.
  animateFontSize.Duration = TimeSpan.Parse("0:0:1");  ← Set the duration.
                                            Include
                                            the suffix.
                                                ↓
  myButton.BeginAnimation( FontSizeProperty, animateFontSize );
}       ↑           ↑                      ↑                  ↑
     Target    Start the              Target              Animation
     Object    animation.        Dependency Property        Object
```

Animation Object Basics

To apply animation to a property, you must use an animation class that corresponds to the type of that property. For example, if the property is of type double, then you must use an animation object of type DoubleAnimation.

WPF provides a set of animation classes for many built-in .NET and WPF types. Basic animation classes are named *XXX*Animation, where *XXX* is the name of a .NET type or a WPF type. There are 17 of these classes. Each of these classes is derived from a base class called Timeline, which supplies most of its animation properties.

Table 19-1 lists the types for which animation classes exist. Notice that the animation types don't use the C# names. Instead, they use the .NET type names to which the C# types correspond.

Table 19-1. *The Basic Animation Types*

Category	Types
.NET types	Byte, Decimal, Double, Int16, Int32, Int64, Single
WPF types	Color, Point, Point3D, Quaternion, Rect, Rotation3D, Size, Thickness, Vector, Vector3D

Once you have an animation object of the right type, you need to set its properties so that it describes the timeline you want for the animation. Figure 19-2 shows a DoubleAnimation object on the right and a timeline on the left. The timeline is labeled showing which parts of an animation are affected by the different property values.

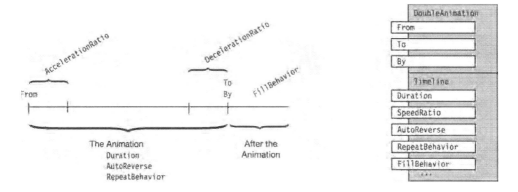

Figure 19-2. *An animation contains the information about how the dependency property should be changed.*

Although the meanings of the From, To, and Duration properties shown in the figure seem pretty clear, some of the other DoubleAnimation properties need more explanation.

I'll start with the three properties shown at the top of the DoubleAnimation figure. These three are declared in the DoubleAnimation subclass that extends the Timeline base class. If the From and To properties are set, then when the animation starts, WPF begins by setting the dependency property's value to the From value and starts from there. That is, the From and To animation object properties specify the exact beginning and ending values for the animated dependency property.

Rather than specifying an exact beginning and ending value, however, you can skip the From and To properties and use the By property instead. In this case, when the animation starts, the first thing it does is check the current value of the dependency property and use that as the From value. To that value, it adds the value assigned to the By property and uses the result as the To property. In other words, the By property acts as an offset from the dependency property's beginning value.

The Duration property specifies how long the animation should run. The longer the Duration, the slower the rate at which the property will change. The shorter the duration, the faster the property will change.

The AutoReverse, RepeatBehavior, and FillBehavior properties specify how the animation should act after the animation's duration is complete. Their behaviors are the following:

- AutoReverse: This is a bool type property you can use to specify whether the animation should reverse and go in the opposite direction when the Duration time is complete. If AutoReverse is set to true, the complete animation takes twice the Duration time.

- RepeatBehavior: This property specifies whether the animation should be repeated immediately upon completion. If the AutoReverse property is set to true, then the forward and backward processes combined are considered one iteration of the animation. Three types of values are accepted by the RepeatBehavior property:

  - An iteration count, such as 3 or 2.7. This double value specifies how many times the animation should repeat.

```
RepeatBehavior rb = new RepeatBehavior(2.7);
animateFontSize.RepeatBehavior = rb;
```

  - A TimeSpan object, which specifies exactly how long the animation should continue. The animation will continue to repeat until the time specified expires. If the TimeSpan value is less than the Duration, the animation terminates before completing one time. The following TimeSpan lasts for seven seconds.

```
RepeatBehavior rb = new RepeatBehavior( new TimeSpan( 0, 0, 7 ) );
animateFontSize.RepeatBehavior = rb;
```

  - The value Forever, which of course continues to repeat indefinitely.

```
animateFontSize.RepeatBehavior = RepeatBehavior.Forever;
```

- FillBehavior: This property specifies what should be done with the dependency property after the animation ends. It has two possible values:

  – If it's set to HoldEnd, then the animated property is left with the value it had at the end of the animation. This is the default.

  – If it's set to Stop, then the animated property is set to the value it had before the animation started.

By default, WPF determines the rate of an animation by taking the difference between the start point and the end point and dividing by the duration. This gives a constant rate. Several properties, however, allow you to modify the speed:

- The SpeedRatio property holds a value of type double, which specifies the rate of speed relative to the default speed. For example, if you set SpeedRatio to 2.0, the rate of change will be twice as fast, and the actual duration of the animation will be half what it would otherwise be.

- The AccelerationRatio property holds a double value between 0.0 and 1.0. This value represents a proportion of the animation's timeline starting at the beginning. For example, a value of 0.25 represents the first quarter of the distance of the animation. If this value were set, WPF would accelerate for the first quarter of the animation and then maintain a constant rate until the end.

- The DecelerationRatio property is similar to the AccelerationRatio property except that it controls a deceleration at the *end* of the animation. For example, if you set this value to 0.25, the animation spends the last quarter of its timeline decelerating.

Table 19-2 summarizes the most common animation properties.

Table 19-2. *The Basic Properties of an Animation Object*

Category	Property	Description
Limits and increments	From Type: double	Use this property to specify the value of the animated property at the start of the animation. If the From property isn't set, the animation starts at the animated property's current value.
	To Type: double	Use this property to specify the value of the animated property at the end of the animation.
	By Type: double	Use this property, instead of the To property, to specify the endpoint relative to the start point. The endpoint will be the initial value plus the value specified by the By parameter.
	Duration Type: double	Use this property to specify the duration of the animation from beginning to end. This doesn't include time required for AutoReverse or for repeated execution.
Variable rates	AccelerationRatio Type: double	Use this property to specify the proportion of time the animation should use accelerating at the start of the animation before evening off to a linear rate. This value must be between 0 and 1.
	DecelerationRatio Type: double	Use this property to specify the proportion of time the animation should use decelerating at the end of the animation before reaching the end value. This value must be between 0 and 1.
After the animation	AutoReverse Type: bool	Use this property to specify whether the animation should immediately run in reverse upon completion.
	RepeatBehavior Type: RepeatBehavior	Use this property to specify whether the animation should immediately halt, repeat some number of times, or repeat indefinitely upon completion of the first execution of the animation.
	FillBehavior Type: FillBehavior	Use this property to specify what the value of the animated property should be after the animation completes.

The AnimationClock Class

So far you've seen the structure and properties of animation objects. But an animation object itself is just an object that can generate a sequence of values. For every animation, WPF produces an AnimationClock object, which manages the value of the animated dependency property.

For example, at the beginning of the chapter, you saw a program that animated the FontSize property of a button from 12.0 points to 22.0 points. Figure 19-3 illustrates the components involved in this process. At the left of the figure is the button whose text is being animated. At the right are the objects that define and drive the animation:

- The AnimationClock object: This object keeps track of the amount of time since the beginning of the animation.

  - It queries the animation object to get the next value and assigns that value to the dependency property.

  - WPF produces the AnimationClock behind the scenes.

- The DoubleAnimation object: This object describes the timeline and produces a value of type double when queried by its AnimationClock object.

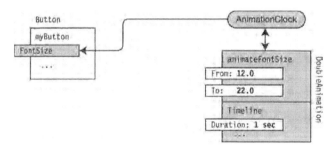

Figure 19-3. *The animation's AnimationClock object gets the next value from the animation object and sets the dependency property.*

Every dependency property that is animated must be associated with an animation object. However, an animation object can be shared by multiple animations, as illustrated in Figure 19-4.

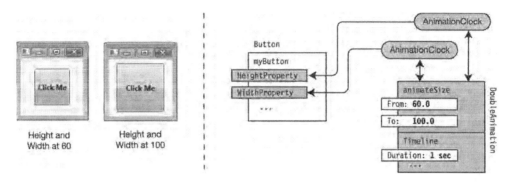

Figure 19-4. *A single animation object can be associated with multiple animations.*

The following is the markup for this program:

```
<Window x:Class="WidthAndHeight.Window1" ...
    Title="Window1" Height="130" Width="120">
    <Grid>
        <Button Name="myButton" FontWeight="Bold">Click Me</Button>
    </Grid>
</Window>
```

The following is the code-behind. Notice that both calls to BeginAnimation use the same animation object—animateSize.

```
public partial class Window1 : Window
{
    public Window1()
    {   InitializeComponent();

        DoubleAnimation animateSize = new DoubleAnimation();
        animateSize.From = 50.0;
        animateSize.To   = 80.0;

        myButton.BeginAnimation( HeightProperty, animateSize );
        myButton.BeginAnimation( WidthProperty,  animateSize );
    }
}
```

Storyboards

You now know how to animate a single dependency property using an animation object, by using the target object's BeginAnimation method. More frequently, however, you'll want to set up a group of animations that are performed as a set. The Storyboard class allows you to do exactly that. Figure 19-5 illustrates the structure of the Storyboard class. There are several important things to notice about the class:

- A Storyboard object has a property called Children, which is a collection of animation objects. These animations are started when the Storyboard is started.

- Like the animation classes, the Storyboard class derives from Timeline and therefore has its own instances of Duration, AutoReverse, and so on.

- The Storyboard class also has its own set of methods for starting, stopping, pausing, and resuming animation actions.

- A Storyboard object has its own clock, called a ClockGroup, that is used to synchronize the AnimationClocks of the animations in its Children collection.

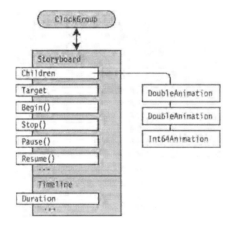

Figure 19-5. A Storyboard contains a group of animations, which are managed as a group.

Figure 19-6 shows screenshots of a program that uses a Storyboard containing two animation objects: one to animate the Height of the button and the other to animate the FontSize.

Figure 19-6. *A Storyboard animating the Height and FontSize of a button*

The following is the markup for the program. It simply declares the button. The animation code is contained in the code-behind.

```
<Window x:Class="Storyboard1.Window1" ...
    Title="Storyboard" Height="150" Width="200">
  <Grid>
    <Button Name="myButton" FontWeight="Bold" Height="40" Width="150">
        Click Me</Button>
  </Grid>
</Window>
```

Figure 19-7 shows the annotated code-behind for the program.

```
public partial class Window1 : Window
{
    public Window1()
    {
        InitializeComponent();

        DoubleAnimation animateFontSize = new DoubleAnimation();    ⎫  Create the animation object for
        animateFontSize.From = 12.0;                                 ⎬  use with the FontSize property.
        animateFontSize.To   = 22.0;                                 ⎭
        animateFontSize.Duration = TimeSpan.Parse( "0:0:2" );

        DoubleAnimation animateHeight = new DoubleAnimation();      ⎫  Create the animation object for
        animateHeight.From = 40.0;                                   ⎬  use with the Height property.
        animateHeight.To   = 80.0;                                   ⎭
        animateHeight.Duration = TimeSpan.Parse( "0:0:2" );

        Storyboard sb = new Storyboard();                            ⎫  Create the Storyboard object.
        sb.Duration = TimeSpan.Parse( "0:0:3" );                     ⎭

        sb.Children.Add( animateFontSize );                          ⎫  Add the animation objects to
        sb.Children.Add( animateHeight );                            ⎭  the Storyboard object.

        Storyboard.SetTargetName( animateFontSize, "myButton" );     ⎫  Connect the font size animation
        Storyboard.SetTargetProperty( animateFontSize,               ⎬  object to the button's FontSize
                new PropertyPath(Button.FontSizeProperty));          ⎭  property.

        Storyboard.SetTargetName( animateHeight, "myButton" );       ⎫  Connect the height animation
        Storyboard.SetTargetProperty( animateHeight,                 ⎬  object to the button's Height
                new PropertyPath( Button.HeightProperty ) );         ⎭  property.

        sb.Begin(myButton);                     ◄───────  Start the Storyboard.
    }
}
```

Figure 19-7. *A Storyboard contains and controls a set of animations.*

Figure 19-8 illustrates the structure of the program. The Storyboard architecture is shown on the left, and the button being animated is shown on the right. Notice that the two animation clocks are being driven by the Storyboard's ClockGroup object.

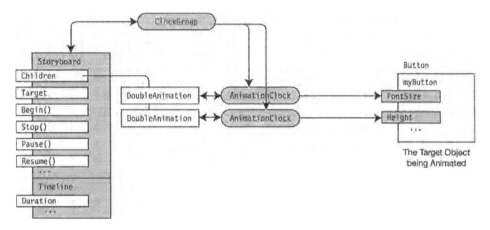

Figure 19-8. *The structure of a Storyboard with two animations*

Figure 19-9 shows the timelines of the three animation components—the Storyboard and the two animations it contains.

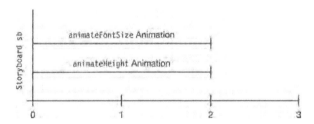

Figure 19-9. *The timelines of the three animation components*

You might have noticed that there are two ways to implement animations: directly hooking up an animation object with a dependency property and Storyboards. The names for these two architectures are *local animations* and *storyboard animations*, respectively.

Storyboards in Markup

So far, you've only seen how to implement animation using imperative code. That is, the examples have used the code-behind to create the animation objects and to set their properties. Local animations can only be done this way, with imperative code. Storyboard animations, however, can be created in markup. Where to place the Storyboard in the markup, however, isn't at all obvious. Storyboard animations must be placed inside EventTriggers.

Since an animation has a start point, you need to place it in the markup where it can be started when the appropriate trigger occurs. In Chapter 12, I introduced Triggers but saved EventTriggers for this chapter. The following are some important things to know about EventTriggers:

- EventTriggers occur at a single point in time and don't have duration. This is in contrast to the triggers you saw before, which remain "triggered" as long as the condition remains true and then become "untriggered."

- EventTriggers require actions as their content. When an EventTrigger's condition occurs, it kicks off the actions it contains.

- EventTriggers are usually placed inside Styles, but they can also be placed directly in objects.

All this is fine, but animations aren't actions and can't, therefore, be placed directly inside an EventTrigger. To get around this, you need to place a Storyboard inside a BeginStoryboard element.

- A BeginStoryBoard element represents an action and is therefore eligible to be placed in an EventTrigger. This element corresponds to the BeginAnimation method you saw in the code-behind of local animations.

- A BeginStoryBoard element can contain one or more StoryBoard objects.

- A StoryBoard can contain one or more animation objects.

Besides BeginStoryboard, EventTriggers can also contain the following actions: StopStoryboard, PauseStoryboard, RemoveStoryboard, ResumeStoryboard, SeekStoryboard, SetStoryboardSpeedRatio, SkipStoryboardToFill, and SoundPlayerAction. Notice that all but the last action affect a StoryBoard object.

The markup shown in Figure 19-10 is the XAML version of the previous example program that created a storyboard animation of the FontSize and Height properties. There are several important things to notice in the figure:

- The nested boxes show the required structure of EventTrigger, BeginStoryBoard, StoryBoard, and animation objects.

- The EventTrigger requires a RoutedEvent as its trigger. As I mentioned, this is a "durationless" event, which starts the BeginStoryBoard action.

- The animation object requires a TargetProperty to know what property to animate. Notice, however, that here in the XAML you *must* use the CLR wrapper name of the property—that is, *without* the Property suffix. This is in contrast to creating an animation in the code-behind, where you *must use* the suffix.

```xml
<Window x:Class="StoryboardXAML.Window1" ...
    Title="Storyboard" Height="150" Width="200">
  <Grid>
    <Button Name="myButton" Height="40" Width="150" FontWeight="Bold">
      <Button.Triggers>
        <EventTrigger RoutedEvent="Button.MouseEnter">
          <EventTrigger.Actions>
            <BeginStoryboard>
              <Storyboard Duration="0:0:2">
                <DoubleAnimation From="40.0" To="80.0"
                                 Storyboard.TargetProperty="Height"/>
                <DoubleAnimation From="12.0" To="22.0"
                                 Storyboard.TargetProperty="FontSize"/>
              </Storyboard>
            </BeginStoryboard>
          </EventTrigger.Actions>
        </EventTrigger>
      </Button.Triggers>
      Click Me
    </Button>
  </Grid>
</Window>
```

Figure 19-10. *The XAML architecture for using an animation*

Other Variations on Animation

In the animation examples you've seen so far, the rate of change in the dependency property value has been a linear interpolation between the starting value and the ending value.

There are, however, two other variations on animation that allow you to change the values in other ways. These are called *animation with keyframes* and *animation along a path*.

- Animation with keyframes allows you to set specific values of the property at various points in the progression.

- Animation along a path allows you to move the position of an object along a path.

Not all types of dependency properties can be animated with each of the three types of animation. Table 19-3 shows the three types of animation and the types with which they can be used.

Table 19-3. *Types for the Standard Built-in Animation Classes*

.NET Type	Basic Animation	Keyframes	Path	WPF Type	Basic Animation	Keyframes	Path
Boolean		✓		Color	✓	✓	
Byte	✓	✓		Matrix		✓	✓
Char		✓		Point	✓	✓	✓
Decimal	✓	✓		Point3d	✓	✓	
Double	✓	✓	✓	Quaternion	✓	✓	
Int16	✓	✓		Rect	✓	✓	
Int32	✓	✓		Rotation3D	✓	✓	
Int64	✓	✓		Size	✓	✓	
Object		✓		Thickness	✓	✓	
Single	✓	✓		Vector	✓	✓	
String		✓		Vector3D	✓	✓	

Keyframe Animations

The first nonlinear type of animation I'll cover is animation with keyframes. This type of animation allows you to specify specific values at specific points in the timeline. The following are some important things to know about keyframe animation:

- A *keyframe* is an object that represents a point in the animation's timeline. It contains two properties: KeyTime and Value.

    - The KeyTime attribute specifies a time on the timeline. This is represented as an offset from the animation's starting time.

    - The Value attribute specifies the value the dependency property must have at that time.

- Between each pair of keyframes, the animation performs a linear interpolation to determine the value of the animated property.

- Each keyframe animation object contains a collection of keyframe objects.

Each of the standard animation classes has a corresponding keyframe class. For example, the corresponding keyframe class of the DoubleAnimation class is the DoubleAnimationUsingKeyFrames class. The keyframe animation classes have most of the same properties as their corresponding animation classes. For the keyframe classes, however, there is no need for the From, To, or By properties, since these values are given explicitly as keyframe objects.

There are three types of keyframe classes—*linear, spine,* and *discrete.* I'll cover each type in the following sections.

Linear Keyframe Animation

I'll start by showing an example of a linear keyframe animation. The markup in Figure 19-11 shows an example of an animation object that moves an object left and right in a Canvas panel. There are several important things to notice in the markup:

- You need to use the appropriate *XXX*AnimationUsingKeyFrames class, where *XXX* is one of the supported .NET or WPF types. In this case, it's DoubleAnimationUsingKeyFrames.

- If the TargetProperty is an attached property on the object you are animating, you must enclose the attached property name in parentheses, as shown.

- You need to use a collection of keyframe objects. This example uses the LinearDoubleKeyFrame type.

```
<DoubleAnimationUsingKeyFrames
                Storyboard.TargetProperty="(Canvas.Left)" Duration="0:0:5">
    <LinearDoubleKeyFrame KeyTime="0:0:0" Value="0"/>
    <LinearDoubleKeyFrame KeyTime="0:0:1" Value="160"/>
    <LinearDoubleKeyFrame KeyTime="0:0:2" Value="40"/>
    <LinearDoubleKeyFrame KeyTime="0:0:3" Value="120"/>
    <LinearDoubleKeyFrame KeyTime="0:0:4" Value="80"/>
    <LinearDoubleKeyFrame KeyTime="0:0:5" Value="100"/>
</DoubleAnimationUsingKeyFrames>
```

Figure 19-11. *The XAML for an animation using keyframes*

Figure 19-12 shows screenshots of a button being animated by this keyframe animation object. At various points in the timeline the button has different values for its Canvas.Left property and is therefore in different places on the screen. What the screenshots can't show is that the button is continuously moving throughout the entire five seconds.

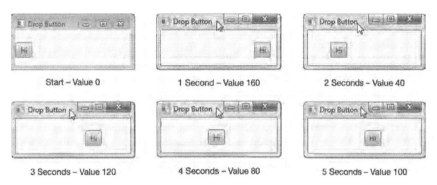

Figure 19-12. *Animating the Canvas.Left property with keyframes*

Now consider the following markup, which animates the Canvas.Top attached property and does *not* use keyframes. Figure 19-13 shows the result of animating a button with this animation object. The button drops slowly over the period of five seconds.

```
<DoubleAnimation Storyboard.TargetProperty="(Canvas.Top)"
                 Duration="0:0:5" From="20" To="120"/>
```

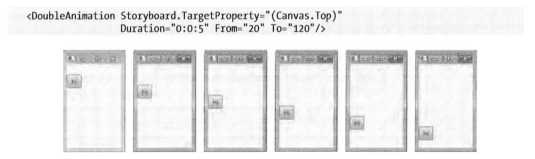

Figure 19-13. *Animating the Canvas.Top property with normal animation*

If you use these two animations together in the same Storyboard, the first animation moves the button back and forth, and the second animation moves it steadily downward. The dashed line in Figure 19-14 illustrates the movement of the button.

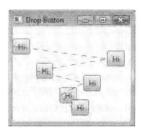

Figure 19-14. *Animating both the Canvas.Left and Canvas.Top properties together*

The following code is the full markup of the program:

```
<Window x:Class="DropFigure.Window1" ...
    Title="Drop Button" Height="197" Width="215">
   <Canvas>
      <Button Canvas.Top="20" Canvas.Left="0" Content="Hi" Padding="7,3">
         <Button.Triggers>
            <EventTrigger RoutedEvent="Button.MouseEnter">
               <EventTrigger.Actions>
                  <BeginStoryboard>
                     <Storyboard>

                        <DoubleAnimationUsingKeyFrames
                              Storyboard.TargetProperty="(Canvas.Left)"
                              Duration="0:0:5">
                           <LinearDoubleKeyFrame KeyTime="0:0:0" Value="0"/>
                           <LinearDoubleKeyFrame KeyTime="0:0:1" Value="160"/>
                           <LinearDoubleKeyFrame KeyTime="0:0:2" Value="40"/>
                           <LinearDoubleKeyFrame KeyTime="0:0:3" Value="120"/>
                           <LinearDoubleKeyFrame KeyTime="0:0:4" Value="80"/>
                           <LinearDoubleKeyFrame KeyTime="0:0:5" Value="100"/>
                        </DoubleAnimationUsingKeyFrames>

                        <DoubleAnimation From="20" To="120"
                              Storyboard.TargetProperty="(Canvas.Top)"
                              Duration="0:0:5"/>

                     </Storyboard>
                  </BeginStoryboard>
               </EventTrigger.Actions>
            </EventTrigger>
         </Button.Triggers>
      </Button>
   </Canvas>
</Window>
```

Spline Interpolation Animations

The keyframe animations you saw in the previous section perform straight linear interpolations between each of the two successive keyframes. The rate of change at each of these keyframes can be abrupt. A spline keyframe animation uses Bezier curves to make each transition from the previous timeline segment smoother.

The following markup is an example of a simple animation that has only two points. The first point uses a simple LinearDoubleKeyFrame keyframe, since it doesn't have a point before it. The second point, however, uses a SplineDoubleKeyFrame keyframe. Besides the KeyTime and the Value, it also has a KeySpline property that takes two pairs of numbers. These two pairs of numbers represent the anchor points of the Bezier curve. The first pair represents the anchor point with respect to the beginning point of the timeline segment, and the second pair represents the anchor point with respect to the end point.

```
<DoubleAnimationUsingKeyFrames Storyboard.TargetProperty="(Canvas.Left)"
                                               Duration="0:0:4">
    <LinearDoubleKeyFrame KeyTime="0:0:0" Value="20"/>
    <SplineDoubleKeyFrame KeyTime="0:0:4" Value="220"
                        KeySpline=".06,.94 .90,0"/>
</DoubleAnimationUsingKeyFrames>
```

Figure 19-15 shows this Bezier curve. To understand what the graph means, notice that the x-axis represents time and the y-axis represents the rate of change. Notice also that at the beginning of the graph, the speed goes up very quickly, but at about one second it levels off and moves only slowly. At about three seconds it picks up its speed again and accelerates to the end.

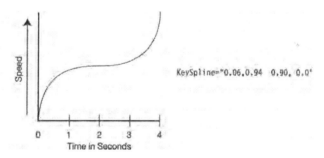

Figure 19-15. *The Bezier curve graph for a particular KeySpline*

473

If you use this animation object to animate the Canvas.Left attached property of a button, the button moves from left to right, as illustrated in Figure 19-16. What's interesting about the movement is that it starts by accelerating toward the right for the first second and then slows down so that it's moving very slowly. Then, at about three seconds it picks up speed again and races to the end. The picture on the right of the figure shows the button at five points in its progression.

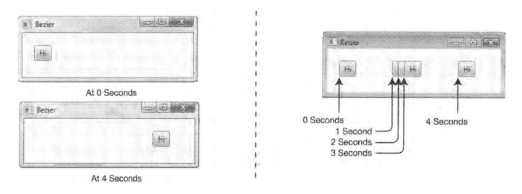

Figure 19-16. *A button animated using a spline interpolation*

The following is the markup for this program:

```
<Window x:Class="Bezier.Window1" ...
    Title="Bezier" Height="109" Width="308">
    <Canvas>
        <Button Canvas.Top="20" Canvas.Left="20" Content="Hi" Padding="7,3">
            <Button.Triggers>
                <EventTrigger RoutedEvent="Button.MouseEnter">
                    <EventTrigger.Actions>
                        <BeginStoryboard>
                            <Storyboard>
                                <DoubleAnimationUsingKeyFrames
                                        Storyboard.TargetProperty="(Canvas.Left)"
                                        Duration="0:0:4">
                                    <LinearDoubleKeyFrame KeyTime="0:0:0" Value="20"/>
                                    <SplineDoubleKeyFrame KeyTime="0:0:4" Value="220"
                                        KeySpline=".06,.94 .90,0"/>
                                </DoubleAnimationUsingKeyFrames>
                            </Storyboard>
                        </BeginStoryboard>
                    </EventTrigger.Actions>
                </EventTrigger>
            </Button.Triggers>
        </Button>
    </Canvas>
</Window>
```

Discrete Keyframe Animation

The last type of keyframe animation is discrete keyframe animation. In this method, there is no interpolation between the keyframes. Instead, at the time designated by the next keyframe, the value immediately changes to the specified value, without any interpolation.

Figure 19-17 shows the path of the button if you use the code for the Drop Button program used at the beginning of the section on keyframe animation and change the type of the keyframe from `LinearDoubleKeyFrame` to `DiscreteDoubleKeyFrame`. The button starts by traveling downward and then at one second immediately moves to the right to the new value of 160. Continuing to move downward, it immediately changes the value to 40, and so forth, at each keyframe.

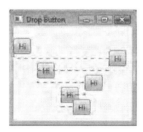

Figure 19-17. *With discrete keyframe animation, the value of the controlled property changes immediately, without any interpolation in between.*

The following is the animation part of the markup. Again, the animation with keyframes is moving the button left and right, and the standard `DoubleAnimation` below it is moving the button downward.

```
<DoubleAnimationUsingKeyFrames Storyboard.TargetProperty="(Canvas.Left)"
                    Duration="0:0:5">
            <DiscreteDoubleKeyFrame KeyTime="0:0:0" Value="0"/>
            <DiscreteDoubleKeyFrame KeyTime="0:0:1" Value="160"/>
            <DiscreteDoubleKeyFrame KeyTime="0:0:2" Value="40"/>
            <DiscreteDoubleKeyFrame KeyTime="0:0:3" Value="120"/>
            <DiscreteDoubleKeyFrame KeyTime="0:0:4" Value="80"/>
            <DiscreteDoubleKeyFrame KeyTime="0:0:5" Value="100"/>
</DoubleAnimationUsingKeyFrames>

<DoubleAnimation From="20" To="120" Storyboard.TargetProperty="(Canvas.Top)"
            Duration="0:0:5"/>
```

Path Animations

The last type of animation I'll cover is called *path animation*. Path animation allows you to move an object along a path on the screen. The path is described by a PathGeometry object. I covered PathGeometry objects in Chapter 18. If you refer to Table 19-3, you'll find that there are only three types that support animation along a path—Double, Matrix, and Point. The animation class names have the form *XXX*AnimationUsingPath.

Instead of using a From and a To property or using a set of keyframes, path animations animate properties along a path. For example, Figure 19-18 shows a button moving along a crooked line.

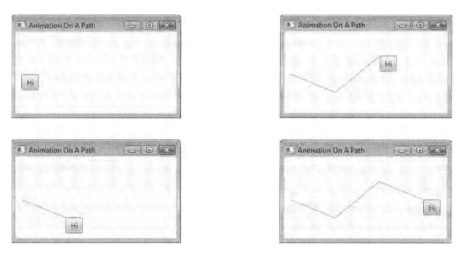

Figure 19-18. *Example of a button being animated on a crooked path*

Figure 19-19 shows the syntax for an animation using a path. The syntax looks similar to the others, but there's one new attribute: the Source attribute. The Source attribute has two possible values: X or Y. What this means is that the value of the dependency property being animated is the value of either the X or Y coordinate of the path.

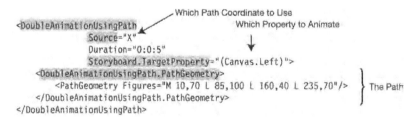

Figure 19-19. *The syntax for a path animation*

The following is the markup for animating the button along the path as shown in Figure 19-18:

```
<Canvas>
    <Button Canvas.Left="10" Canvas.Top="70" Content="Hi" Padding="7,3">
        <Button.Triggers>
            <EventTrigger RoutedEvent="Button.MouseEnter">
                <EventTrigger.Actions>
                    <BeginStoryboard>
                        <Storyboard>

                            <DoubleAnimationUsingPath
                                    Storyboard.TargetProperty="(Canvas.Left)"
                                    Source="X"                  ← Use the X coordinate.
                                    Duration="0:0:5">
                                <DoubleAnimationUsingPath.PathGeometry>
                                    <PathGeometry
                                        Figures="M 10,70 L 85,100 L 160,40 L 235,70"/>
                                </DoubleAnimationUsingPath.PathGeometry>
                            </DoubleAnimationUsingPath>

                            <DoubleAnimationUsingPath
                                    Storyboard.TargetProperty="(Canvas.Top)"
                                    Source="Y"                  ← Use the Y coordinate.
                                    Duration="0:0:5">
                                <DoubleAnimationUsingPath.PathGeometry>
                                    <PathGeometry
                                        Figures="M 10,70 L 85,100 L 160,40 L 235,70"/>
                                </DoubleAnimationUsingPath.PathGeometry>
                            </DoubleAnimationUsingPath>

                        </Storyboard>
                    </BeginStoryboard>
                </EventTrigger.Actions>
            </EventTrigger>
        </Button.Triggers>
    </Button>
</Canvas>
```

Summary

Animation is the process of having WPF automatically vary the value of a dependency property over a set period of time. You can set a number of properties on the animation, allowing it to be a simple linear interpolation, to be based on keyframes, or to be based on a `PathGeometry` object.

CHAPTER 20

Audio and Video

Overview of Audio

In most of the areas I've covered throughout this text, WPF allows the programmer far more expressiveness than in previous frameworks. The audio features it provides, however, aren't particularly impressive. Instead, they are little more than wrappers around Win32 APIs or the Windows Media Player.

WPF provides four classes for producing sound. They are the following—starting with the simplest (and least useful) and progressing to the most useful:

- The SystemSounds class can produce several of the commonly used operating system sounds.

- The SoundPlayer class is used for short, simple .wav format files where the only thing you require is to be able to start the sound file.

- The MediaPlayer class allows you to use a wide variety of sound file formats and allows you to control their playback. This class, however, can be used only in the code-behind; it can't be used in markup.

- The MediaElement class gives you the same control as the MediaPlayer class but can also be used in XAML.

SystemSounds

The SystemSounds class is the simplest of the four classes used to produce sounds. The following are the important things to know about the SystemSounds class:

- It can produce five operating system sounds: Asterisk, Beep, Exclamation, Hand, and Question.

- The SystemSounds class doesn't offer any way to modify or control the playback of these sounds.

- You can use this class only in imperative code. That is, you can't use it in markup.

For example, the following code is the event handler for a button. The code simply plays the system's Asterisk sound.

```
...
using System.Media;                 ← Must use this namespace.

private void Button_Click( object sender, RoutedEventArgs e )
{
    SystemSounds.Asterisk.Play();
}
```

Before using this class, you might want to consider whether the user might be confused by hearing operating system sounds coming from your application.

SoundPlayer

The SystemSounds class is pretty limiting in that it can produce only five specific sounds. The SoundPlayer class allows you a broader range. The following are the important things to know about the SoundPlayer class:

- The SoundPlayer class is a very lightweight wrapper around the Win32 PlaySound API.

- It can only play sound files in the pulse-code modulation (PCM) .wav format.

- The three operations SoundPlayer allows are starting playback, stopping playback, and changing the source of the sound file.

- The sound source can be a local file, a URL, an Embedded Resource (not a Resource—but an Embedded Resource) or a Stream. (Stream objects are beyond the scope of this text.)

The following code shows a simple example of using this class. It consists of creating a SoundPlayer object, specifying the location of the .wav file to play, and calling the Play method.

```
private void Button_Click( object sender, RoutedEventArgs e )
{
    SoundPlayer sp = new SoundPlayer( );     ← Create SoundPlayer object.
    sp.SoundLocation = "Shuffle.wav";        ← Specify the location of the sound file.
    sp.Play();                               ← Load and play asynchronously.
}
```

By default, the SoundPlayer object doesn't load the sound file until the Play method is called. If the file is coming from a URL and you want to load it ahead of time, you can call the LoadAsync method to preload the file. If the sound file isn't accessed through a URL, though, this command is ignored.

The Play method loads the sound file asynchronously and then plays it in another thread. This means that your main thread is free to continue working as the sound plays.

If you want the program to play the sound synchronously—in your main thread—you can use the PlaySync method.

Figure 20-1 illustrates the SoundPlayer class's most important members.

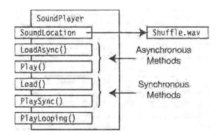

Figure 20-1. *The main exposed components of the SoundPlayer class*

SoundPlayerAction

The SoundPlayer class isn't a WPF element and therefore can't be placed in the markup. To get around this, the WPF designers created the SoundPlayerAction class, which is a wrapper around the SoundPlayer class. SoundPlayerAction is derived from the TriggerAction class and can therefore be used as an EventTrigger.

The SoundPlayerAction class has even fewer options than the SoundPlayer class. For example, it doesn't allow you to preload the .wav file, and you can't play the sound synchronously.

The following markup shows the button used in the previous example, but this time, there's no event handler in the code-behind. Instead, clicking the button trips the button's EventTrigger, which contains the SoundPlayerAction element. Notice the following about the markup:

- The SoundPlayerAction element takes an attribute named Source, which takes the file path or URL of the .wav file.

- If you include the .wav file in the Visual Studio project, you can specify it as an assembly resource. I covered assembly resources in Chapter 11—but in short, after adding it to the project, you can set the file's properties in one of the following two ways:

  - Set the file's Build Action option to Resource. This compiles it into the executable.

  - Set the Build Action property to None, and set the Copy to Output Directory option to Copy always. This leaves the .wav file as a loose file that is copied to the output directory.

```
<Grid>
    <Button>

        <Button.Triggers>
            <EventTrigger RoutedEvent="Button.Click">
                <EventTrigger.Actions>
                    <SoundPlayerAction Source="Shuffle.wav"/>
                </EventTrigger.Actions>
            </EventTrigger>
        </Button.Triggers>

        Click Me
    </Button>
</Grid>
```

MediaPlayer

With the SoundPlayer class, your only control over playing a sound is starting it, stopping it, or setting it to play repeatedly in a loop. The MediaPlayer class gives you much more control.

The following are the important things to know about the MediaPlayer class:

- MediaPlayer uses components of the Windows Media Player (WMP), which must be installed on the target machine. The installed version of WMP must be version 10.0 or later. Since MediaPlayer uses components from WMP, it can use any sound file format that WMP can use.

- MediaPlayer gives you much greater control of sound playback. It allows you to start, stop, and set the speed of the playback. You can also set the position in the file and even adjust the balance of the left and right channels.

- Unlike most of the classes you've seen in this text, the properties of the MediaPlayer class are not dependency properties, and its events are not RoutedEvents.

- MediaPlayer can be used only in imperative code. That is, you cannot use it in XAML.

The following code is a simple example of using the MediaPlayer class. The process consists of creating the MediaPlayer object, opening the media file using a URI, and then calling the Play method.

```
public partial class Window1 : Window
{
    MediaPlayer player;                        ← Declare the MediaPlayer variable.

    public Window1()
    {
        InitializeComponent();

        player = new MediaPlayer();            ← Create the MediaPlayer object.
          Open the media file
               ↓
        player.Open( new Uri( "music.wma", UriKind.Relative ) );
        player.Play();
    }            ↑
}        Play the media file
```

Table 20-1 lists the most important methods and properties of the MediaPlayer class.

Table 20-1. *Some of the MediaPlayer Class's Important Methods and Properties*

Name	Description
Balance	Gets or sets the proportion of the sound signal sent to the left and right channels. The value ranges from -1.0, representing all the volume going to the left speaker, to +1.0 where all the volume is going to the right speaker.
Close()	Closes the media file.
Open()	Opens the media file.
Pause()	Pauses playback.
Play()	Plays the media file.
Position	Gets or sets the position in the media file. This is a TimeSpan object.
SpeedRatio	Gets or sets the speed of playback. Normal speed is 1.0. Less is slower; more is faster.
Stop()	Stops playing the media file and returns the position to the beginning.
Volume	Gets or sets the playback volume. This is a double value from 0.0 to 1.0. The default value is 0.5.

The markup shown next produces the UI for a simple music player that uses MediaPlayer. The program allows the user to start, stop, or pause the playback. The user can also set the balance so that the sound is coming from the left speaker, the right speaker, or both.

```
<StackPanel>
    <GroupBox Header="Balance" Margin="5" >
        <StackPanel Orientation="Horizontal">
            <RadioButton Margin="10,5" GroupName="balanceButtons"
                         Checked="radioButton_Checked" Name="radioLeft"/>
            <RadioButton Margin="10,5" GroupName="balanceButtons"
                         Checked="radioButton_Checked" Name="radioCenter"/>
            <RadioButton Margin="10,5" GroupName="balanceButtons"
                         Checked="radioButton_Checked" Name="radioRight"/>
        </StackPanel>
    </GroupBox>
    <StackPanel Orientation="Horizontal" HorizontalAlignment="Right"
                VerticalAlignment="Top">
        <Button Click="Play_Click"  Margin="3" Padding="6,3">Play</Button>
        <Button Click="Pause_Click" Margin="3" Padding="6,3">Pause</Button>
        <Button Click="Stop_Click"  Margin="3" Padding="6,3">Stop</Button>
    </StackPanel>
</StackPanel>
```

Figure 20-2 shows a screenshot of the UI with the balance set so that equal amounts of volume are sent to the left and right speakers.

Figure 20-2. *Simple music player that allows the user to set the balance*

The following is the code-behind for the program. Notice that this program only plays a single media file—music.wma. You can see from the Uri that the program expects that file to be in the same folder as the executable. One additional detail is that Play starts from the current position. So, when playback completes, you have to call Stop, which resets the position to the beginning, before you can play the file again.

```
public partial class Window1 : Window
{
    MediaPlayer player;

    public Window1()
    {   InitializeComponent();

        player = new MediaPlayer();
        player.Open( new Uri( "music.wma", UriKind.Relative ) );

        radioCenter.IsChecked = true;
    }

    private void Play_Click( object sender, RoutedEventArgs e )
    { player.Play(); }

    private void Pause_Click( object sender, RoutedEventArgs e )
    { player.Pause(); }

    private void Stop_Click( object sender, RoutedEventArgs e )
    { player.Stop(); }

    private void radioButton_Checked( object sender, RoutedEventArgs e )
    {
        if (radioLeft.IsChecked.Value )
            player.Balance = -1.0;
        else if (radioRight.IsChecked.Value )
            player.Balance = 1.0;
        else
            player.Balance = 0;
    }
}
```

MediaElement

The MediaElement class is similar in features to the MediaPlayer class described in the previous section but is derived from UIElement, and therefore it acts more like the WPF classes you're used to seeing. The following are some of the important things to know about the MediaElement class:

- Like the MediaPlayer class, MediaElement uses components of the installed Windows Media Player. And like MediaPlayer, the installed version of the WMP must be at least version 10.0.

- Unlike the MediaPlayer class, however, the properties of MediaElement are dependency properties, and its events are RoutedEvents.

- Because MediaElement derives from UIElement, you can place it in the markup.

The following markup produces a simple music player that plays a file called music.wma, by setting the Source attribute to the file name. This program loads the media file and immediately starts playing it.

```
<Window x:Class="MediaElementSimple.Window1" ...
    Title="Simple Player" Height="120" Width="200">
    <StackPanel>
        <MediaElement Source="music.wma"/>
    </StackPanel>
</Window>
```

Although this is a perfectly fine program, you'll usually want more control of the media than just having it start up when the window initializes. You can do this in several ways.

The first way is to use the MediaElement in the markup and create buttons with event handlers for the Click events. The following markup shows this approach. Notice that the LoadedBehavior attribute must be set to Manual if you want to control the MediaElement from the code-behind.

```
                                  Must Be Set to Manual
                                          ↓
<StackPanel>
    <MediaElement Name="player" LoadedBehavior="Manual"/>

    <StackPanel Orientation="Horizontal" VerticalAlignment="Top">
        <Button Click="Play_Click"  Margin="3" Padding="6,3">Play</Button>
        <Button Click="Pause_Click" Margin="3" Padding="6,3">Pause</Button>
        <Button Click="Stop_Click"  Margin="3" Padding="6,3">Stop</Button>
    </StackPanel>
</StackPanel>
```

Figure 20-3 shows a screenshot of the simple player produced by this markup. The code-behind is essentially the same as in the MediaPlayer example and is shown next.

Figure 20-3. *Simple music player using the MediaElement with event handlers*

```
public partial class Window1 : Window
{
    public Window1()
    {   InitializeComponent();

        player.Source = new Uri( "music.wma", UriKind.Relative );
    }

    private void Play_Click( object sender, RoutedEventArgs e )
    {
        player.Play();
    }

    private void Pause_Click( object sender, RoutedEventArgs e )
    {
        player.Pause();
    }

    private void Stop_Click( object sender, RoutedEventArgs e )
    {
        player.Stop();
    }
}
```

Another way, however, is to control the MediaElement from the XAML. The first part of the markup looks similar to the previous markup. The major difference is that the buttons are now named and do not include Click handlers.

```
<StackPanel>
    <MediaElement Name="player"/>

    <StackPanel Orientation="Horizontal">
        <Button Name="playButton"   Margin="5" Padding="3">Play</Button>
        <Button Name="stopButton"   Margin="5" Padding="3">Stop</Button>
        <Button Name="pauseButton"  Margin="5" Padding="3">Pause</Button>
        <Button Name="resumeButton" Margin="5" Padding="3">Resume</Button>
    </StackPanel>

    ...
```

The question that arises now, however, is how do you handle the button clicks? You can, of course, use EventTriggers to catch the button clicks, but what do you do inside the EventTrigger.Actions? Actions can only set the values of dependency properties, but the states of the MediaElement object are controlled by methods such as Play and Pause.

The answer to this dilemma is that you don't directly control the MediaElement. Instead, you create an object of a special type of Timeline, called a MediaTimeline, and associate the MediaElement with it. Then, instead of manipulating the MediaElement, you manipulate the MediaTimeline.

The markup in Figure 20-4 shows how to do this. The following are some of the important things to notice in the markup:

- The MediaElement, named player, is placed in the StackPanel.

- The StackPanel contains a collection of four EventTriggers—one for each of the Click events from the four buttons.

- The EventTrigger for the Play button performs the BeginStoryboard action and associates it with the MediaElement element, through the TargetName.

- Each of the other three Actions operates on the Storyboard named in the BeginStoryboard Action.

```
<StackPanel>
    <MediaElement Name="player"/>

    <StackPanel Orientation="Horizontal">
        <Button Name="playButton" Margin="5" Padding="3">Play</Button>
        <Button Name="stopButton" Margin="5" Padding="3">Stop</Button>
        <Button Name="pauseButton" Margin="5" Padding="3">Pause</Button>
        <Button Name="resumeButton" Margin="5" Padding="3">Resume</Button>
    </StackPanel>

    <StackPanel.Triggers>
        <EventTrigger RoutedEvent="Button.Click" SourceName="playButton">
            <EventTrigger.Actions>        Name the BeginStoryboard object.

                <BeginStoryboard Name="musicStoryboard">
                    <Storyboard SlipBehavior="Slip">
                        <MediaTimeline Source="music.wma" Storyboard.TargetName="player"/>
                    </Storyboard>
                </BeginStoryboard>
            </EventTrigger.Actions>            Associate the BeginStoryboard object
        </EventTrigger>                        with the MediaElement object.

        <EventTrigger RoutedEvent="Button.Click" SourceName="stopButton">
            <EventTrigger.Actions>
                <StopStoryboard BeginStoryboardName="musicStoryboard"/>
            </EventTrigger.Actions>
        </EventTrigger>

        <EventTrigger RoutedEvent="Button.Click" SourceName="pauseButton">
            <EventTrigger.Actions>
                <PauseStoryboard BeginStoryboardName="musicStoryboard"/>
            </EventTrigger.Actions>
        </EventTrigger>

        <EventTrigger RoutedEvent="Button.Click" SourceName="resumeButton">
            <EventTrigger.Actions>
                <ResumeStoryboard BeginStoryboardName="musicStoryboard"/>
            </EventTrigger.Actions>
        </EventTrigger>

    </StackPanel.Triggers>

</StackPanel>
```

Figure 20-4. *The markup to control playback of the MediaElement*

Table 20-2 lists the Action elements you can use to manipulate the Storyboard.

Table 20-2. *The Actions Used to Manipulate the Storyboard*

Name	Description
BeginStoryboard	Starts the Storyboard playing from the beginning.
PauseStoryboard	Pauses the Storyboard at its current location.
RemoveStoryboard	Removes the Storyboard, freeing up resources.
ResumeStoryboard	Resumes playing the Storyboard if it's currently paused.
SeekStoryboard	Moves the current position of the Storyboard to an offset from the beginning.
SkipStoryboardToFill	Moves the current position to the fill position, if there is one.
SetStoryboardSpeedRatio	Sets the speed of playback of the Storyboard. The default SpeedRatio is 1.0.
StopStoryboard	Stops playing the Storyboard.

Video

To play video in WPF, you use the MediaElement class, just as you did to play sounds. Just as with sounds, you can control the video from the code-behind, using with the class's methods, or you can use EventTriggers to manipulate a Storyboard.

For example, the following markup creates the UI for a simple video viewer that plays a video named Bear.wmv. It can play, stop, and pause the video. There are several important things to notice about the markup:

- As with the audio playback, the LoadedBehavior property must be set to Manual in order to be able to control the video playback from the code-behind.

- By default, if the video is paused and you programmatically change the position in the video file, the new current video frame isn't shown until you start the video playing again. If you want the new frame to be shown immediately, even though the video is paused, set the ScrubbingEnabled property to true.

```
<StackPanel>
    <MediaElement Name="videoElement" LoadedBehavior="Manual"
                  ScrubbingEnabled="True" Source="Cat.wmv"/>
    <StackPanel Orientation="Horizontal">
        <Button Margin="3" Padding="3" Click="Play_Click">Play</Button>
        <Button Margin="3" Padding="3" Click="Stop_Click">Stop</Button>
        <Button Margin="3" Padding="3" Click="Pause_Click">Pause</Button>
    </StackPanel>
</StackPanel>
```

Figure 20-5 shows a screenshot of the program.

Figure 20-5. *The simple video viewer using the MediaElement class*

The following is the code-behind for the program. Notice that to show the first frame, the code starts the video playing and immediately pauses it. It then sets the Position to the beginning of the file.

```
public partial class Window1 : Window
{
   public Window1()
   {  InitializeComponent();

      // To show the first frame. Make sure ScrubbingEnabled = true;
      videoElement.Play();
      videoElement.Pause();
      videoElement.Position = TimeSpan.Zero;
   }

   private void Stop_Click( object sender, RoutedEventArgs e )
   {
      videoElement.Stop();
   }

   private void Play_Click( object sender, RoutedEventArgs e )
   {
      videoElement.Play();
   }

   private void Pause_Click( object sender, RoutedEventArgs e )
   {
      videoElement.Pause();
   }
}
```

Summary

WPF provides four classes for playing back audio. The simplest of these is the SystemSounds class, which can play five of the operating system sounds. The other three classes are not quite so trivial, and Table 20-3 shows a comparison of their features.

Table 20-3. *Summary of the Sound Playback Classes*

	SoundPlayer	MediaPlayer	MediaElement
Implementation	Lightweight wrapper around the Win32 PlaySound API	Uses Windows Media Player (WMP).	Uses Windows Media Player (WMP)
Formats Supported	Only .wav files	All formats supported by WMP	All formats supported by WMP
Control of Sounds	Only start and stop; no other control of sound, including volume	Can control starting, stopping, pausing, seeking, and so on	Can control starting, stopping, pausing, seeking, and so on
Concurrent Sounds	Only one sound at a time	Only one sound at a time	Multiple sounds if multiple elements
Used in XAML	Wrapped by the SoundPlayerAction element	Procedural code only; no use in XAML	Use stand-alone or in MediaTimeline element
Namespace	System.Media	System.Windows.Media	System.Windows.Controls

To play video, you can use either the MediaPlayer or MediaElement class.

Index

XBAPs (XAML Browser Applications), 13,
332–335
x:Key attribute, 273

■Z

z-order, Canvas, 136–137

You Need the Companion eBook

Your purchase of this book entitles you to buy the companion PDF-version eBook for only $10. Take the weightless companion with you anywhere.

We believe this Apress title will prove so indispensable that you'll want to carry it with you everywhere, which is why we are offering the companion eBook (in PDF format) for $10 to customers who purchase this book now. Convenient and fully searchable, the PDF version of any content-rich, page-heavy Apress book makes a valuable addition to your programming library. You can easily find and copy code—or perform examples by quickly toggling between instructions and the application. Even simultaneously tackling a donut, diet soda, and complex code becomes simplified with hands-free eBooks!

Once you purchase your book, getting the $10 companion eBook is simple:

❶ Visit **www.apress.com/promo/tendollars/**.

❷ Complete a basic registration form to receive a randomly generated question about this title.

❸ Answer the question correctly in 60 seconds, and you will receive a promotional code to redeem for the $10.00 eBook.

233 Spring Street, New York, NY 10013

Offer valid through 4/10.

15761409R00281

Made in the USA
Lexington, KY
17 June 2012